2 Litchfield Road
Londonderry, NH 03053
Meetinghouseofnhdems@gmail.com

FROM THE FOLKS WHO BROUGHT YOU
THE WEEKEND

A SHORT, ILLUSTRATED HISTORY OF LABOR IN THE UNITED STATES

Priscilla Murolo and
A. B. Chitty

ILLUSTRATIONS BY JOE SACCO

THE NEW PRESS · NEW YORK

Published in the United States by The New Press, New York, 2001
Distributed by W. W. Norton & Company, Inc., New York

Designed by Kathryn Parise

LIBRARY OF CONGRESS CATALOGING-IN-PUBLICATION DATA
Murolo, Priscilla.
From the folks who brought you the weekend: a short, illustrated history
of labor in the United States / Priscilla Murolo and A. B. Chitty;
illustrated by Joe Sacco.
p.   cm.
Includes index.
ISBN 1-56584-444-0 (hc.)
1. Labor—United States—History.   2. Working class—United States—
History.   3. Labor movement—United States—History.
I. Chitty, A. B.   II. Title.
HD8066 .M86 2001
331'.0973—dc21   2001030978

The New Press was established in 1990 as a not-for-profit alternative to the large, commercial publishing houses currently dominating the book publishing industry. The New Press operates in the public interest rather than for private gain, and is committed to publishing, in innovative ways, works of educational, cultural, and community value that are often deemed insufficiently profitable.

The New Press, 450 West 41st Street, 6th floor, New York, NY 10036
www.thenewpress.com

Printed in the United States of America

2   4   6   8   10   9   7   5   3   1

For David, Marty,
and Meridith

CONTENTS

FOREWORD AND ACKNOWLEDGMENTS

Why this book now? For two reasons, mainly. When we started this project in 1998, no comprehensive survey of U.S. labor history for the general reader had appeared for more than a decade. Recent scholarship had added new dimensions and many details to the story of working people in America. It was past time to compile these insights into a new general history.

Also, the labor movement itself had changed—most dramatically in the 1995 election of the "New Voice" slate to the leadership of the American Federation of Labor-Congress of Industrial Organizations. This change reflected a belated recognition that the labor-government-management accord achieved after the Second World War had already been scuttled by both corporations and government, that without reorientation to new economic and political realities unions and the federation itself could become as irrelevant as any boss or banker might wish, and just wither away. Compared to the men they succeeded, the new generation of leaders had different ideas about the role of organized labor in society. These ideas are not new: They are revivals and developments of labor traditions that had long been subordinated to the demands of the scuttled accord of the Cold War era. It was a good time to look again at these traditions.

As we began drafting the story, a third reason appeared and became clearer as we continued. Even a casual look at American history reveals how much of what we learn and teach in school is just not true. Sometimes these misreadings are errors of fact—the extent of the U.S. war in the Philippines at the turn of the last century is one example. More often they are errors of omission—the African American role in the Civil War, for example. Mostly they concern perspective: Looking at historical events from the bottom up alters our understanding of historical agency and causation. Adopting the perspective of people organizing to achieve common goals gives an account of historical events that is truer, and surely more useful.

Compared to conventional labor history, we tried mainly to be more inclusive in terms of "workers" and "working peoples' movements," and to incorporate as much recent research, historiography, and events as we could. Almost none of the material comes from our own research. We found an abundance of materials—in fact, too much. To keep the narrative from expanding beyond our publisher's mandate, or our control, we had to exclude more than we could include at every turn. There are some interesting books we did not write. We did not write a comprehensive account of trade unions, their internal affairs, or their complicated relationships with one another in and out of federations. We did not write a history of work, nor a history of labor and capital. We did not write a history of labor politics. These would be good and useful books. We also tried to keep from straying too far into major reinterpretations of American history, perhaps with mixed results. That would be a great book too, but beyond our ambition, and probably our competence.

Besides, for us the significance of the past is found in the present, and the present moment is full of rapid changes, even surprises. We are hopeful for the future, but certain of very little. We do know that in the past people have always found a way to struggle to make life better for themselves and their posterity. We know their struggles have generally been effective in proportion to the range and depth of the solidarity of their movements. We know the incessant and implacable adversary is privilege, legitimated by law, custom, and popular ideology, which never yields without challenge, to which democracy is anathema. We side with democracy. We write for the people who work too hard for too little, whose families and communities are hostage to the greed and arrogance of the same privilege that deforms our humanity and threatens our common welfare. We write for the people who can change history.

Our debts to historians and activists are too numerous to list. Our publisher, André Schiffrin and The New Press, and our editors, first Matt Weiland, then Marc Favreau, encouraged our work. Copyediting by David Allen helped to reconcile inconsistencies and force clarification. A Flik grant from

Sarah Lawrence College gave Priscilla some money for travel. Feedback from students in labor history courses at Sarah Lawrence, the Midwest Summer School for Women Workers, and summer workshops sponsored by Hospital and Health Care Workers District 1199 in Ohio, West Virginia, and Kentucky sharpened the analysis and the narrative. Friends and comrades like Kim Scipes, David Cline, and Gideon Rosenbluth helped us at particular points. Without the intellectual, emotional, and logistical support of Mary Reynolds, Associate Director of the Graduate Program in Women's History at Sarah Lawrence College, this book most likely would never have appeared.

We dedicate this book to three people. David Montgomery has been our personal intellectual guide to American labor history. His life and work combine the long view with mastery of historical detail and with activism to a degree all too rare in the profession of history. Martel Montgomery, David's wife, has been our good friend, steadfast and practical in seeing the possibility of change for the better, constant in her conviction that the principles by which we work for social justice apply with equal force to our everyday lives. Finally, our student and friend Meridith Helton learned labor history and then lived it, long enough at least to realize a personal dream working for the union victory at the Fieldcrest Cannon mills in North Carolina. She died too suddenly and too soon, leaving us with an indelible and fiery memory of beauty, youth, and energy, love of music, adventure, and life, and passion for justice. She and her generation carry our hopes and quiet our fears. They have already started making our history.

Yonkers, New York
January 2001

LIST OF
ILLUSTRATIONS

LIST OF
ABBREVIATIONS

1199	Hospital and Health Care Workers Union 1199
AAFLI	Asian American Free Labor Institute
AAPL	Alliance of Asian Pacific Labor
ACORN	Association of Communities for Reform Now
ACTWU	Amalgamated Clothing and Textile Workers Union
ACW	Amalgamated Clothing Workers
AFL	American Federation of Labor
AFL–CIO	American Federation of Labor and Congress of Industrial Organizations
AFSCME	American Federation of State, County, and Municipal Employees
AFT	American Federation of Teachers
AIFLD	American Institute for Free Labor Development
AIM	American Indian Movement
APALA	Asian Pacific American Labor Alliance
APRO	Asian Pacific Regional Organization of the International Confederation of Free Trade Unions
ARU	American Railway Union
AUD	Association for Union Democracy

AWO	Agricultural Workers Organization
AWOC	Agricultural Workers Organizing Committee
B&O	Baltimore and Ohio Railroad
BAGL	Bay Area Gay Liberation
BIA	Bureau of Indian Affairs
BRU/SdP	Bus Riders Union/Sindicato de Passajeros
CAP	Congress of African Peoples
CAT	Contract Action Teams
CBTU	Coalition of Black Trade Unionists
CFI	Colorado Fuel & Iron
CFUN	Committee for a Unified Newark
CGT	Confederación General de Trabajadores
CEO	chief executive officer
CIA	Central Intelligence Agency
CIO	Committee for Industrial Organization; later, Congress of Industrial Organizations
CIO-PAC	CIO Political Action Committee
CLUW	Coalition of Labor Union Women
CNLU	Colored National Labor Union
COF	Congreso Obrero de Filipinas
COINTELPRO	Counter Intelligence Program of the Federal Bureau of Investigation
COLA	cost of living adjustment
COPE	Committee on Political Education
CORE	Congress on Racial Equality
COSH	Committee on (or Coalition for) Occupational Safety and Health
CP	Communist Party
CROC	Confederación Revolucionario de Obreros y Campesinos
CTM	Confederación de Trabajadores Mexicanos
CUA	Chinese Unemployed Alliance
CUTW	Connecticut Union of Telephone Workers
CWA	Communications Workers of America
EEOC	Equal Employment Opportunity Commission
ENA	Experimental Negotiations Agreement
ERP	employee representation plan

FAT	Frente Autentico de Trabajo
FBI	Federal Bureau of Investigation
FEPC	Fair Employment Practice Committee
FLOC	Farm Worker Organizing Committee
FLT	Federación Libre de Trabajadores
FLU	federal labor union
FOTLU	Federation of Organized Trades and Labor Unions
FSLA	Fair Labor Standards Act
FTA	Food, Tobacco, Agricultural, and Allied Workers
FTUI	Free Trade Union Institute
FWIU	Food Workers Industrial Union
G&W	Gulf & Western Corporation
G.E.	General Electric Corporation
G.M.	General Motors Corporation
HERE	Hotel Employees and Restaurant Employees
IBEW	International Brotherhood of Electrical Workers
ICC	Interstate Commerce Commission
ICFTU	International Confederation of Free Trade Unions
ILA	International Longshoremen's Association
ILGWU	International Ladies' Garment Workers Union
ILO	International Labor Organization
ILWU	International Longshore and Warehouse Union
INS	Immigration and Naturalization Service
IUE	International Union of Electrical, Radio, and Machine Workers
IWW	Industrial Workers of the World
JMLA	Japanese-Mexican Labor Association
JwJ	Jobs with Justice
K of L	Knights of Labor
LAANE	Los Angeles Alliance for a New Economy
LCFO	Lowndes County Freedom Organization
LCLAA	Labor Council for Latin American Advancement
LFLRA	Lowell Female Labor Reform Association

MFDP	Mississippi Freedom Democratic Party
MFLU	Mississippi Freedom Labor Union
Mine Mill	Mine, Mill, and Smelter Workers' Union
MOU	Movimiento Obreros Unidos
NAACP	National Association for the Advancement of Colored People
NAFTA	North American Free Trade Agreement
NAM	National Association of Manufacturers
NCA	National Contractors Association
NCF	National Civic Federation
NEA	National Education Association
NFU	Newfoundland Fishermen's Union
NFWA	National Farm Workers Association
NIRA	National Industrial Recovery Act
NLC	National Labor Committee
NLRA	National Labor Relations Act (Wagner Act)
NLRB	National Labor Relations Board
NLU	National Labor Union
NRA	National Recovery Administration
NTU	National Trades Union
NTU	National Typographical Union
NWLB	National War Labor Board
NWRO	National Welfare Rights Organization
OAAU	Organization of African American Unity
OCAW	Oil, Chemical, and Atomic Workers
OPA	Office of Price Administration
OPM	Office of Production Management
ORIT	Inter-American Regional Organization of Workers
OSHA	Occupational Safety and Health Administration
PACE	Paper, Allied-Industrial, Chemical, and Energy International Union
PAFL	Pan-American Federation of Labor
PASSO	Political Association of Spanish-Speaking Organizations
PATCO	Professional Air Traffic Controllers Organization
PAW	Pride at Work
PSP	Partido Socialista Puertorriqueño

RUM	Revolutionary Union Movement
RWDSU	Retail, Warehouse, and Department Store Workers Union
SCLC	Southern Christian Leadership Conference
SEIU	Service Employees International Union
SFWR	Stewardesses for Women's Rights
SNCC	Student Non-Violent Coordinating Committee
SP	Socialist Party of America
SWOC	Steel Workers' Organizing Committee
SWP	Socialist Workers Party
TSEU	Texas State Employees Union
TUEL	Trade Union Educational League
TUUL	Trade Union Unity League
UAW	United Auto Workers
UCAPAWA	United Cannery, Agricultural, Packing, and Allied Workers of America
UE	United Electrical, Radio, and Machine Workers
UFCW	United Food and Commercial Workers
UFW	United Farm Workers
ULU	United Labor Unions
UMW	United Mine Workers
UNIA	Universal Negro Improvement Association
Union WAGE	Union Women's Alliance to Gain Equality
UNITE	Union of Needletrades, Industrial, and Textile Employees
UOPWA	United Office and Professional Workers of America
UPW	United Public Workers
URW	United Rubber Workers
U.S.S.R.	Union of Soviet Socialist Republics (Soviet Union)
USWA	United Steelworkers of America
UTU	United Transportation Union
UTW	United Textile Workers
VVAW	Vietnam Veterans Against the War
WBA	Workingmen's Benevolent Association
WFM	Western Federation of Miners

WFTU   World Federation of Trade Unions
WMC   War Manpower Commission
WPA   Works Progress Administration
WTO   World Trade Organization

YLP   Young Lords Party

CHAPTER

LABOR IN COLONIAL AMERICA:
THE BOUND AND THE FREE

The New World looked much like paradise to European voyagers in the fifteenth and sixteenth centuries. Christopher Columbus's first expedition (1492–93) took him to the Bahamas, Cuba, and Hispaniola, all of which he claimed as colonies for Spain's King Ferdinand and Queen Isabella and described as modern-day Edens in his report to the crown. He found Hispaniola especially breathtaking: "In that island . . . there are mountains of very great size and beauty, vast plains, groves, and very fruitful fields, admirably adopted for tillage, pasture and habitation. The convenience and excellence of the harbors in this island, and the abundance of rivers, so indispensable to the health of man, surpass anything that would be believed by one who had not seen it . . . and moreover it abounds in various kinds of spices, gold, and other metals." The island's inhabitants seemed "exceedingly liberal with all that they have; none of them refusing any thing he may possess when he is asked for it, but on the contrary inviting us to ask them."

Such impressions were not confined to the balmy Caribbean. In the 1580s, Englishmen hoping to colonize the rougher shores of today's North Carolina thought they had found an Eden on Roanoke Island. There, wrote Arthur Barlowe, "The earth bringeth forth all things in abundance, as in the first creation, without toil or labor." Thomas Harriot forecast a happy relationship with Roanoke's natives, whose desire for "friendship & love" seemed certain to imbue them with "respect for pleasing and obeying us." These were stock images in the earliest reports from European colonists in the Americas.

Many also told of astonishingly rich mineral deposits, which caught Europe's attention above all else. These rumors began with Columbus, who announced at the end of his first voyage that the islands he had claimed would supply Ferdinand and Isabella with "as much gold as they need." The islanders would presumably be happy to serve it up. In fact, Caribbean gold deposits fell far below Columbus's estimates, and only brutal force could make mine slaves out of the region's natives, a collection of tribes known in retrospect as the Arawaks. The islands he likened to paradise in 1492 soon became hellholes where Spain enforced its rule with troops, heavy armaments, and attack dogs as the Arawaks were literally worked to death harvesting gold. The same befell Puerto Rico, Jamaica, and other islands that came under Spanish control in later years. By the 1530s, the Caribbean's goldfields had been stripped bare; the Arawak population had dwindled from about ten million to a few thousand at best, and a new cycle of misery had begun as colonists turned from mining to cultivating sugar cane with captive labor from Africa as well as the Americas.

Dreams of mineral wealth in the New World remained alive and well thanks to Spain's conquests of the Aztec empire in Mexico (1519–21) and the Inca empire in Peru (1532), both exceptionally rich in gold and silver. For decades to come, colonists throughout the Americas would dig for ore before getting down to the more mundane business of farming. Over the long haul, however, agriculture—the production of cash crops for European markets—proved more lucrative than mining; and so did the commerce in slaves, who raised the lion's share of colonial crops.

These developments vindicated Columbus's first impressions of the New World in one respect. Though the soil did not teem with gold and the people would not volunteer for servitude, the profits Europe extracted from American enterprises fully met his expectations. Many nations partook of the wealth: Portugal, England, France, and Holland joined Spain as major colonial and slave-trading powers, and their proceeds fueled economic growth throughout Europe.

Commerce across the Atlantic was not an entirely new phenomenon. Pre-Columbian journeys both to and from the Americas may have been numerous to judge from fragmentary evidence such as Roman coins found in the Americas, Eskimo harpoon heads unearthed in Ireland and Scotland,

and ancient Mayan sculptures that bear faces with African features. The Norse voyages described in Icelandic sagas are confirmed by archeological evidence of a short-lived settlement in Newfoundland in the early eleventh century, and timber from the region was shipped to Greenland for another 300 years. Columbus himself found evidence of commerce between Africans and Americans: Arawaks sometimes used spearpoints of "guanine," an alloy of gold, silver, and copper developed and used in West Africa, where it was also called guanine. The Arawaks said the alloy had come from dark-skinned traders. Columbus's son Ferdinand met people "almost black in color" in what is now eastern Honduras; the Balboa expedition to Panama encountered a "tribe of Ethiopians."

While transatlantic travel and trade predated Columbus, colonial ventures were something new. Unlike their predecessors, the voyagers of 1492 and after came from societies that had developed military technology to unprecedented levels during the Christian Crusades to seize the Holy Land from Muslims in the eleventh through thirteenth centuries. The new tools of war went hand in hand with the certainty of entitlement to any and all lands inhabited by non-Christians. And just as merchants had bankrolled the Crusades in return for trade monopolies, the men who pioneered Europe's colonization of the New World combined Christian piety with a keen eye for business opportunities.

Exploiting the colonies was never a simple matter, however. European monarchs gave giant tracts of American land to favorite courtiers, explorers, military men, and merchants, but land in and of itself could not make the recipients rich. It seldom contained precious metals; when it did, someone had to mine the ore. Contrary to Europeans' first impressions, moreover, the soil would not feed people without cultivation, let alone yield up cash crops. To make a colony pay, its proprietors had to acquire and control a labor force.

Though colonial labor systems differed from place to place and changed over time, bondage was invariably their linchpin. Slaves, indentured servants, and other captives vastly outnumbered wage workers, and the latter enjoyed few civil liberties beyond the enviable right to quit an unbearable job. For free laborers as well as the unfree, subordination was the central fact of life. Yet both groups repeatedly challenged their masters' authority. The things they endured and the ways they resisted form the core themes of colonial labor history in territories now part of the United States.

LEGACIES OF CONQUEST

The first colonists to arrive in the future United States were Spaniards who explored Florida in the early 1500s, hunting for gold and for Indian captives to work Caribbean gold mines. By 1565, when Spain claimed Florida as a colony, Spanish expeditions had also explored much of what is today the southwestern U.S. and had established outposts as far north as Virginia and Kansas. By the mid-1700s, the Spanish frontier in North America was confined to southern latitudes but stretched all the way from Florida to California. Free laborers—Spaniards, Native Americans, Africans, and many people of mixed ancestry—were part of the work force on this frontier. They included artisans, domestic servants, cotton sharecroppers, and herders on cattle and sheep ranches. Indian servitude was the mainstay of Spanish colonies, however, and fairly common in the sections of North America controlled by England and France.

In the late 1500s, the Spanish crown forbade the outright enslavement of Indians, but other forms of Indian bondage remained legal, and slavery was often practiced despite the law. From Florida to California, Spain's North American colonies were dotted with missions established by Franciscan friars working to convert Indians to Christianity. This project proceeded on an especially large scale in the colony of New Mexico, established in 1598. By 1629, there were fifty Franciscan missions in the colony, and a reported 86,000 Pueblo Indians had been baptized. The majority of the converts lived in the mission settlements, where men, women, and children spent most of their waking hours at labor under the friars' supervision. Mainly, they raised crops and livestock, not only feeding the settlement but also producing surpluses that the friars marketed for consumption in America or for shipment to Spain.★ While Spanish law did not define mission Indians as slaves, neither were they free to come and go as they wished. Floggings awaited those who failed to do their assigned work, missed the compulsory religious services, or otherwise broke the friars' rules. Soldiers guarded the missions to keep marauding Indians out and the converts in.

Still, many Indians preferred mission life to their treatment under secular Spanish rule. In New Mexico, colonists regularly violated the law by sending Navajo and Apache captives into slave labor in Mexico's mines. Outside the missions, Pueblo peoples labored under the *encomienda* system in which re-

---

★ Mission industries expanded as time went on and grew especially large in California. By the early 1800s, the products included butter, tallow, hides and chamois leather, maize, wheat, wine, brandy, vegetable oils, and textiles.

cipients of royal land grants collected tribute from the land's inhabitants. Under this system, the Pueblos produced maize, cotton blankets, and hides for export to Mexico or Spain. Tribute in the form of forced labor was prohibited by the crown, but *encomenderos* repeatedly ignored that rule.

In both New Mexico and Florida, colonists also foisted *repartimiento* and *rescate* on native peoples. The system of *repartimiento de indios* drafted Indians for labor on public works projects—unloading ships, transporting supplies, building and repairing roads, bridges, and fortifications. By law, the draftees served for limited terms, labored only on public projects, and received fair compensation. In practice, colonial officials often extended service beyond the legal term, dispensed with wages, and compelled *repartimiento* workers to labor for private businesses and households. *Rescate* was practiced in all Spanish colonies: Indians taken captive by other Indians were ransomed and bound over for domestic service in colonists' households. Technically these *indios de depósito* were not slaves, and did not pass their condition to their children. But they could be bought and sold, and some were sold into slavery in Mexico.

In New Mexico unbaptized Indians—especially women and children—were often seized and sold as domestic slaves in violation of the law. Officials tolerated the practice on the theory that it "civilized" the slaves; but like most forms of slavery, this one was more likely to barbarize the masters. In 1751, the wife of Alejandro Mora complained to authorities in Bernalillo, New Mexico, that he mistreated the Indian woman Juana, a slave in the Mora household. The investigating constable found Juana covered with bruises and burns, her ankles raw from manacles, her knees festering with sores. Mora had broken her knees to keep her from running away and periodically reopened the wounds with a flintstone. Juana gave this testimony:

> I have served my master for eight or nine years now but they have seemed more like 9,000 because I have not had one moment's rest. He has martyred me with sticks, stones, whip, hunger, thirst, and burns all over my body. . . . He inflicted them saying that it was what the devil would do to me in hell, that he was simply doing what God had ordered him to do.

Mora protested that he was only looking out for Juana's welfare. He had raped her, he said, only to test her claim to virginity, and he had tortured her only to keep her from becoming a loose woman. Authorities removed Juana from the Mora household; that was her master's only penalty.

English and French colonists enslaved Indians too, though never in the same numbers as did the Spanish. In 1622, Virginians sold Indian survivors of Powhatan's War into slavery in the West Indies; in 1637, Indian survivors of the Pequot War in New England were enslaved in Bermuda. During the Tuscarora and Yamasee Wars (1711–15), Englishmen and their Indian allies captured and enslaved natives of the Carolina interior. In 1731, the French in Louisiana rounded up most of the surviving Natchez nation for sale to West Indies plantations. And while English and French colonies typically sent Indian captives to the Caribbean, quite a few were enslaved on the mainland. About a tenth of the slaves in French Louisiana were Indians, mostly women assigned to domestic work. French settlers in Detroit bought Pawnee, Osage, and Choctaw captives and held them and their descendants as slaves for most of the 1700s. A census of South Carolina in 1708 counted 3,960 free whites, 4,100 African slaves, 1,400 Indian slaves, and 120 indentured whites. In New York in 1712, about a quarter of all slaves were Indians. In Kingston, Rhode Island, in 1730, a census counted 935 whites, 333 African slaves, and 223 Indian slaves. By the late 1700s, Indian and African slaves had amalgamated to the point that census takers did not distinguish between the two, instead listing all slaves as "colored."

Indians also labored for Europeans in relationships that did not involve bondage. Many hunted and trapped for pelts to sell to colonial fur traders. Since Indians valued commodities differently than Europeans, they often failed to get market value for their goods. From the mid-1600s onward, some New England Indians were wage earners, working as farmhands, domestics, whalers, and construction laborers. This movement into wage work—a pattern that would eventually extend across the continent—reflected the losses of land that undermined Native American's ability to live without hiring out.

In 1742, the Seneca leader Canassatego spoke to Pennsylvania officials on behalf of the Iroquois nations: "We know our lands are now become more valuable. The white people think we do not know their value; but we are sensible that the land is everlasting, and the few goods we receive for it are soon worn out and gone. . . . Besides, we are not well used with respect to the lands still unsold by us. Your people daily settle on these lands, and spoil our hunting. We must insist on your removing them, as you know they have no right to settle." In this instance and countless others, colonial authorities failed to remove the squatters, and Indians' economic independence eroded.

INDENTURED LABOR IN BRITISH COLONIES

Indentured workers—commonly called "servants"—were a key source of labor for British colonies. They planted the first crops at the Jamestown colony founded in Virginia in 1607, Britain's first permanent settlement in what is now the United States. Twelve of them were aboard the *Mayflower* when it brought the Pilgrims to Plymouth, Massachusetts, in 1620. By the time the American Revolution broke out in the mid-1770s, more than half of all European immigrants to the colonies had entered as indentured servants. Estimates put their proportion at 60 to 77 percent. In the 1600s, the vast majority came from England as individuals, and the males far outnumbered the females. The next century saw a large influx of Irish and German families, and the sex ratio grew more even.

Until the 1660s, most black immigrants to British North America arrived as indentured workers too. The first twenty, at least three of them women, landed in Jamestown on a Dutch ship in 1619. Over the next forty-odd years, many hundreds of black indentured servants entered Britain's mainland colonies, from New England in the north to the Carolinas in the south. The majority came from England, Spain, or Portugal, where Africans had lived for two generations or more; others came from the West Indies.

Indenture placed workers in bondage for a limited term—typically three to five years, though some served considerably more time. What had promised to be a short term might stretch into a long one. Magistrates routinely extended the terms of servants hauled into court for fleeing their masters or otherwise breaking the law. For the duration of the indenture, they were their master's property, and many were repeatedly bought and sold before their terms expired.

Mostly they were put to hard labor, clearing land and plowing new fields, cultivating crops that required constant work, draining swamps and building roads, scrubbing and cooking, hauling heavy loads. A man with special skills might enjoy lighter duty as an artisan's helper. That was the lot of William Moraley, an apprentice watchmaker back in England and for three years the servant of a New Jersey clockmaker who purchased him fresh off a ship that docked in Philadelphia in 1729. Craft work was seldom the whole of a servant's assignment, however; in addition to cleaning timepieces, Moraley herded livestock and labored in an iron foundry. He was fortunate in that the clockmaker beat him only once, as a punishment for trying to run away. Other masters had less self-control. Writing from Maryland in 1756, Elizabeth Sprigs complained of regular floggings in a letter to her family in London: "I one of the unhappy Number, am toiling almost Day and Night . . . and then tied up and whipp'd to that Degree that you'd not serve an Annimal."

Despite reports of such abuses, a great many people indentured themselves voluntarily in return for transportation to the New World and, they hoped, better opportunities than Europe offered. The volunteers signed indentures with labor contractors who paid their passage and then sold them to American employers. Because there was room to haggle, men and women indentured under this arrangement served relatively short terms. But quite a few servants had no choice in the matter. Some were English convicts sentenced to servitude in the colonies. Others were destitute children kidnapped off the streets of England's seaports or ordered into indenture by colonial authorities. Still others were debtors bound by law to work off their obligations to creditors. Among these groups—especially convicts and children—terms of up to fourteen years were not at all uncommon.

Indentured servants faced the hardest times during the early decades of colonial settlement. Newcomers routinely succumbed to the deadly fevers that struck the colonies every summer. And the "seasoned" servants who had survived their first summers were far from safe—especially the thousands indentured to tobacco planters in the Chesapeake region of Virginia and Maryland. Nearly two-thirds of these workers died before their indentures ended. Following an Indian attack that killed 347 Jamestown residents in March 1622, the Virginia Company back in England inquired into the fate of the 700 people in the colony as of spring 1619 and the 3,570 immigrants who had arrived since then. A head count showed that just 1,240 remained alive. Some probably envied the dead. As one of Virginia's women servants wrote in 1623, "I thought no head had been able to hold so much water as hath and doth daily flow from mine eyes."

Endurance had its rewards. On fulfilling the term of service, each worker except for the convicts and debtors received "freedom dues"—a sum of money, a parcel of land in some colonies, and perhaps other things, too, such as clothing, tools, a horse or a cow. In theory, the dues would turn released servants into proprietors of American farms, craft shops, or other small businesses. In fact, such happy endings were rare. Surviving records suggest that, of all the people indentured in British North America between 1607 and 1776, just 20 percent went on to self-employment in the colonies or newborn United States. About half did not outlive their indentures; most of the rest became wage workers or paupers or returned to their countries of origin.

In the mid-1700s, the indenture system developed a new twist as shipping merchants devised a scheme that forced many thousands of free immigrants into terms of servitude. Recruitment agents commissioned by the shippers visited European towns and depicted America as a land where no one worked hard and everyone got rich. People who signed up for transport to this paradise were promised a cheap fare and easy credit if they could not afford the full price. By the time the passengers arrived in America, nearly all were in debt to the ship's captain, who had levied surprise charges for tariffs, duties, and provisions. Nobody could leave the ship without first clearing accounts, and no sooner was that announced than entrepreneurs came on board with offers to redeem people who signed indenture contracts for themselves and their children. Exhausted and frightened, the captives often agreed to exceptionally long terms of service. Most of these immigrants, known as "redemptioners," came from Ireland or Germany.

One eyewitness to their predicaments was Gottlieb Mittelberger, whose *Journey to Pennsylvania* (1756) publicized the miseries he had seen. In 1750 Mittelberger left his home in the Duchy of Württemberg and joined a party of fellow Germans sailing for Philadelphia. The ship was so crowded with families and so poorly stocked with food that over half the passengers died in transit, their debts to the captain devolving to their kin. Desperate to leave the vessel when it finally docked, the survivors were ready to sign virtually any indenture contract. Adults committed themselves for terms of three to six years if they were lucky, six to twelve if their spouses were too sick to work or had died at sea. Minor children were bound over by their parents, or the ship's captain in the case of children orphaned during the voyage. Those between ten and fifteen years old were sold into service until age twenty-one. The youngest, who could not by law be sold, were given away to anyone who promised to maintain them.

One of a handful who had paid in full for his passage, Mittelberger escaped indenture, but he saw what awaited his less fortunate shipmates. As a schoolteacher in rural Pennsylvania, he watched "soul-drivers" march lots of fifty or more redemptioners into the backcountry and sell them into labor on farms where they were "beaten like cattle." Returning to Württemberg in 1754, he published his book in hopes that it would persuade fellow Germans to remain at home: "Let him who wants to earn his piece of bread honestly and who can only do this by manual labor in his own country, stay there rather than come to America." Such warnings had little if any impact. As the century wore on, redemptioners arrived in Philadelphia in growing numbers—by 1770 at an average rate of twenty-four shiploads a year.

SLAVERY

In 1505, a Spanish ship carried a cargo of slaves from West Africa to Hispaniola, inaugurating one of the most hideous and profitable business enterprises in world history. Over the next centuries, the transatlantic trade in African slaves would grow to gigantic proportions and involve merchants and shippers from virtually every European and American seafaring power. By the time the trade ended in 1870, an estimated 15 to 20 million Africans had been forcibly transported to the Americas, about 1 million to the United States or the colonies that preceded it. Countless other captives—up to five times the number who reached American shores—died en route to the slavers' ships or during the ocean crossing.

Britain's colonies in North America enslaved Africans almost from the beginning, as did the Dutch colony of New Amsterdam (which became British New York in 1664). As black indentured servants arrived in the early and mid-1600s, so did black slaves, though not yet in large numbers. The Dutch West India Company transported them to New Amsterdam as early as 1626. Others arrived in Boston in 1638 and in Connecticut the following year. Some indentured servants meanwhile became slaves in fact if not in name. Starting in the 1640s in Virginia, colonial courts sentenced black servants who fled their masters to lifelong bondage.

The decisive turn toward slavery came in the later 1600s, with Maryland and Virginia taking the lead. In 1663, Maryland's lawmakers declared all of its black residents slaves for life and imposed the same status on all persons henceforth born to enslaved women. In 1670, Virginia condemned all Africans entering the colony to slavery, and a 1682 law extended the sentence to all offspring of enslaved women. Thus started a juggernaut. By 1710, every colony had passed laws that enslaved Africans and their descendants as well as Indian captives. Georgia, founded in 1732 with a charter that outlawed slaveholding, reversed that stand in 1750. Between 1700 and the start of the American Revolution in 1775, the number of slaves in British North America rose from about 25,000 to 500,000, about 90 percent laboring in the southern colonies of Virginia, Maryland, Georgia, and the Carolinas.

Slavery expanded in northern colonies too. By the mid-1700s, nearly every wealthy family in northern port cities owned household slaves, up to a third of the artisans in these cities used slave labor in their shops, and grain farmers from Pennsylvania to southern New England were replacing indentured servants with slaves. In Philadelphia and New York City, slaves constituted 20 percent of the whole labor force in artisan shops and did an even larger share of the work in maritime trades such as shipbuilding and sail making. In some grain-producing counties in northern New Jersey, the Hudson Valley, and Long Island, slaves far outnumbered free workers. The major slaveholding colony north of Maryland was New York, whose slave population rose from 9,000 in the 1740s to almost 20,000 in the 1770s. New England's 16,000 slaves as of 1770 were concentrated in Connecticut, Massachusetts, and Rhode Island, but some 2,000 worked in the more sparsely settled areas to the north.

The merchants and shippers of Newport, Rhode Island, became the leading North American participants in the transatlantic slave trade. Other cities whose ships regularly bore down on Africa included Providence, Rhode Island, Salem and Boston, Massachusetts, and Portsmouth, New Hampshire. While southern colonists dealt mostly with British slave traders, Yankees dominated the business in northern ports and shipped up to 10 percent of the slaves arriving in southern ports in 1700s.

Africans' experience en route to America is vividly described in *The Interesting Narrative of the Life of Olaudah Equiano,* the autobiography of a former slave published in 1791. Born in 1745 in the Essaka province of Benin, Equiano was kidnapped at age ten or eleven, passed from hand to hand, and finally sold to the Guinea coast, where in 1757 he was carried aboard an English slave ship bound for Barbados. To guard against a revolt, crewmen placed the adults in iron chains and allowed just a few captives at a time to leave the hold and breathe fresh air on deck. Then, when the ship got under way, all were put below. As Equiano later wrote,

> The stench of the hold, while we were on the coast, was so intolerably loathsome, that it was dangerous to remain there for any time; but now that the whole ship's cargo were confined together, it became absolutely pestilential. The closeness of the place, and the heat of the climate, added to the number in the ship, being so crowded that each had scarcely room to turn himself, almost suffocated us. This produced copious perspirations, so that the air soon became unfit for respiration, from a variety of loathsome smells, and brought on a sickness among the slaves, of which many died. . . . The shrieks of the women and the groans of the dying rendered it a scene of horror almost inconceivable.

Such was the setting on every slave ship, and Equiano recounted incidents that typified the voyage. Beatings and force-feeding awaited those who refused to eat, for the same business logic that prompted slave traders to jam-pack their ships made them anxious to keep the cargo alive. When captives nearing death were brought on deck for resuscitation, some threw themselves overboard; two men on Equiano's ship succeeded in drowning while a third was rescued and flogged.

When the ship docked in Bridgetown, Barbados, merchants and planters came on board to inspect the captives, who were then taken ashore and penned into a yard. Several days later, Equiano remembered, we were sold after the usual manner, which is this:—On a signal given, such as the beat of a drum, the buyers rush at once into the yard where the slaves are confined, and make choice of that parcel they like best. . . . In this manner, without scruple, are relations and friends separated, most of them never to see each other again.

The West Indies sugar planters who bought most of Equiano's companions rejected him, just twelve years old and frail "from very much fretting." So he and a few others in similar condition were transported to Virginia. There, he was sold to an English ship's captain and began a twenty-year maritime career during which he managed to purchase his freedom.

Some others enslaved in British North America gained their liberty through self-purchase, manumission, lawsuits, or flight. Until the American Revolution, however, such deliverance was rare. Of the nearly 5,000 "free colored people" in the colonies on the eve of the Revolution, the majority were freeborn descendants of indentured servants, both black and white, or noncaptive Indians. They were free by virtue of that ancestry, not soft spots in the fortress of slavery.

Slavery's tenacity reflected its economic value to the colonies, which exploited slaves' minds and muscles in remarkably elaborate ways. The typical slave of the colonial era was a field hand raising tobacco, rice, or indigo on a southern plantation; this was the most common labor for the men, women, and children. But slaves worked in many other capacities too. They tilled land on the giant estates that lined New York's Hudson Valley and on many a small farm from New Hampshire to Georgia. Their labors on southern plantations encompassed carpentry and blacksmithing, leather tanning and shoemaking, bricklaying and plastering, spinning woolen thread, weaving cloth, and sewing clothes. In northern colonies, they could be found in virtually all skilled trades, from maritime crafts to goldsmithing, printing, and cabinetmaking. Every colonial port counted slaves among its sailors and dock workers. In many white households—rural and urban, northern and southern—enslaved women fetched water, hauled firewood, cooked meals, scoured kitchens, tended infants and children, and saw to other chores.

In addition to a wide variety of labor, slaveholders demanded deference. Nothing better illustrates this than the 1701 court case in which a Massachusetts slave identified only as Adam sued his master John Saffin for reneging on a 1694 promise to free him in seven years. Saffin's defense was that Adam had been "intollerably insolent, quarrelsome and outrageous," daring to work at his own pace, talk back when insulted, and resist beatings. Though the jury sided with Saffin, Adam won his freedom in 1703 by appealing the decision to the colony's Superior Court. His appeal and indeed the original lawsuit would have been impossible outside of New England; elsewhere, slaves had no rights to sue or testify against whites.

Against this backdrop, assault, homicide, and rape became part and parcel of slavery; and while slaves on southern plantations were the most vulnerable to abuse, others were scarcely immune. New Jersey slaves were flogged to degrees that shocked the indentured servant William Moraley. "For the least Trespass," he wrote, "they undergo the severest Punishment . . . and if they die under the Discipline their Masters suffer no Punishment, there being no Law against murdering them." A British visitor to colonial South Carolina recorded the following in his diary: "Mr. Hill, a dancing-master in Charleston, whipped a female slave so long that she fell down at his feet, in appearance dead; but when, by the help of a physician, she was so far recovered as to show some signs of life, he repeated the whipping with equal rigour, and concluded the punishment by dropping scalding wax upon her flesh: her only crime was overfilling a tea-cup!" A New Englander who hobnobbed with Charleston's most prominent men was astonished to hear them speak with "no reluctance, delicacy or shame" about molesting women in the slave quarters.

The most common forms of abuse, however, were starvation and overwork. In the 1990s, preservationists blocked the construction of a skyscraper atop the "African burial ground" in the oldest part of New York City and reburied over 400 skeletons* that testify to the grueling toll on slaves' bodies. The majority of the dead were children twelve and under, half of them infants. The adult skeletons showed lesions on shoulder, arm, and leg bones where muscles were torn away by strain, and some showed circular fractures at the base of the skull, a sign that excessively heavy loads were carried on the head. One skeleton belonged to a boy about age six who died in the early 1700s. Though his remains indicated that he was malnourished and anemic from birth, the anchor points on his arm bones revealed that his muscles were unusually well developed from lifting, and the many healed fractures in his neck show that his head, too, bore large weights. Whatever disease or trauma ended his life, it is fair to say that he was worked to death.

FREE LABOR

Though bondage lay at the core of colonial labor systems, the numbers of free men and women hiring out for wages steadily increased. This work

---

* An estimated 20,000 burials took place there.

force included free immigrants, former indentured servants, Native Americans pushed off their lands, the lucky few who made their way out of slavery, and descendants of all these groups. Wage earners were a minority among free people, most of whom made a living through a family farm, a family craft shop, or some combination of the two. Almost from the start, however, the colonies were home to at least some wage workers, and by the early 1700s wage labor was a fast-rising trend in British North America, especially its coastal cities and towns.

The largest sectors of the wage-earning labor force were sailors, journeyman artisans, women and girls employed as domestic workers or in cloth and clothing production, and men and boys who plowed fields, hauled freight, and performed other backbreaking jobs that fell under the heading of "common labor." Except for the journeymen, whose craft skills won them higher wages than the rest, these workers belonged to the poorest segments of free society. Though nearly all earned substantially more than their European counterparts, their lives were scarcely enviable by free Americans' standards.

Single women with dependent children got the worst of it, often trudging from place to place in search of a job that would pay enough to feed and shelter their families. Their chances of finding one were so slim that the overseers of Connecticut, Massachusetts, Rhode Island, and numerous towns in other colonies barred single mothers from settling down unless they relinquished the right to solicit help from local charities. Starting in the mid-1700s, agencies such as Boston's Society for Encouraging Industry and Employing the Poor opened cloth and clothing "manufactories" where women and children worked for a pittance, just enough to keep them alive.

Most women wage earners escaped such dire circumstances, as did the majority of sailors and common laborers; but very few were comfortably situated. Domestics and farmhands typically lived with their employers, working sixteen hours a day and more in return for a tiny cash wage plus room and board. Even in Philadelphia, North America's most prosperous city in the late colonial era, sailors and common laborers almost never found steady jobs. Those who did earned about £50 per year—£10 less than a family of average size needed to survive in Philadelphia.* To make ends meet, the wives and children of male wage earners often hired out too.

Workers' troubles in some occupations went beyond hard labor and low pay. Many sailors lost their lives at sea, many more suffered from what they called "Falling Sickness"—dizziness caused by recurrent beatings at the

---

* Despite occasional unemployment, the city's journeyman artisans earned slightly or substantially more than £60 a year depending on their crafts.

hands of their captains. Domestic workers sometimes faced physical abuse as well. In 1734, a group of them announced in the *New York Weekly Journal* that "we think it reasonable we should not be beat by our Mistrisses Husband[s], they being too strong, and perhaps may do tender women Mischief."

For all of these reasons, most free people did everything in their power to build lives that did not revolve around wage work. More often than not, they succeeded. Just as wages were higher than in Europe, alternatives to wage earning were more plentiful.

Family farming was by far the most common alternative; it occupied well over half of free people, both black and white. Land to the west of the well-established settlements was cheap enough for a great many people to buy. Others obtained acreage as part of their "freedom dues" or squatted on land the colonies had reserved for Indians. A good number of people rented farms, especially in Massachusetts, New Jersey, New York's Hudson Valley, and interior Pennsylvania and Maryland. Though farming was a family affair, it was also a commercial venture in most cases. Nearly every household marketed products such as corn, butter, and woolen goods; many also produced cash crops for export—tobacco in southern colonies, wheat in New England and the mid-Atlantic region. In the Northeast, whose winters brought farm work to a halt for several months each year, numerous households filled the time with craft work, chiefly leather tanning and shoemaking. Farm families were often hard-pressed, even destitute, the land owners as well as the tenants. "Inconsiderable people," the colonial elite called them. Even so, they lived and worked without a boss breathing down their necks; therein lay the great attraction of farming.

Craft work in cities and towns offered another route to independence, an astonishingly fast route by European measures. In Europe, an artisan spent many years preparing for self-employment as a master of his craft. First, he completed a seven-year apprenticeship, serving under a master craftsman in return for room and board; then he worked a long stint as a journeyman, perfecting his skills as he slowly saved money to finance a shop of his own. In America, it was easy to find shortcuts, for the craft guilds that oversaw the system in Europe almost never took root in the colonies. Absent guild oversight, few apprentices put in a full seven years. Some served less time by mutual agreement with their masters; others reneged on their contracts and ran away, eluding the law by moving to a different colony. Skilled labor was in such short supply that almost anyone with a few years of apprenticeship under his belt could get work as a journeyman, and journeymen usually earned enough to finance swift transitions to self-employment.

Benjamin Franklin exemplifies this mobility. Born in 1706 in Boston, he was a candlemaker's son who at age twelve undertook an apprenticeship in printing—a much more prestigious craft, not far below silversmithing at the very top. His master was his older brother James, whom Ben contracted to serve for seven years. By all accounts the boy learned quickly, but James's foul temper made it a difficult apprenticeship. So in 1723, two years before his obligation expired, Ben ran away to Philadelphia, where he passed himself off as a journeyman and soon opened a printshop of his own. By 1748, he was sufficiently rich to retire from the shop and give himself full time to the almanac writing, political activity, and scientific experiments that made him one of the most famous Americans of the eighteenth century.

The unregulated craft system could also undermine the very advantages it bestowed. By the mid-1700s, some trades were so crowded with master craftsmen that bankruptcies were common in slack times. Some masters lowered costs by retaining fewer journeymen and more apprentices—more than they could train in all aspects of the craft. Others turned to slave labor or imported out-of-town journeyman to glut the local job market and thus reduce wages. For the time being, though, such problems were confined to certain trades in certain locales. Most practitioners of most crafts still had good reason to believe Ben Franklin's adage, "He that hath a Trade, hath an Estate."

This "he" was frequently a she. While midwives practiced a prestigious, wholly female trade, many more women engaged in male-dominated crafts from silversmithing on down. Excluded from formal apprenticeships, they acquired craft skills by working in shops owned by their fathers, husbands, or other male kin. Virtually every master craftsmen counted on women's assistance; it took more than his own labor and that of male employees to make the shop pay. A handful of women opened crafts shops of their own. In Baltimore, for example, Mary Minskie and two male assistants made metal corset stays and men's and women's clothing. But the vast majority of master craftswomen were widows carrying on their husbands' businesses—women like Ann Smith Franklin, who ran James Franklin's printshop for twenty-three years following his death.

UNRULY LABOR

The first labor rebellion in colonial North America preceded the establishment of permanent colonies. In the summer of 1526, 500 Spaniards and 100 enslaved Africans made camp near the mouth of the Pee Dee River in present-day South Carolina. That November the slaves rose up, killed most of their captors, and escaped to nearby Indian settlements. The Spanish survivors retreated to Hispaniola; the Africans stayed on. Over the next 250 years, North America saw many more acts of resistance by colonial laborers, both bound and free.

Slaves and indentured servants frequently challenged authority in the much the same ways Adam defied John Saffin. "Stubborn, refractory and discontented," in the words of one Connecticut official, they paced their work as they saw fit, objected aloud to insults, and refused to march dutifully to whipping posts. Many took aim at their masters' property, breaking tools, injuring farm animals, setting fire to houses and barns. Some took aim at the masters themselves, along with anyone who got in the way. In 1678, the Englishman Thomas Hellier, indentured on a Virginia plantation called Hard Labour, axed to death his master, mistress, and a woman servant who tried to assist them. In 1747, the Comanche Pedro de la Cruz led his tribesmen in an armed raid on the New Mexico town where he had been enslaved. In 1771, two African slaves in New Orleans were arrested for flogging their master and burning his hayloft. Stories of such incidents appeared in colonial newspapers on a fairly regular basis.

For both slaves and indentured servants, however, the most common form of resistance was flight. Newspapers carried column upon column of advertisements describing runaways and promising rewards for their capture and return. In British colonies, which were more thickly settled than those of France and Spain, most of the fugitives wound up caught. As one indentured Pennsylvanian wrote, " 'Tis certain that nothing is more difficult than for a Slave or a Servant in America to make his Escape without being retaken." The penalties for those apprehended included whipping, branding, and the amputation of an ear. But attempts at escape continued nonetheless, inspired by the fact that some people managed to get away for good. Those who beat the odds typically found refuge among Native Americans or by fleeing to French or Spanish territory.

In Spanish Florida, escaped slaves from the Carolinas founded a town of several hundred in 1739. Located just north of Saint Augustine, surrounded by stone walls, and guarded by a town militia about 100 strong, this settlement—known as Fort Mose*—became a barrier against British invasion as well as a beacon for runaways. In 1740, when an army of South Carolinians marched into Florida, their defeat at Fort Mose persuaded them to retreat. Welcoming new arrivals from the Carolinas and, later, Georgia as well, the town survived until Spain ceded Florida to Britain in 1763 and Fort Mose's residents moved to Cuba.

---

* Its full name was Gracia Real de Santa Teresa de Mose.

Resistance to servitude also took the form of armed rebellion. Colonial records describe the suppression of hundreds of plots by would-be rebels, including indentured servants in Maryland in the 1650s, an alliance of Indian and African slaves in Massachusetts in 1690, slaves in French New Orleans in 1730 and 1732, about 150 slaves and 25 white allies in New York City in 1741, and the Pueblos in Spanish New Mexico in 1784, 1793, and 1810. If authorities exaggerated some plots and dreamed up some others, their suspicions are understandable. Experience proved time and again that bondage begat revolts.

The largest by far occurred in New Mexico in August 1680, when 17,000 Pueblos rose up against Spanish demands for tribute under the *encomienda* system and Indian conversions to Christianity. A model of strategic planning, this offensive mobilized Pueblos from over two dozen far-flung villages that spoke at least six different languages and widely varied dialects, many of them mutually unintelligible. The revolt also seems to have won strong support from the tens of thousands of baptized Pueblos laboring for Franciscan missions. By October, the rebels had driven every Spaniard out of New Mexico, and only a few hundred Pueblos from the missions had joined the exodus. Spain did not retake the colony until 1693 and never reestablished the *encomienda*. Following a smaller Pueblo uprising in 1696, the colonists also softened their demands for religious conversion and for labor from mission Indians and *repartimiento* draftees.

Slaves and indentured servants in British colonies launched scores of smaller-scale revolts that made up in daring what they lacked in size. The early 1660s ushered in thirty years of unrest in Virginia. Both slaves and servants fled their masters in record numbers. Authorities discovered plots for armed rebellion by servants in York County in 1661, an alliance of slaves and servants in Gloucester County in 1663, and slaves in the Northern Neck region in 1687. Bands of fugitive slaves staged repeated raids on plantations in various counties in 1672 and again in 1691. In 1682, when planters' overproduction of tobacco plunged the colony into depression, slaves, servants, and impoverished free people laid waste to the tobacco crop on plantations throughout Gloucester County.

For Virginia's elite, the most frightening of all the uprisings in this period was Bacon's Rebellion in 1676. It began that spring as a revolt by backcountry farmers, most of them former servants working land they had received as freedom dues. In April some 500 farmers united behind the tobacco planter Nathaniel Bacon to wage an unauthorized war on neighboring Indians. By summer Bacon's troops were also plundering wealthy planters' property, and in September they attacked the colony's capital in Jamestown, where hundreds of slaves and servants joined the uprising. Within days the rebels had burned Jamestown to the ground and fanned out into the surrounding countryside to loot plantations. Chaos reigned for the rest of the year, with slaves and servants fighting on long after Bacon died of dysentery in late October and the farmers started to trudge home.

Following Bacon's Rebellion, the large planters of coastal Virginia and nearby Maryland rethought their labor policies. The indenture system seemed terribly risky now that former servants had inaugurated a mass revolt in which black and white fought side by side. Slavery might prove safer, as long as slaves could be isolated from poor whites. To secure their dominion, the planter elite would henceforth purchase as many slaves as possible, use indentured workers only in a pinch, and try to minimize contact between the two. Colonial officials meanwhile criminalized marriage across the color line and granted servants certain rights and protections denied to slaves—the right to own property, for example, and protection from dismemberment as a penalty for insubordination. As other British colonies institutionalized slavery, they, too, passed laws designed to eliminate common ground between servants and slaves. Labor revolts that united black and white were soon a thing of the past.

Both slaves and servants continued to resist bondage, however, and especially bold mutinies broke out in New York, South Carolina, and Florida following its transfer to England's hands. In April 1712, about twenty-five slaves in New York City—including two Indians and a visibly pregnant black woman—armed themselves with guns, clubs, and knives, set fire to a building on the northern edge of town, and attacked the men who came to put out the fire. Soldiers garrisoned in the city quickly rounded up the rebels, save for six who chose suicide over capture; and some fifty more slaves were arrested on the suspicion that they had helped to plan the revolt. In the end, twenty-one people were executed in gruesome ways designed to terrify potential rebels into submission.

The South Carolina rebellion began in the town of Stono on September 9, 1739, when about twenty slaves led by an Angolan named Jemmy seized guns and powder from a warehouse and set out for Spanish Florida, waving flags, beating drums, and shouting "Liberty!" About sixty more slaves soon joined the column, which attacked every plantation in its path and killed about twenty-five whites along the way. A militia detachment tracked down the rebels in a matter of hours but failed to stop their march for another ten days. While most were finally killed or captured, as many as ten or fifteen got away.

In Florida, a revolt erupted in summer 1768 among Italian and Greek immigrants indentured to ten years' labor on an indigo plantation at New Smyrna on the colony's Atlantic coast. The plantation's British proprietors had recruited them with promises of comfortable lodgings, a half-share of the crop, and their own acreage as freedom dues. Arriving at New Smyrna in June and July 1768, the immigrants found an arid wilderness of uncleared land, severe shortages of food and shelter, and epidemics of gangrene and scurvy. On August 18, some 300 rebels led by Carlo Forni of Livorno, Italy, helped themselves to firearms from the plantation storehouse and locked up their English overseer. About 100 then crowded onto the only ship at the settlement's dock and set sail for Cuba. The British navy soon intercepted them, but a few of the rebels, including Forni, escaped in a rowboat and remained at large for another four months. The only fatalities stemming from this revolt occurred when Forni and one of his lieutenants were captured and beheaded by British authorities. Back at New Smyrna, the deaths were many; close to 900 workers had succumbed to disease by 1773. Four years later, the survivors deserted en masse, and the African captives who replaced them ran away in droves. By 1783, when Spain snatched Florida back from Britain, the plantation lay in ruins.

Free workers resisted subordination in ways that sometimes paralleled those of slaves and indentured servants. Save for the sailors, wage earners in British North America almost never staged strikes. Historians have so far discovered just two definite exceptions to this rule—a 1636 strike in northern Massachusetts (now Maine) by fishermen whose employer had withheld their earnings and a 1768 strike for higher pay by journeymen tailors in New York City. But wage earners repeatedly joined with others from the lower and middle classes to protest harms from above. Most of these protests took place in cities, and Boston saw an especially large share. In 1713, when the city's grain supplies dwindled and its food prices soared, some 200 hungry Bostonians ransacked the ships and warehouses of a merchant exporting corn to the West Indies. In 1747, a crowd of several thousand armed with clubs and swords stopped a British commander from press-ganging Boston seamen into compulsory service in the Royal Navy. A city official who vigorously backed this riot's suppression soon lost his house to arson as hundreds gathered in the street hollering, "Let it burn!"

On a more mundane level, free workers asserted their rights to dress and amuse themselves in ways the elite deemed inappropriate. As often as they could afford, they wore bits of finery such as a handkerchief, a garment of brightly colored chintz, or a collar of fine linen. Many working men and more than a few of the women congregated in taverns in their spare hours. Some showed up at entertainments intended for the gentry. All of this the upper classes abhorred. No less a body than the Massachusetts General Court denounced wage earners for desiring clothes "altogether unbecoming their place and rank" and for frequenting "taverns and alehouses where they idled away their time." A British musician performing in Lancaster, Pennsylvania, was horrified to find three farmhands in the audience; he had thought the ticket price "sufficient to exclude such characters." An important issue underlay these small conflicts. The elite resented free workers' liberty to do as they wished in at least some corners of their lives; and that was the very thing the workers valued most.

Nowhere was this more evident than in their responses to destitution, a constant danger for all wage earners save craft journeymen. From the mid-1600s onward, colonial officials complained about the numbers of "idle and unprofitable" people who could not find steady wage work yet refused to volunteer for the security of indentured service. They scavenged, begged, engaged in petty crime, squatted on other peoples' land, searched endlessly for a few days' work here and there—anything to avoid bondage. Officials who tried to intervene met strong, sometimes violent resistance. In 1715, a sheriff served an eviction notice on a squatters' camp in Schoharie County, New York; Magdalena Zeh and her women neighbors attacked him with rakes and hoes, rode him out of the camp on a rail, and dumped him on the road back to Albany. In later decades, city governments opened poorhouses where the destitute could work in return for bed and board in strictly regimented dormitories. No one went there voluntarily; instead, authorities filled the dormitories with people who were too weak to flee. Philadelphia's poorhouse reported in the 1770s that inmates arrived "emaciated with Poverty and Disease to such a Degree that some have died in a few days of their Admission."

Women sometimes resisted subordination in another way too: they fled their husbands. English law, which applied in the colonies, defined a wife as her husband's chattel. Whatever he desired, she should desire. Whatever wages she earned, property she obtained, or children she bore belonged to him. He was entitled to her labor in the household and entitled as well to give her "reasonable chastisement," meaning any physical punishment that did not inflict permanent injury or death. Most wives seem to have worked out tolerable domestic arrangements nonetheless, but quite a few did not. The same newspaper columns that described runaway slaves and servants also described runaway wives, warning that anyone who assisted these women would be prosecuted to "the utmost Rigour of the Law." Such ads were placed by free men of all stations, from merchants and planters to silversmiths, tailors, bricklayers, and sailors.

Labor organizations were few and far between in colonial America and confined to men in skilled trades. Master craftsmen founded a handful of guilds. The largest, chartered in 1724, was the Carpenters' Company of Philadelphia, which regulated the prices masters charged their customers, the wages they paid to journeymen, and their treatment of apprentices. But guilds had a minuscule impact on the helter-skelter American craft system, for they operated city by city in a tiny minority of trades. Local benevolent societies sprang up in a somewhat larger number of trades. Encompassing masters, journeymen and sometimes apprentices, these societies provided members with sick benefits, small loans, and assistance in times of dire need.

Journeymen occasionally formed ad hoc organizations in order to make demands on employers, as when the Journeyman Caulkers of Boston suddenly appeared in 1741 to announce that its members would no longer work for promissory notes. More commonly, master craftsmen came together to stop production in protest of statutory caps on the prices they could charge. Masters of all crafts subject to price controls—carters, coopers, bakers, chimney sweepers, and others—took part in such actions. The courts routinely convicted them of conspiracy, and black craftsmen in particular risked more brutal retaliation. Rage sufficient to spawn violence permeated the *South Carolina Gazette*'s report in October 1763 that Charleston's black chimney sweepers "had the insolence by a combination amongst themselves, to raise the usual prices, and to refuse doing their work, unless their exorbitant demands are complied with."

Among wage earners, sailors were by far the most militant. They included men of all colors and a few women who went to sea disguised as men. They displayed a legendary contempt for wielders of arbitrary authority, from constables to kings. Several thousand of them became pirates, whose declared purpose was to "plunder the rich." And no one outshone sailors when it came to labor solidarity, for shipmates were quite literally all in the same boat. They often quit a ship en masse, refusing to leave port on vessels that were undermanned or in poor repair. They also staged numerous strikes, not only in port but also at sea. Safety was often the issue. In 1719, the crew of the *Hanover Succession,* sailing from Charleston to London, tired of pumping seawater out of the ship's leaky hold and refused to work until the captain agreed to return to port. In other instances sailors struck to protest floggings, to stop captains from changing the itinerary once a ship was at sea, or to demand time off when they reached the next port. Work stoppages are called strikes on account of sailors; they would "strike"—that is, lower—a ship's sails when they were no longer willing to work.

On the eve of the American Revolution, the vast majority of people in the colonies that would form the United States lacked rights enjoyed by the colonial elite. Slaves, indentured servants, apprentices, women of all stations, free men without property: none had the right to vote and hold office. Together, they made up at least 90 percent of colonial society, and most of them were poor as well as politically disfranchised. Therein lay the heart of the "labor problem" from labor's point of view. It was a problem shared by bound and free workers and one that both groups were determined to solve.

CHAPTER

THE AMERICAN REVOLUTION

On July 4, 1776, the Continental Congress in Philadelphia unanimously adopted the Declaration of Independence, announcing to the world that thirteen North American colonies intended to throw off British rule and found a new nation based on republican government. Penned by Thomas Jefferson of Virginia, this document was designed to stir souls:

> We hold these truths to be self-evident, that all men are created equal, that they are endowed by their Creator with certain unalienable Rights, that among these are Life, Liberty, and the pursuit of Happiness.—That to se-cure these rights, Governments are instituted among Men, deriving their just Powers from the consent of the governed—That whenever any Form of Government becomes destructive of these ends, it is the Right of the People to alter or to abolish it, and to institute new Government, laying its Foundation on such Principles, and organizing its Powers in such Form, as to them shall seem most likely to effect their Safety and Happiness.

There, in plain language, was the spirit of the American Revolution.

The Declaration's signers came late to that spirit. American colonists had been at war with Britain since April 1775, when Massachusetts militiamen battled the British army; and the war followed more than a decade of anti-British protests by common people, especially artisans and wage workers in the coastal cities. Wealthy colonists had sometimes sponsored and supported these protests but had also viewed them with alarm. When they finally came around to the revolutionary program, they commandeered the movement.

Jefferson was one of the wealthiest slaveholding planters in North America, and the Declaration's other signers were well-to-do planters, lawyers, and merchants. They believed that the right to self-government belonged to people like themselves—white men of substantial means. But such men could not win a war or found a nation without rallying common people, whose quarrels with the British regime targeted privilege based on wealth and rank as well as royal prerogatives and imperial edicts. Thus the founding fathers signed on to a declaration that expressed a spirit much more egalitarian than their own.

Nowhere was that spirit stronger and more unruly than among working people. Building on over a century of colonial labor rebellions, both the free and the unfree fought for "Life, Liberty, and the pursuit of Happiness" in many ways that the gentlemen of the Continental Congress did not appreciate. And these struggles grew all the more contentious after Britain's defeat, when men of wealth constructed a republic that reneged on egalitarian ideals.

From Resistance to Independence

Britain's empire in North America reached its zenith in 1763, when protracted wars with France and Spain ended in a treaty that brought all lands east of the Mississippi under British control. No one could have guessed that just twelve years later American colonies would take up arms against the mother country. But the seeds of that revolt had already been planted, for Britain's imperial wars bankrupted its treasury. To meet the costs of empire, the British Parliament sought to squeeze more revenues from the colonies, touching off protests that led inexorably to revolution.

The first round of protests took aim at the Stamp Act of 1765, which required that legal documents and other printed materials bear a stamp purchased from British agents. Marriage licenses, land deeds, indenture agreements, commercial contracts, playing cards, books and newspapers, handbill advertisements: all this and more were subject to the new tax. And to add insult to injury, revenues from the Stamp Act financed Britain's colonial army and administrative apparatus—the very power structure that kept Americans under Parliament's thumb.

Anger at this arrangement sparked militant resistance, mainly among working people in coastal cities. Men from the maritime trades organized demonstrations that swelled with artisans, common laborers, housewives, and children, and sometimes targeted the property of British officials. In New York City, sailors and other maritime workers formed the anti–British Sons of Neptune and staged what observers called an "insurrection" against the Stamp Act. In Boston, the shoemaker Ebenezer MacIntosh led a crowd of 2,000 workingmen that demolished the local stamp agent's office and vandalized his home.

Some members of the wealthy and middle classes joined the movement against the Stamp Act. In Boston, Newport, New York, and other cities, protest committees called the Sons of Liberty included merchants, lawyers, doctors, ministers, shopkeepers, and master craftsmen along with larger numbers of wage workers. Other gentlemen, fearful of British reprisals, supported protests behind the scenes. These were fragile alliances, however, for common people's anger at Britain's heavy hand routinely spilled over into anger at the rich. Less than two weeks after Boston workingmen attacked the stamp agent's office and home, a second crowd ransacked the mansion of Massachusetts's lieutenant governor. In Newport, workingman John Weber led Stamp Act protests whose participants said such radical things about redistributing wealth that the city's merchants—who had hired Weber to organize the demonstrations—soon demanded his arrest.

Assaults on the rich persisted even after Parliament caved in to American protests and repealed the Stamp Act in March 1766. That May, in New York City, a crowd turned out to jeer at the fancy attire and manners of people attending the opening of an expensive new theater. Before the night was out, the demonstrators had torn down the theater, then marched through town shouting "Liberty! Liberty!"

With the Stamp Act gone, Parliament soon turned to a new plan for taxing the colonies. The Revenue Act of 1767 imposed tariffs known as the Townshend Duties on key goods Americans imported from abroad: paint, lead, glass, paper, and tea. Rebellious colonists responded with a "nonimportation" movement, a boycott of all British imports. A wide network of boycott committees—called Sons of Liberty, Regulators, Associators, or Liberty Boys—extended from Massachusetts to South Carolina and from major cities to the backwoods. Merchants and shopkeepers who sold British goods were denounced as public enemies and often tarred and feathered too.

Women played crucial roles in the boycott by producing alternatives to British imports. They brewed herbal drinks and "Rye Coffee" as substitutes for tea; replaced paint with homemade whitewash; and virtually eliminated the colonies' dependence on British textiles by spinning gigantic volumes of cloth from wool, flax, and hemp. Hundreds of local women's committees—

often called the Daughters of Liberty—organized spinning bees and promoted slogans like, "Better to wear a Homespun Coat than to lose our Liberty." In Kinderhook, New York, when a man scolded a spinning circle for meddling in politics, the women stripped off his clothes, covered him with molasses and flax down, and sent him on his way.

As the boycott movement gained momentum, Britain enlarged its army in North America, stationing most of the reinforcements in New York City and Boston, the movement's most militant centers. The soldiers liked to supplement their meager pay by moonlighting in waterfront jobs. Local workers competed for the same jobs, ever harder to find once the boycott curtailed commercial shipping. Tensions mounted, punctuated by occasional fistfights, until pitched battles erupted in 1770. In January, workers and soldiers in New York City slugged it out in a two-day street fight known as the Battle of Golden Hill. Push came to shove in Boston that March, when British troops brawled with rope makers who had insulted a soldier looking for work. Two days later, on the night of March 5, a crowd of workingmen taunted soldiers from the same regiment, who suddenly opened fire. Five workers were killed and another six wounded in what colonists called the Boston Massacre.

The dead were seamen Crispus Attucks and James Caldwell, rope maker Samuel Gray, apprentice leather maker Patrick Carr, and apprentice ivory turner Sam Maverick. Attucks—a fugitive slave of mixed African and Indian ancestry, then a free mariner for 20 years—had been a member of the Sons of Liberty and a leader of the crowd. Ten thousand Bostonians marched in the martyrs' funeral procession, and the dead were commemorated in many surrounding towns. Well into the nineteenth century, much of Massachusetts celebrated March 5th as the American Revolution's premier holiday.

On the very day of the Boston Massacre, well before the news reached London, Parliament rescinded the Townshend Duties except for the tax on tea. With that, the nonimportation coalition began to fragment. Merchants wished to resume the lucrative trade with Britain. Well-to-do families had tired of giving up imported luxuries. And as much as colonial elites might resent British rule, most distrusted the "mob" of common people who clung to a boycott abandoned by the upper classes.

In fact, this so-called mob mounted well-organized resistance to the British. While the gentry vacillated, the movement spread. In New York City, Philadelphia, and Charleston, South Carolina, master craftsmen and journeymen formed mechanics' associations to press the boycott cause in colonial assemblies and councils. In November 1772, a Boston town meeting established a Committee of Correspondence to communicate with other cities and coordinate resistance. Within a few months identical committees had been authorized by town meetings and popular assemblies in every colony. The committees' leaders typically came from the ranks of master craftsmen, professionals, or the handful of wealthy men still loyal to nonimportation, but small farmers, journeymen, and other wage workers made up most of the rank and file. One merchant complained that "the lowest Mechanicks discuss upon the most important points of Government with the utmost Freedom."

The committees carefully planned direct-action protests, breaking British laws in orderly ways. A prime example was the famous Boston Tea Party of December 1773, in which squads of men boarded British ships, dumped their cargo of tea into the harbor, and left without claiming any booty. That winter, similar "tea parties" took place in other ports, and though jobs were scarce, workingmen in Boston and New York City conformed to strict boycotts on labor for the British army. When General Thomas Gage called for workers to build military fortifications in Boston, no one from that city stepped forward, and later efforts to recruit New Yorkers failed as well. In the end Gage had to import carpenters and bricklayers from as far away as Nova Scotia.

If organization and discipline strengthened the resistance movement, so did British reaction to the Boston Tea Party. To punish Massachusetts, Parliament passed a series of laws known in America as the Intolerable Acts. They closed Boston Harbor to all trade; forbade communities throughout the colony to hold more than one town meeting a year; allowed British officials indicted for crimes in Massachusetts to stand trial elsewhere; and empowered the British army to quarter troops in colonists' homes. These statutes ignited resistance in every part of Massachusetts, whose citizens stockpiled weapons, formed local militias, and held town meetings in defiance of British orders. Expressions of sympathy poured forth from other colonies, and Committees of Correspondence grew in size and number as they collected food, clothing, and money for the blockaded Bostonians. The new forces included members of the wealthy classes, not only merchants but also Virginia's big planters, who forged an anti-British alliance with that colony's poor whites.

For six weeks in fall 1774, representatives from every colony but Georgia gathered in Philadelphia for the first Continental Congress, which hammered out a common program for resistance. Though most of the delegates were men of wealth, the militant spirit of popular protests carried the day. The Congress launched a Continental Association, which decreed a total embargo on trade with Britain—no imports, no exports—and called for the formation of local committees to enforce the ban. By the end of the year embargo committees and anti-British militias had sprung up in all colonies, and the Association was forging them into a national movement.

Outright war began on April 19, 1775, when Massachusetts militia companies fought the British troops General Gage had sent to seize a colonial arsenal in Concord. Within days, militiamen closed in on Boston, besieging Gage's forces. In a matter of weeks, militia units from Connecticut, Rhode Island and New Hamphire went to aid the siege, and another band of New Englanders routed British troops from Fort Ticonderoga in upper New York.

In Philadelphia, the second Continental Congress laid plans to spread the fight. The delegates issued a formal declaration of war against Britain and authorized the creation of a Continental Army to be commanded by Virginia planter George Washington. But when they debated the question of American independence, caution prevailed. Their declaration of war explicitly rejected independence, and another resolution implored Britain's King George III to reconcile with the colonies.

As the war wore on, however, popular anger at Britain reached new heights, and radical agitators channeled that anger into sentiment for independence. The most influential agitator was the journalist Thomas Paine, a former artisan whose plain language and democratic politics struck a deeply responsive chord among common people. In January 1776, Paine published a fifty-page pamphlet titled *Common Sense* that argued for an independent America under republican government. Readers snapped up more than 100,000 copies, and *Common Sense* was even more widely discussed—read aloud to people who were not literate enough to read it for themselves. Echoing Paine, the Declaration of Independence signaled the Continental Congress's conversion to a program that the rank and file of revolutionaries had already embraced.

Not all common people backed the cause. Contemporaries estimated that about one-third of free colonists favored independence, another third opposed it, and the rest stayed neutral. Only in New England and Virginia did the revolution have majority support. On the whole, it was more popular among the laboring and middle classes than among the elite, but local resentments sometimes produced countercurrents. In 1771, the North Carolina militia had crushed the Regulator Movement in which backcountry farmers rallied to stop judges and land speculators from confiscating the homesteads of tax delinquents. When the Regulators' wealthy enemies later endorsed the revolution, much of the backcountry chose the other side. Revolutionary sentiment among large landowners had the same effect on many tenant farmers in New York's Hudson Valley and poor whites in Eastern Shore Maryland.

For slaves—about 20 percent of the colonial population in 1775—the war fueled hopes for their own independence, and that repeatedly placed them at odds with white revolutionaries. The contradiction had been brewing since the days of the Stamp Act protests. Charleston, South Carolina, had declared martial law for a week when slaves echoed white protestors' shouts for "Liberty." The crowd of Boston artisans led by Ebenezer McIntosh had excluded all blacks so as not to encourage their insubordination. By the time the revolutionary war began, a rising tide of slave conspiracies, mutinies, and petitions for freedom had made it clear that slaves stood ready to fight for whichever side offered better possibilities for emancipation.

Black men both slave and free served in the New England militia units that mobilized against the British in spring 1775 and in the Continental Army's earliest regiments. All of these troops were volunteers. Slaves usually enlisted with their owners' consent and always with the understanding that military service would render them free. That crack in the edifice of slavery agitated the Continental Congress, whose unity in behalf of the war rested on an agreement that it would not liberate slaves. In February 1776, following months of debate among Congressmen and military commanders, George Washington ordered that free black men who had already served could reenlist in the Continental Army but that no other black or Indian soldiers would be accepted. By summer, militia laws in the various colonies had been amended to exclude all but white men.

As Continental leaders debated black enlistment, slaves in Virginia made a bid for freedom under British auspices. In November 1775, the colony's royal governor, Lord John Dunmore, issued a proclamation promising freedom to all slaves who belonged to American rebels and bore arms for Britain. In the few weeks that elapsed before Continental troops drove Dunmore from the mainland, some 700 slaves made their way to his camp near Norfolk. About 1,000 more later managed to reach his ships anchored off Virginia's shore, and in summer 1776, when he sailed to Staten Island, slaves from New York and New Jersey reinforced his black regiment. By the end of the war, tens of thousands of escaped slaves—men and women alike—would serve Britain's army as soldiers or workers behind the lines.

Native Americans fought for both sides too, though most would have preferred to stay neutral. From Pequot towns in New England to Catawba villages in South Carolina, Indians in the heartlands of white settlement joined the revolution's troops in 1775 and resisted exclusion the following year. But the vast network of Indian nations on the colonies' frontiers spurned overtures from the Continentals and the British. As the Seneca chief Kayashuta explained, "We must be Fools indeed to imagine that they regard us or our Interest who want to bring us into an unnecessary War." In the end, though, few frontier nations could avoid the fight. Combatants from both sides penetrated more and more of Indian country and tolerated no neutrals. Forced to choose, many nations split into opposing camps, but most people sided with Britain, which pledged to uphold Indian claims to land the colonists had time and again tried to grab.

The Declaration of Independence pointedly ignored the revolution's incongruities: that slaveholders shouted for liberty; that black and Indian volunteers for the cause had been turned away; that the Continental Congress still sought allies among frontier Indians who did not wish to fight; that republican values ran deeper at the revolution's grassroots than among its official leaders in Congress. Thomas Jefferson revised his first draft of the Declaration to delete the charge that King George disgraced himself by abetting slavery and the slave trade. The final draft's bill of grievances climaxed with the complaint that he incited "domestic insurrections" (a euphemism for slave revolts) and courted military assistance from "merciless Indian Savages." To defend slavery and condemn Indians contradicted the statement that "all men are created equal," but this was a political document, not a treatise on logic. If the congressmen thought themselves more equal than most—"an aristocracy of virtue and talent," as Jefferson later put it—they also knew that the revolution could not succeed unless masses of commoners saw it as their own.

THE PEOPLE'S WAR AND THE GENTLEMEN'S REPUBLIC

As Tom Paine observed in 1792, "The Independence of America, considered merely as a separation from England, would have been a matter but of little importance, had it not been accompanied by a Revolution in the principles and practice of Governments." Common people, who bore the brunt of the war with Britain, took part in the political revolution as well. The elite remained in command, however, and concessions to those below were not evenly distributed.

After the Continental Congress declared independence, the rebel colonies—now members of the United States of America—began to draw up constitutions for state government. Virtually all of the men involved in this process agreed that politics should remain a male affair and that governments should be elected. But there was no consensus as to how much political power should belong to ordinary men compared to men of the elite.

Pennsylvania fashioned the most democratic constitution, adopted in summer 1776. It gave all taxpaying freemen the right to vote and hold office, created a unicameral legislature to be elected every year, and authorized the governor to do little more than execute the legislature's decisions. Except in emergencies, legislators could not pass a bill into law unless its text had first been distributed for discussion by the general public. In 1777, when small farmers in upper New York broke away to form the new state of Vermont (not formally part of the United States until 1791), they wrote a constitution modeled on Pennsylvania's.

By and large, however, state constitutional conventions were dominated by conservatives and strictly limited democracy. In Maryland and Virginia, for example, planters preserved their political clout by instituting stiff property qualifications for both voters and officeholders and by setting long intervals between elections. In New York and Massachusetts, merchants and lawyers drafted constitutions that provided for powerful governors and bicameral legislatures in which assemblies chosen by the whole electorate (male taxpayers) shared lawmaking with senates elected by wealthy men. New Jersey was the only state that enfranchised women—as long as they were unmarried and met the same high property requirements as men.

Whatever their formal rights to a voice in politics, both men and women of the lower classes made their voices heard. When wartime shortages pushed food prices through the roof, popular protests forced every state north of Maryland to enact price controls. Angry crowds of women meanwhile raided the storerooms of merchants and shopkeepers guilty of price gouging or suspected of hoarding necessities. In the port cities, sailors and craft journeymen struck for pay hikes to meet the rising cost of living. In 1779, militiamen in Philadelphia assaulted the home of a prominent lawyer opposed to price controls and even wheeled up a piece of artillery before they were dispersed by a unit of light cavalry. The countryside was also in turmoil. Many tenant farmers stopped paying rent and joined with small freeholders to appropriate land owned by wealthy men who sided with Britain.

Slaves fled their masters in unprecedented numbers, 30,000 in Virginia alone, according to Thomas Jefferson's estimate. Petitions for freedom poured into state courts and legislatures, often echoing the Declaration of Independence. One petition presented in Massachusetts in January 1777 argued that slaves "have in common with all other Men a Natural and Unalienable Right to that freedom which the Great Parent of the Universe hath bestowed equally on all menkind."

Quite a few fugitive slaves joined the Continental Army, whose color bars disintegrated as the fighting dragged on. The turning point came in 1777, when Congress scrambled to reinforce the military. American diplomats stepped up efforts to win European allies and eventually brought France, Spain, and Holland into the war. Various blends of diplomacy and coercion yielded Indian allies from the Delawares, Tuscaroras, Penobscots, and other frontier nations. Mainly, however, Congress looked to the states. Starting in January 1777, each had to supply the army with a certain quota of regular troops. Unlike state militiamen, who enlisted for three to twelve months, the regulars served for three years. Volunteers for such duty were so scarce that state recruiters usually welcomed one and all, ignoring legalities as to who could and could not serve.

Every state soon instituted a military draft, which ushered in more drastic changes in the army's makeup. While the draft laws typically conscripted white men only, that did not determine who actually served. A man who was summoned could send his slave, his indentured servant, his apprentice or any paid substitute to take his place. Many draftees did just that, and many a town hired outsiders to substitute for its residents, if only to keep the local militia intact. By the end of the decade, the Continental Army bore little resemblance to the volunteer force that had mustered in 1775. Most of the soldiers were now conscripts or their stand-ins. Artisans, journeymen, and small landowners, the core of the old army, were now outnumbered by lowlier groups—common laborers and landless farmers along with apprentices, servants, and slaves.

The enlistment of bound workers pitted private-property rights against the public need for troops. Numerous petitioners called on Congress to stop military recruiters from inducting bondsmen without their masters' consent or compensation. A county committee in Cumberland, Pennsylvania, protested on the grounds that "all apprentices and servants are the property of their masters and mistresses, and every mode of depriving such masters and mistresses of their property is a violation of the rights of mankind." Jonathan Hobby of Concord, Massachusetts, sued the army to return a teenaged slave who had enlisted while Hobby was out of town. Military judges agreed that Hobby's property rights had been violated but declined to rule on his suit. Congress waffled too, telling the military to return runaway bondsmen at their masters' request but ignoring the routine violations of this order. The sharpest controversies concerned state laws on the enlistment of slaves. Northern and middle states quickly approved this practice once Congress assigned troop quotas. Maryland followed suit in 1780, after three years of debate and failure to meet its quota. Virginia, the Carolinas, and Georgia resisted to the bitter end, though they allowed black freemen to substitute for white conscripts. From the late 1770s until the fighting ceased, emissaries from Congress and General George Washington badgered these states to raise slave battalions. Every request was, to quote one of Washington's aides, "drowned by the howlings of a triple-headed monster in which prejudice, avarice and pusillanimity were united."

A different sprit prevailed among the army's rank and file, where men of every color—and some women disguised as men—soldiered for meager pay almost always in arrears. There were a few all-black regiments. Enlistees from Indian towns sometimes signed up in groups and formed their own squads. But most units were fully integrated, and they all merged in battle, with common soldiers of every description fighting side by side. The Massachusetts rosters included Ben Russell, a white apprentice printer from Worcester; Ezekiel Brown, a white Concord schoolmaster fresh out of debtor's prison; Cesar Perry, a free black laborer from Bristol County; Charlestown Edes, a black slave from Groton; and the farmer Daniel Nimham, a Wappinger Indian elder from Stockbridge who died in battle near New York City. At least one woman was also part of this mix: Deborah Sampson, a white woman from Middleborough who grew up as an indentured servant and, at age twenty-one, went off to war under the name of Robert Shurleff.

Up to 20,000 women served the army in other ways. Most were soldiers' wives or widows, sometimes with children in tow. Since the Continental Army did not provide family allowances, poor women often had little choice but to follow the troops and work for rations. They served as cooks, seamstresses, laundresses, and nurses, and in the heat of battle, quite a few fought. The most famous was Mary Hays McCauley, who earned the nickname Molly Pitcher by carrying water to soldiers on the front lines. When her husband fell from wounds or fatigue, she took his place as a cannon loader. Though General Washington called women "camp followers" a nuisance, he was known to assign them to cannon crews when he ran short of men.

Tensions between the troops and their commanders ran high throughout the war. From the moment they took charge, Washington and his corps of officers complained about undisciplined foot soldiers. One captain described them as "the strangest mixture of Indians, Negroes, and whites, with old men and mere children, which together with a nasty lousy appearance make a shocking spectacle." The three-year enlistments instituted in 1777 were supposed to whip the army into shape; but recruits who entered under the draft proved even more unruly than their predecessors. Several times in 1780, units from Pennsylvania and New Jersey mutinied over short rations and pay, and the ringleaders were executed on Washington's orders.

If ragtag troops were hard to govern, however, they defeated the world's foremost imperial power. Of the 200,000 troops who fought Britain, about half served in local militias. Assembling at need, harassing the enemy with sniping fire, they made every British expedition costly. But Continental regulars endured the heaviest combat, casualties, and privations. The victory belonged first and foremost to them.

The fighting ended suddenly in October 1781, when the British army in Virginia was trapped between American and French forces. That winter Parliament voted to abandon the war, and in 1782 the British troops withdrew from all states, accompanied by some 30,000 former slaves who had assisted them in the war. In the Treaty of Paris, signed in 1783, Britain formally recognized American independence and transferred to the United States all territory east of the Mississippi River, south of the Great Lakes, and north of Florida. Slavery, Indian land rights, and other issues Congress had sidestepped in the Declaration of Independence would now come sharply to the fore.

Settlers and speculators rushed into the northwestern frontier, snatching land from Indian allies as well as those who had sided with Britain. To restore law and order, Congress made the thefts legal. By 1790, treaties signed at gunpoint had deprived Indians of nearly all their land between Lake Ontario and the Ohio River. Back east, Indian veterans of the Continental Army did not fare much better. Debts incurred when the men were away compelled many households to sell off their land. Massachusetts rescinded Indians' right to self-government, putting their towns under the authority of white overseers. In the space of a few years the new republic made explicit the principle that Indians were not "created equal," not even those who had bled for the revolution; and hardly anyone save for Indians themselves disputed that injustice.

Servitude became a more contentious issue. Master craftsmen pushed for stricter laws to control apprentices, who ran away even more frequently than during the war. Starting in 1783, state after state stiffened the penalties for runaway apprentices and anyone who helped them abscond. But in most cases the new statutes also extended republican rights to apprentices, declaring that they could not be bound to labor beyond age twenty-one and spelling out procedures by which they could sue their masters for cruelty or neglect.

The indenture of European immigrants came under fire too. Right after the war, societies to protect indentured servants from abuse sprang up in

New York, Maryland, and Pennsylvania. German immigrants, many of whom had arrived as redemptioners, were especially active in this cause. In 1784, one group in New York City paid off the indentures of a shipload of new immigrants and condemned the "traffic in White People" as a British custom at odds with "the idea of liberty this country has so happily established."

Movements against slavery gathered on a larger scale, inspired by republican ideals, religious fervor, and the emancipation of several thousand black war veterans. In northern states, slave trading was outlawed and slavery itself edged toward extinction. Vermont had set the example in 1777, abolishing slavery under its constitution. In 1783, New Hampshire did the same, and Massachusetts courts ruled slavery illegal. Elsewhere in the North, freedom came at a snail's pace under gradual emancipation laws enacted by Pennsylvania (1780), Connecticut (1784), Rhode Island (1784), New York (1799), and New Jersey (1804). Designed to reconcile slaves' rights to liberty and masters' rights to property, these statutes freed enslaved women's future offspring but only after they reached ages ranging from eighteen to twenty-eight.

In the southern states slavery expanded, despite opposition from some quarters. During the 1780s, a number of slaveholders in the upper South caught the "contagion of liberty" and voluntarily freed their slaves. By the early 1790s, local societies to promote manumission had formed statewide networks in Delaware, Maryland, and Virginia. No southern legislature moved to abolish slavery, however. Nor did manumission societies spread to the lower South, or even make a sizable dent on their home ground.

From Delaware to Georgia, the great majority of slaveholders sought to increase holdings depleted in wartime. They tracked down runaways, purchased the slaves southern states had confiscated from people who sided with Britain, imported tens of thousands of captives from Africa or the Caribbean, and enslaved some free blacks kidnapped from as far north as Massachusetts. In other cases masters reasserted claims to slaves freed during the war so that they could substitute for white conscripts.

These efforts more than offset freedom's progress in the North. By 1790, the free black population reached almost 60,000, up from just a few thousand at the start of the revolution; but slaves numbered about 698,000, compared to 500,000 in 1775. Some 658,000 slaves lived in the South, a little over 100,000 in Maryland and in each of the Carolinas. The largest slaveholder by far was Thomas Jefferson's Virginia, where the census of 1790 counted 292,627 slaves.

Though political conflicts over slavery would dwarf all others in decades to come, the most explosive issue in the postwar era was a debt crisis that wreaked havoc on family farms. When American ports reopened to British trade, wartime shortages and inflation gave way to peacetime glut and depression. Small farmers were the hardest hit, for agricultural prices were the first to fall. By 1786, many farms were so heavily mortgaged that their owners stood on the brink of bankruptcy, and to make matters worse, merchants who had earlier extended credit now demanded that customers pay their accounts in full. In state after state, farmers pressed legislatures to lower taxes on farmland, suspend debt collection, abolish imprisonment for debt, and ease the depression by issuing large sums of paper money.

Nowhere was this agitation more ferocious than in Massachusetts, whose lawmakers resisted the debtor's demands. In August and September 1786, many hundreds of armed farmers—most of them Continental Army veterans—seized courthouses to suspend debtors' trials. Daniel Shays, a captain during the war, emerged as the movement's leader. That fall he organized 1,000 men to march on Boston, whose merchants spent $200,000 to raise a private militia that turned back Shays's troops. In January 1787, they regrouped to besiege the Springfield armory but this time suffered a decisive defeat. Rural uprisings were also suppressed in New Hampshire, New Jersey, Pennsylvania, Maryland, Virginia, and South Carolina.

In the wake of these rebellions, the wealthy classes moved to consolidate their political power. From late May to mid-September 1787, delegates from every state but Rhode Island held a closed-door convention in Philadelphia. George Washington chaired the gathering, whose participants came from the revolutionary elite. They included ambassadors, high-ranking army officers, Continental Congressmen, and the revolution's financiers. As far as the public knew, the delegates would amend the Articles of Confederation that had established a national government during the war. Instead, they wrote an entirely new Constitution of the United States.

The Constitution divided the government into legislative, executive, and judicial departments, each authorized to curb action by the others. On the legislative side there was a bicameral U.S. Congress, made up of the House of Representatives and the Senate. Delegates to the House would be elected every two years by voters who met the minimum qualifications to cast ballots for their state legislature; and the number of seats apportioned to each state would depend on the size of its population. The senators—two for every state regardless of population—would be chosen by state legislatures and serve six-year terms. The president and vice president would be chosen every four years by appointees to an "electoral college" where each state had as many votes as it had seats in the House and Senate. From the Supreme

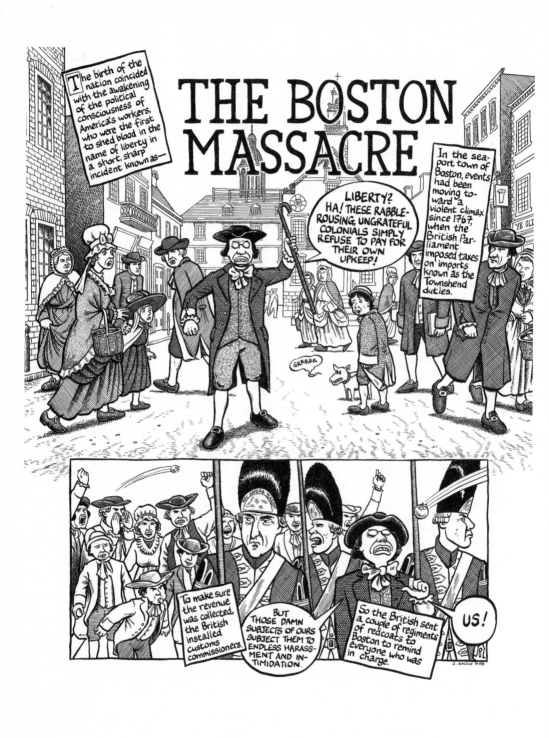

The tension had not abated by March 2, when a British grenadier strolled into a ropewalk—a place where workers wound hemp into ropes and cables—in search of a part-time job to supplement his meager soldier's income.

SOLDIER, WILL YOU WORK?

I WILL, FAITH.

THEN YOU CAN GO CLEAN MY SHIT-HOUSE.

Y'SEE THE SORT OF VULGAR LOUTS WE'RE TRYIN' TO GOVERN HERE?

The insult led to a series of brawls between soldiers and the rope makers—and then other citizens of Boston—that would culminate in tragedy a short time later.

On the night of March 5, a large group of disaffected dockyard workers and seamen, led by a runaway slave and sailor, Crispus Attucks, joined a crowd of Bostonians taunting and menacing several British soldiers outside the Customs House.

YOU DAMN LOBSTER!

I'LL HAVE ONE OF YOUR CLAWS!

DAMNED IF I WON'T!

The soldiers fired into the crowd, killing four men, including Attucks, and mortally wounding another.

All the dead — who included a ship's mate, a journeyman leathermaker, a rope maker, and an ivory turner's apprentice — were working men.

At the trial of the British soldiers that followed, the chief defense attorney was none other than that ostensible patriot and future U.S. president, John Adams.

AND EVEN HE CALLED THE BOSTON MOB—

—A MOTLEY RABBLE OF SAUCY BOYS, NEGROES AND MULATTOES, IRISH TEAGUES AND OUTLANDISH JACK TARS!

But the sacrifice of laborers that fateful night underscored the stake workers had in the revolution that was about to come and the nation that was about to be born.

J. SACCO 10·98

Court to lower courts, federal judges would be selected by the president (subject to Senate approval) and serve indefinite terms.

Unlike the Articles of Confederation, the Constitution empowered the national government to levy taxes and tariffs, pay the war debt, regulate commerce, coin money and set its value, standardize bankruptcy laws, and otherwise look out for businessmen's needs. New prohibitions on the states outlawed actions demanded by indebted farmers. No state could issue its own money, allow debts to be paid in anything but gold and silver coinage, or make laws that impaired contracts such as mortgages and loans.

Southern planters won a favorable compromise when the Philadelphia convention debated whether slaves should be counted for the purpose of apportioning seats in the House of Representatives. Under the "three-fifths clause," 60 percent of the slave population was factored in and southern states got many more seats than they would otherwise possess. The Constitution also stipulated that states could import slaves from overseas for the next twenty years. Another clause obligated every state to return runaway slaves to their masters.

By summer 1788, the Constitution had been ratified by the required quorum of states, whose voters elected special conventions to debate the pros and cons. The patchwork of state restrictions on voting rights placed these proceedings in the hands of men who owned property—at least enough to make them taxpayers. This did not guarantee agreement, however. More often then not, ratification won by a nose.

While the wealthy generally endorsed it, state officials anxious to preserve their powers often came down on the other side. Popular radicals divided, many backing the Constitution as a means to solidify the republic, many others rejecting it as a yoke on democracy, and some waffling back and forth. Urban artisans championed ratification as the key to prosperity; a national government empowered to tax imports could protect American industries from foreign competition. Small farmers mounted the most resolute opposition, fearful that the new government would tax them into bankruptcy. As one farmer charged at the Massachusetts convention, the rich aimed to "get all the power and all the money into their own hands, and then . . . swallow up all us little folks."

When the Constitution became law, cities across the country celebrated with parades that included everyone from merchants and lawyers to apprentices and common laborers. The largest took place in Philadelphia on July 4, 1788, led by local dignitaries, regiments of Continental Army troops, and a marching band. Some 17,000 people turned out, and artisans formed more than forty contingents representing their various crafts. But riots were brewing in rural Pennsylvania; just one week earlier, a band of farmers near Wilkes-Barre had kidnapped a judge involved with land speculators. In other states, too, the backcountry was as angry as the cities were joyous.

In spring 1789, the new government took power, with George Washington as president, both houses of Congress controlled by the well-to-do, and a great many citizens wary of or outright opposed to this concentration of power. That fall Congress proposed a series of constitutional amendments aimed at "extending the ground of public confidence in the Government." Ten of these provisions, known as the Bill of Rights, were subsequently ratified by the states and added to the Constitution in December 1791. The First Amendment declared that Congress would not abridge popular rights to religious freedom, to free speech and a free press, to peaceful assembly, or to petition government to redress grievances. Other amendments guaranteed rights to bear arms, to protection from unwarranted searches and seizures, to trial by an impartial jury, and to other safeguards against abuse by criminal and civil courts.

So ended the American Revolution, the Bill of Rights pledging to protect the many from persecution by the governing few. For forty years both the presidency and Congress belonged to the revolutionary elite and their protégés. In the 1790s, they split into rival parties, the Federalists backed by merchants and financiers, and the Democratic-Republicans favored by planters, farmers, and artisans. By the mid-1820s, the Federalists had collapsed into the Democratic-Republicans, whose rival sectors would regroup as the Democratic Party and the Whigs. These factional divisions and redivisions were intensely acrimonious, but however federal elections turned out, certain basics remained the same: a coalition of planters and urban businessmen ran the government; federal policies fostered slavery, industrial development, and national expansion; the U.S. Army was perpetually at war with Indian nations resisting encroachment on their land.

REPUBLICAN LEGACIES

In 1794, Independence Day gatherings outstripped anything the nation had seen since the Philadelphia parade of 1788, and this time their tone was more defiant than triumphant. In city after city craftsmen came out to damn the reigning Federalist Party, cheer Democratic-Republicans, and celebrate the Fourth of July as "a memento to the oppressed to rise and assert their rights." These sentiments resonated with broader patterns. In years to come working people of all sorts challenged oppression on republican grounds, defining liberty and equality not as privileges or prizes but as inherent rights. Common ideals did not, however, mean common cause in a political system increasingly open to white men, closed to other free workers, and tryannical toward slaves.

The Federalist regime of the 1790s enraged masses of Americans by ruling like British aristocrats. National and state legislators repeatedly held secret sessions and passed laws written in such arcane language that the general public could not decipher their meaning. In 1792, Congress enacted a militia law that authorized the states to draft men into service. In 1794, President Washington sent some 13,000 militiamen into Pennsylvania's backcountry to crush popular resistance to a federal tax on whiskey, which farmers distilled from their excess corn. In 1798, Congress tried to silence anti-Federalists with a Sedition Act that made it a crime punishable by fine and imprisonment to publish statements that subjected the government to "contempt or disrepute." Especially damaging to craftsmen, the Federalists constructed a legal system based on British law, which treated labor unions as criminal conspiracies.

The earliest American unions appeared in the 1790s. They were established by white craft journeymen, starting with Philadelphia shoemakers in 1792. Other pioneers included tailors in Baltimore and printers and cabinetmakers in New York City. In the early 1800s, the movement spread to carpenters, masons, and tailors in New York; shoemakers in Baltimore and Pittsburgh; and printers in seven cities from Boston to New Orleans. Condemning employers for "depriving free men of their just rights," unionists aimed to carry republican self-government into the workplace—to regulate wages and hours of labor, to secure jobs for union members and to keep others out of union shops. Whenever they made progress on these goals, unionists were hauled into court and convicted on charges of conspiracy. Long after the Federalist Party was a dead letter, the jurists it had appointed and the legal doctrines it had embraced undercut union organizing.

Politics offered a clearer field. In the mid-1790s, white craftsmen, seamen, and farmers joined with some well-to-do dissidents in a large network of political clubs that soon merged into the Democratic-Republican Party headed by Thomas Jefferson. The clubs championed causes the aristocratic Federalists despised: extensions of voting rights, an end to closed-door lawmaking, the establishment of public schools. They held dinners to honor the French Revolution of 1789–99, circulated radical pamphlets such as Tom Paine's *Rights of Man* (1791–92), and in 1800 helped to propel Jefferson into the presidency.

Jefferson's election ushered in twenty-four years of Democratic-Republican administrations headed by Virginia planters and widely supported by white workingmen. In some respects democracy advanced. Federalists slowly lost their hold on state and local governments, which began to provide for public education and to increase the portion of public officials who were elected rather than appointed. By 1825, all but three states (Virginia, Rhode Island, and Louisiana) granted voting rights to every white male citizen, and all but two (South Carolina and Delaware) chose presidential electors by polling voters instead of state legislators. White servitude receded as the white electorate expanded. State and local courts stopped enforcing indenture contracts for craft apprentices. The indenture of European immigrants died out as state lawmakers eliminated imprisonment for debt and thus liberated redemptioners from debt bondage.

Jeffersonian democracy did not expand women's rights, however. As under British rule, the legal system gave husbands absolute title to their wives' personal property, including any wages they earned. As in the past, husbands could legally subject their wives to beatings that did not cause irreparable bodily harm. As white men gained wider access to the ballot, moreover, women were left behind. They even lost what little ground they had gained in New Jersey, where Democratic-Republican lawmakers disfranchised women in 1807.

Industrial development added to women's subordination in some ways and liberated them in others. The earliest U.S. factories—textile mills in northern states—recruited a white workforce largely composed of women and girls. Some mills hired whole families, and in such cases male heads of household received the wages for all of their kin. By the 1820s, however, it was more common for textile manufacturers to staff their mills with young unmarried women, especially farmers' daughters. Mill jobs regimented their lives. They worked at least twelve hours a day, six days a week, and resided in company-owned boarding houses that imposed strict rules regarding curfews, bedtimes, church attendance, and so forth. But their wages went into their own pockets, and that gave most mill women a greater sense of independence than they had ever before known.

As one worker later recalled of newcomers to the mill complex in Lowell, Massachusetts, "When they felt the jingle of silver in their pocket, there for the first time, their heads became erect and they walked as if on air." While many women sent money to their families, just as many spent their earnings on themselves, buying new clothes, saving up dowries, sometimes sending themselves to school. Writing home from Lowell, a worker told her family, "Others may find fault with me and call me selfish, but I think I should spend my earnings as I please."

Mill women's independent spirit sparked labor protests as well. In December 1828, a strike by women at the Cocheco mill in Dover, New Hamshire, forced the company to rescind new rules that fined workers for lateness and forbade them to talk on the job. To publicize their demands, the strikers staged a parade that resembled Fourth of July celebrations. Accompanied by a brass band, they marched through town carrying flags, setting off firecrackers, and shouting their determination to resist "the shocking fate of slaves."

If slavery shocked some white Americans, it flourished nonetheless. As agreed at the Constitutional Convention, Congress outlawed the importation of slaves as of January 1, 1808. By then, however, slaves numbered about 1 million; and new births together with illegal importations would double that figure by 1830. The free black population grew at a slower pace, from about 180,000 in 1808 to 320,000 in 1830.

Congressional policy on admitting new states to the federal union helped slavery spread far beyond its old strongholds. From the 1790s onward, admissions proceeded according to a quota system designed to equalize the numbers of slave states and "free states" (where slavery was either illegal or marked for death via gradual emancipation). Slaveholders thus controlled half of the U.S. Senate, where their spokesmen could derail legislation unfriendly to slavery. This arrangement almost broke down in 1820, when Congress debated the admission of Maine as the twelfth free state and Missouri as the twelfth slave state. Northerners in the House of Representatives vehemently objected to slavery in Missouri, which lay in territory earlier designated "free soil." In the end, however, conciliation carried the day. Under a plan called the Missouri Compromise, Congress agreed that Missouri could come in with slavery intact, that additional slave states would have to lie to the south of Missouri, and that slave states and free states would continue to join the union in pairs.

While politicians sought to reconcile slavery and liberty, rebellious slaves carried republican doctrines to more radical conclusions. In fall 1800, Virginia militiamen broke up an underground army of about 600 slaves and some free black workers poised to march on the capital city of Richmond. Their leader was a young blacksmith named Gabriel, one of the 5 percent of U.S. slaves who could read and write. He had worked in Richmond since 1798, identifying white abolitionists, mixing with white craftsmen active in the Democratic-Republican movement, and avidly following news from the island of San Domingo (Hispaniola), where slaves' successful war for emancipation had widened into a fight for national independence. Along the way he came to believe that a slave revolt in Virginia could spark a more general uprising. His army planned to enter Richmond behind a banner proclaiming "Death or Liberty," rally support from many whites as well as the black populace, and force the state government to complete the American Revolution by ending slavery and upholding equal rights for every man.

Gabriel and twenty-five of his lieutenants went to the gallows for daring to think such things possible. One of them told the court, "I have nothing more to offer than what General Washington would have had to offer had he been taken by the British and put to trial. I have adventured my life in endeavoring to obtain the liberty of my countrymen, and am a willing sacrifice in their cause." Within a year some veterans of Gabriel's army regrouped under a ferryman named Sancho and laid plans for a rural uprising along the border of Virginia and North Carolina, once again expecting help from poor whites. When authorities got wind of the project in spring 1802, another twenty-five bondsmen were hanged. Following the executions in Virginia, the American Revolution receded as a reference point for slave resistance. But republican ideals remained a rich source of inspiration thanks to events in San Domingo, where black revolutionaries overthrew French colonialism and founded the independent republic of Haiti in 1804.

In 1822, authorities in Charleston, South Carolina, hanged thirty-five men for inciting a plot to replicate what Haiti modeled. The mastermind was the carpenter Denmark Vesey. A former slave who had purchased his freedom in 1800, he was the only freeman in the conspiracy's inner circle. Like Gabriel, Vesey could read, and Charleston's slaves had long relied on him for news of Haiti. In 1821, when Haitian troops overcame a protracted Spanish effort to recolonize their country, he turned from agitation to organizing. As one recruit later testified: "He said, we were deprived of our rights and privileges . . . and that it was high time for us to seek our rights, and that we were fully able to conquer the whites, if only we were unanimous and courageous as the St. Domingo people were." The result was the largest slave conspiracy in U.S. history. At least several thousand people took part; some said as many as 9,000.

While few free blacks took part in slave rebellions, a great many shared Denmark Vesey's identification with Haiti. By the mid-1820s, free black communities in both northern and southern cities gathered annually to celebrate Haitian independence as proof, to quote one speaker in Baltimore, "that the descendants of Africa were never designed by their Creator to sustain an inferiority, or even a mediocrity, in the chain of being." That was a crucial point for free African Americans, whose rights before the law had steadily declined since the Constitution took effect.

Federal action set the stage for discrimination by the states. The immigration law of 1790 reserved naturalized citizenship for "free white

Pre-Industrial Era Workers

SHOE MAKERS

SUGAR PLANTATION SLAVES

FAMILY FARMERS

persons"; the Militia Act of 1792 excluded black men from service; and in 1810, the U.S. Post Office stipulated that only whites could carry the mail. Congress repeatedly welcomed new states that deprived black citizens of fundamental rights, and it never censured old states for withdrawing rights previously extended.

Close to 60 percent of free African Americans resided in southern states, whose lawmakers enacted the harshest restrictions. Starting with Virginia in 1793, states across the South prohibited or severely limited the entry of free black people, ordered those already resident to document their freedom before local authorities, and treated all who did not comply as fugitive slaves. By 1810, every southern state but Delaware had barred free blacks from testifying against white people in court, and in 1811, Georgia denied them the right to jury trials. Northern states passed a hodgepodge of discriminatory statutes that in some cases rivaled the South's. By 1820, for example, most northern school systems were either segregated or entirely closed to black children, both Ohio and Illinois outlawed the entry of black settlers, and Massachusetts was the only northern state where an African American could serve as a juror.

In both the North and the South, black voting rights eroded too. As of 1800, with sixteen states in the union, all but Virginia, South Carolina and Georgia enfranchised free black men on the same basis as white men. But over the next half century just one incoming state (Maine) gave black men equal access to the ballot, and nine older states took it away—often at the same time that they removed property restrictions on the white electorate. By the 1850s, black men could participate in politics in just five of thirty-one states: Massachusetts, Rhode Island, New Hampshire, Vermont, and Maine.

In free black communities, then, activism generally centered in churches and benevolent associations. Virtually all of them worked against slavery in some fashion, surreptitiously in the South and openly in the North. As the southern communities helped fugitive slaves make their way to free states, the northerners built a network of abolitionist societies—more than fifty by the late 1820s. Most of these groups were run by men, but a fair number were women's organizations like the Colored Female Religious and Moral Society of Salem, Massachusetts, whose members gathered to "write and converse on the sufferings of our enslaved sisters."

Black abolitionism was especially dynamic in Boston, whose General Colored Association agitated for racial equality as well as an end to slavery and worked tirelessly to knit free African Americans into a national movement. One of the Association's leaders was David Walker, a tailor who galvanized black activists with his militant *Appeal to the Coloured Citizens of the World* (1829). Condemning all manifestations of white supremacy and racism, this pamphlet called black America to rebel against every violation of the doctrine that "ALL MEN ARE CREATED EQUAL!!" The Boston abolitionists also included a pioneer for women's rights: Maria W. Stewart, a widowed domestic worker who became the first American-born woman to lecture in behalf of equality for her sex.

The most radical elaboration on republican ideals came from the printer Thomas Skidmore, a New York City labor activist who had grown up in an old Yankee farm family in Newtown, Connecticut. In 1829, Skidmore published a manifesto titled *The Rights of Man to Property!*, which proposed sweeping redistributions of wealth and power. The country belonged equally to all of its people, Skidmore proclaimed, and "the same eternal and indissoluble rights exist for all." Every form of servitude should be abolished; every man and unmarried woman—white, black and Indian—should get a 160-acre homestead to call their own; factories, railroads, and other industrial property should be collectively owned; every adult should have full and equal voting rights; and government should consist of "a great judicial tribunal of all our citizens sitting in judgment over and deciding for themselves." Skidmore promoted this program through the New York Working Men's Party, which he helped to found in 1829. Less radical voices prevailed, however. Within a few months he and his handful of followers were pushed out of the party, and their independent efforts fell apart with Skidmore's death in 1832.

His ideas lived on in piecemeal form. Over the next three decades, working people took part in various movements for land redistribution, for the abolition of slavery, for the establishment of cooperative workshops, for racial equality and for women's rights. But many more years would pass before significant numbers came together, as Skidmore endorsed, to "oppose everything of privilege . . . in whatever shape it might present itself."

CHAPTER

SLAVERY AND FREEDOM IN
THE NEW REPUBLIC

On January 10, 1860, the Pemberton Mill, a cotton textile factory in Lawrence, Massachusetts, collapsed like a house of cards. Of the 670 workers
buried in the rubble, 90 died and another 120 suffered severe injuries.
Erected in 1853 at a cost of $800,000 and equipped with the latest in steam-
powered machinery, the mill had been touted as the finest example of the
vast northern textile industry, in which wage workers wove cloth from the
cotton grown by slaves. In many ways the Pemberton epitomized the nation
as a whole, a grand edifice standing on shaky pillars.

The Constitution's ratification ushered in seventy years of national
growth and prosperity. Land purchases and seizures extended the United
States across the continent, from Florida to California and from New England to the Pacific Northwest. The population swelled from about 4 million in 1790 to over 31 million in 1860. Each decade brought a larger influx
of immigrants, mostly from northwestern Europe and the British Isles. Close
to 600,000 people arrived in the 1830s, 1.7 million in the 1840s, 2.6 million
in the 1850s. Cities increased in numbers and size. In 1790 there were just six
municipalities with more than 8,000 residents; by 1860 there were 141.
New York's population reached 1.2 million, Philadelphia's 566,000, and

six other cities topped 100,000—Boston, Baltimore, Cincinnati, St. Louis, Chicago, and New Orleans.

Agriculture, industry, and commerce flourished as never before. Cotton plantations spread across the lower South from the Atlantic coast to eastern Texas; corn, wheat, hog, and cattle farming proliferated in the Midwest; merchant wealth funded an industrial revolution that centered in the North but penetrated other regions too. More and more commodities were produced in factories, not only textile mills but also iron foundries, machine shops, printing plants, sugar refineries, meatpacking houses, boot and shoe factories, and furniture works. To fuel iron furnaces and power machinery, coal mining expanded from about 50,000 tons of output in 1820 to 14 million tons in 1860. East of the Mississippi, a giant network of new canals, paved roads, and over 30,000 miles of railroad track linked farms, plantations, factories, and mines to distant markets for their products. By 1860, the United States was the world's fourth biggest industrial power (behind England, Germany, and France) and second to none in commercial agriculture. It produced two-thirds of the world's raw cotton and industrial goods valued at more than $1.8 billion, with cotton textiles in the lead.

Injustice and inequality abounded as well. The 1860 census counted nearly 4 million slaves. Free workers and their dependents, about 12 million people in all, lived on wages that averaged under $1 a day. Restrictions on free African Americans were harsher than ever. Women of all colors still lacked political rights. Federal law still stipulated that only white immigrants could become citizens and required that they wait for five years. In addition to dispossessing Indians, westward expansion involved the seizure of 1.2 million square miles of Mexican land. Two ruling classes—the South's richest planters, the North's industrial capitalists—dominated their respective regions and jockeyed for control of the federal government. Both regarded labor as nothing more than a commodity. The planters' regime supported a thriving interstate slave trade, buying and selling an average of 7,500 people a year from 1820 to 1860. The Pemberton Mill's owners calculated the market value of lives lost in the collapse at $500 for male heads of household down to $50 for children and paid just that to the dead's survivors.

As oppression mounted, so did resistance. Working people asserted themselves through labor unions, political action, cooperatives, strikes, and countless challenges to slavery. As in the past, different groups of workers fought on different fronts. Inequality and plain bigotry divided women and men, white workers and workers of color, U.S. natives and immigrants, the free and the unfree. Amidst these divisions, however, a critical mass of people coalesced against slavery's expansion into new territories. By 1860, this

"Free Soil" coalition realigned American politics, and the compromises that had once secured slavery's future frayed beyond repair.

"IF YOU CAN'T FIGHT, KICK"

The planters' regime spared no effort to preserve and defend slavery. Only a third of the South's white households owned slaves in 1830, and the proportion fell to a fourth by 1860. For that very reason, the planter elite—the richest 1 percent who owned one-quarter of all slaves—ruled the region with a heavy hand, organizing southern life to serve the slaveholding minority. Yet they never managed to squelch the tradition of resistance exemplified by the Tennessee slave who advised her children to, "Fight, and if you can't fight, kick; and if you can't kick, then bite."

Planters' supremacy in the South and their influence in Washington, D.C., owed a great deal to the cotton boom. While other cash crops—chiefly tobacco, rice, and sugar cane—remained important in parts of the South, cotton production soared from about 100,000 bales in 1800 to 5.4 million bales in 1860. The South's wealthiest planters made their fortunes in this business, which also profited smaller planters, family farms, cotton brokers, cotton shippers, and slave traders. Northern capitalists had a big stake in the business too; many of them engaged in cotton trading, advanced loans to cotton planters, and invested in cotton textile factories. What served the planter elite thus appealed to a good portion of the white South and to much of the North's ruling class.

At bottom, though, the planters' regime rested on force. Armed and mounted posses policed country roads every night, on the lookout for "disturbances" among the slaves. Sentries patrolled cities and towns. Enormous state militias—more than 100,000 strong in Virginia alone—drilled frequently and mobilized at the least sign of trouble. Free people likely to inspire slave unrest faced increasing suppression. By the mid-1820s, nearly every southern abolitionist had been expelled from the region or intimidated into silence. White workers ran afoul of the law when they tried to organize; the courts routinely crushed their unions and strikes. Free blacks, who by 1860 numbered about 250,000 in slaveholding states, were now subject to curfews, public whippings for giving the slightest offense to whites, automatic imprisonment for possessing abolitionist literature, and statutory exclusion from learned professions and the majority of skilled trades.

Thousands of state and local laws targeted slaves. They were forbidden to raise a hand against any white person, to assemble without white super-

vision, to buy or sell anything without their masters' permission, to leave
a plantation at any time, to walk city streets after dark without written
passes . . . the list went on and on. Most states made it a crime to teach slaves
to read or write. By 1860, several states in the Deep South had prohibited
manumission.

Whatever their knowledge of the statutes, every day reminded slaves of
their status as chattel. The slave trade besieged family life, breaking up a
quarter to a third of all marriages and snatching countless children from
their parents. One of the first things adolescent girls learned about sex was
that white men could rape black women with impunity; not a single slaveholding state defined such assaults as crimes. Attempts at book learning
carried tremendous risks. As Hannah Crasson of Wake County, North Carolina, later remembered, "You better not be found trying to learn to read.
Our marster was harder down on that than anything else." Some masters forbade slaves to worship on their own. Mary Reynolds grew up on a Louisiana
sugar plantation whose manager lurked around slaves' cabins at night and
threatened to "come in there and tear the hide off your backs" whenever he
heard prayers or hymns.

Labor conditions varied considerably. As plantations multiplied, more
and more slaves were field hands working in large, tightly supervised gangs.
This system prevailed on the lower South's cotton plantations, the upper
South's tobacco plantations, and the sugar plantations of Louisiana. But
most slaves did other kinds of work. As late as the 1850s, roughly half were
household servants, craftsmen, or field hands on farms too small to qual-
ify as plantations (units with at least twenty slaves). Some of this group—
mainly urban craftsmen and servants—hired out for wages, saw to their
own maintenance, and paid their owners a weekly fee. Another 5 percent of
slaves worked for industrial enterprises such as mines, railroads, and factories. While the vast majority of industrial slaves were owned or leased by
the businesses that employed them, a few were hired for a wage. Not all
plantation field hands did gang labor, moreover. The rice plantations of
South Carolina, Georgia, and Louisiana used the task system, under which
each slave got a daily assignment, worked with minimal supervision, and
could stop once the job was done. Task labor was also the norm on the cotton plantations on the Sea Islands along the coasts of Georgia and South
Carolina.

Whatever the setting, slaves who broke work rules risked physical assault
from masters and mistresses, the overseers they hired, or the slaves they appointed as foremen or "drivers." Some of this violence was simply sadistic.
One tobacco manufacturer whipped a teenaged girl to death as his wife

burned her with an iron. The Richmond *Dispatch* congratulated a factory overseer for shooting a bondsman who left the premises without permission. Jenny Proctor, born on an Alabama cotton plantation, spent her childhood working under a relentlessly cruel driver: "the least little thing we do he beat us for it and put big chains around our ankles and make us work with them on until the blood be cut out all around our ankles."

By all accounts, though, most slaveholders took a businesslike approach to labor discipline and insisted that their agents do the same. A popular manual on the management of slaves summarized the strategy: "Never fail . . . to notice the breach of an established rule, and be equally unfailing in punishing the offender justly, according to the nature and circumstance of the offence. Never inflict punishment when in a passion, nor threaten it; but wait until perfectly cool." Solomon Northrup, a free New Yorker kidnapped into slavery in Louisiana, saw this strategy at work during picking season on a cotton plantation: "It was rarely that a day passed without one or more whippings. This occurred at the time the cotton was weighed. The delinquent whose weight had fallen short, was taken out, stripped and made to lie on the ground, face downward, when he received a punishment proportioned to his offense. The number of lashes is graduated according to the nature of the case."

But slavery was more than a business, and work rules were not the only dictates slave masters enforced with the whip. As one North Carolina jurist wrote in 1852, any hint of insolence on the part of a slave "violates the rules of propriety, and if tolerated, would destroy that subordination upon which our social system rests." Masters promoted "propriety" by doling out countless punishments of the sort described here by Frederick Douglass, the abolitionist leader who had been a slave in Maryland:

> A mere look, word, or motion . . . are all matters for which a slave may be whipped at any time. Does a slave look dissatisfied? It is said, he has the devil in him, and it must be whipped out. Does he speak loudly when spoken to by his master? Then he is getting high-minded, and should be taken down a button-hole lower. Does he forget to pull off his hat at the approach of a white person? Then he is wanting in reverence, and should be whipped for it. Does he ever venture to vindicate his conduct, when censured for it? Then he is guilty of impudence,—one of the greatest crimes of which a slave can be guilty.

These humiliations—like armed patrollers, draconian laws, and everything else that propped up the planters' regime—were designed to control slaves' minds as well as their behavior. To make the system run smoothly, slaveholders had to make emancipation unthinkable.

The effort failed. Slaves repeatedly thought, sang, and dreamed about freedom, and defiant hopes often sparked rebellious action. Both forms of resistance required personal courage. Both were also collective projects, deeply rooted in the families and communities slaves constructed outside the meticulously supervised world of work. Labor from dawn to dark or longer absorbed most but not all of their waking hours. Work usually ended early on Saturdays, Sunday was virtually always a holiday, and most people could squeeze some spare minutes from the rest of the week. These spaces between the demands of work provided seedbeds for resistance.

Family life inspired and supported innumerable challenges to masters' authority. In Maryland, Harriet Ross (mother of the famous Harriet Tubman) refused to give her youngest child to the Georgia slave trader to whom he had been sold. An older son later described her response when the trader and her master came knocking late at night: "She ripped out an oath and said, 'You are after my son; but the first man that comes into my house, I will split his head open.' That frightened them, and they would not come in. So she kept the boy hid until the Georgia man went away." In Virginia, John Jones Middleton left the plantation where he was repeatedly beaten and lived in nearby woods, his wife and children supplying him with food and harboring him in their cabin many a night. Stories like this abound in the memoirs written or dictated by former slaves. They do not always have happy endings; but their sheer volume illustrates how deeply family love and loyalties undercut slavery's "rules of propriety."

Community was family writ large, centered in gatherings that broke the rules in both tacit and overt ways. With or without permission, slaves regularly came together for prayer and praise, for parties and dances, and for self-education. This united people who did not normally cross paths at work—field hands and artisans, household servants and industrial laborers, slaves held by different masters, and sometimes free blacks as well. When it was impossible to congregate in the open, they met in secluded corners of the woods or in cabins with shutters drawn tight. To facilitate safe travel to and from the meetings, they frequently strung grape vines across the roads to trip the patrollers' horses. Sometimes they confronted a patrol head on. Betty Jones remembered one such incident in Virginia, when patrollers showed up at a cabin where a meeting was in progress: "Just as we heard 'em, ol' man Jack Diggs and Charlie Dowal shoveled fire and coals right out the door on them devils. They ran from the fire we ran from them. Ain't nobody get caught that time."

These gatherings were subversive in other respects too. At parties slaves satirized masters and mistresses in songs, jokes, and imitations of their high-handed ways. Educational meetings took place at "midnight schools" where literate slaves taught others how to read and write. In Natchez, Mississippi, Milla Granson ran such a school for seven years and graduated hundreds of pupils, a number of whom forged travel passes and ran away to Canada. In their religious meetings slaves shared a faith starkly different from the gospel heard at the services and Sabbath schools masters arranged. There, every sermon echoed Ephesians 6:5: "Servants, be obedient to them that are your masters." But the underground slave church fostered a religion of liberation exemplified in the lyrics of spiritual songs such as,

> *O, gracious Lord! When shall it be,*
> *That we poor souls shall all be free;*
> *Lord, break them slavery powers—*
> *Will you go along with me?*

An ethic of solidarity permeated all of these activities. Participants trusted each other to keep secrets from masters and their agents; they also fostered secrecy by nurturing the independent spirit slaveholders tried so hard to kill.

The Reverend Charles Jones of Georgia, a white clergyman determined to save slaves from the sin of disobedience, was constantly frustrated by their refussals to identify wrongdoers. "Inquiry elicits no information," he complained. "No one feels at liberty to disclose the transgressor; all are profoundly ignorant; the matter assumes the sacredness of the professional secret." Solidarity was not seamless. Every community had traitors and informants from time to time, but solidarity was sturdy enough to support a rich network of group activities that slaveholders did not control.

These activities shaded over into more radical challenges to masters' power and to slavery itself. At least 100,000 bondspeople escaped from slave-holding states between 1800 and 1860, and many more tried to get away. Other forms of resistance dating back to the colonial era continued as well: arson, vandalism, assaults on masters, guerilla raids by bands of runaways, and armed rebellion. Nearly every year brought news of slave revolts or conspiracies. In addition to the efforts led by Gabriel, Sancho, and Denmark Vesey, the most famous incidents included an uprising in 1811 of some 500 slaves on plantations near New Orleans and a mutiny in 1841 by slaves on the *Creole,* who took over the ship as it carried them down the Mississippi River and eventually reached freedom in the Bahamas.

But nothing shook the planters' regime like the 1831 insurrection led by the field hand Nat Turner in Southampton County, Virginia. Turner, who had learned to read the Bible, often preached at religious meetings. As he later told a lawyer who recorded his confession, the Holy Spirit had appeared to him in 1828 and said that "I should . . . fight against the Serpent, for the time was fast approaching when the first shall be last and the last shall be first." On the night of August 21, 1831, he and five disciples armed themselves and set out on a crusade against bondage. Their first blows were aimed at Turner's master and his family, all of whom the rebels executed. As the group pushed on toward the county seat, a town named Jerusalem, more and more slaves joined the march. By the morning of August 23, when militiamen put them to flight, the rebels numbered about seventy and at least fifty-seven whites had been killed. Turner, who eluded capture for another two months, was hanged in Jerusalem on November 11. Nineteen of his comrades—including three freemen—had already been tried and hanged, and over 100 black residents of Southampton County had been massacred in retaliation for the revolt.

Following the Turner cataclysm, American slaveholders fortified the machinery of repression. There were more patrols, bigger militias, harsher pressures on abolitionists and free blacks, more brutal penalties for slaves deemed guilty of impudence. Slave communities survived nonetheless, waiting for the time when they could successfully act on the hopes expressed in their spiritual about Samson: "If I had my way, I'd tear this building down."

WAGE WORKERS AND ACTIVISM

While cotton production dominated the South, manufacturing transformed the North. At the close of the American Revolution, about three-quarters of free people in New England and the mid-Atlantic states had lived and worked on family farms. By 1860, farm families made up just 40 percent of the population in these states, where nearly a million people now did industrial work. As manufacturing boomed, so did wage labor. Like slavery in the South, the wage system became the core institution of the northern economy, steadily supplanting other means of making a living.

Wage workers came from various backgrounds. Some were the descendants of the eighteenth century's tiny wage labor force of maritime workers, domestic servants, and common laborers. Some others were former slaves or their descendants. Many were craftsmen from trades such as printing and shoemaking, where competition from factories was driving artisan shops out of business and foreclosing journeymen's routes to self-employment.

Wage work also absorbed numerous immigrants, especially people of Irish, German, and British descent. But by far the largest cohort were native-born men and women from farming districts plagued by land shortages, debt, and competition from midwestern agriculture.

Like slaves' labor, wage work varied in terms and conditions. Domestic servants—the biggest occupational group among women workers—usually lived in their employers' homes, got cash payments in addition to room and board, and had almost no time to themselves. Other wage earners typically worked twelve to fourteen hours a day with Sundays off, but pay arrangements differed from group to group. Women routinely got one-half of what men earned for comparable work. Many miners and factory workers received at least a portion of their wages in goods from a company store. Like young women employed in textile mills, railroad and canal construction laborers were often paid partly in cash and partly in room and board. Some workers, such as carpenters, bricklayers, and blacksmiths, earned a set amount for each day on the job; garment workers, printers, cigar makers, and others received "piece wages" that depended on their output.

Manufacturing was a world of contrast with regard to technology and the organization of production. By 1860, many industrial workers operated power-driven machinery in factories, but many more used hand tools and worked in small shops. Garment and shoe manufacturers still relied extensively on "outworkers"—women, children, and sometimes whole families who sewed clothing or stitched shoes at home.

Job opportunities depended on workers' color, sex, and national origin as well as their levels of skill. Factory jobs were reserved for whites and the best-paying positions for men. Craft shops owned by whites typically employed white men only except in a few trades—printing, shoemaking, and tailoring—where white women might work alongside male kin. German and British immigrants, who usually arrived with craft skills, formed ethnic networks that gave them a leg up in the U.S. labor market. Newcomers from Ireland, most of whom lacked industrial experience, concentrated in unskilled jobs, and anti-Irish bigotry further limited their options. A typical want ad read: "WOMAN WANTED.—To do general housework . . . English, Scotch, Welsh, German, or any country or color except Irish."

In the end, color trumped nationality; all European immigrants found wider opportunities than African Americans. While Irish women clustered in domestic work, many had moved into factory employment by the 1850s, and Irish men had made inroads into crafts such as plumbing, carpentry, blacksmithing, and glassmaking. Black women, on the other hand, were almost wholly confined to jobs as laundresses, domestic servants, or outworkers for garment shops. Black men worked mostly as construction laborers, stevedores, sailors, waiters, or cooks, and their small numbers in skilled trades had declined as immigrants poured in. In Philadelphia, for instance, the ranks of black mechanics (both master craftsmen and journeymen) dwindled from 506 in 1838 to 286 in 1849.

Wage workers across the board shared some general problems: poverty and insecurity despite long hours of labor, driving by bosses who continually tried to get more for less, inequality under political and legal systems designed by and for the elite. In every sector of the work force, activists addressed these issues through collective action, not only unionism but many other projects too. Mutualism had boundaries, however. Specific conditions of life and labor differed sharply for men and women, skilled and unskilled, citizens and aliens, white and black; and labor activism reflected these distinctions. White citizens and craftsmen in particular—workers with the most resources and options—were the first to organize.

In December 1827, Philadelphia's craft unions formed the Mechanics' Union of Trade Associations, the first U.S. labor organization that encompassed workers from various trades. The following summer its member unions founded another first: a local Working Men's Party that ran its own candidates for municipal and state office, calling on craftsmen to use the ballot box "to take the management of their own interests, as a class, into their own immediate keeping." By the early 1830s similar parties had appeared in at least sixty cities and towns, from Portland, Maine, to Washington, D.C., and as far west as Cincinnati. They called for improvements in public education, for an end to compulsory militia musters, for repeal of conspiracy laws applied to unions, and for other reforms beneficial to the laboring classes. The Democratic Party soon embraced enough of these causes to coopt independent labor politics, but craftsmen continued to organize across occupational lines.

From 1833 through 1836, craft unions established central federations in thirteen cities, including New York, Philadelphia★, Boston, Albany, Pittsburgh, and Louisville. Coordinating efforts through the National Trades Union (NTU) founded in 1834, these "city centrals" spawned labor newspapers, mobilized strike support, helped to build new unions, and championed reforms workingmen's parties had endorsed. First and foremost, they agitated and organized to reduce the standard workday from twelve or more hours to ten. While the NTU petitioned the federal government to grant its

★ The Mechanics' Union of Trade Associations had disintegrated along with the Philadelphia Working Men's Party in 1831.

employees the ten-hour day, local activists staged strike after strike demanding the same from their bosses.

The largest of these strikes occurred in June 1835, when the Philadelphia Trades Union organized unionists from seventeen crafts to join a walkout initiated by Irish "coal heavers" who unloaded barges along the Schuylkill River. This was the first general strike in U.S. history and a resounding success. After three weeks the City Council announced that municipal workers would henceforth work ten hours a day with no reduction in pay, and private employers quickly followed suit. Inspired by Philadelphia's example, craft unions across the mid-Atlantic states launched ten-hour strikes that summer and fall, and in most cases they won.

The National Trades Union was part of a wider uprising among white workers. As craft unions mobilized for the ten-hour day, women and unskilled men built their own organizations and struck for better pay. Women activists included tailoresses in New York City and Baltimore; shoebinders in New York, Philadelphia, and Lynn, Massachusetts; and textile operatives in Lowell. In June 1835, against the backdrop of Philadelphia's general strike, some 500 workingwomen from various trades formed a citywide federation—the Female Improvement Society—that won wage increases for seamstresses who sewed uniforms for the U.S. Army. Among unskilled men, no one outshone Irish canal workers for militancy. They staged at least fourteen strikes in the 1830s and in January 1834 clashed with federal troops sent to put down a strike on the Chesapeake and Ohio Canal in Maryland. New York City's docks became a hub of strike activity in 1834–36, when sailors, stevedores, and coal heavers walked off their jobs and Irish construction laborers stopped work on nearby projects.

Employers fought the labor movement by firing and blacklisting activists and by taking unions to trial. In 1835, in a case involving a shoemakers' union in Geneva, New York, the state's supreme court ruled that both unions and strikes were illegal under conspiracy law. In June of the following year, twenty journeymen tailors in New York City were convicted of criminal conspiracy for striking shops that had nullified wage agreements with the tailors' union and discharged union members. A crowd of 27,000, about a fifth of New York's adult population, jammed into City Hall Park to protest the verdict, and their outrage reverberated through the labor press. A Philadelphia paper declared: "It is our prerogative to say what institution we will be members of, that being bequeathed to us by our forefathers—the toilworn veterans of '76 who Nobly moistened the Soil with their Blood in defence of equal rights." But the law clearly did not recognize workers' right to organize, and that threatened everything the labor movement had achieved.

Following the tailors' conviction, leaders of the National Trades Union debated the movement's future. Some endorsed political action with an eye to repealing antiunion laws. A more radical contingent favored cooperative production, calling for the establishment of craft shops collectively owned and managed by their workers. Within months, however, the debates were moot. In spring 1837, a financial panic among bankers and speculators ushered in a seven-year depression, and mass layoffs quickly destroyed the National Trades Union, the city centrals, and nearly all unions.

Reforms the NTU had endorsed made some headway as the Democratic and Whig parties vied for working-class votes. In 1840, President Martin Van Buren endeared the Democrats to workingmen by instituting the ten-hour day for employees on federal construction projects. Not to be outdone, Whigs in command of the Massachusetts Supreme Court gave unionism a landmark legal victory in 1842. Overturning a conspiracy verdict against a bootmakers' union in Boston, the court ruled in the case of *Commonwealth v. Hunt* that workers had the right to organize and strike for "useful and honorable purposes." These concessions had limited impacts, however. Unions were so few and weak that labor conspiracy trials had virtually disappeared, and workers could not force state governments to follow Van Buren's example.

As the depression deepened, many working people poured into the nation's first mass movement for abstention from alcohol. In 1840, six Baltimore craftsmen who had recently sworn off drinking formed the Washington Temperance Benevolent Society to convert other men to sobriety. This crusade spread like wildfire in white working-class communities. By 1843, Washingtonian lodges had sprung up across the Northeast, and they claimed an aggregate membership of three million. The great majority of members were workingmen, though men of other classes also took part and women organized Martha Washington auxiliaries. Unlike older temperance groups sponsored by employers and churches, the Washingtonians did not moralize about drinking. They opposed it on the very practical grounds that it made hard times more difficult. Their lodges and auxiliaries dispensed aid to the down and out, hosted a steady round of parties, picnics, and other amusements, and held weekly "experience meetings" where reformed drinkers testified about the satisfactions of getting sober. When the economy recovered the movement faded, but its veterans would carry the temperance cause into many labor organizations.

The depression also fueled popular interest in projects that offered a refuge from capitalism. Workers and their families joined with middle-class reformers to establish new communities based on communal living, collective ownership of property, and equal rights for all members. The most radical experiment was the Northampton Association of Education and Industry, which operated a farm and a silk mill in Northampton, Massachusetts. Founded by abolitionists in 1842, the Northampton Association welcomed both black and white members, including fugitive slaves. It was governed by community meetings where everyone had an equal voice. By vote of the membership, the workday at Northampton was ten hours; wages were replaced by a system of subsistence allowances and profit sharing, and those who did housework got the same pay as others. The ideas of the French socialist Charles Fourier inspired the establishment of twenty-six communes from 1843 through 1845. The first Fourierist settlement—the Sylvania Association in western Pennsylvania—was a cooperative farm organized by craftsmen from New York City and Albany.

Except for those sponsored by religious sects like the Shakers and Mennonites, cooperative settlements seldom survived for more than a few years. The main problem was lack of capital; members could not come up with enough cash to build decent housing, equip farms and workshops, and tide everyone over until the commune was self-supporting. As one veteran of the Hopedale Community in Milford, Massachusetts, explained: "The rich and well-to-do derided our scheme . . . the poor, needy, and homeless eagerly applied . . . [and] less than a third of our reliable associates had sufficient money at command to meet their own family expenses—much less to help others."

While communes faltered, less elaborate cooperatives proliferated. The most common were consumers' cooperatives modeled on the Working Men's Protective Union founded by Boston craftsmen in 1845. Protective unions ran nonprofit stores where members could purchase food, fuel, and other necessities at reduced prices. They also functioned as mutual benefit societies, providing sick pay and old-age pensions. By the mid-1850s, workers organized close to 800 protective unions, mostly in New England and New York State but also as far west as Wisconsin.

Cooperative production gained a following too. Just before the depression, some craft unionists in Philadelphia, New York, and several other cities had set up their own workshops, but none of these projects had survived the economic collapse. Starting in the late 1840s, producers' cooperatives reappeared in greater numbers, most of them organized by reborn unions. Some cooperatives, such as the Journeymen Molders' Union Foundry in Cincinnati, were established by strikers as a temporary source of income but then developed a life of their own. Others had more radical purposes. In New York City, where unions in more than a dozen trades opened workshops in 1850, most agreed with the painters who declared their aim to dismantle the whole system by which employers "always obtain and retain the profits of our labor."

Another popular cause was the "land reform" campaign that called on the federal government to give public lands to families who wished to homestead in the West. This movement was the brainchild of George Henry Evans, an English-born printer, editor of labor newspapers, and former leader of the New York Working Men's Party and the National Trades Union. In 1844, a committee of veteran labor activists headed by Evans founded the National Reform Association to rally workingmen for political action in behalf of land reform. While would-be homesteaders flocked to the campaign, so did many more workers who viewed land reform as way to improve life in the East. An exodus of homesteaders promised to reduce competition in eastern labor and housing markets; those who stayed behind would presumably enjoy higher wages, better labor conditions, and lower rents. By the late 1840s, legions of workingmen had joined National Reform clubs, pledging to vote only for politicians who had agreed in writing that all public lands should be set aside "for the full and exclusive use of actual settlers."

Factory workers from Maine to Georgia meanwhile agitated for the ten-hour day. This loose-knit movement did not generate a national organization, but it had a de facto headquarters in the New England Workingmen's Association, founded by Massachusetts activists in 1844. Despite its masculine name, the Workingmen's Association included workers of both sexes, most of them employed in textile mills. They came together to fight for the ten-hour day not only as an end in itself but also as the first step toward a new social order. As one of the Association's organizers explained, shorter hours of labor would enable workers to "take the business of *reform* into [their] own hands" and find solutions to "the general evils of social life *as it is*." This message spread far and wide through the Massachusetts labor press, read by mill workers across New England and in other regions as well.

In contrast to craft unions of the 1830s, the ten-hour day organizations of the 1840s and 1850s sought to decrease the workday through political reform. They organized petition drives and mobilized voters to demand that state lawmakers prohibit private industry from employing anyone more than ten hours a day. A number of legislatures yielded to the pressure. New Hampshire passed a ten-hour law in 1847, as did Pennsylvania and Maine in

1848 and six more states★ over the course of the 1850s. Loopholes rendered these statutes unenforceable, however. They allowed for "special contracts" to extend the workday beyond ten hours, and factory owners routinely ordered workers to sign such contracts or find other jobs. In Massachusetts, textile corporations had such a stranglehold on the legislature that ten-hour bills never even came up for a vote.

Some ten-hour activists took up other issues too. Nowhere was their agenda broader than in the Lowell Female Labor Reform Association (LFLRA), the biggest of several women's unions in the New England Workingmen's Association. Members of the LFLRA organized a temperance group and a Fourierist club, raised money for the Society for the Abolition of Capital Punishment, and sent aid to Ireland during the Potato Famine of the late 1840s. Their newspaper, the *Voice of Industry,* promoted these causes along with protective unions and land reform. And in sharp contrast to most of the labor movement, the LFLRA both condemned slavery and championed women's rights.

SOLIDARITY AND FRAGMENTATION

The labor movement that emerged after the depression was more diverse than the movement of the 1830s and less cohesive. Printers, machinists, building trades workers, and cigar makers organized national craft unions, the first of which was the National Typographical Union founded in 1852 and still alive today. For the most part, however, union building was a local affair. Labor conventions and federations generally paid much more attention to issues like land reform, ten-hour legislation, and worker cooperatives than to organizing on the job. That was invariably the case at the National Industrial Congresses that convened annually from 1845 through 1856 and brought together unionists, land reformers, cooperationists, and assorted radicals. In 1850, forty-six organizations in New York City formed a local federation also known as the Industrial Congress. In addition to trade unions, participating groups included National Reform clubs, mutual-benefit societies, Christian labor reform groups, German socialist lodges, and both consumers' and producers' cooperatives. They tried in vain to construct a common program, and the federation fell apart in less than two years.

Divisions on the basis of sex, nationality, and color permeated the labor movement as well. Women were mostly excluded or treated as men's under-

★ New Jersey, Connecticut, Rhode Island, Ohio, Georgia, and California

lings and helpmeets. While immigrants and American natives cooperated in some parts of the movement, other parts were hostile to the foreign-born. Black workers were the ultimate outsiders—routinely the targets of violence as well as exclusion. Many white labor activists embraced the movement to abolish slavery, but a great many more did not.

"You have been degraded long enough," the *Voice of Industry* told its female readers in 1846. "Resolve that you will think, reason, judge, love, hate, approve and disapprove, for yourselves, and at your own volition; and, not at the dictation of another." Most of all, the Lowell Female Labor Reform Association urged workingwomen to defy the notion that social activism was unwomanly. Sarah Bagley, the Association's president, declared at a meeting of ten-hour organizers:

> For the last half century it has been deemed a violation of woman's sphere to appear before the public as a speaker; but when our rights are trampled upon and we appeal in vain to legislators, what shall we do but appeal to the people? Shall not our voice be heard and our rights acknowledged?

One of Bagley's coworkers, writing under the name of Julianna, urged mill women to rally behind the motto, "EQUAL RIGHTS or death to the corporations."

Though New England's factory operatives sent no delegates, some other workingwomen attended the nation's first women's rights convention, which met in Seneca Falls, New York, in July 1848. Among the participants was the nineteen-year-old Charlotte Woodward, an outworker who sewed deerskin gloves for leather shops in Seneca County. She dreamed of becoming a typesetter but could not find a printer willing to teach a woman the trade. "I wanted to work," she later wrote, "but I wanted to choose my task. . . . That was my form of rebellion against the life into which I was born." As the convention closed she put her name to a Declaration of Principles that updated the Declaration of Independence: "We hold these truths to be self evident: that all men and women are created equal . . ."

Workingwomen had voiced such sentiments as early as 1831, when Sarah Monroe, the president of New York City's Tailoresses Society, chided workingmen for making light of a wage strike by her union. In a speech reprinted by the labor press, she asked, "if it is unfashionable for the men to bear oppression in silence, why should it not also become unfashionable with the women? or do they deem us more able to endure hardships than they themselves?" In many cases workingmen actively supported women's militancy. During the strike wave of the mid-1830s, journeymen's unions backed women strikers, and women and men struck jointly in Philadelphia's shoe and textile factories. A decade later the ten-hour campaign in western Pennsylvania's cotton mills was punctuated by rip-roaring strikes of women operatives who rallied male friends to help. In 1845 and again in 1848, the strikers tore down factory gates and stormed in to oust workers who had remained on the job. Hundreds of men showed up to cheer these actions and dissuade police from stepping in. "Let 'em hit one of them gals if they dare, and we'll fetch them out of their boots," one man told the *Pittsburgh Journal*.

Chivalry was one thing, however, and comradeship another. Even the most generous workingmen did not generally accept women as equals, and many craftsmen were profoundly disturbed by women's very presence in industrial jobs. The National Trades Union, whose locals supported many a women's strike, excluded women's unions and voted at its 1835 convention to oppose "the multiplying of all description of labor for females." The shoemaker William English, head of Philadelphia's city central during its general strike for the ten-hour day, appealed to workingwomen to restrict their hours of labor in order to create more and better-paying positions for men. What nature intended, he said, was that men be the breadwinners so that women could devote themselves to housework, each generation training the next for the "sober duties of wives, mothers and matrons."

In 1836, the NTU appointed a Committee on Female Labor that echoed English. In its report to that year's convention, the committee urged journeymen's unions to help workingwomen organize for better labor conditions, but only as a stopgap effort "to curb the excess before we destroy the evil." The ultimate goal, the report insisted, should be women's removal from workshops and factories. Since workingwomen were "very blind to their real interest," they had so far failed to recognize the beauty of that goal, and so it was imperative that union men enlighten them. Every woman had to be made to understand that "her labor should be only of a domestic nature" and that taking industrial work was "the same as tying a stone around the neck of her natural protector, Man."

When craft unions regrouped in the late 1840s and early 1850s, their posture toward women was much the same. They defined female industrial labor as an evil and proposed as a solution that workingmen receive a "family wage" sufficient to keep the womenfolk at home. A handful of unions helped to organize sister locals of workingwomen. The Journeymen Tailors of Cleveland admitted women in 1850 in return for their support of a union strike. That same year, the Journeymen Cordwainers (shoemakers) in New York City established a local for women workers related to union men. Otherwise craft unions excluded women, as did most of the National Industrial Congresses.

There were moments of unity. Women and men cooperated closely in the New England Workingmen's Association, whose constitution granted women's unions "all the rights, privileges and obligations" enjoyed by the men's. President Sarah Bagley of the Lowell Female Labor Reform Association presented an address at the first National Industrial Congress in 1845, and women took part in the land reform movement under the National Reform Association.

The most celebrated example of labor solidarity between men and women was the Great Shoemakers Strike of 1860, in which some 20,000 shoe workers in factory towns across New England staged a six-week strike for better pay. The strike was led by journeymen's unions but included a good many women, those who did outwork at home as well as those employed in the factories. Women were especially active in Lynn, Massachusetts, where they staged the strike's most widely reported parade. On March 7, two weeks into the strike, about 800 women braved a snowstorm to march through town behind a banner proclaiming that "AMERICAN LADIES WILL NOT BE SLAVES. GIVE US FAIR COMPENSATION AND WE LABOR CHEERFULLY." Cooperation between the sexes was another important theme. Male strikers marched behind the female contingents, and a group of women from the town's Fourth Ward presented the men with a flag that read, "Weak in Physical Strength but Strong in Moral Courage, We Dare to Battle for the Right, Shoulder to Shoulder with Our Fathers, Husbands, and Brothers."

Behind this show of unity, however, lay a split. Lynn's journeymen said they were striking "not as citizens and men merely but as heads of families," and in that spirit they requested that women strikers restrict their pay demands so that the men might win more. Outworkers readily agreed; since most lived in family households whose men worked in the shoe factories, they stood to benefit from a male raise. But there was resistance from factory women, most of them entirely self-supporting and about half from out of town. Just days before the March 7 parade, factory women angrily abandoned the strike when outworkers altered the high female wage demands earlier approved at a mass meeting. Other shoe towns saw the same division in less dramatic forms. Workingwomen related to male shoe workers ardently supported the strike while the rest generally sat it out. If the Great Shoemakers' Strike epitomized labor solidarity between men and women, it also revealed the boundaries of solidarity centered in the family.

Another fault line among working people was that between immigrants and natives. Labor campaigns of the 1840s and 1850s coincided and in some instances overlapped with an anti-immigrant movement that especially targeted Irish Catholics. During the depression, nativism surged under the auspices of the American Republican Party, which was founded in 1841 and had major branches in New Orleans, Charleston, Boston, New York, Newark, Philadelphia, and St. Louis by late 1843. The American Republican platform called for immigrants' exclusion from politics. Public offices, it said, should be reserved for native-born citizens, and immigrants should have to wait twenty-one years before they could file for naturalized citizenship and gain the right to vote. The party also charged that Catholicism—Irish Catholics in particular—caused most of the poverty, crime, and political corruption that plagued American cities. These arguments attracted a fair number of Protestant working men, especially those from skilled trades that employed few immigrants. In 1844, American Republican candidates swept municipal elections in New York City, and a wave of anti-Irish riots in Philadelphia claimed more than thirty lives.

A year later the party had sharply declined, but nativism flourished in new fraternal orders for white, native-born Protestants. While some were founded and led by men of the elite and attracted predominantly genteel followings, other nativist fraternities had working-class roots. The most popular of was the Order of United American Mechanics, which began in Philadelphia in 1845 and quickly spread to other cities in both the North and the South. Craft journeymen made up the great bulk of OUAM members, though master craftsmen with small shops joined as well. American Mechanics helped each other find jobs, promoted abstinence from alcohol, profanity, gambling, and sexual vice, and maintained a mutual insurance system that provided sick, unemployment, and death benefits. They also boycotted immigrant-owned businesses, pledged not to work with immigrant labor, and gathered on patriotic holidays to proclaim Protestant America's superiority to Catholic nations. Some of the journeymen's unions that sprang up in the 1840s and 1850s recruited their charter members from OUAM lodges or kindred groups.

Immigrants also built unions and in some cities became the labor movement's driving force. The Laborer's Union Benevolent Association—organized in 1843 by Irish workingmen on New York City's docks and construction sites—became the country's biggest labor organization, with 6,000 members in 1850. By then, New York's craft unions were largely composed of Irish, German, and British immigrants, and the same pattern prevailed in all of the North's major cities. In 1849, British coal miners in

Schuylkill County, Pennsylvania, established the country's first miners' union, one of many U.S. labor organizations founded by veterans of radical reform campaigns led by the Chartist movement in England. Many German unionists had radical backgrounds; the most militant were the "Forty-Eighters," who had taken part in Germany's failed democratic revolution of 1848. Irish immigrants often had old-country experience in the radical Society of Ribbonmen or secret associations like the Whiteboys, which waged a guerrilla war against British colonialism. Infusing the American labor movement with new traditions of struggle, immigrants also expanded its awareness of struggles abroad. Native as well as foreign-born labor activists attended mass meetings to congratulate British workers when Parliament passed a ten-hour law in 1847, to hail the revolutions that swept across Europe in 1848, and to express solidarity with Irish resistance to British rule.

In factory towns, on the other hand, immigrants and natives generally kept their distance. That was especially true in New England's cotton mills, where Irish workers became the largest ethnic group over the course of the 1850s. Unions formed in connection with the ten-hour campaign had mostly died out by the start of the decade, and working conditions were on the decline. Yankee workers often blamed the decline on the Irish, who entered the mills at substandard pay and worked at speeds the Yankees had resisted. Sometimes employers recruited Irish strikebreakers. In 1851, mill overseers in Amesbury and Salisbury, Massachusetts, brought Irish immigrants to town to replace local people on strike over an increase in the workday. For the most part, however, Irish workers replaced Yankee women departing for better jobs, and complaints against them were nothing more than bigotry dressed up as a grievance.

Some of the loudest complaints came from conservative quarters like the *New England Offering,* a journal edited by a former mill worker, largely written by Yankee operatives, and subsidized by textile companies. Editor Harriet Farley thought wages would fall on account of defects in immigrants' character. Their poor work, she predicted, would compel the companies to reduce pay, and the Irish would submit "since they have little energy, few aspirations to be ministered unto by their gains, and . . . little of the home sentiment." That was the gist of all nativist thinking: attribute unsavory traits to immigrants, then blame those traits for whatever is going wrong.

In the mid-1850s, a new nativist political movement gathered across the country, and nowhere did it garner more support than in Massachusetts. In 1852, nativist fraternities organized the American Party, often called the "Know Nothings" because its founders disclaimed knowledge of secret societies to which they belonged. The party's national platform replicated that of the American Republicans, but local Know Nothings often linked nativism and anti-Catholicism to other causes. In Massachusetts, where they endorsed labor reform, abolitionism, and women's rights, Know Nothings swept the state elections of 1854, winning the governorship, every seat in the state senate, and all but a few in the assembly. Once in power, they fired immigrants from state jobs, excluded them from the state militia, formed a committee to investigate Catholic convents, and instituted a literacy test for voters. They also enlarged the public school system, required that industrial workers under fifteen attend school several months of the year, abolished imprisonment for debt, granted property rights to married women, and passed resolution after resolution against slavery.

Conditions in the mills continued to deteriorate, all the more swiftly after the economy slipped into a depression in 1857. In 1859, about 500 women—all immigrants and mostly Irish—struck several Lowell mills to protest wage cuts. None of the Yankee women supported the strike, and the low rates remained in force.

The most persistent and pernicious division among American workers was the color line. Not a single labor union federation included both black and white workers. The National Trades Union was entirely white and not by happenstance; its member unions and city centrals admitted whites only. Black activists were invited to a National Industrial Congress exactly once, in 1851, and the white Mechanics' Assembly of Philadelphia stormed out in protest.

A fair number of white workers supported the abolition movement. In upstate New York, the Workingmen's Parties of the early 1830s included antislavery planks in their platforms. Later that decade, craft journeymen provided the lion's share of signatures on the petitions that New York City's abolitionists sent to Congress. Mill workers in Lowell organized a Female Anti-Slavery Society in 1832, and twenty years later abolitionism had a large following in factories throughout New England. After touring the region in 1852, an organizer for the American Anti-Slavery Society reported: "The factory operatives felt that the northern capitalist was closely akin to the southern slaveholder, and that the design of the Slave Power and the Money Power is to crush both black and white." German labor radicals also took strong stands for abolition. In San Antonio, Texas, the Forty-Eighter Adolph Douai published the Deep South's only abolitionist newspaper, until a proslavery mob ran him out of town in 1856.

For the most part, however, white workers were indifferent or hostile to abolitionism. Many argued that reform should begin at home, that white labor should focus on its own grievances. Some were put off by antislavery agitators who regarded the wage-labor system as a model of social justice. William Lloyd Garrison, the Boston editor who became the country's most prominent white abolitionist, alienated legions of working people in the 1830s, when he attacked unionism as a "pernicious doctrine" that encouraged workers "to consider the opulent as the natural enemies of the laboring classes." In the 1850s, abolitionists' alliances with the Know Nothings alienated immigrants. Worker opposition to abolitionism also stemmed from desires to preserve the Democratic Party, whose core constituencies were workingmen in the North and slaveholders in the South. The Democratic press encouraged worries that the emancipation of slaves would "lower the conditions of the white laborer" by flooding the job market with new competitors.

At bottom, antiabolitionism rested on the same hard-core racism that made race riots part of the American landscape. Rioters often directed their fury at antislavery activists and symbols. For eight full days in July 1834, white mobs in New York City attacked antislavery meeting halls, stormed the home of a wealthy white abolitionist, and rampaged through black neighborhoods. Between 1832 and 1849, Philadelphia was the site of five major riots in which white workingmen invaded black districts to club and stone residents and destroy the churches and other buildings where abolitionists gathered. The Philadelphia riot of 1842 commenced with an assault on a black parade in honor of Britain's emancipation of slaves in the Caribbean.

In black communities, abolitionism was the most vibrant social movement. In Boston, New York, Philadelphia, Cincinnati, and other cities with substantial black populations, antislavery work went hand in hand with agitation for equal voting rights, for the right to serve on juries, and for the desegregation of public schools and transportation. Black abolitionists also took direct action to liberate fugitive slaves who had been recaptured. In 1833, an armed crowd in Detroit stopped a sheriff and his deputies from returning a Kentucky fugitive to his former master. In 1836, a group of women barged into a Boston courthouse and rescued two women fugitives. Starting that same year in New York City, many communities formed "vigilance committees" to harbor fugitive slaves, defend recaptured fugitives in the courts, and organize direct action in their behalf.

Black and white activists cooperated in the "Underground Railroad," a clandestine network that helped up to 50,000 slaves escape to freedom. The railroad's best conductor was Harriet Tubman. Born a slave on the Eastern Shore of Maryland around 1820, she ran away to Pennsylvania in 1849 and became a hotel waitress in Philadelphia and Cape May, New Jersey. During the 1850s, she made some twenty trips back to Maryland, led out hundreds of slaves, and inspired thousands to escape on their own.

In the workplace, as in unions, the color line was rigidly enforced. In 1838, Frederick Douglass arrived in New Bedford, Massachusetts, the center of the U.S. whaling industry and home to mariners of all colors from all over the world. The black community numbered over 1,000 in a city of 12,000, and included African Americans, West Indians, and Africans from the Cape Verde Islands. Black men voted, the public schools were integrated, and abolitionism had broad support among whites. But when Douglass applied for caulking work at a shipyard, he was told that the white caulkers would strike rather than work alongside a black man.

There were occasions when black and white workers made common cause. In 1835, they went on strike together at shipyards in Baltimore and Washington, D.C. Racial clashes were more typical, however, especially between black workers and white immigrants. In 1842, Irish coal miners in eastern Pennsylvania violently drove black men out of the mines, and Philadelphia's coal heavers warned that a riot would ensue if their employers hired any black men. In 1853, armed black laborers replaced Irish strikers on the Erie Railroad. In 1855, there were brawls between Irish longshoremen on strike in New York City and black men who went in to work. As Frederick Douglass observed of the longshore strike, "Colored men can feel under no obligation to hold out in a 'strike' with the whites, as the latter have never recognized them."

Black workers organized local unions of waiters, barbers, sailors, and ship caulkers. Sometimes a black union cooperated with its white counterpart. In 1853 in New York City, white hotel waiters who had just organized a union sought the counsel of the Waiters Protective Association, a black union that had already won a raise. A black waiter named Peter Hickman told them, "Gentlemen, I advise you to strike . . . for $18 a month, and if the landlords of this city do not give it, that you turn out, and be assured that we will never turn in in your places at less." When white waiters did strike, a second black union hastily formed and sent its members to take the strikers' places. The Protective Association denounced the new group as a tool of the hoteliers and supported the strike to the end.

Mostly, black and white unions were in conflict if they were in touch at all. One of the worst confrontations erupted among caulkers in Baltimore's shipyards, where caulking was traditionally a black trade. In 1850, members of a black Caulkers' Association virtually monopolized the work, but over the next decade shipyards hired more and more German and Irish caulkers, sometimes bringing them in when the Association called a strike. In 1858, the immigrants organized a rival union whose mission was to make caulking an entirely white trade. Union members mobbed black workers and petitioned the state legislature to bar them from the shipyards. As violence flared, the Caulkers' Association was dissolved by court order, and employers recognized the white union.

Speaking for the National Reform Association, the Irish-born radical Thomas Devyr typified the white labor movement's response when the issues of slavery and the rights of free blacks came up. "Emancipate the white man first," he declared, "free him from the thraldom of his unsupplied wants and the day this is done, we'll commence the manumission of the much wronged black man within our borders." That was hardly a formula for solidarity across the color line, but it could work in unintended ways. Though many land reformers opposed abolitionism, they found themselves on a collision course with slaveholders as Americans debated slavery's extension to the West.

Westward Expansion and Irrepressible Conflict

The nation's expansion to the Pacific coast started largely as a Southern drive to acquire new lands for cotton and new states for slavery. The Deep South was mostly cleared of Indians in the 1830s. Choctaws, Chickasaws, Cherokees, Creeks, and Seminoles were relocated to the "Indian Territory" in what is now Oklahoma. Resistance succeeded in only few cases. In Florida, Seminole villages and sister communities of fugitive slaves fought off the U.S. Army in a seven-year war starting in 1835, and some escaped relocation. In North Carolina and Tennessee, some Cherokees got away in the winter of 1837–38, when U.S. troops rounded up 17,000 people for a forced march to Oklahoma.

In the 1820s, American cotton growers and land speculators established slaveholding settlements in Texas, a province of newly independent Mexico. They clashed with the Mexican government after it abolished slavery in 1829 and the next year enacted laws to stop the Anglos from importing slaves under the ruse that they were indentured. In 1835, Anglos rebelled, and in spring 1836 at San Jacinto they defeated an army led by Mexico's president President General Antonio Lopez de Santa Anna. Captured in battle, Santa Anna bought his release by ceding independence to the province. It became the Republic of Texas, whose President Sam Houston had earlier been the governor of Tennessee. Almost immediately, Texas began to petition for annexation to the United States, and in 1845 it became the twenty-eighth state.

The next year Congress declared war on Mexico, and by fall 1847, U.S. troops occupied Mexico City. In return for peace, the Americans demanded the northern half of Mexico, from California to what is now western Texas. It was transferred to the United States in February 1848, under the Treaty of Guadalupe Hidalgo. The treaty stipulated that Mexicans living on this land would be treated as full-fledged U.S. citizens. Very quickly, however, the Americans set up special courts that reviewed Mexicans' land claims and nullified them by the hundreds. In New Mexico, about 3.7 million acres were confiscated; in California, the Southern Pacific Railroad wound up with 11 million acres. In Arizona (part of the New Mexico territory until 1863), U.S. companies took over the copper and silver mines, bringing in white workers and a two-tier wage system, one rate for whites and a lower "Mexican wage" for people of color.

The sharpest changes occurred in California, the site of a gold rush. Just a week before the Treaty of Guadalupe Hidalgo was signed, a mechanic struck gold on a construction site at Sutter's Mill in the New Helvetia colony near modern-day Sacramento. New Helvetia belonged to the German-Swiss entrepreneur John Sutter, who oversaw a gigantic wheat farm, a distillery, a hat factory, a blanket factory, a tannery, and various other businesses. The work was done by Indian laborers recruited from local Miwok and Nisenan settlements, paid in disks that could be redeemed for goods at Sutter's store, and policed by his private army of 200 Indians commanded by German officers. Native Americans in California would face much worse than this after gold was discovered.

Gold seekers swarmed into California from all over the United States and Mexico and from Europe, South America, Australia, and China. Once there, they made a beeline for Indian country in the interior, where the gold was. Some Native communities were massacred, many others pushed off their land. At first they survived through wage work in mines and on ranches, but before long most of them were displaced by the many unlucky gold prospectors who needed jobs. In 1855, the U.S. Army forced California Indians onto five reservations where they would supposedly feed themselves by growing wheat, but the farms were too small to support everyone. The Indian population fell from about 150,000 in 1848 to 30,000 in 1860.

The new Anglo elite in California dreaded Mexican resistance. In July 1856, Los Angeles raised four vigilante companies to guard against "Mexican revolution" after a Californio crowd liberated a man from the city jail. Another alarm went out the following year when a young man named Juan Flores escaped from San Quentin Prison, organized a band of more than fifty Californios, and skirmished with Anglo lawmen. Again Los Angeles raised vigilantes. After an eleven-day campaign, they captured Flores and most of his men and hanged him and three others before delivering the rest to legal authorities.

Some Tejanos (Mexican Texans) took up arms as well. In 1859, Juan Cortina, son of a prominent ranching family in the Brownsville area, led some sixty guerrillas—mostly ranch hands—in a campaign to redress Tejano grievances. Proclaiming their "sacred right of self-preservation," the band freed Mexicans from the Brownsville jail, raided the stores of Anglo merchants, and executed four Anglos who had gone unpunished for killing Mexicans. By the end of the year, Cortina had more than 1,000 followers. On December 27, they were defeated by the U.S. Army, but skirmishing continued into 1860 and Cortina was never caught.

The annexation of northern Mexico intensified the national debate over slavery. In 1848, the House of Representatives endorsed a proposal to ban slavery from the lands annexed under Guadalupe Hidalgo, but the measure failed in the Senate. That same year antislavery Democrats and Whigs broke away to form the Free Soil Party, which carried on the fight against slavery's extension. Growing numbers of white workers and farmers supported the cause in the name of land reform, demanding that western lands be set aside for poor homesteaders, not slaveholding planters. New York's Senator William Seward hit the nail on the head in a famous speech on the rising discord: "It is an irrepressible conflict between opposing and enduring forces, and it means that the United States must and will, sooner or later, become either entirely a slaveholding nation, or entirely a free-labor nation."

Congress tried vainly to put the conflict to rest with a package of laws known as the Compromise of 1850. California joined the federal union as the sixteenth free state, and the number of slave states remained at fifteen. New Mexico and Utah were recognized as formal U.S. territories without any prohibitions on slavery. Slave trading was banned from Washington, D.C., but not slavery itself. Congress pledged not to interfere with the interstate slave trade: It also passed a Fugitive Slave Act that commissioned federal marshals to hunt down runaway slaves and set up special courts to facilitate the reenslavement of anyone who got caught.

In defiance of the Fugitive Slave Act, black communities' vigilance committees stepped up rescue activities, and more and more whites lent a hand. In one famous incident in 1851, abolitionists in the rural town of Christiana, Pennsylvania, battled a posse of slaveholders and federal agents who arrived with warrants for four runaways. Thirty-one blacks and five whites were arrested for this incident, which left a slaveholder dead and another seriously wounded. Just one person, a white man, was brought to trial, and a sympathetic jury found him not guilty.

Tensions escalated in 1854, when Congress passed the Kansas-Nebraska Act that called for "popular sovereignty"—each new state would decide for itself whether to be slave or free. This plan enraged Free Soilers and antislavery factions among the Democrats, Whigs, and Know Nothings. In summer 1854, they came together to found the Republican Party. Advancing the slogan "Free Soil, Free Labor, and Free Men," the new party called for an end to slavery's expansion and to federal laws supporting its existence. Warfare meanwhile erupted in Kansas; as it moved toward statehood under the popular-sovereignty plan, both slaveowners and abolitionists organized guerrilla bands to stamp out the opposition. In May 1856, violence penetrated the halls of Congress. A few days after the Republican Senator Charles Sumner of Massachusetts denounced slaveholders for the "rape" of Kansas, South Carolina's Democratic Congressman Preston Brooks beat Sumner almost to death on the floor of the Senate.

In the South, slave resistance heightened. Group escapes, plots, and mutinies were reported in Missouri and Virginia in 1850; North Carolina, Texas, and Virginia in 1851; Virginia again in 1852; Louisiana in 1853 and 1854; and Maryland, Mississippi, and Louisiana in 1855. The momentum accelerated in mid-1856, against the backdrop of a presidential election in which slavery was the principal issue. In Tennessee, four slaves working in an iron foundry near Dover were sentenced to death for plotting insurrection, and 150 black men marched on the town in an attempt to free the prisoners. In North Carolina, fugitive slaves living in the swamps near Lumberton stepped up guerrilla attacks on slaveholders and fought off posses that tried to clear the swamps. By the end of the year, every slaveholding state but Delaware was rife with news of slave riots and conspiracies, some of which involved white abolitionists. Tejanos also aided rebel slaves. In September 1856, authorities in Colorado County, Texas, expelled Tejanos for helping to arm more than 200 slaves conspiring to revolt. The Austin *State Gazette* reported that month that, "the lower class of the Mexican population are incendiaries in any country where slaves are held."

In the North, the Republican Party won substantial working-class support in 1856. Increasingly, white workers defined slavery and slaveholders as menaces not only to land reform but also to free labor. A Republican labor convention in Pittsburgh made the case at length in an address to the workingmen of Pennsylvania. The heart of the argument was simple:

In another section of our country exists a practical aristocracy owning labor, and made thereby independent of us. With them Labor is servitude and Freedom is compatible only with mastership. . . . These aristocrats desire to extend this system over all the Territories of the nation. To extend it over the Territories is to give them supreme power over the government, and then they will extend it to us.

This was not an unreasonable fear; some prominent defenders of slavery did suggest that in a better world all labor would be enslaved.

In 1857, the U.S. Supreme Court gave its seal of approval to slavery and further galvanized the opposition. The case involved a lawsuit by Dred Scott, a Missouri slave who claimed to be legally free because his owner had taken him into Illinois and Wisconsin, where slavery was prohibited. The Court ruled against Scott, finding that he was not entitled to sue in federal court because slaves were not U.S. citizens. According to Chief Justice Roger Taney, free blacks were not citizens either. That question had been settled long ago, he wrote, for the republic's founders had made clear their conviction that all black people were "so far inferior that they had no rights which the white man was bound to respect." The Supreme Court now affirmed that opinion, and ruled in addition that federal laws to restrict slavery's spread were unconstitutional because they deprived slaveholders of property without due process.

Across the North, antislavery forces protested the Dred Scott decision; across the South, slave resistance continued. Then, on October 16, 1859, the white abolitionist John Brown—already notorious for the savagery of his guerrilla campaigns in Kansas—led a raid on the federal arsenal at Harper's Ferry, Virginia. Brown and his band, eighteen men both black and white, were all killed or captured after two days of fighting. Their action attracted national attention, as did the trials of the survivors, convicted of treason and sentenced to death. As John Brown awaited his execution, black communities throughout the North held meetings in honor of the "old man." A resolution passed in New Bedford, Massachusetts, was typical: "Resolved, that the memory of John Brown shall be indelibly written upon the tablets of our hearts, and when tyrants cease to oppress the enslaved, we will teach our children to revere his name." More immediately, over the summer of 1860, at least eleven slave plots and insurrections led or abetted by whites were suppressed in Georgia, Alabama, Mississippi, and Texas. At least twenty slaves and a dozen white men were hanged or lynched in Texas alone.

Many Americans continued to hope that slavery's defenders and enemies

He was the great African-American abolitionist who said he'd graduated from the institution of slavery with the scars on his back for a diploma.

But on his road to freedom, Frederick Douglass would discover the difficulty of reaching across the color line to those who might seem to be natural allies, the white working class.

SLAVE and WORKER

Young Frederick was a Maryland slave sent to work as a field hand in 1834 under a man with a reputation as a "nigger-breaker."

Frederick needed "breaking," it seemed, for helping other slaves do what he'd done — learn to read.

YOU GOTTA LOOK AT THIS FROM A SLAVE OWNER'S PERSPECTIVE.

HE WANTS A SLAVE WHO'LL LET THE THINKING BE DONE FOR HIM.

NO POINT HAVING A SMARTY-PANTS PLOWING THE FIELD.

"I was broken in body, soul, and spirit," he would later write. "My natural elasticity was crushed, my intellect languished ... the dark night of slavery closed upon me; and behold a man transformed into a brute."

J. SACCO 10-00

One day, Frederick fought back rather than endure another whipping.

DO YOU MEAN TO RESIST, YOU SCOUNDREL?

YES, SIR!

"I felt as I had never felt before... my long-crushed spirit rose, cowardice departed, bold-defiance took its place; and I now resolved that, however long I might remain a slave in form, the day had passed forever when I could be a slave in fact."

In 1836, Frederick was back in his home-town of Baltimore, working at a shipyard as an apprentice caulker.

Free blacks had been forced out of their skilled positions at the shipyards by Irish immigrants. Frederick was tolerated only because his wages were going to his owner, Hugh Auld.

J. SACCO 10.90

BUT FREDERICK ALWAYS SEEMS TO BE GETTING HIMSELF INTO SCRAPS. HE'D DO HIMSELF WELL TO LEARN THE PECKING ORDER.

On one occasion Frederick was set upon by four white apprentices who beat him severely before an approving crowd.

KILL HIM! KILL HIM!

KILL THE DAMNED NIGGER!

KNOCK HIS BRAINS OUT!!

could peacefully coexist. Many white workers remained loyal to the Democratic Party, which supported the popular-sovereignty doctrine and the Dred Scott decision. But votes from small farmers and workingmen were enough to elect Republican Abraham Lincoln to the presidency in 1860. The Republican platform called for a ban on the admission of slaveholding states; the abolition of slavery in the District of Columbia, all U.S. territories, and American ships on the high seas; the end of the interstate slave trade; strict enforcement of the ban on importing slaves from abroad; and the exclusion of slaveowners from federal jobs at all levels, from local post offices to Capitol Hill.

Even before Lincoln took office, the South's planter elite organized insurrection, and the slave states began to secede from the federal union. By mid-April 1861, the country was at war. On his way to execution, John Brown had left behind a note predicting that slavery "will never be purged away but with blood." Now that prophecy would be fulfilled.

CHAPTER

CIVIL WAR AND RECONSTRUCTION

By the eve of the Civil War, slavery gripped more Americans, ruled more states, and produced more dollars than ever before. The federal government had protected it from the earliest days of the republic but never more vigorously than in the 1850s. When Abraham Lincoln's election threatened this arrangement, the South's master class confidently decided to break away from the federal union of states.

South Carolina seceded in late December 1860. The rest of the lower South soon followed: Mississippi, Florida, Alabama, Georgia, Louisiana, and Texas. In February 1861, the secessionists founded the Confederate States of America, later joined by Virginia, North Carolina, Tennessee, and Arkansas. In his inaugural address that March, Lincoln declared secession unlawful and assured the South, "I have no purpose directly or indirectly to interfere with the institution of slavery in the States where it exists." Confederate states could return to the union without reprisal and with full faith that slavery would stay intact. But things had gone too far for that.

In mid-April, South Carolina answered Lincoln by bombarding the U.S. garrison at Fort Sumter in Charleston's harbor. On April 15, the President called for volunteers to fight the Confederacy; within days, troops were skirmishing along its northern borders. Confederate leaders fully expected to win the war. Since slaves did much of the work, many white men were free to fight, and most had received military training in the large militias southern states maintained. The war had some powerful opponents in the North, whose bankers and merchants generally wanted peace and a resumption of trade with southern planters. Britain, whose giant textile industry depended on American cotton, seemed likely to side with the Confederacy. If the North had more men and factories to equip an army, the South's prospects still looked bright.

What the Confederates did not anticipate was that slaves would mobilize for the South's defeat. By running away, by sabotaging production, by working and fighting for the Union Army, slaves doomed the Confederacy. If Southern leaders did not foresee that, Lincoln did when his Emancipation Proclamation declared the Confederacy's slaves forever free and ordered that freedmen be received into the Union's forces. Abolitionism surged in the North; by the end of the war, Congress had passed a Constitutional amendment to eradicate slavery and the states were certain to ratify. The Fifty-Fourth Massachusetts, one of the Union Army's black regiments, meanwhile marched into Charleston, followed by columns of black civilians who burned down the city's slave market.

These were the opening scenes of a second American revolution in which the victory over slavery sparked other insurgencies. Southern freedpeople struggled to claim their rights as workers and citizens. Northern workers revived the labor movement and organized on the political front. The women's rights movement launched its first campaign for female suffrage. Like the first revolution, however, this one was incomplete. Women would not win the vote for another fifty years, and most of the gains made by freedpeople and northern workers were soon wiped out.

THE CIVIL WAR

The war defied the expectations of political and social leaders on both sides. Confederate and Union officials alike thought the war would be over in short order and involve minimal casualties. The fighting began in a festive atmosphere, with high-society Charleston toasting the bombardment of Fort Sumter and upper-class residents of Washington, D.C., driving their carriages out to northern Virginia to watch and cheer the early battles. Moreover, neither side at first identified the war as a conflict over slavery. The Confederacy claimed to fight for states' rights to independence; the Lincoln administration's only declared aim was to "Save the Union." Contrary to expectations on both sides, the war dragged on for four long years and the casualties were enormous. Against this backdrop, slavery's abolition became a central Union cause.

The Civil War was the bloodiest conflict in U.S. history. It claimed the lives of 618,000 troops and uncounted numbers of civilians, and maimed hundreds of thousands more. New military technology—the Winchester repeating rifle and the Gatling revolving machine gun—produced some of this carnage. Military tactics—long-term bombardment, mass charges against defensive formations and fortifications—produced even more. Most died of the complications of mass warfare: two-thirds of the casualties came from disease, hunger, or sheer exhaustion. Military camps were rife with mumps, measles, malaria and typhoid; prisoners of war were packed into stockades with little food and less care, and died of starvation or disease by the thousands. Yet out of this carnage came one of the most glorious chapters in U.S. history—the eradication of chattel slavery.

African Americans argued from the start that the Union's war against the Confederate secession could not be won unless it became a war against slavery as well. "Never wound a snake, but kill it," declared Underground Railroad activist Harriet Tubman. Since the Confederacy's wealth and power rested on slavery, the Union would ultimately be compelled, in the words of Tubman's comrade John Rock, "to take slavery by the throat, and sooner or later . . . choke her to death." With that idea in mind, free black men were among the first to form volunteer companies when Lincoln called for troops to fight the Confederacy. In the spring of 1862, Tubman herself went to the Sea Islands of South Carolina to work with the 10,000 former slaves who had stayed behind after their masters fled the previous December.

The federal government dragged its feet. Fearful of alienating the "loyal" slaveholding states, it not only hesitated to "take slavery by the throat" but also refused to enlist black regiments during the opening years of the war. A handful of white regiments admitted black men, and a few light-skinned blacks enlisted by "passing" as white. For the most part, however, African Americans were turned away. As Union casualties mounted and Confederate victories multiplied, however, the Lincoln administration had no choice but to change its stand toward slavery and the enlistment of black troops. Only then did the Union start to win the war.

This shift in Union fortunes on the battlefield galvanized abolitionists on the home front. Their movement swelled, as did their political clout. By the time the war ended in April 1865, Lincoln had issued his famous Emancipation Proclamation declaring that the Confederacy's slaves were "forever free"; abolition had triumphed in Missouri, Maryland, and West Virginia, and Congress had approved and northern states had begun to ratify a Constitutional amendment that would erase the last vestiges of slavery from U.S. soil.

Working people had a major hand in transforming the Union's war from a fight against secession into a fight against slavery. Slaves played the leading role. As soon as the war started, they seized every opportunity to flee their masters and make their way to Union Army camps. These refugees from bondage numbered about half a million by the end of 1862. The U.S. government called them "contrabands of war." The historian W.E.B. Du Bois has more aptly described them as participants in a "general strike" against the Confederacy—a strike waged not only by those who escaped bondage but also by the legions of slaves who were unable to flee but weakened the Confederacy from within by engaging in slowdowns, arson, and other forms of sabotage.

Though some of the refugees soon left military camps for northern cities, large numbers stayed on to work for the Union Army as scouts, spies, construction laborers, stevedores, mariners, laundresses, nurses—and, in some cases, as soldiers, even though federal policy barred them from formal enlistment. In recognition of this assistance, several Union generals declared the refugees free by military order, and in summer 1862 Congress proclaimed that all slaves who escaped from Confederate masters would be "forever free."

The fact that the so-called contrabands had proved a crucial military asset—and could be even more valuable if allowed to enlist as soldiers—was clearly on Abraham Lincoln's mind when he penned his famous Emancipation Proclamation, issued January 1, 1863. This document, which proclaimed the freedom of all slaves under Confederate rule, did not immediately change anyone's actual status, for it applied only to slaves in areas that the U.S. government did not control. The proclamation did have immense repercussions, however. It foreclosed the possibility that Confederate states would be brought back into the Union as slaveholding states—an arrangement the Lincoln administration had repeatedly offered in the early days of the war. The Emancipation Proclamation also turned the Union Army into an army of liberation that dismantled slavery as it advanced into Confederate territory. And, most important for the Union's military fortunes, the Emancipation Proclamation announced that the U.S. armed forces would henceforth welcome black men. They had previously fought in very small numbers, under the banners of white regiments; now they would form all-black regiments and fight en masse.

Following the Emancipation Proclamation, about 186,000 black men entered the U.S. armed forces, nearly 35 percent of all troops enlisted by the Union during the final two years of the war. Of the 186,000 black troops, about 134,000 (72 percent) had been slaves when the war began. African

American regiments served in the war's most vicious battles and distinguished themselves for bravery under fire. Harriet Tubman again was exceptional. After a stint in Florida nursing Union soldiers sick with dysentery, she returned to South Carolina and from 1863 through 1864 she headed a corps of pilots and scouts supporting guerrilla raids deep into rebel parts. Dressed as a soldier, wearing pants, carrying a rifle, Tubman personally led many of these raids. A notice in the *Boston Commonwealth* dated July 10, 1863, reported a foray up the Combahee River:

HARRIET TUBMAN

Colonel Montgomery and his gallant band of 300 black soldiers, under the guidance of a black woman, dashed into the enemy's country, struck a bold and effective blow, destroying millions of dollars worth of commissary stores, cotton and lordly dwellings, and striking terror into the heart of rebeldom, brought off near 800 slaves, and thousands of dollars worth of property, without losing a man or receiving a scratch.

The actual numbers were 150 soldiers and 756 slaves. After she reconnoitered the area, Tubman insisted that the colonel lead the raid—he had fought in Kansas with John Brown. She herself mustered the fugitives on the three gunboats used in the raid.

Conditions of service were much harsher for black soldiers than for whites. The Confederates executed black prisoners as armed rebels—the most notorious incident was the April 1864 massacre at Fort Pillow in east Tennessee. The federal government itself did not make service easy. Recruiters promised black soldiers the regular pay—$13.00 a month plus $3.50 for clothing—but Congress authorized the same pay for black troops as for black workers—$10.00 a month less $3.00 deducted for clothing. The *Christian Recorder* printed a communication from Sergeant Gabriel Iverson of the Fifty-fifth Massachusetts:

Resolved, that even as the founders of our Republic resisted the British tax on tea on the ground of principle, so did we claim equal pay with other volunteers, because we believed our military and civil equality at issue—and independently of the fact that such pay was actually promised; and not because we regulated our patriotism and love of race by any given sum of money.

In protest, many black soldiers refused to take any pay at all. Some did more: Sergeant William Walker of the Third South Carolina Volunteers was executed for leading a group that stacked arms to protest unequal pay. Congress finally granted retroactive equal pay to free black recruits in June 1864, to ex-slaves in March 1865.

The Emancipation Proclamation and the arming of black troops electrified African Americans still enslaved. They fled bondage and made for Union Army camps in ever greater numbers, and those unable to flee stepped up their sabotage against the Confederacy.

Free labor also played an important role in the Union's war against slavery. From the start, the Union Army was mainly composed of laboring men—small farmers and wage workers. They made up the vast bulk of all adult males in Northern society and an even larger proportion of those who signed up to fight the Confederacy when Lincoln called for volunteers. In some cases, the members of local labor unions signed up as a group. The federal government estimated at the end of the war that up to 750,000 men had left industrial jobs for the Union Army. Wage earners—both industrial workers and farm hands—served in higher proportions than any other sector of Northern society and composed more than ninety percent of a great many Union regiments.

White workers in the North were by no means unanimous in opposition to the Confederacy. That was quite clear in the federal elections of fall 1862; the Democratic Party, which advocated peace with the Confederacy, gained Congressional seats as pro-war Republicans lost ground. During the months preceding the election, white working men in a number of Northern cities had struck or rioted to protest the hiring of black men. The Democratic Party fanned these flames by declaring that Republicans planned to "turn the slaves of the Southern states loose to overrun the North and enter into competition with the white laboring masses."

In the minds of many white workers, the Emancipation Proclamation proved such predictions correct. This fueled old resentments against African Americans and the Republican Party, both of which came to a head after the federal government instituted a military draft in March 1863. Draftees could avoid service by paying a $300 fee or hiring others to take their places, and many rich men exercised these options. When poor men were drafted, however, they had no choice but to serve. In July 1863, anger at this inequity combined with racial hostility to spark a bloody four-day riot in New York City, where white mobs terrorized black communities with arson, assaults, and lynchings, and attacked the property of wealthy white Republicans. Estimates of the number of people killed in the riots range from 400 to a thousand.

For the most part, however, Northern workers supported the war; and their determination to see it through often grew deeper and stronger after the Emancipation Proclamation was issued in January 1863. Pro-war Republicans swept most local elections in the fall of that year. Their success at the polls is largely attributable to the fact that the Union Army was scoring significant victories now that black men were allowed to enlist. Union victories also grew more politically inspiring now that the U.S. Army was an army of liberation.

As pro-war sentiment swelled, so did active opposition to slavery. This was partly in recognition of the African Americans' crucial contributions to the Union's war but also a result of abolitionists' increased activity following the Emancipation Proclamation. Now that one of the Union's official aims was to dismantle slavery in the Confederacy, slavery's very heart, abolitionists became the most ardent war supporters. They took the lead in organizing a giant network of Loyal Leagues, Union Leagues, and Equal Rights Leagues that coordinated and linked pro-war and anti-slavery agitation in both black and white communities. Abolitionist agitation persuaded the "loyal" slave-holding states of West Virginia, Maryland, and Missouri to adopt anti-slavery constitutions. Petitions calling for a new, anti-slavery amendment to the U.S. Constitution flooded into Congress. Lincoln won re-election in fall 1864 on a platform that endorsed such an amendment and uncompromising prosecution of the war. On the last day of January 1865, Congress passed the Thirteenth Amendment and sent it to the states for ratification.

The following April the Confederacy collapsed like a house of cards. The Thirteenth Amendment, outlawing slavery everywhere in the United States, meanwhile moved inexorably toward ratification. On December 18, 1865, it was added to the Constitution, and slavery was entirely banished from U.S. soil. (By then only Kentucky and Delaware had not yet already abolished slavery.) Though everyone who backed the Union's war contributed to this revolutionary advance, it originated in the wartime actions of slaves themselves.

Much remained to be done. Returning north from her service in South Carolina, Harriet Tubman was forcibly removed from a passenger train car by the conductor and three other white men, who refused to recognize her military pass. She rode from Virginia to New York City in a baggage car.★ And throughout the Union outside New England, black veterans returned to states where they could not vote. A convention of veterans from Iowa's

---

★ This was not her last slight by officialdom: her claim to a war pension was denied until 1899. She died in 1913 at her home in Auburn, New York; the local post of the Grand Army of the Republic gave her a military funeral.

Sixtieth U.S. Colored Infantry declared in October 1865, "that he who is worthy to be trusted with the musket can and ought to be trusted with the ballot."

SOUTHERN RECONSTRUCTION AND COUNTERREVOLUTION

The Confederacy's defeat raised two key questions. On what terms would the rebel states be readmitted to the Union? What would happen to the 4 million African Americans who had been slaves when the war began? The answers were related.

The Southern world had turned upside down. News of the Confederacy's surrender set off celebrations throughout the South. When the news came to a Mississippi slave woman in a field,

> Caddy threw down her hoe, she marched herself up to the big house, then, she looked around and found the mistress. She went over to the mistress, she flipped up her dress, and told the white woman to do something. She said it mean and ugly. This is what she said: "Kiss my ass!"

But the old order did not disappear. Andrew Johnson, the Tennessean who became President after Lincoln's assassination on April 14, 1865, sought quick reconciliation. He pardoned most of the rebels, and put them in charge of reconstructing state governments. He directed the vast tracts of lands seized by the Union army returned to their old owners. He asked only that the rebel states ratify the Thirteenth Amendment and repudiate the Confederate debt to earn readmission to the Union. White Southern leaders moved quickly. They drafted state constitutions incorporating Black Codes, which denied black men the right to vote and hold office, excluded black children from public schools, and imposed harsh labor laws designed to keep ex-slaves at work. Under the Black Codes, for instance, freedpeople could be charged with vagrancy if they did not sign year-long labor contracts with white employers. By December 1865, ten of the former Confederate states (all but Texas) had met the president's requirements for readmission.

Freedpeople made the best they could of their limited liberty. They reunited with family members sold away under slavery. They moved to cities to find alternatives to plantation labor. They organized to improve their conditions of work: on the New Orleans levees, black and white workers together struck for higher wages (though the whites demanded and got more). They sent their children to the "freedmen's" schools set up by the federal government. Some managed to get farms of their own, often purchased with the discharge bonuses received by Union army veterans. They petitioned Congress for equal rights as citizens.

Violence against freedpeople had become widespread—beyond the many individual beatings and murders, there were mass slaughters. In Memphis, Tennessee, on May 1–3, 1866, forty-six blacks (mostly Union veterans) and two whites were killed by mobs who also torched much of the black community and raped several black women. A white mob rioted in New Orleans on July 30, killing at least thirty-five blacks and injuring more than a hundred others. Both riots were suppressed by federal troops, not local police.

Congressional Republicans had had enough. "Radical" Republicans supported black equality under the law and opposed negotiations with former rebels. Moderate Republicans feared Democratic challenges to protective tariffs and possible moves to default on the war debt (owed to Northern financiers), and hoped to maintain Republican control of the government with black Southern votes. In June 1866, Congress refused to seat the newly-elected Southern delegates.

Reconstruction stalled. Congress failed to override Johnson's veto of an act establishing military courts to prosecute the multitudes of civil rights violations. But Congress did override another veto to pass a Civil Rights Act (1866) that entitled all Americans except Indians to the "full and equal benefit" of citizenship without regard to race. Congress also passed the Fourteenth Amendment, which prohibited states from violating any citizen's rights or failing to give every citizen "equal protection" under the law. The Civil Rights Act was routinely ignored; the Amendment failed to win ratification, rejected by every state legislature from the former Confederacy, except Tennessee.

On March 2, 1867, over another presidential veto, Congress passed a new Reconstruction Act. The ten former Confederate states that had rejected the Fourteenth Amendment came under martial law. To rejoin the Union, these states were now required to allow black men to vote and hold office, to exclude former Confederate officials from voting and holding office, and to ratify the Fourteenth Amendment. About 1.3 million men became eligible to vote, about 700,000 of them African Americans. The first elections held under Radical Reconstruction chose delegates to constitutional conventions that overhauled the state governments between 1867 and 1869.

The new state governments were the most democratic the South had ever known. Freedpeople poured tremendous energy into grassroots political organizing, sometimes in alliance with poor whites, often under the auspices of Union and Loyal Leagues, and Republican Clubs. In the lower

South where black voters were often the majority, African American men were elected to local and state offices. Mississippi, Louisiana, and South Carolina sent black men to Congress. In the 1868 election, freedmen's ballots provided the margin of victory for the Republican candidate, General Ulysses S. Grant.

Reconstructed governments ratified the Fourteenth Amendment (adopted July 1868), and also the Fifteenth (adopted March 1870), which prohibited states from depriving citizens of voting rights "on account of race, color, or previous condition of servitude." They eliminated all property requirements for voting and holding office. They rescinded the Black Codes. They recognized labor's right to organize. They abolished imprisonment for debt. They built public hospitals, orphanages, and asylums. They created the South's first free public school systems.

Black workers organized to improve their wages and working conditions. In March 1866, field workers on a Louisiana plantation stopped work when the proprietor was late paying monthly wages. Black "washerwomen" (as they called themselves) in Jackson, Mississippi, announced on June 20 that year that they would no longer work for less than $1.50 a day. Black stevedores in Savannah, Georgia, went out on strike in February 1867, to protest a new municipal tax imposed on them. In April, black stevedores went on strike in Richmond, Virginia, and Mobile, Alabama.

Radical Reconstruction had severe limitations. One was the failure to reconfiscate and redistribute the vast acres of farmland President Johnson had returned to the planters. Few freedpeople ever acquired their own farms: most became sharecroppers, sometimes on the same plantations where they had been enslaved, employed by the same men who had owned them before the war.

Sharecropping rested on debt and credit. Contracts ran a calendar year, bound an entire family, provided a small monthly wage, and promised landlords a share (one-fourth to one-half) of the crop. On the annual "counting day," the landlord first deducted various levies against the proceeds—payments for seed, tools, and draft animals supplied by the landlord, and for goods and supplies purchased on credit; fines for days missed for sickness, bad weather, or absence, and for disobedience or insubordination. After deductions, the worker's share might amount to only a few dollars; sometimes the deductions were so large and the proceeds so small (from a poor crop, a fall in prices for agricultural commodities, or plain cheating) that the worker owed money to the landlord. A family that ended the year free and clear could look for a new contract with a new landlord, but families still in debt had to work another year. Sharecropper Henry Blake later recalled: "A man that didn't know how to count would always lose. He might lose anyhow. The white folks didn't give no itemized statement . . . you just had to take their word. . . . If you didn't make no money, that's all right; they would advance you more. But you better not try to leave and get caught. They'd keep you in debt." For some families, "debt peonage" continued for generations.

Other compromises were made. The public school systems, hospitals, asylums, and other institutions remained segregated. The color line in employment was not challenged: like their northern counterparts, southern blacks had fewer job opportunities than whites and earned lower wages for their work. Even education might not help: Women trained as school teachers often worked as laundresses or domestic servants, and men with college degrees had to settle for manual labor.

Neither the Freedmen's Bureau nor the U.S. Army could stop the violence. Organizations like the Ku Klux Klan and the Knights of the White Camelia unleashed a wave of arson, beatings, rapes, and murders targeting the black community: political leaders and activists, school teachers, professionals like doctors and lawyers, independent farmers and small business people, and anyone who organized unions, strikes, or other labor actions.★ But trouble came with little provocation: a Georgia witness to a Congressional committee testified about sharecroppers in the early 1870s that

> Just about the time they got done laying by their crops, the Ku-Klux would
> be brought in upon them, and they would be run off, so that [the planter]
> could take their crops.

Violence became so common by the late 1860s that whole communities were "lying out" at night—sleeping in the fields and woods to avoid the nightriders.

By 1870, every ex-Confederate state had been readmitted. An 1872 Amnesty Act restored electoral rights to most ex-Confederates. Following his reelection, President Grant appointed prominent white Southerners to federal jobs and pardoned Klansmen convicted of violating freedpeople's civil rights. The Freedmen's Bureau was dismantled. The planters and their allies went to work on the Radical governments. Conservative Democrats—sometimes in alliance with white Republicans—had come to power

---

★ The Klan specialized in labor discipline: its founder, Nathan Bedford Forrest, had been the largest slave trader in Memphis, Tennessee, before the war, served as a Confederate general (commanding the troops who committed the Fort Pillow massacre), and became a railroad executive who often used convict labor on his Selma and Memphis line.

in most of the states where white voters were the majority (Georgia, North Carolina, Tennessee, Virginia by 1871); now the counterrevolution turned to states where black men formed substantial voting blocs. Combining terror campaigns to keep African Americans from voting with fraudulent electorial tallies when they did, Democrats had come to power in Alabama, Arkansas, Mississippi, and Texas by 1875, and Florida, Louisiana, and South Carolina in 1876.

Freedpeople resisted heroically. Henry Adams—born a slave in Georgia in 1843, sold onto a plantation near Logansport, Louisiana, emancipated at the end of the war—served three years in the Union Army, where he learned to read and write. Discharged in September 1869, he settled in Shreveport, working as a rail-splitter, plantation manager, and faith healer. In 1870, he joined other black veterans to form the "Committee," some 500 people who organized Republican Clubs, advised freedpeople of their legal rights, distributed ballots at elections, and investigated fraud at the polling places, swindles by landlords, and terrorist attacks. Adams became president of Shreveport's Republican Club in 1874, and was fired from his plantation job. That year's elections were accompanied by unprecedented "bulldozing"—assassinations, beatings, arson—and the Republican Clubs fell apart in the countryside. Adams and his Committee tried hard to rebuild the Clubs for the 1876 elections, but the local "White League" stepped up its terror, and the Democrats won easily. Though they knew about voter fraud and intimidation, federal officials did not intervene. The last Union occupation troops were withdrawn from South Carolina and Louisiana in April 1877.

The Radical governments were replaced with regimes that legally subordinated African Americans and controlled their labor. They redirected funding away from public education and projects like poor relief. They stifled black political activity with terror and fraud, and drove many black officials from their positions—those who remained depended on white patronage. They passed statutes reminiscent of the postwar Black Codes, criminalizing unemployment ("vagrancy") and quitting a job before the end of a contract ("enticement"). They developed extensive convict labor systems, leasing prisoners to work without pay for railroad, mining, and lumber companies. They refined sharecropping laws to make sure landlords, received their profits whether or not crops brought enough money to cover workers' wages too.

Many freedpeople abandoned any hope of building a decent life in the South and organized to leave for some other place, "where a man can enjoy his political opinions without being murdered." Despite Klan opposition, organizations promoting black emigration sprang up all over the South. In 1877, Henry Adams's Committee became the Colonization Council and held meetings throughout the region. The next year was worse. Fifty-nine African Americans—Adams among them—went to New Orleans to testify about the terror, then could not return home where the White League had marked them for murder. In the spring of 1879, 6,000 black people from Louisiana, Mississippi, and eastern Texas migrated to Kansas by riverboat, joined the next winter by 3,000 to 4,000 more from Texas who came by wagon or rail. "Exodusters" settled as farm laborers, railroad workers, miners, domestics, and laundresses—by 1880 about a third had acquired their own land. Adams himself remained in New Orleans advocating migration until at least 1884.

Though the counterrevolution was aimed at freedpeople, it had a deleterious effect on all labor, not just in the South but in the nation as a whole. The *de facto* disenfranchisement of freedpeople—a large portion of working-class Americans—increased the employing classes' edge in both regional and national politics. By giving American manufacturers a low-wage haven to run to, the repressive labor system of the "New South" would eventually discipline workers in other regions too.

LABOR MOVEMENTS AND STRUGGLES

As Reconstruction and counterrevolution wracked the South, labor struggles elsewhere in the country traced a parallel course. The war years themselves saw a wave of workplace organizing in Northern states as the economy boomed on war production and inflation hit rents and prices. Despite the occasional use of troops to break strikes against firms engaged in war-related production, wartime strikes for higher wages were often short and successful. Hundreds of local unions sprang up, citywide assemblies of local unions reappeared, and about a dozen "national" unions connected local assemblies in various cities. African Americans in Union states began to build a black labor movement: in 1862, black sailors in New York City formed the American Seaman's Protective Association—the first seamen's union in the United States.

Peace permitted an even broader effort. At a mass meeting celebrating the Confederate surrender in April 1865, Boston workers approved this resolution:

> While we rejoice that the rebel aristocracy of the South has been crushed
> . . . we want it to be known that the workingmen of America will

demand in the future a more equal share of the wealth their industry creates . . . and a more equal participation in the privileges and blessings of those free institutions defended by their manhood on many a bloody field of battle.

But workers faced many obstacles. The postwar economy was unstable. Corruption flourished in government, nourished by profiteering in military procurement and land speculation, which mocked the Republican commitment to "Free Soil."★ Employers used imported contract labor (authorized by Congress in 1864) to replace strikers.

Labor was itself divided, especially by widespread racial animosities, and organized actions often stopped at the color line. Some labor activists recognized the problem. The *Boston Daily Evening Voice,* founded in late 1864 by white printers fired for union activity, advocated labor solidarity across occupation and race. An editorial from October 15, 1865, shows a characteristic blend of principle and expediency:

> If we insist that employers are no better than we, we must not pretend to be better than others. If we claim justice, we must do justice. . . . The workingman's success is simply impossible without united and harmonious action. If the machinist says to the wielder of the pick and shovel, I will not associate with you,—if you want better wages you must get it on your own hook; if the clerk says to the coal-heaver, between you and I there is a gulf fixed; or if the white man says to the black, I do not recognize you as a fellow workman; and these feelings prevail, there is the end of hope for the labor movement.

The history of the National Labor Union (NLU) shows both labor's high hopes for radical change and the difficulties of achieving it. Founded in 1866 at a labor convention in Baltimore, the NLU drew together a large network of local and national unions of metal workers, coal miners, clothing and shoe makers, construction workers, typographers, and other trades. The NLU supported union organizing, producer and consumer cooperatives, and po-

---

★ After the Homestead Act of 1862, speculators staked bogus claims and bought the land at bargain prices. This was only a small part of the land grab. Between 1862 and 1864, Congress gave 70 million acres to three railroads—the Union Pacific, the Central Pacific, and the Northern Pacific—and turned over 140 million acres to states, which made their own bargains with speculators.

litical action for a range of goals: making eight-hour workdays the law in every state; reforming the banking, currency, and tax systems to benefit people of small means; abolishing convict labor; securing the distribution of public lands to homesteaders; and building a National Labor Party to work for these and other reforms.

William Sylvis was instrumental in the NLU's formation. Born in 1828, one of twelve children of a poor white wagon maker in rural Pennsylvania, he began an apprenticeship at the age of eighteen in a local iron foundry. When the foundry went out of business a few years later, and now married with a family to support, he moved to Philadelphia. In 1855, he joined Philadelphia's Stove Molders' Union, and became one of its leading organizers. In 1859, he helped found the National Molders' Union, which collapsed at the outbreak of war when its members—including Sylvis—joined the Union Army. By 1863, he was back home, working to revive the union, which elected him president. A tireless organizer, he travelled thousands of miles to organize molders in city after city, living on donations from members of new locals. The union became one of the strongest in the country: In 1864, it stopped a New York City company from operating a foundry at Sing Sing prison with convict labor bought from the state for 40¢ a day (the Molders' rate was $3 a day). In 1866, Sylvis helped found the National Labor Union.

Sylvis held strong views. "Capital blights and withers all it touches. It is a new aristocracy, proud, imperious, dishonest, seeking only profit and exploitation of the workers." But "Labor is the foundation of the entire political, social and commercial structure . . . the attribute of all that is noble and good in civilization." So "Let our cry be REFORM. . . . Down with a monied aristocracy and up with the people." He hoped that by organizing workers' cooperatives, "we will become a nation of employers—the employers of our own labor." Elected NLU president in 1868, he literally worked himself into the grave, dying suddenly shortly before the NLU's 1869 convention.

The NLU preached and sometimes practiced labor solidarity across gender and racial lines. Several women's unions participated, including the newly founded Daughters of St. Crispin, the female counterpart of the shoemakers' Knights of St. Crispin, and the first national union of women industrial workers. The NLU held the first national labor convention to endorse organizing workingwomen, urging them to join existing unions or build new ones to force employers to "do justice to women by paying them equal wages for equal work."

The NLU never endorsed women's right to vote, though it did seat Elizabeth Cady Stanton from the Women's Suffrage Association at its 1868 convention. But relations with the suffragists were uneasy. Some women unionists—the New York and Massachusetts Daughters of St. Crispin, for example—supported them; others argued that workingwomen could move to better their lives more by organizing unions than by agitating for the vote.

The early career of Augusta Lewis illustrates the complexity of gender relations. After starting as a newspaper reporter, she learned typesetting, and in 1867, went to work as a typesetter for the New York *World*. At the time, about 200 women worked as typesetters in the city's print shops, though the National Typographical Union (NTU) barred them from membership. That December NTU Local 6 struck the *World* when members were ordered to set type for another newspaper that other local members were striking. The women typesetters stayed on the job, and the paper hired more women to replace the strikers. When the *World* settled with Local 6 in September 1868, most of the women were fired. Lewis quit in protest, and within days joined a small group of women workers and prominent suffragists (including Elizabeth Cady Stanton and Susan B. Anthony) to start the New York Working Women's Association, dedicated "to act for the interests of its members, in the same manner as associations of workingmen now regulate the wages, etc., of those belonging to them." A week later she called a meeting of women typesetters to discuss unionism, and the Women's Typographical Union was founded on October 13, 1868, with Lewis (not yet twenty-one years old) as president.

Lewis forged an alliance with the men's local. They supplied financial assistance and a meeting hall; in turn, the women boycotted employers who paid women less than men for the same work. When Local 6 went on strike for higher pay in book and specialty print shops in January 1869, the Women's Typographical Union refused to work for these shops, and encouraged other women typesetters to shun them too. Susan B. Anthony saw a different kind of opportunity. Backed by print shop employers, she started "training schools" where women could learn typesetting and be quickly readied to replace strikers.

In June 1869, at the insistence of Local 6 leadership, the NTU chartered the Women's Typographical Union as an official local. And when Anthony went to the National Labor Union's 1869 convention as a representative of the New York Working Women's Association, Lewis challenged her credentials, arguing that the Association was not a true friend of organized labor. The convention declined to seat Anthony as a delegate.*

Labor solidarity across racial divisions proved harder to practice. The NLU's founding convention's final statement ended with stirring words:

> What is wanted is for every union to help inculcate the grand, ennobling idea that the interests of labor are one; that there should be no distinction of race or nationality; no classification of Jew or Gentile, Christian or infidel; that there is but one dividing line—that which separates mankind into two great classes, the class that labors and the class that lives by others' labor.

But beginning with this same convention, the NLU repeatedly called for the exclusion of Chinese immigrants from the United States, considering them naturally submissive workers who happily undercut American wage standards and working conditions.

The movement against Chinese labor started in California, where it had been brewing since the 1850s, when white miners formed vigilante gangs to drive Chinese miners from the gold fields. In the 1860s, the Central Pacific Railroad hired 12,000 Chinese men—90 percent of its construction force, and paid at two-thirds the going rate for white laborers—to build the western run of the first transcontinental railroad. By 1870, close to 50,000 Chinese immigrants lived in California—12,000 of them in San Francisco.

Eastern and southern employers also experimented with using Chinese immigrants to replace other workers. In 1870, when the Knights of St. Crispin (mostly Irish immigrants) struck Massachusetts shoe factories for higher wages and the eight-hour day, a North Adams factory owner fired the strikers and replaced them with Chinese workers brought from San Francisco. An attempt to form a Chinese lodge of the Knights collapsed in mounting racial hostility, and the strike collapsed too, in North Adams and nearby towns. Over the next few months, Chinese workers recruited by labor contractors on the West Coast also replaced white workers in a steam laundry in Belleville, New Jersey, and a cutlery factory in Beaver Falls, Penn-

---

* Lewis became the NTU's corresponding secretary, charged with investigating industry working conditions. Her report to the 1871 convention criticized male typesetters: the women generally found "that they are more justly treated by what is termed 'rat' foremen, printers and employers than they are by union men." She married fellow typesetter Alexander Troop in 1874, and moved to New Haven, Connecticut, where she raised seven children, wrote articles for her husband's labor paper, agitated for suffrage, and worked on behalf of the city's Italian immigrants.

sylvania. Black workers were affected too: some plantation owners in Louisiana and Mississippi tried replacing black workers with Chinese, though they found the Chinese all too quick to respond to mistreatment with mass protests.

In fact the NLU stereotype of Chinese was quite undeserved. In 1867, Chinese laborers staged an exceptionally large and brave strike for a favorite NLU cause—the eight-hour day. Five thousand Chinese men blasting tunnels and laying track through the Sierra Nevada mountains downed their tools and told their boss, "Eight hours a day good for white men, all the same good for China men." As white workers scabbed, the Chinese held out, and finally returned to work only after the Central Pacific blocked the wagons carrying food to the strikers' remote mountain camps.

The NLU was somewhat more consistent with black workers: it endorsed organizing black workers from the start, and by 1869 delegates from black organizations were attending NLU conventions. Nonetheless, the NLU never made an effective alliance between black and white workers, and almost none of the federation's constituent unions admitted black workers.

In December 1869, Isaac Myers, leader of Baltimore's Colored Caulkers' Trade Union Society, joined other labor activists and black reformers in Washington, D.C., to found the Colored National Labor Union (CNLU). The call for this convention had come out of the State Labor Convention of Colored Men of Maryland the previous July. State and local meetings convened across the country to select delegates and discuss issues to be addressed by the national federation. Response was especially enthusiastic in the South, where large local meetings convened in Macon, Georgia, and Columbia, South Carolina. Like many local meetings, the Macon convention itself produced a network of local unions and a statewide Colored Mechanics and Laboring Man's Association.

Delegates from eighteen states came to Washington. They proposed to work for equal employment opportunities for black workers. They called also for equality before the law (equal access to public schools, eligibility for jury service). They sought land for freedpeople. They endorsed the Republican Party as the best (though imperfect) safeguard for freedpeople in the South. But the CNLU remained a labor organization. Its key goal was expressed in the organization's newspaper, the *New Era,* on January 13, 1870:

> By argument and appeal addressed to the white mechanics, laborers and trade unions of our country, [and] to our legislators and countrymen at large, to overcome the prejudices now existing against us so far as to secure

a fair opportunity for the display and remuneration of our industrial capabilities.

Compared to the NLU, the CNLU took a broader view of racial solidarity. Black workers also worried about Chinese competition. At the preliminary meeting in November, in Cumberland County, Pennsylvania, a resolution condemning the use of "contract Chinese or Coolie labor" that was "forcing American laborers to work for Coolie wages or starve, and crowding us out on all sides, and reducing the workingman to a state worse than slavery." But the Macon local meeting passed a resolution extending "the right of fellowship to John Chinaman or any other man," and the national meeting agreed:

> With us, too, numbers count. . . . Hence, our industrial movement, emancipating itself from every national and partial sentiment, broadens and deepens its foundations, so as to rear . . . a superstructure, capacious enough to accommodate . . . the Irish, the Negro, and the German laborer . . . the "poor white" native of the South . . . the white mechanic and laborer of the North . . . as well as the Chinaman.

All together could "aid in the protection and conservation of their and our interests."

The CNLU also addressed the woman question. Indeed it also appeared during the preliminary meetings. At the meeting in Newport, Rhode Island, an unnamed workingwoman complained that "in all your deliberations, speeches, and resolutions, which were excellent so far as the men are concerned, the poor woman's interests were not mentioned or referred to." The meeting responded by naming a woman to Newport's delegation to Washington. Nevertheless, though some CNLU activists (like school teacher Mary Ann Shadd Cary) campaigned for votes for women, the federation never formally endorsed women's suffrage.

Isaac Myers and his comrades hoped to coalesce with the white NLU, but that never happened. From 1870, the NLU concentrated on its National Labor Party project, running candidates in 1872. But black labor leaders and activists supported Radical Reconstruction in the South, and remained committed to the electoral success of the Republican Party. The CNLU survived into the late 1870s, mainly as a paper organization that endorsed Republicans.

Labor organizations everywhere faced harsh repression when the economy collapsed following the Panic of 1873. Five thousand businesses closed, unemployment soared, and employer resistance escalated—more and more often coordinated by industry-wide and local employers' associations. Countless locals and several national unions were entirely wiped out; the rest shrank sharply. In 1870, more than thirty national unions functioned, and union membership totaled about 300,000; by 1877, just nine national unions remained, and union membership had fallen to less than 50,000. Nationwide that year only one-fifth of the labor force had steady, full-time jobs.

Employers took advantage of racial divisions among workers to procure scabs during strikes. In June–July 1874, white coal miners in southern Ohio's Hocking Valley struck against a wage cut, and mine owners imported black workers to replace them. The following October, the St. Bernard Coal Company in Earlington, Kentucky, recruited a mostly black scab force to replace striking white miners. The color line could be crossed in the other direction. In April 1877, black stevedores in Richmond, Virginia, struck the Powhattan Company shipping firm against a 25 percent wage cut. The company immediately hired forty white scabs, and police escorted them to work, dispersing a black crowd that had gathered to enforce the strike.

Where the workers cooperated across the color line, they were stronger. In April 1873, black workers led a strike for four months' back pay by about a thousand track men—both black and white—on the Chesapeake and Ohio Railroad near Beckley in southern West Virginia. This was an especially militant strike—the trackmen seized a switching station, wrecked a locomotive, and blocked tracks with stones and stumps. But only a few months later, in November, with the depression now underway, 200 black Chesapeake and Ohio Railroad laborers on a tunnel project near Richmond, Virginia, also struck for back pay, about two months' worth. Within days the company had replaced them with newly arrived Italian immigrants. The strike was lost, and the black strikers lost their jobs and their back pay.

WHOSE GOVERNMENT?

In the South, state and local governments could not bring force and law fully into the service of employers until Radical Reconstruction was brought down. In August 1876, black workers on the rice plantations in South Carolina's Combahee River district staged a mass strike for cash wages instead of chits good only at plantation stores. Ten strikers were tried before a black judge in Beaufort, South Carolina, and set free to the applause of supporters gathered in front of the courthouse. The planters finally agreed to pay cash wages, as required by state law. That fall's state elections overturned Reconstruction in South Carolina and foreclosed any possibility for such victories in future.

As the South descended into its long night of apartheid, state and local governments elsewhere also rushed to repress labor unrest. During the hungry winter of 1873–74, labor activists in New York City organized mass meetings and demonstrations demanding public assistance to the unemployed. On January 13, 1874, thousands of men, women, and children rallied in Tompkins Square on the city's Lower East Side, expecting to be addressed by Mayor William Havemeyer. Instead, the mayor sent the police, who charged into the Square without warning, clubbing right and left as mounted officers chased down people fleeing through the side streets. Hundreds of demonstrators and bystanders were injured, several arrested and sentenced to prison terms for resisting arrest. The city's unemployed movement stalled and dissipated in the wake of this brutality.

In eastern Pennsylvania's Schuylkill County, the Philadelphia and Reading Railroad enlisted local courts in its assault on labor activists in the anthracite mines that produced fuel for the railroad's locomotives. The miners' union—the Workingmen's Benevolent Association—disintegrated in 1875 when it lost a long and bitter strike against a 20 percent wage cut. But Franklin Gowen, the Railroad's president, was not satisfied with the union's defeat; he wanted to get the strike's grassroots leaders, the Irish American miners whose ethnic fraternal lodge, the Ancient Order of Hibernians, harbored labor activists after the WBA's demise. Gowen hatched an elaborate plan. In 1873, he hired James McParlan, a detective from the Pinkerton Agency (which specialized in labor activists and political radicals), to infiltrate the Hibernian lodge in Schuylkill County. During the 1875 strike, Gowen placed stories in the newspapers alleging that a secret society of Irish immigrants calling themselves the "Molly Maguires" conspired to destroy American society by starting labor uprisings and attacking the forces of law and order. In 1876, McParlan surfaced to charge nineteen miners with murder. Gowen arranged to serve as prosecutor in several of the trials. Carefully screened juries ignored the inconsistencies in McParlan's testimony, and all the miners were convicted. Their public hangings began on June 21, 1877.

The miners in Schuylkill County had hardly finished burying their dead when the Great Railroad Strike swept across the country, taking the railroad magnates by surprise. Railroad workers had absorbed wage cut after wage cut, amounting to over 60 percent since the Panic of 1873. Their strikes were broken up by Pinkerton agents, and their fraternal brotherhoods blacklisted. When the Baltimore & Ohio Railroad imposed a new 10 percent cut on Monday, July 16, only forty firemen and brakemen in Baltimore refused to work, and were quickly dispersed and replaced. The strikers gathered at Camden Junction outside the city, stopped a freight train, and were again dispersed by police.

But at Martinsburg, West Virginia, a couple dozen more firemen left their freight trains, and a crowd gathered in support. When the mayor arrested three leaders, the crowd freed them. When the company tried to send out freight trains with new firemen, the brakemen walked off, and the strikers blocked the trains. On Tuesday, B&O officials called on Governor Henry M. Mathews, who ordered two companies of militia into Martinsburg. The militiamen refused to fire on the strikers. The strike spread to other junctions, and by the end of the day 500 men were out, joined by 200 boatmen on the Chesapeake & Ohio Canal, and the freight blockade at Martinsburg had stalled 70 trains with 1200 cars, many fully loaded.

The B&O suggested that Governor Mathews ask President Rutherford Hayes for help. The president complied: on the morning of Wednesday the 18th, 400 soldiers—many just returned from South Carolina—left Washington and Baltimore for Martinsburg, riding a special train provided by the B&O. There the troops pushed the crowds back with bayonets and manned two trains, one going in each direction. The next day thirteen trains moved, all manned with troops.

The strike spread along the lines. On Friday, July 20, in Baltimore, state militia companies were stranded at Camden Station, surrounded by an angry crowd. In Pittsburgh, where the local militia again refused to fire on the crowds supporting the strikers, Governor John P. Hartranft ordered a Philadelphia militia company to the scene. Arriving on Saturday, they fired on the crowd, retreated into the Pennsylvania Railroad's roundhouse, then withdrew under fire after a blazing rail car was rolled into the building. At least 40 civilians were killed; 500 rail cars, 104 locomotives, and 39 buildings went up in flames. At Johnstown, the troops were stoned. At Reading on Tuesday the 24th, the militia company from Morristown threatened to fire on the company from Easton, then stacked their arms and refused to deploy against the citizens. Three thousand federal soldiers were sent to Pennsylvania, and Governor Hartranft led troop convoys around the state for two weeks, opening fire on every crowd until it dispersed.

Within a week of Camden Junction, strikes had occurred on more than a dozen lines north to New York state, west to the Rockies, and south to Texas. Mass rallies were staged in Buffalo, Albany, Trenton, Boston, and New York City. After a 10,000-strong rally of workers at the Halsted Viaduct in Chicago beat off a police attack on Thursday the 26th, Secretary of War

George W. McCrary ordered General Philip Sheridan to suspend his campaign against the Sioux and take his troops to Chicago.

In St. Louis, a general strike developed, and lasted five days. The railroads had quickly restored wage cuts, but the Relay Depot in East St. Louis was controlled by a committee representing workers from four lines. The Relay committee appealed to their brothers across the river, who went out in sympathy. An "Executive Committee" formed and over the next couple of days delegations visited every factory and shop to call out the workers. The Executive Committee called on Missouri Governor John S. Phelps to convene the legislature to pass laws enforcing an eight-hour day and prohibiting the employment of children under fourteen in factories or dangerous occupations. It called on Mayor Henry Overstolz to arrange for the distribution of food to destitute families (promising that the unions would pay for the food), and offered to help maintain public order.

But the tide had turned. Martinsburg had been pacified by Thursday the 19th, the Baltimore riots were over by the following Monday, and Pittsburgh was subdued the next day (though the B&O lines were not cleared until August 1, after three days of fighting). The Chicago and St. Louis strikes ended with the arrests of their leaders by Saturday, July 28. Overall, more than 100,000 railroad workers—about half the total, and affecting about two-thirds of the nation's lines—had gone on strike, and cities from Baltimore, Buffalo, and Albany to St. Louis and Chicago had been occupied by troops.

Aside from the wartime contraband movement, the railroad strike was the largest strike to date in U.S. history. It had many notable features. The railroad workers were widely supported by other workers and their families. Women participated as fiercely as men; the *Baltimore Sun* reported that

> The singular part of the disturbances is in the very active part taken by the women, who are the wives or mothers of the firemen. They look famished and wild and declare for starvation rather than have their people work for the reduced wages. Better to starve outright, say they, than to die by slow starvation.

Women and children were among the strike supporters killed in Pittsburgh.

Both blacks and whites participated. Many people in the Martinsburg crowd were black. Black and white coal miners together halted trains in the surrounding countryside. Black workers in St. Louis closed the canneries and docks, black boatmen stopped steamboats on the Mississippi, and the Executive Committee's five-person delegation to the mayor included one black man. In Galveston, Texas, a strike began with black track layers and construction workers, and won a 30 percent increase. But racial animosity had prevailed in San Francisco: a July 24 mass meeting to discuss news of the disturbances spawned a mob of young men who rampaged through the city's Chinatown, wrecking laundries and other small businesses. Anti-Chinese riots continued two more nights, and one Chinese laundryman was killed.

The strike was suppressed by the first peacetime deployment of federal troops, required when some state militia units proved unreliable. In addition to the regular troops, city and state governments mobilized other armed forces—regular police, special deputies recruited and armed for the emergency, and civilian patrols, often organized and armed by the railroad companies.

The speed and scale of government intervention on the side of the railroad barons showed clearly that labor unrest—whatever the hardships of the workers and the merits of their complaints—had come to be seen as pathological social disorder. Business leaders, and the politicians and journalists they employed, saw everywhere the specter of "communism"—the insurrectionary spirit of the Paris Commune of 1871, spread by immigrant revolutionaries inciting tramps and hooligans to destroy civilized society. "RIOT OR REVOLUTION?" screamed the New York *World* headline on Monday, July 23. The federal government certainly feared revolution. President Hayes met daily with his cabinet from Friday the 20th through Sunday the 29th to review the crisis and military deployments. Sailors and marines were ordered to Washington to protect the Treasury.

From the vantage of 1877, the high hopes with which labor activists had celebrated the Confederacy's defeat in 1865 seemed quite ironic and almost naive. They had looked forward to "a more equal share of the wealth"; now they endured progressive wage cuts. They had expected to enjoy "the privileges and blessings" of citizenship; now they were targeted by police riots, kangaroo courts, and regular army troops. Labor had defended the Republic on the bloody battlefields of the Civil War, only to see it seized by capital.

The second American Revolution—like the first—was deeply inspiring and woefully incomplete. The Constitution was amended to abolish bondage and guarantee equality before the law—revolutionary advances that were thwarted and stalled but never obliterated by the reactionary triumphs of the planters of the South and the industrialists of the North. Many workers still believed in the vision of America articulated in a poem by a member of the National Molders' Union on the centennial of the Declaration of Independence:

> For though slaves in their eyes we now may seem to be
> Created by God for their pleasure alone;
> The day's not far distant, when we shall be free,
> And tyrants their unpitied downfall bemoan.
> Then gird on the sword in our glorious cause,
> Every lover of liberty—all who'd be free,
> And rescue thy children from tyranny's jaws,
> Break the chains that now wait for the child at thy knee.

CHAPTER

LABOR VERSUS MONOPOLY IN
THE GILDED AGE

The economic crash of 1873 helped to douse the democratic revolution sparked by the Civil War. It also ushered in the Gilded Age, a quarter century of glittering riches for American capitalists and leaden poverty for masses of working people. Even more than in the past, politics and law protected class privilege and the accumulation of wealth.

The fortunes and influence of wealthy Americans exceeded anything the nation had ever seen. At the top of the heap stood a new group of monopoly capitalists like Jay Gould, whose empire included a slew of railroads and controlling interests in the Western Union Telegraph Company and several steamship lines. Gould was notorious for more than mere wealth. His corrupt stock transactions ruined so many people that he retained a phalanx of plainclothes police to protect him from assault and bombproofed his office in the Western Union headquarters near Wall Street. He bought a daily newspaper (the New York *World*) so the public could read good things about him. He stocked the greenhouse of his country estate with $40,000 worth of orchids, surrounded himself with European artwork, relaxed on a 230-foot yacht, and bestowed lavish gifts on state and federal lawmakers and judges. When he died in 1892, he left $77,000,000 to his heirs.

As for labor, he boasted, "I can hire one-half of the working class to kill the other half."

For the vast majority of workers and their families, the Gilded Age brought unceasing economic insecurity in a churning national economy. The depression of 1873–78 was followed by a sharp recession in 1883–85, and another, deeper depression that stretched from spring 1893 through most of 1897. Even in the relatively good years between depressions and recessions, working people suffered repeated wage cuts and layoffs. At the same time, government officials serviced the interests of their business friends. In 1886, the U.S. Supreme Court declared that corporations were entitled to the same protections guaranteed to citizens under the Fourteenth Amendment. State courts nullified laws that limited hours of labor, set minimum wages, or otherwise restricted employers' "rights." Judges routinely issued injunctions against strikes, demonstrations, boycotts, and organizing drives.

"There are too many millionaires and too many paupers," observed the *Hartford Courant* in 1883. In 1890, the richest 1 percent of Americans had a combined annual income larger than the poorest 50 percent. Captains of finance and industry feasted at lavish banquets. The guests at one dinner puffed cigarettes wrapped in $100 bills; at another, rare black pearls were tucked into the oysters served as appetizers. Workers, meanwhile, scavenged for firewood. Bernardo Vega, a Puerto Rican immigrant to New York City, recalled his Aunt Dolores during the winter of 1879–80: "The price of coal had gone up, and what made it worse was that it was hard to come by. . . . Every day she would go out with the children in search of firewood to heat the house." Each summer, millionaires caught the night ferry from Fall River, Massachusetts, to their summer homes in Newport, Rhode Island. As the ferry pulled out, passengers could view mill workers on the beaches digging for clams to supplement their meager diets. Children of the rich grew up with ponies, private tutors, and grand tours of Europe. In immigrant ghettos like New York City's Lower East Side, children lived in tenement flats with little daylight, less ventilation, and no running water. The census of 1880 counted more than a million wage workers under sixteen years of age. While millionaires built mansions modeled on European castles, many families had no shelter at all. In city after city, homeless people lined up every night to sleep in police stations.

The poet Walt Whitman saw in the increase in capitalist wealth "a sort of anti-democratic disease and monstrosity." But to big businessmen and their spokesmen, their ascendancy was inevitable, natural, and sanctioned by God—the beneficent result of social evolution based on "the survival of the fittest." The steel tycoon Andrew Carnegie wrote in 1889 that, "Individualism, Private Property, the Law of Accumulation of Wealth, and the Law of Competition" were "the highest result of human experience." John D. Rockefeller, Sr., the oil and mining potentate, declared in a lecture to Sunday-school students: "The growth of a large business is merely a survival of the fittest. . . . This is not an evil tendency in business . . . merely the working-out of a law of nature and a law of God." William Graham Sumner, Yale professor of political and social science and a favorite lapdog of the rich, opined that, "The millionaires are a product of natural selection, acting on the whole body of men to pick out those who can meet the requirement."

Capitalists did not have to rely on natural law alone; they could buy favors from legislators and judges. State lawmakers passed a raft of anti-labor statutes that made picketing and strikes illegal and authorized corporations to use their own police in company towns. Anything an employer did to discourage unions (short of actual mayhem and murder) was a perfectly legal defense of his property rights. As in the past, labor activists were repeatedly indicted for conspiracy. Prosecutors did not have to prove criminal intent or action: under the law, the mere existence of a combination of workers violated an employer's freedom to run a business in a profitable manner. In *Moores v. Bricklayers' Union* (1890), Ohio's supreme court ruled it illegal to make an employer conduct business according to union regulations.

Conspiracy trials were inefficient, however; they took time, required witnesses, and left it to juries to render a verdict. In 1877, a new, more streamlined legal device appeared—the labor injunction, applied first to striking railroad workers. Injunctions had several advantages over conspiracy indictments. They were issued by "equity" courts, where judges alone determined all issues of fact and law and decided what actions constituted contempt of court. Labor injunctions prohibited any activity that might cause irreparable harm to employers' property: both tangible possessions like machinery and buildings and intangibles like the right to hire and sell.

Against this backdrop, working people mobilized on a scale that caught the upper classes by surprise. Though the labor movement had been devastated by the depression of the 1870s, the insurgent spirit so evident in the great railroad strike had not died out. In September 1880, a labor newspaper in Detroit predicted that the quiet of the past three years would prove to be the calm before a storm: "Labor is waking from its long slumber. The rising giant is just now stretching and . . . will make [its] strength felt in every phase of American life." These were prophetic words. The 1880s and 1890s saw unprecedented levels of labor organizing, strike militancy, and political action by working people—initiatives aimed first and foremost at curbing the power of capitalist monopoly.

INDUSTRIAL CAPITALISM: CONSOLIDATION AND CRISIS

The Union's victory in the Civil War cleared the way for the swift expansion of American industry, and railroads drove the trend. The first transcontinental line was completed in 1869; by the late 1890s, more than 100,000 miles of new track had produced the largest rail system in the world. This massive construction rippled through feeder industries such as lumber, iron, and steel. Increased iron and steel production swelled demand for coal. The railroad network in turn linked producers everywhere to new markets, prompting a tremendous boom in industrial and agricultural output. Metal mining (gold, silver, copper, iron) proliferated in the West. Farming and ranching took more and more land. The South planted about 9 million acres of cotton in the early 1870s, about 24 million by the late 1890s. Annual wheat production in the North Central states rose from 67 million bushels in 1869 to 307 million in 1899. Meanwhile, in the Rocky Mountain states, wool production zoomed from 1 million to 123 million pounds a year.

Much of the land newly devoted to farming and grazing came from the railroads. They sold vast amounts to small homesteaders and to agribusinesses like the Miller and Lux partnership that owned more than 1 million acres in California's San Joaquin Valley. About 150 million acres of the railroads' land came from the government, which took it from Native Americans, by fiat or by deadly force.

Federal campaigns against Indians had resumed during the Civil War. In 1863–64 in Arizona, U.S. troops destroyed Navajos' sheep, corn fields, and orchards, then rounded up 8,500 starving people for a "Long March" to a prison camp in New Mexico, where they were held four years before returning to Arizona under a new treaty. At Sand Creek, Colorado, soldiers overran a camp of Cheyennes and Arapahos in November 1864, killing 450 people. Immediately after the Civil War, Dakotas contested the construction of a road through their lands in the northern Great Plains (Montana and Wyoming); the five-year confrontation ended with their confinement to a reservation in Dakota Territory.

Indian wars continued throughout the Gilded Age. In 1870, Modocs left their reservation in Oregon to return home to northern California, where they fought the Army in 1872–73, before surrender and exile to Oklahoma.

In 1871, Chiricahua resistance to reservation confinement started the Apache War in New Mexico and Arizona. It ended in 1886, when Geronimo's band was captured, imprisoned in Florida until 1894, transferred to Oklahoma, and finally dispersed to several small southwestern reservations in 1913. An 1875 gold strike in the Black Hills on Dakota land brought out troops to protect prospectors. War parties led by Sitting Bull and Crazy Horse annihilated General George Armstrong Custer and 264 soldiers at Little Big Horn, but the Dakotas were defeated in October 1876. When the Nez Perce community in Oregon's Wallowa Valley was ordered to Idaho in 1877, Chief Joseph led resisters on a three-month retreat towards Canada, but the Army pursued and caught them. They, too, were interned in Oklahoma (which they called *eeikishpah,* the "hot place"); the survivors were transferred to Washington's Coleville Reservation in 1885.

Some relocations were accomplished without wars. Pawnees and Poncas from Nebraska, Comanches from Wyoming, Tonkawas from Texas: all were moved to Indian Territory in Oklahoma. Some military campaigns against Indians had no goal other than cultural suppression. In 1890, soldiers harried the adherents of what whites called the "Ghost Dance"—a ritual originated by the Paiute visionary Wovoka to commemorate the dead. In December 1890, the campaign climaxed in the massacre of a Dakota encampment at Wounded Knee Creek in South Dakota. The U.S. Army reported killing 146 people, though the actual number was closer to 400, mostly women, children, and old men. Congress awarded twenty Medals of Honor to soldiers who had participated in this last Indian battle of the era.

The federal government also seized Indian lands by statute. In 1887, the General Allotment Act (known as the Dawes Act) divided tribal lands into individual holdings, assigning 160 acres to each head of a family and 80 to each single adult. The government then bought unassigned land and opened it to settlers. In 1891–92, 3.9 million acres—parts of the Sauk and Fox, Pottawatomie-Shawnee, and Cheyenne-Arapaho reservations—were taken in Oklahoma alone.

If none paid more dearly than Native Americans for industrial capitalism's swift growth, many other Americans suffered too. While the rail system expanded commerce, it also destabilized the economy. Railroad companies established many parallel routes in the northeastern industrial heartland and engaged in cutthroat competition, slashing freight rates to beat out rivals. To offset shrinking profit margins, the companies jacked up rates in other regions and cut railroad workers' wages. And the less the railroads charged for transporting industrial goods, the more manufacturing firms expanded production to capture national markets—and the more sharply they vied with

other firms.* Wage cuts helped to finance price wars, and the losers curtailed production and laid off employees.

Regions developed unequally. Monopoly capitalists headquartered in
the Northeast dominated development in the South and West. Southern
and western farmers, usually served by a single railroad, paid top dollar to
transport crops to market. This exacerbated other problems: the exorbitant
interest charged by merchants who extended credit to cotton farmers; the
sky-high fees wheat farmers paid to store their crops in grain elevators; and
the decline in agricultural prices as production increased. (In 1896, the average price for farm products was half what it had been in 1870.) In the Cotton Belt and on the Great Plains, many family farms went bankrupt. Kansas
alone saw 11,000 farm mortgage foreclosures between 1889 and 1893. By
1900, more than a third of all U.S. farms were worked by tenants or sharecroppers rather than owners, debt peonage was increasingly common, and
farmhands' wages remained exceedingly low. Agriculture played a central
role in the national economy, with cotton the single largest export and grain
and grain products not far behind, but most of the people who produced this
wealth were locked into poverty.

Monopolists also restricted industrialization in the South and West.
Hampered by higher freight charges, the iron and steel industry centered in
Birmingham and the cotton textile industry in the Carolina Piedmont were
not only smaller than their northern counterparts but also paid significantly
lower wages and used more child labor. In 1896, 25 percent of textile workers in North Carolina were under age sixteen, compared to 5 percent in
Massachusetts.

San Francisco was the West's only manufacturing center. Most of the
region's economy was designed to supply eastern factories with raw or
semiprocessed materials—agricultural produce, lumber, cattle, wool, coal,
and smelted metal ores. Western industries followed the boom-and-bust
cycles of eastern manufacturing, further destabilizing a labor market already
weakened by only seasonal work in farming, ranching, and logging, and
temporary railroad construction jobs. Though labor was in short supply in
the West and workers in most occupations averaged higher daily wages
than their eastern counterparts, they worked less often, and many of
them—mainly but not only single men—migrated from place to place to
find jobs.

---

* Rail and manufacturing corporations tried combining to fix prices and divide up markets.
The courts outlawed such combinations, but they were weak anyway. Their members repeatedly
reneged on promises to cooperate, touching off new free-for-all price wars and market grabs.

THE WORKING CLASSES

As industrial capitalism expanded, so did the ranks of wage workers. By 1900, they numbered about 18 million, up from 6.7 million in 1870; together with their families, they added up to at least three-quarters of the U.S. population of 76 million. They came from ever more diverse backgrounds, and their working conditions varied tremendously. Indeed, Americans in the Gilded Age often spoke of the "working classes" instead of a single working class.

Immigration was a key source of working-class growth and diversity. From 1873 through 1897, 10 million immigrants entered the United States, more than during the previous fifty years; and they came from more places than ever before. European immigrants still outnumbered the rest, but more and more arrived from Italy, Austria–Hungary, Russia, and Poland, and, in smaller numbers, from Portugal, Spain, Greece, Romania, and Turkey. Syrians and other Arabs came from the Middle East. Japanese as well as Chinese arrived from Asia. In addition to English- and French-speaking Canadians, immigrants from the Western Hemisphere included Mexicans, Caribbean islanders, and South Americans. Nearly all immigrants had one thing in common: they depended on wage work for their livelihoods during their first years in the United States, if not longer.

Some were fleeing ethnic persecution in their homelands. Armenians fled brutality at the hands of Ottoman Turkey. Jews from eastern Europe sought relief from Russia's Czarist regime, which attacked them with pogroms, barred them from owning land, and confined them to *shtetls,* Jewish towns in restricted zones.

Most immigrants came in search of better economic opportunities. Many planned to go back home once they had saved enough, and quite a few did. Plans often changed, however. In 1882, Mihailo Evanich's family in the Croatian village of Smisliak selected him to go to America to earn money to send home. He found work in the copper mines in Calumet, Michigan. A year later he brought over his wife to keep house for him and several of his coworkers. By 1891, the couple had decided to stay and set up a saloon, which they ran as a club for Croat and Slovene miners. Evanich was called "Mike Evans" by his foremen and became a citizen under that name. Some immigrants came and went several times. From the 1890s into the 1920s, Elias Garza moved back and forth between Mexico and the United States, working at a variety of jobs—from meatpacking to railroad track maintenance—in Kansas, California, Texas, and Arizona.

Many immigrants moved from wage work to self-employment. Kinji Ushijima, who arrived from Japan in 1887, worked first as a potato picker but then became a labor contractor. By the 1910s, his business cultivated potatoes on 10,000 acres he had purchased or leased. John Starkku came from Finland in 1890, and for five years worked his way westward, taking jobs in mines and lumber camps and saving every penny he could. When he reached Oregon's Hood River Valley, he bought land and planted orchards.

Many more immigrants never managed to save much. This was especially true for women who had to make it on their own, with substandard female wages. An Irish-born sewing machine operator told investigators from the Colorado Labor Bureau in 1886: "My parents live in Ireland and are entirely dependent on myself and my sisters for support. . . . I am a good seamstress and work hard. I try but I can not make over one dollar per day." In 1884, Rosa Cassetari came from the Lombardy region of Italy to join her husband who worked in the iron mines in Union, Missouri. When they saved enough, he bought a brothel, but she refused to live there and moved to Chicago, where she supported her children by washing clothes and cleaning houses. She recalled walking everywhere with her children, nearly freezing to death: "I never took the streetcar. We needed those five cents to eat." She ended up a cleaning woman in the Chicago Commons, one of many "settlement houses" established by genteel reformers who reached out to the urban poor.

Immigrant groups generally clustered in particular occupations. Chinese men were the majority of migrant farm laborers in California in the 1880s and 1890s. Many Irish women entered domestic service. Slavic men worked mainly in coal mines, steel mills, and railroad maintenance. Italians and Russian Jews of both sexes tended to concentrate in the garment industry. Puerto Ricans and Cubans often worked in cigar factories in New York City and Tampa and Key West, Florida.

A great many new additions to the wage labor force came from within U.S. borders. As railroads penetrated the Southwest, more and more Mexican Americans went to work in railroad construction and maintenance, in mining, in large-scale commercial farming and ranching, as domestics in Anglo households, and as laundresses and seamstresses in mining and railroad camps. Laguna Pueblos built and maintained the section of the Santa Fe Railroad on their reservation in New Mexico. Mi'kmaq families from northern New England harvested potatoes in Maine and wheat in Wyoming, Montana, and Canadian Alberta and Saskatchewan. Ottawas in Michigan worked seasonally as fruit and berry pickers, as lumberjacks, and in service jobs in resort hotels. Kumeyaays and Luiseños held most of the stevedore jobs on the docks of San Diego, California, and also worked on farms and ranches as fruit pickers, vaqueros, sheep herders, and shearers.

Ninety percent of African Americans lived in the South, where they slowly moved from sharecropping into jobs paying an individual wage. Their choices were severely limited: as of 1890, agriculture and domestic service employed the vast bulk of African American workers, 96 percent of the women and 85 percent of the men. Exceptions included stevedores and teamsters in New Orleans, iron foundry workers in Birmingham, brick makers in Richmond, coal miners in West Virginia, Kentucky, Tennessee, and Alabama, teachers in black schools, and clerical and sales employees of black-owned businesses.

The industrial Northeast saw a steep rise in the ranks of wage-earning women. Wives took jobs when their husbands' pay could not support a family, or stopped entirely; this was especially common in black communities. The numbers of working-class daughters earning wages rose even more sharply. Before the 1870s, only the poorest families had regularly put daughters out to work. During the Gilded Age, even relatively prosperous working-class households began to send their daughters into the labor market once they had finished grammar school (around age fourteen). Though they spent some of their pay on themselves, virtually all of these workers contributed most of their earnings to family coffers, sometimes to cover bare necessities and in other cases to finance luxuries like parlor furniture or good clothes. The new "working girls"—the vast majority white and nativeborn—usually took jobs in factories or as saleswomen in department stores but also included office clerks, school teachers, and custom dressmakers and milliners. Most remained wage workers until they married and became mothers, typically in their mid-twenties; those who did not marry often remained wage workers for life.

Income was unevenly distributed within the working class. Higher paying skilled jobs belonged almost exclusively to American-born white men or male immigrants from northwestern Europe. For their households, living standards rose despite the roller coaster economy. Thanks to falling prices, the cost of living declined even faster than employers cut wages in skilled trades.

Workers on every rung of the occupational hierarchy generally disdained those below. As Lucy Warner, a Connecticut cotton mill operative, wrote in 1891: "The teacher considers herself superior to the sewing girl, and the sewing girl thinks herself above the mill girl, and the mill girl thinks the girl who does general housework a little beneath her." Stratification combined with the diversity of culture and language to divide the working class by color, ethnicity, gender, and occupation. Resentments and conflicts repeatedly led to violence across racial and ethnic lines.

The anti-Chinese movement accelerated. In October 1880, a white mob drove out the residents of Denver's Chinatown, lynching one man along the way. In 1881, Texas railroad workers—Tejanos and Apaches as well as whites—repeatedly assaulted Chinese coworkers. In 1882, Congress passed the Chinese Exclusion Act, barring the immigration of Chinese laborers for ten years. The violence continued. In September 1885, after Chinese and Welsh coal miners brawled in Rock Springs, Wyoming, a mob attacked the Chinese section of the mining camp, killing twenty-eight and chasing the rest into the wilderness. White "ouster committees" drove Chinese from Tacoma, Washington, in November 1885 and from Seattle the following February.

African and Mexican Americans faced continued discrimination and violence. More than 2,500 African Americans were lynched between 1885 and 1900, mainly in Mississippi, Alabama, Georgia, and Louisiana. White craftsmen barred black men from most skilled trades. In August 1897, 1,400 white workers went on strike at the Fulton Bag and Cotton Mill in Atlanta to protest the hiring of twenty black women. From the 1870s through the 1890s, Mexican Americans were lynched in Texas, California, Arizona, and Colorado, and Anglo cowboys repeatedly raided Tejano towns such as Socorro and Tascosa.

Native-born white workers or immigrants from northwestern Europe often despised Slavs, Italians, and Russian Jews. Slavs were vilified as dumb and docile, though they were in fact quicker than most immigrants to organize and strike. In 1891, coal miners in Wheeling, West Virginia, walked off the job when their employer refused to fire Italians, and 500 boys employed in a New Jersey glass factory rioted when fourteen Russian Jews were hired. Even when people worked together in relative peace, social life was typically segregated by color and ethnicity.

Within working-class communities, different perspectives contended. For some people, personal advancement took precedence. Others were consumed by the daily struggle for survival. But a critical mass of activists proposed collective remedies for common problems. They aimed to rally workers to defend "the rights of labor" and build a better world for one and all. As the labor editor John Swinton put it, workers united had "the power to establish . . . an industrial community, under which neither the 'bloated millionaire' nor the abject starveling shall dishonor the country in which they dwell."

Working people from every background and occupation had more in common than dependency on wages. Everyone was affected by the economic crises that defined the Gilded Age. Everyone saw how governors, legislators, and judges served the interests of the moneyed classes. Everyone beheld the arrogance of business spokesmen like John Hay, the corporate lawyer and Republican statesman who pontificated: "That you have property is proof of industry and foresight on your part or your father's; that you have nothing is a judgment on your laziness and vices, or on your improvidence. The world is a moral world, which it would not be if virtue and vice received the same reward." Jay Gould's New York *World* insulted all working people when it declared that, "Men must be contented to work for less wages. In this way the workingmen will be nearer to that station in life to which it has pleased God to call them."

Working-class communities were also bound together by traditions of struggle and resistance. Leading labor activists often had a keen sense of the movement's history in the United States, from the National Trades Union of the 1830s and ten-hour agitation of the 1840s to the National Labor Union and Colored National Labor Union of the Reconstruction era. These legacies blended with other militant traditions rooted in U.S. soil or imported from immigrants' homelands.

Black communities harbored a rich heritage of resistance to slavery and included many veterans of the Civil War and Radical Reconstruction. One of the younger activists who carried on this legacy was Ida Wells. Born in 1862 in Holly Springs, Mississippi, she attended a freedmen's school and went to work as a teacher at age fourteen, supporting herself and four siblings after their parents died of yellow fever. At twenty-two she moved to Memphis, Tennessee, where she taught school until 1891, when she was fired for writing about conditions in the city's segregated black schools. The following year, she published a report on the lynching of three black grocers and had to flee the South for her own safety. She continued to crusade against lynching, travelling and speaking widely in the United States and twice taking her campaign to Britain. Pausing only briefly after her marriage to Chicago civil rights activist Ferdinand Barnett, Ida Wells-Barnett organized black women in support of many causes, including women's right to vote.

Working women sustained other activist traditions too. Like the mill workers who joined with genteel labor reformers to agitate for ten-hour laws in the 1840s, women trade unionists in Chicago came together with middle-class groups to form the Illinois Women's Alliance in 1888. The Alliance campaigned for laws against sweatshops and child labor. Like the women who rallied behind the 1877 rail strike, Mary Septek organized an "Amazon army" of Hungarian, Polish, and Italian women to battle scabs during a miners' strike near Hazelton, Pennsylvania, in September 1897.

Mexican American resistance to Anglo domination continued in the Southwest and increasingly targeted corporate power and privilege. In San Miguel County, New Mexico, Juan José Herrera and his brothers Pablo and Nicanor formed an underground organization known as Las Gorras Blancas ("The White Caps") in 1887, recruiting up to 1,500 members within a couple of years. They conducted a guerilla campaign against the Santa Fe Railroad and cattle corporations, cutting barbed wire fences and torching company property. Las Gorras also rallied behind an insurgent political party, El Partido del Pueblo Unido.

In the tradition of Chinese railroad workers' 1867 strike for higher wages, Chinese farm workers organized against unequal pay. Fruit pickers in California's Santa Clara Valley went on strike in 1880, as did hops pickers in Kern County in 1884. In 1890, California newspapers reported that Chinese immigrants had formed a labor union that demanded $1.50 a day for work in orchards and vineyards. Other immigrant groups drew on their own militant traditions, including German socialism, Bohemian (Czech), Italian, and Mexican anarchism, Irish resistance to English occupation, Jewish radicalism forged under Czarist persecution, Puerto Rican and Cuban rebellion against Spanish colonialism.

The labor movement of the Gilded Age tapped into all of these legacies. And if labor organizations sometimes failed to unite even their own ranks, workplace and community solidarity provided a bedrock for resistance to corporate assaults on labor and dominance of American life.

THE KNIGHTS OF LABOR

The Gilded Age labor movement was as diverse as the working class itself. From 1881 through 1897, the United States saw more than 18,000 strikes for higher wages, the eight-hour day, union recognition, and other goals. Labor activists promoted their objectives in many different languages and accents, and they gathered in arenas ranging from trade unions to political parties, social clubs to revolutionary organizations, and neighborhood saloons to national conventions. At every point this movement challenged monopoly capitalists, but by the end of the era, the boldest initiatives had been crushed, and the prevailing spirit had retreated from audacity to caution.

The largest and most influential labor organization of the Gilded Age was the Noble and Holy Order of the Knights of Labor, founded in 1869 as a secret organization of garment workers led by Philadelphia tailor Uriah Stephens. When Stephens stepped down in 1879, he was replaced by Terence Powderly, a railroad machinist who had recently been elected mayor of Scranton, Pennsylvania, on a "Labor Reform" ticket. Secrecy protected Knights from blacklisting by employers and involved elaborate codes. The cryptic message "★★★★★ 8 610/75" chalked on a wall meant "Knights meet 8 PM June 10 Assembly 75." Members gathered in Local Assemblies that included both "trade assemblies" organized by industry and "mixed assemblies" of people from various industries and walks of life. Locals reported to District Assemblies; annual conventions known as General Assemblies debated and adopted policy; and a General Executive Board oversaw the Order between conventions. The Knights' basic principle was solidarity, their motto "An Injury to One is an Injury to All."

In 1881, the Knights went public, issuing a Declaration of Principles that began with an attack on monopoly:

> The alarming development and aggressiveness of great capitalists and corporations, unless checked, will inevitably lead to the pauperization and hopeless degradation of the toiling masses. It is imperative, if we desire to enjoy the full blessings of life, that a check be placed upon unjust accumulation, and the power for evil of aggregated wealth. This . . . can be accomplished only by the united efforts of those who obey the divine injunction, 'In the sweat of thy face shalt thou eat bread.'

The Knights regarded monopolists as monarchs in all but name. To quote George McNeill, a longtime labor activist among the leaders of Boston's District Assembly:

> The railroad president is a railroad king, whose whim is law. He collects tithes by reducing wages. . . . He can discharge (banish) any employee without cause. He can prevent laborers from following their usual vocations. He can withhold their lawful wages. He can delay trial on a suit of law, and postpone judgment indefinitely. He can control legislative bodies, dictate legislation, subsidize the press, and corrupt the moral sense of the community. He can fix the price of freights, and thus command the food and fuel-supplies of the nation.

If this "iron heel of a soulless monopoly" undermined democracy, so did wage labor, which forced workers into dependency on employers. As Mc-

Neill wrote, "These extremes of wealth and poverty are threatening the existence of the government. In light of these facts, we declare that there is an inevitable and irresistible conflict between the wage-system of labor and the republican system of government,—the wage-laborer attempting to save the government, and the capitalist class ignorantly attempting to subvert it."

The Knights proposed to replace the wage system with a "cooperative commonwealth." Workers would be their own masters. Only then, proclaimed the Declaration of Principles, could they have "the full enjoyment of the wealth they create, sufficient leisure in which to develop their intellectual, moral and social faculties; all of the benefits, recreation and pleasures of association; in a word . . . to share in the gains and honors of advancing civilization."

This message had a very broad appeal. The Order's membership climbed steadily—from 28,000 Knights in 1880 to 43,000 in 1882, 71,000 in 1884, and 110,000 by 1885. At the movement's peak in 1886, about 750,000 Knights gathered in more than over 15,000 locals across country, and only seventy counties had no assembly at all. Up to 200,000 more belonged to assemblies founded in Canada, England, Ireland, Belgium, France, Italy, Australia, and New Zealand.

The Knights of Labor became the most inclusive U.S. labor organization of the nineteenth century. It welcomed to its anti-monopoly coalition all of the "producing classes"—not only wage workers but also housewives, farmers, clergymen, shopkeepers, doctors, writers, editors, and other professionals. Employers could join too, if they had once been wage earners and now treated their employees fairly by paying good wages and observing the eight-hour day. The only groups summarily excluded were liquor dealers, stockbrokers, bankers, professional gamblers, and corporate lawyers.

The Knights formally admitted women in 1882, after women shoe workers in Philadelphia had organized their own assembly. In 1886, when women made up about 10 percent of the Order's membership, the General Assembly established a national Women's Department headed by Leonora Barry, an Irish-born hosiery mill operative who led a female trade assembly in Amsterdam, New York. Chicago's giant District Assembly was headed by Elizabeth Rodgers, a housewife and mother of twelve children. The Order was the first U.S. labor organization to endorse female suffrage, and the local assemblies hosted many lectures on women's rights.

The Order also welcomed immigrants, translated its literature into various languages, and chartered numerous foreign-language assemblies, with one major exception. Though the New York City and Philadelphia districts tried to organize Chinese assemblies in 1886–87, western districts were deeply involved in the anti-Chinese movement, and the organization's national spokesmen often proclaimed that, "The Chinese must go." When Wyoming Knights led the mob that massacred Chinese in Rock Springs in 1885, Terence Powderly blamed the violence on Chinese evasion of the Exclusion Act.

Black-white cooperation was more impressive. The Order's *Journal of United Labor* declared in 1880: "We should be false to every principle of our Order should we exclude from membership any man who gains his living by honest toil, on account of his color or creed." By 1886, African American Knights numbered at least 60,000. They made up about half the membership in Virginia, North Carolina, and Arkansas, and a third of the whole southern membership. Even after the Knights went public, black members in southern states often had to organize in secret. After touring the South, one member of the General Executive Board observed, "It is as much . . . as a person's life is worth to be known as a member of the Knights of Labor there." Southern assemblies were sometimes integrated: Ida Wells, who attended a Memphis assembly in the late 1880s, reported that "everyone who came was welcomed and every woman from black to white was seated with courtesy usually extended to white ladies alone in this town."

The Order's most dramatic confrontation with the color line came in October 1886, when the annual convention met in Richmond, Virginia. A local hotel refused to accommodate Frank Ferrell, an African American official in New York City's District Assembly 49 and a member of the General Executive Board. The whole New York delegation boycotted the hotel in protest and lodged with black families. At the convention's opening session, the Knights were welcomed by Virginia's Governor Fitzhugh Lee. The next speaker was Frank Ferrell, who had been selected to introduce Terence Powderly. "One of the objects of our Order," he reminded his audience, "is the abolition of those distinctions maintained by creed or color." The convention endorsed civil equality "with no distinction on account of color," called for the admission of black apprentices to skilled mechanical trades, and recommended a southern drive "to organize all classes of laborers" irrespective of race. When the meeting adjourned, the 660 delegates and 2,000 local Knights marched to a picnic ground, joined by thousands of Richmond's black residents. The Cleveland *Gazette,* a black newspaper, called this parade "the most remarkable thing since Emancipation."

The Knights of Labor sponsored social and educational programs, ran candidates for office in over 200 cities and towns in 1885–86, and sponsored hundreds of consumer and producer cooperatives. First and foremost, however, K of L assemblies functioned as labor unions. Many craft unions wiped out by the 1870s depression reconstituted themselves within the Order. Local assemblies frequently went on strike to force employers to negotiate wages and working conditions, and trade assemblies in the same industry frequently backed each other with sympathy strikes. Walkouts grew more common as the Order expanded. Across the country, K of L strikes averaged about 450 a year from 1881 through 1884; but they numbered 645 in 1885 and more than 1,400 in 1886 and again in 1887. In 1885, a successful strike against wage cuts on Jay Gould's southwestern rail lines greatly boosted the Order's prestige and attracted many new recruits.

The proposal for the Knights' biggest campaign originated outside the Order, in the Federation of Organized Trades and Labor Unions. The FOTLU was a relatively small network of national craft unions not affiliated with the Knights, and it seldom did more than pass resolutions. But in September 1882, its Central Labor Union in New York City staged a "labor holiday" parade; instead of going to work, some 30,000 men and women marched for labor's rights. Labor Day parades henceforth became annual events in New York and other cities, including Cincinnati, Buffalo, and Lynn, Massachusetts.★ Many marchers carried placards and banners emblazoned with the slogan "Eight Hours for Work, Eight Hours for Sleep, Eight Hours for What We Will." Earlier campaigns for the eight-hour day had aimed at winning legislation, but FOTLU leaders like P. J. McGuire of the Brotherhood of Carpenters held that unionists should take direct action to shorten the workday. The FOTLU convention of 1884 resolved that "eight hours shall constitute a legal day's labor from and after May 1, 1886," and called for nationwide strikes to enforce this edict.

The Knights' General Executive Board declined to endorse the plan, and Terence Powderly secretly ordered his lieutenants to discourage its adoption by local and district assemblies. But the FOTLU's call galvanized rank-and-file Knights. Assembly after assembly pledged support, and organizers built multitudes of new assemblies on the eight-hour platform. That accounted for most of the Order's astonishing sevenfold growth between 1885 and 1886.

The eight-hour movement generated tremendous optimism—more than enough to sustain the Order through a crushing rematch with Jay Gould. In February 1886, Knights on his southwestern railroads struck to enforce a demand for union recognition. This time around, Gould refused to give in, and lawmen mobilized to smash the strike. Many workers were arrested; in East St. Louis, Illinois, seven were killed during a battle with

★ Congress declared Labor Day a federal holiday in 1894.

militiamen and police. By mid-April, it was clear that the strike would go down to defeat, that monopolists like Gould could find the wherewithal to vanquish mass revolts. But the Knights' eight-hour assemblies continued to multiply. As John Swinton wrote in the spring, "Never has there been such a spectacle as the march of the Order of the Knights of Labor at the present time."

On Saturday, May 1, about 350,000 workers at more than 11,000 establishments across the country went on strike for the eight-hour day. In Chicago, 65,000 strikers staged weekend rallies and parades. Counterattacks began on Monday; police fired into a group picketing the McCormick Harvester Works and killed at least four workers. Anarchist leaders of the city's eight-hour coalition called a protest meeting, held the night of May 4 at Haymarket Square. A few thousand showed up, but the crowd had dwindled to a few hundred by the time policemen arrived to disperse the gathering a little after ten o'clock. As the police entered the square, someone—the culprit was never identified—threw a bomb that killed one officer and wounded another sixty-six, seven of whom later died.

For several weeks police rounded up labor activists by the hundreds. Meeting halls and residences were raided; entire families were jailed; evidence of incendiary plotting was seized—and planted when it could not be found. Newspapers reported daily on the police department's progress in solving the "crime of the century." On May 27, eight anarchists—August Spies, Albert Parsons, Adolph Fischer, George Engel, Louis Lingg, Samuel Fielden, Oscar Neebe, and Michael Schwab—were indicted for conspiracy to commit murder. Their trial began on June 21.

Only two of the defendants, Spies and Fielden, had been present when the explosion occurred, but the prosecution did not care who actually threw the bomb. The anarchists had been indicted for their radicalism and militant leadership of the eight-hour movement, not for their actions in Haymarket Square. As the state's attorney told the jury:

> Law is on trial. Anarchy is on trial. These men have been selected, picked out by the grand jury and indicted because they were leaders. . . . Gentlemen of the jury: convict these men, make examples of them, hang them and you save our institutions, our society.

The jury convicted all of the defendants. Neebe was sentenced to fifteen years; the others were condemned to death.

Trade unionists and social reformers campaigned widely for clemency or pardon. Albert Parsons's wife was especially active. A Texan of black, Mexican, and Native American ancestry, Lucy Eldine Gonzalez Parsons worked tirelessly for the amnesty campaign, speaking to 200,000 people in sixteen states and inspiring widespread support. John Brown, Jr., sent the convicted men baskets of grapes and a letter that quoted his father's statement shortly before execution: "It is a great comfort to feel assured that I am permitted to die for a cause,—not merely to pay the debt of nature as all must." Petitions in behalf of the Haymarket martyrs came from as far away as Russia. Just days before the execution, the governor of Illinois commuted the sentences of Fielden and Schwab to life in prison. The night before the execution, Lingg cheated the state by committing suicide. On November 11, 1887, Spies, Parsons, Fischer, and Engel went to the gallows. Some 25,000 people marched in their funeral procession.

The eight-hour movement had already fizzled, and the Knights were on the wane. Within a week of the bombing, strikers across the country were straggling back to work, brutalized by police and vilified by the press as dupes of an "anarchist plot." Terence Powderly and his General Executive Board joined the conservative chorus. Denouncing anarchism, they refused to contribute to the Haymarket defense fund, and they tried their best to stamp out militancy among the Order's rank and file.

In October 1886, trade assemblies of meatpacking workers led a strike of 25,000 at Chicago's Union Stock Yard, which had adopted the eight-hour day that spring and now declared a return to ten hours. Powderly told the striking assemblies to go back to work; when they defied him, he threatened to revoke their K of L charters. Smelling blood, the company broke off negotiations and announced that it would no longer employ any member of the Knights of Labor. A week later the strikers conceded defeat, and the meatpackers' assemblies soon died out.

There followed a long series of strikes that pitted rank-and-file Knights against their national leaders as well as corporate employers. Workers lost nearly all of these battles, and the Knights of Labor shrank almost as swiftly as it had grown. Membership fell from 750,000 in 1886 to 220,000 in 1888, 100,000 in 1890, and only 20,000 by 1896.*

THE AMERICAN FEDERATION OF LABOR

As the Knights of Labor declined, a new national labor organization came to the fore. The American Federation of Labor (AFL) was founded in Decem-

---

* The last K of L assembly—motion-picture projectionists in Boston—merged into the American Federation of Labor in 1949.

ber 1886 in Columbus, Ohio, at a convention called by the Federation of Organized Trades and Labor Unions. The AFL's founding president—re-elected almost every year until his death in 1924—was the cigarmaker Samuel Gompers, an English immigrant of Dutch Jewish descent. An alliance of thirteen national craft unions, the newborn Federation advanced two fundamental principles: "pure and simple unionism" (a narrow focus on wages, hours and working conditions) and "voluntarism" (strict reliance on only the union and its members). Defining itself as a better alternative to the Knights of Labor, the AFL practiced what one historian has aptly called "prudential unionism," a defensive strategy that accepted the wage-labor system and tried to avoid government intervention in labor disputes.

In some respects the early AFL took up where the Knights had left off. In 1890, the Federation revived the eight-hour campaign, selected the Brotherhood of Carpenters to be the first union to strike, and urged all unionists to demonstrate in support on May 1. The business journal *Bradstreet's* reported more strikes started that day than on any previous day on record, and the Carpenters won the eight-hour day for more than 46,000 members. Sympathy strikes characterized AFL style in the early years. Of the 7,500 strikes its unions staged from 1890 through 1894, nearly one in ten was a sympathy strike.

Otherwise, the Federation sharply distinguished itself from the Knights. It did not run candidates for public office. In contrast to the Order's centralized structure, the AFL Executive Council upheld the autonomy of affiliated unions. The Council intervened only to mediate between affiliates disputing jurisdictions and to provide support for organizing drives and strikes. Critical of rank-and-file Knights' penchant for going on strike without adequate resources, the AFL also encouraged affiliates to set high initiation fees and dues so that union treasuries would be large enough to sustain members through long work stoppages. And the Knights' diversity gave way to homogeneity in the AFL, which focused on organizing highly skilled workers—those with the most social clout. The AFL's initial membership was overwhelmingly male and white, reflecting the composition of skilled trades. Of the thirteen founding unions, only the cigarmakers and the typographers admitted women, and none included many men of color.

By 1892, another twenty-seven national unions had affiliated, many of them formed by defectors from the Knights of Labor. Newcomers included the Boot and Shoe Workers International Union, the United Mine Workers, the National Union of Textile Workers, and the United Garment Workers. The textile, garment, and shoe unions all had substantial female membership.

About a fifth of the United Mine Workers' members in the coal fields were black men.

AFL headquarters lent verbal support to women's organizing drives but seldom came through with much more. In May 1892, the Executive Council hired the Chicago bookbinder Mary Kenney as the Federation's first general organizer of women. That summer she toured northeastern cities, establishing female locals of bookbinders and garment workers in New York City, Albany, and Troy, and making contact with interested women from a variety of trades in and around Boston. In October, however, the Executive Council abolished Kenney's post. Several prolonged strikes by male unions had recently decimated AFL coffers, and now that every penny counted, most of the Council regarded outreach to women as an expendable luxury. In December 1893, the AFL hired a second woman organizer—the Boston typographer E. Frances Pitts—and she, too, was let go within a few months. A permanent post did not materialize until 1898, when Eva McDonald Valesh, former editor of a labor newspaper in Minneapolis-St. Paul, was hired into the dual job of union organizer and assistant editor of the AFL monthly, the *American Federationist*.

If outreach to women had a low priority, the AFL did generally respond to those who came knocking at its door. Women's unions were often chartered as "federal labor unions"—locals that did not belong to a national union. By the late 1890s, all but a handful of the Federation's national affiliates had amended their constitutions to allow for female membership; but a great many kept women out in other ways—through high initiation fees, for instance, or special examinations for female applicants. In the federal labor unions and in the nationals, nearly all of the young AFL's women members were native-born whites or immigrants from northwestern Europe.

Male membership grew somewhat more diverse, thanks largely to the Executive Council's early policies on that front. The Council hired male organizers fluent in Italian, Yiddish, Bohemian, Spanish, and other foreign languages and translated union literature into various tongues. The AFL convention of 1890 resolved to deny a charter to the National Association of Machinists, whose constitution included a whites-only clause. The following year, the Executive Council sponsored the establishment of a new group, the National Machinists' Union, that "recognize[d] the equality of all men working at our trade, regardless of religion, race, or color." Much the same thing happened in 1893, when AFL headquarters refused to charter the all-white Brotherhood of Boiler Makers and Iron Ship Builders and set up an alternate union that admitted black men.

Starting in 1891, the Executive Council employed black men as general organizers. The first was George Norton from the Marine Fireman's Union in St. Louis; within a year he was joined by James Porter from the Car Drivers' Union in New Orleans. In 1892, both men helped to lead strikes that transcended the color line. That spring, black workers on the St. Louis riverfront initiated a week-long walkout that soon spread to their white counterparts and ended with wage increases across the board. In late October, black and white workers on the New Orleans docks launched a joint strike that culminated in an interracial walkout of 25,000 workingmen from forty-nine different unions. For four days, November 7–10, everything from printing offices to electrical plants to construction sites shut down tight as employers tried in vain to divide and conquer. Finally, they agreed to negotiate, and the dock workers won their demands for shorter hours, higher wages, and overtime pay. As one local labor leader wrote to Samuel Gompers, the New Orleans strike was "the finest unification of Labor . . . ever had in this or any other city."

The AFL's commitment to unifying workingmen always had boundaries, however, and they grew more restrictive over the course of the 1890s. From the start, the Federation barred workers of Asian ancestry, and Gompers lobbied hard for extensions of the Chinese Exclusion Act when it came up for renewal in 1892 and again in 1902. By the latter year, AFL spokesmen were also calling for laws to limit immigration from eastern and southern Europe, and the Federation's Executive Council no longer refused to charter national unions whose constitutions stipulated that only white workers could join. The policy on racially segregated locals had changed too. The Council had initially defined them as a necessary evil that would disappear over time; black and white locals would presumably merge once white workers were educated away from what Gompers called "the ridiculous attempt to draw the color line in our labor organizations." But by 1900, AFL headquarters regarded segregated locals as a permanent arrangement—the best way to organize workers of color without "arousing bitterness" among whites.

From day one, moreover, the AFL's basic organizing strategy undercut its capacity to promote labor solidarity irrespective of color, nationality, and sex. The stress on craft unionism, together with hefty dues and initiation fees, inevitably distanced the Federation from workers outside the skilled, relatively high-paying trades. A great many of those outsiders were native-born white men; but women, immigrants, and workers of color were all disproportionately confined to unskilled and semiskilled occupations, where craft unionism—not to mention expensive unionism—simply did not make sense.

Nor could the AFL strategy protect union craftsmen from assault by monopoly capitalists. Never was that more evident than when the Amalgamated Association of Iron and Steel Workers squared off against the steel baron Andrew Carnegie in the summer and fall of 1892. The Amalgamated admitted only the most skilled steelworkers. At Carnegie's mill in Homestead, Pennsylvania, less than a quarter of the 3,800 employees belonged to the union, whose agreement with the company placed the skilled men at Homestead among the best paid workers in the land. Determined to expand his power and profits, Carnegie decided that when the Amalgamated's contract expired on June 30, 1892, the Homestead mill would become a nonunion plant. To that end, he turned over the mill's management to Henry Clay Frick, well known in western Pennsylvania for his hatred of unions and ruthless suppression of strikes.

As the Amalgamated's contract neared expiration, Frick announced the company's intention to cut union men's wages by an average of 22 percent. Then, on May 30, he issued an ultimatum: if the men did not accept the new wage scale by June 24, the company would no longer recognize their union. When the Amalgamated held firm, he went to war, shutting down the mill on June 30 and hiring the Pinkerton Detective Agency to reopen it with scab labor.

Nearly all of Homestead's 11,000 residents rallied behind the Amalgamated. Unskilled steelworkers—mostly Slavic immigrants—joined union members in picketing the mill, as did many housewives and schoolchildren. In the wee hours of July 6, about 300 armed Pinkertons tried to sneak into the plant, traveling on barges that silently pulled up to the company's beach on the Monongahela River. But a patrol of workers had spotted the barges and sounded the alarm. As the Pinkertons landed, an angry crowd of Homesteaders streamed down to the beach, and both sides opened fire. The invaders surrendered after a daylong battle that killed seven workers and three Pinkertons.

When Governor Robert Pattison sent 8,000 militiamen to Homestead on July 12, the Amalgamated welcomed the intervention. A union spokesman declared, "On behalf of the Amalgamated Association I wish to say that after suffering an attack of illegal authority, we are glad to have the legal authority of the state here." The militia had arrived at Frick's request, however; it was there to safeguard the company, not the townspeople. By the end of the month, the mill was starting to produce steel with a force of scabs the Pinkerton Agency had recruited in Pittsburgh. Troops escorted them to work.

The criminal justice system came to Frick's aid too. As the mill reopened, he orchestrated mass indictments of strike leaders on charges of murder, conspiracy, and treason (the "usurpation of civil authority"). This campaign only gained momentum after July 23, when Frick was seriously wounded by Alexander Berkman, a young anarchist from New York who had tried to assassinate him. Homestead's chief of police stepped up arrests of strikers on the pretext that local anarchists were "getting ready to carry out some gigantic schemes." By October, 185 criminal indictments had been issued, with some men charged four and five times. No one was convicted, but the legal battles decimated the union's strike fund.

In November, unskilled workers petitioned the Amalgamated for release from their pledge of support, and the union declared the strike over. The defeat shattered the Amalgamated, formerly one of the most powerful AFL affiliates. Workers at Carnegie mills in several other towns had walked out in sympathy with Homestead, and there, too, the Amalgamated lost union recognition. The union's membership fell from 24,000 in 1891 to 8,000 in 1895. Mills owned by the Carnegie Steel Company—later sold to J.P. Morgan and renamed United States Steel—would remain union-free for two generations.

Two years later, troops and courts combined to put down a mass railroad strike led by a new industrial union, whose members came together regardless of skill. Craft organizations had done little for most railroad workers. Independent of the AFL, the five Railroad Brotherhoods (Engineers, Conductors, Firemen, Brakemen, and Switchmen) were all the more exclusive and prudential. They ignored semiskilled and unskilled employees, tried to drive African Americans out of the industry, and seldom honored one another's strikes. Indeed, their leaders condemned strikes altogether. Working conditions and pay were among the worst in the country. Each year, one trainman out of every hundred was killed on the job and another ten injured; in 1890, only engineers and conductors averaged more than $350 in annual wages. In the fall of 1892 rank-and-file railroad workers met secretly in Chicago to plan "an organization built up of 'all classes' of R.R. men." The American Railway Union (ARU) went public on June 20, 1893, its membership open to all white★ railroad employees except superintendents and corporate officials, with a national initiation fee and yearly dues a dollar each.

Eugene Debs, editor of *The Locomotive Firemen's Magazine,* became the ARU's president. After winning an eighteen-day strike against the Great

---

★ At that founding meeting, a proposal to admit black members was defeated 113 to 102. The ARU did admit women and supported equal pay for equal work.

Northern Railroad in April 1894, the union began to sign up 2,000 new members a day. By June it was the nation's largest union, with 150,000 members in 425 lodges.

Among them were 4,000 workers who manufactured railroad passenger cars at the Pullman Palace Car Company complex in Pullman, Illinois, near Chicago. George Pullman ran a company town, keeping rents high while he reduced wages. When the ARU's Pullman lodges went on strike on May 11, 1894, he closed the plants. In June, the strikers appealed to the ARU's first national convention: "It is victory or death . . . to you we confide our cause . . . do not desert us as you hope not to be deserted." The convention authorized a boycott; beginning June 26, no ARU member would work on any train that included Pullman cars. When the railroad companies refused to detach the cars, the boycott became a general railroad strike. Within three days, and despite opposition from the Railroad Brotherhoods, 150,000 strikers shut down eleven lines, to widespread sympathy fed by public resentment of the rail corporations.

Two days into the strike, U.S. Attorney General Richard Olney sought advice from Edwin Walker, counsel to the railroads' General Managers' Association. Walker recommended getting an injunction based on the Sherman Antitrust Act (1890), a vaguely worded and rarely invoked federal law directed against monopolies involved in interstate trade. On July 2, citing damage to interstate commerce and criminal conspiracy to obstruct postal service, the federal district court in Chicago enjoined all interference with rail operations, including any attempt to persuade any railroad employee not to work. The next day President Grover Cleveland ordered federal troops to enforce the order. They arrived in Chicago on Independence Day, and riots broke out. Over the next few days, at least twenty-five civilians were killed, and the Illinois Central railroad yards went up in flames. Across the country, newspaper headlines reported "MOB BENT ON RUIN," "ANARCHISTS ON WAY TO AMERICA FROM EUROPE," and "ANARCHISTS AND SOCIALISTS SAID TO BE PLANNING THE DESTRUCTION AND LOOTING OF THE TREASURY." Eugene Debs and other ARU officers were arrested July 10.

An emergency committee called for a general strike in Chicago the next day, but only 25,000 workers turned out. Many unions awaited the decision of an AFL executive conference, convened by Gompers at Chicago's Briggs House hotel on July 12. It contributed $1,000 to a legal defense fund, but agreed only to help Debs make an offer to call off the boycott if his members could return to their jobs. With that, the strike collapsed. Rearrested on July 17, Debs and other strike leaders were later convicted of violating the federal injunction, and the U.S. Supreme Court denied their appeal. He served six months, fellow defendants three. By 1897, the ARU had all but disappeared; just two dozen delegates showed up at its national convention that June.

Populism and Racism

The 1893 crash and depression hurt farmers and small businessmen as well as wage workers, and resentment of monopoly control of government was widespread. The People's Party—usually called the Populists—provided an opportunity to act. The party grew out of the Farmers' Alliances, which had preached agrarian organization against monopoly since the late 1870s, when the movement was born in Texas. The Alliances had serious weaknesses: they merged the contrary interests of small farmers and large planters, neglected sharecroppers and tenant farmers, and excluded African Americans entirely. But the movement's 1889 convention adopted a "St. Louis Program" that was bold and practical. It called for nationalizing the railroads, breaking up large landholding companies, abolishing national banks, instituting a graduated income tax, and creating federal "subtreasuries" that would lend money at nominal interest.

In 1890, Alliancemen entered electoral politics, gained control of many state governments in the South and Midwest, and won more than forty seats in Congress. At its first convention, held in Omaha, Nebraska, in July 1892, the Peoples' Party expanded the Alliance program to include "bimetallism" (a plan to increase the money supply by supplementing federal gold reserves with silver) and, in a nod to organized labor, called also for a shorter workday and restrictions on immigration. In 1894, Populist candidates received 1.5 million votes, taking enough votes from Democrats to make the Republicans the majority party.

Samuel Gompers did not think much of the Populists, since they included employers. But their state governments were generally friendly to labor, and socialist trade unionists urged the AFL Executive Council to declare independence from the two-party system and endorse the Populist challenge. At the Federation's national convention in Denver in December 1894, the delegates adopted most of the socialists' program, but Gompers managed to defeat two crucial proposals, for social ownership of the means of production and for independent political action.

If the AFL stood back from the People's Party, the surviving assemblies of the Knights of Labor did not. The Order had become a predominantly rural organization, its 75,000 members mostly in the West and the South.

The Knights sent delegates to the Populist conventions in St. Louis and Omaha.

Unfortunately, the Knights could no longer bring cross-racial cooperation to the movement. Though the Order's overall membership declined after Haymarket, its black membership increased; in mid-1887, the Knights had over 90,000 black members in the South, up from 60,000 a year earlier. That year 10,000 Knights—9,000 of them black—went on strike in Louisiana's sugarcane fields. The strike was suppressed by lawmen and vigilante forces, and more than twenty-five 25 black workers were killed. The Order's General Executive Board declined to assist the strikers. By 1894, with radicals like Frank Ferrell long gone, the Board had decided that the "negro problem" could be solved only by deportation. The southwestern Knights' Mexican American membership had also surged in the late 1880s, especially in New Mexico. In 1888, Juan José Herrera—founder of Las Gorras Blancas—was commissioned as a district organizer for the Order and helped start more than twenty local assemblies of Los Caballeros de Labor in San Miguel and neighboring counties. But these assemblies never developed a working relationship with New Mexico's Anglo Knights and clashed repeatedly with the General Executive Board. When Herrera, his brother Pablo, and forty-five other Mexicanos were indicted for Las Gorras activities, neither the Board nor local Anglo Knights extended support. In 1891, Pablo Herrera (recently elected to New Mexico's territorial legislature) was expelled from the Order for his Las Gorras connections.

Racial exclusion undermined the Populists in both western and southwestern states. The Herrera brothers led the establishment of a local Partido del Pueblo in New Mexico, but it never developed ties to the national People's Party. In the South, a Colored Farmer's Alliance had formed alongside the white movement, and many attempts were made to confederate or merge the two. White Populist leader Tom Watson argued for unity, telling Georgia farmers, "You are made to hate each other because upon that hatred is rested the keystone of the arch of financial despotism which enslaves you both. You are deceived and blinded that you may not see how this race antagonism perpetuates a monetary system which beggars you both." But black activists could not count on white support. Farmers in the white Alliance broke a cottonpickers' strike by members of the black Alliance in 1891; Ben Patterson, the strike's thirty-year-old leader in Arkansas, was caught by a white posse and shot to death. Tom Watson went on to build a long political career as an advocate of the Jim Crow system—state laws requiring separation of the races and constitutional amendments restricting black men's voting rights.

Desperate to recoup the losses of 1894, the Democrats took up the Populist call for "bimetallism" and nominated Nebraska's William Jennings Bryan for president in 1896. A former Congressman and popular orator, he had been stumping the country to speak on the silver issue. After rancorous debate and division, the Populists also nominated Bryan, though he did not endorse most of their program. Republican William McKinley swamped him at the polls, and the Populist moment passed.

Labor activists drew different lessons from the devastating defeats of the Homestead and Pullman strikes. Eugene Debs and his comrades saw the need for even greater solidarity. Samuel Gompers and many craft unionists concluded that it was futile to challenge the combined might of big business and government; judicious, "pure and simple unionism" worked best. Years later, Gompers said of the Briggs House conference, "The course pursued by the Federation was the biggest service that could have been performed to maintain the integrity of the Railroad Brotherhoods."

The Populist failure in 1896 likewise offered contradictory lessons. Gompers favored cultivating those business and political leaders least hostile to labor. Debs concluded that only "the ballots of workingmen emancipated from the [old] parties would bring a higher plane of prosperity." Others rejected politics as a game completely controlled by capital.

"How can the trade unions successfully combat the giant monstrosities of the nineteenth century?" asked George McNeill in an 1896 article titled "The Trade Unions and the Monopolies." If many people agreed that unions were powerless against the "power of aggregated wealth," this veteran labor leader thought otherwise, and he proposed a six-point program:

(1) restructure unions to fit mass production in monopolized industries, where unskilled and semiskilled workers had become the majority;

(2) fund a national campaign to organize the unorganized regardless of skill, race, creed, color, nationality, and sex;

(3) promote cooperation among craft unions in monopoly industries

(4) provide financial support to strikers and pensions for workers disabled or blacklisted in strikes;

(5) create antimonopoly alliances with farmers and small businessmen;

(6) develop an educational program to rally the population against the monopolies.

McNeill's article was widely reprinted and discussed. Several unions endorsed it and called on the AFL to convene a conference and get started. The Federation ignored them.

CHAPTER

LABOR AND EMPIRE

In November 1897, Samuel Gompers's monthly column in the *American Federationist* focused on Hawaii. Four years earlier American sugar planters had deposed Queen Liliuokalani, set up a sham "Republic," and asked for annexation to the United States. Now the Senate debated the proposal. Gompers opposed it and he rebuked its advocates for "cover[ing] themselves with the mantle of patriotism." In fact, he wrote, the scheme was merely "corporate power . . . endeavoring to invade acquired, natural, and constitutional rights." Twenty years later Gompers would become one of the nation's leading proponents of America's transformation into a world power. That shift took place in the context of a vast expansion of U.S. capitalism abroad and rapprochement between government and labor leaders willing to support the empire.

Empire Abroad, Empire at Home

In 1898, the United States moved into the ranks of modern world powers by defeating the forces of Spain, one of the oldest European empires. The Spanish-American War's official purpose was to help Cubans free themselves from Spanish colonialism. The Cuban rebellion had been building for decades, and armed insurrection broke out in 1895. Many ordinary Americans sympathized with the rebels. So did U.S. businessmen, who had invested $50 million in Cuban sugar plantations and aimed to invest more once Cuba was free. Early in 1898, President McKinley sent the battleship *Maine* to Havana to demonstrate American interest in Cuba; it blew up on February 15, killing 266 sailors. U.S. newspapers, some of which had called for the acquisition of Cuba as early as the 1850s, screamed for military reprisal. On April 20, Congress declared war on Spain. Fighting began on May 1 in the Philippines, where a rebellion against Spanish rule was already in progress. By the time the war ended in August, U.S. troops had also invaded Cuba, Puerto Rico, Guam, and Wake Island, and Congress had annexed Hawaii. John Hay, U.S. Ambassador to Great Britain, called it "a splendid little war." U.S. combat deaths totaled 379, though over 5,000 troops died from disease or canned rations of rotted beef. Under the peace treaty, the United States acquired Puerto Rico, Guam, and the Philippines as colonies, and the U.S. military administered Cuba until an independent government was formed.

Puerto Rican patriots protested their island's treatment as spoils of war. As a pamphlet stated, "The voice of Puerto Rico has not been heard. Not even by way of formality were its inhabitants consulted. . . . The island and all its people were simply transferred from one sovereign power to another, just as a farm with all its equipment, houses and animals is passed from one landlord to another." U.S. governors abolished local councils, revised laws, and even changed the island's name to "Porto Rico"—easier for English speakers to pronounce. In 1900, Congress made Puerto Rico a "nonincorporated" territory.

In the Philippines, the United States faced an armed movement for independence that controlled most of the archipelago. Under the leadership of Emilio Aguinaldo, the Revolutionary Congress wrote a constitution, and the Philippine Republic was inaugurated in January 1899. Within days, U.S. forces moved against the Republican army, commencing a three-year war that involved 126,000 American troops. On July 4, 1902, Washington declared the war won, but new rebellions gathered and fighting continued for another twelve years.

Overseas expansion was not a novel idea. The United States had seized the island of Navassa from Haiti in 1858, purchased Alaska from Russia in 1867, and the same year claimed Midway in the Pacific. But now expansionism gained more momentum than ever before. A host of politicians, professors, clergymen, editors, and military leaders contended that empire building was essential to national stability.

The nation's industrial capacity significantly exceeded domestic demand; that had been the chief cause of depressions and deflation in the

Gilded Age. U.S. Labor Commissioner Carroll Wright observed in the early 1890s, "It is incontrovertible that the present manufacturing and mechanical plant of the United States is greater . . . than is needed to supply the demand; yet it is constantly being enlarged, and there is no way of preventing the enlargement." An overseas empire promised relief. As historian Henry Brooks Adams wrote in 1900, "The United States must provide sure and adequate outlets for her products, or be in danger of gluts more dangerous to her society than many panics such as 1873 and 1893."

Imperialists also hoped that overseas military adventures would absorb popular energy. The *Atlantic Monthly* magazine endorsed war with Spain partly on the grounds that it would reduce social unrest: "Apostolic fervor, romantic dreaming, and blatant misinformation have each captivated the idle-minded masses. . . . These things all denote a lack of adventurous opportunities." A sociology professor at Columbia University argued that, if Americans did not spend their "reservoir of energy" in overseas conquests, it would "discharge itself in anarchistic, socialistic, and other destructive modes . . . likely to work uncalculable mischief."

Racism bolstered expansionism. "Take up the White Man's burden," urged British writer Rudyard Kipling in a widely reprinted poem that welcomed the United States to the ranks of colonial powers ruling "new-caught sullen peoples" of Asia and Africa. Theodore Roosevelt—Spanish-American War hero and McKinley's running mate in 1900—complained of expansionism's opponents: "Often these stay-at-homes are too selfish and indolent, too lacking in imagination, to understand the race-importance of the work which is done by pioneer brethren in wild and distant lands."

Racist expansionism closely paralleled white supremacy at home. Quoting Kipling's poem, the *Atlantic Monthly* asked in an editorial, "If the stronger and cleverer race is free to impose its will upon 'new-caught sullen peoples' on the other side of the globe, why not in South Carolina and Mississippi?" In 1890, Mississippi had disenfranchised most black men by imposing a literacy test on voters; in 1895, South Carolina had followed suit and instituted a poll tax as well. After the U.S. Supreme Court upheld the Mississippi restrictions in 1898, black disenfranchisement spread to Louisiana (1900), Alabama (1901), and on across the South. Writing to the *Richmond Planet,* Sergeant Major John Galloway, a black soldier stationed in the Philippines, predicted, "The future of the Filipino . . . is that of the Negro in the South." He was right. In 1901 the Supreme Court ruled that residents of the new U.S. colonies did not automatically enjoy rights and protections guaranteed by the Constitution.

Opposition to empire building was widespread at the turn of the century. Old-fashioned republicans despised colonialism; some racial purists fretted that colonial subjects might become citizens; businessmen worried about military costs; farmers feared competition from imported produce. Labor unions played an active role in the antiimperialist movement. Some unionists opposed wars of conquest on principle. Many others feared that militarism abroad would lead to repression at home.

Samuel Gompers denounced cheap colonial products and labor. In November 1898, he became a vice president of the Anti-Imperialist League, joining businessmen like Andrew Carnegie and politicians like Grover Cleveland. The League enrolled 500,000 members but failed to defeat McKinley's bid for re-election in 1900 and faded soon afterward. Criticism of expansion quickly disappeared from the labor press. In 1901, Gompers rejoiced in the *Federationist,* "Never was labor better organized and alive to its interests than now, and never was America's foreign trade so stupendous."

The American Federation of Labor had mixed relations with labor movements in the new colonies. In Puerto Rico, the Federación Libre de Trabajadores (FLT) accepted annexation to the United States and focused on winning an American standard of living for Puerto Rican workers. The AFL hired the FLT's founder Santiago Iglesias as an organizer in 1901. In the Philippines, the Union Obrera Democratica rallied for independence. Suppressed by the U.S. military, it reorganized in 1903 and in Manila led a May Day march of 100,000 demanding an end to U.S. occupation. For this the Union was suppressed once again. In 1904, the AFL declined to organize Manila cigar makers for fear of abetting "agitation of Philippine independence, very strong among the better class of workers." In Hawaii, white craftsmen from the States joined AFL unions, but the white unions had nothing to do with Asian workers organizing on the sugar plantations.

In the wake of the Spanish-American war, the mainland economy flourished. The depression of the 1890s had ended by the time the war began; now the recovery turned into a boom. The wave of corporate mergers, which had paused during the depression, resumed and accelerated. Consortiums of financiers created holding companies beyond the reach of antitrust legislation. Between 1898 and 1903 thousands of firms were absorbed into ever larger holding companies. The largest of all was United States Steel, formed in 1901 by J. P. Morgan of New York and Elbert Gary of Chicago after they bought a controlling interest in Carnegie Steel. Capitalized at $1.4 billion, U.S. Steel held 165 subsidiaries in a constellation of industries— steel, mining, shipping, and construction. Mergers reduced the ruinous competition of the Gilded Age.

Government regulated industry and commerce in business-friendly ways. The first federal regulatory agency—the Interstate Commerce Commission (ICC)—had accomplished virtually nothing since its establishment in 1887. Congress had authorized it merely to investigate freight railroads and make nonbinding recommendations as to the rates they should charge. In 1906, the ICC's powers expanded. Thanks to lobbying by manufacturers and merchants seeking predictable shipping costs, the agency now got jurisdiction over all interstate transportation, and its rulings on rates became binding unless overturned by the courts. A consortium of food companies lobbied for the Pure Food and Drug Act and Meat Inspection Act of 1906, which imposed product standards acceptable to manufacturers. Bankers designed the Federal Reserve System, established in 1913 to regulate finance. The Federal Trade Commission—set up the following year to regulate industrial corporations—was the brainchild of business magnates, most notably George Perkins of U.S. Steel.

Exports helped to sustain the business boom. The dollar volume of U.S. goods sold abroad increased by more than 50 percent between 1901 and 1914. Capital became an even more important export. As an economist pointed out in 1899, "The real opportunity afforded by colonial possessions is for the development of the new countries by fixed investment." U.S. foreign investment—mostly in Latin America and Canada—more than tripled by 1914. Puerto Rican sugar production expanded under a monopoly of four U.S. corporations. The greatest prizes in the Philippines were the "friar lands," close to a half-million acres of estates abandoned by the Spanish Catholic Church. The United States paid the Vatican for their titles and auctioned them off, mostly to American sugar planters.

The most important U.S. import was labor. Immigration to the United States rose from 229,000 arrivals in 1898 to more than 800,000 in 1904 and averaged about a million a year over the next decade. The vast majority of immigrants now came from eastern and southern Europe, and arrivals from Asia, Latin America, and the Caribbean reached new heights. The result, to quote one historian, was "nothing less than the ethnic recomposition of the American working class." The so-called American worker—a descendant of northwestern Europe—became a relatively privileged minority of the labor force.

To native-born "old" Americans, the crowded immigrant ghettoes of modern cities seemed to be cesspools of vice and crime and a threat to social order. Proposed solutions came from many quarters. Old-fashioned evangelists and moral reformers campaigned to eradicate drinking, gambling, and prostitution. Newer ideas came from middle-class reformers who called themselves "progressives." Social workers in immigrant communities promoted vocational training, employment bureaus, and education in American customs and hygiene. Doctors, lawyers, social scientists, and other professionals advocated stricter housing codes and public sanitation. The impulse for reform ranged so widely that the age became known as the "Progressive Era."

Virtually every industrial state saw campaigns to ban child labor, regulate hours and conditions for women and teenagers, set standards for workplace safety and health, and create funds to compensate workers injured on the job. Beginning in Illinois in 1893, reformers in several states had lobbied successfully for labor laws to protect children and women in manufacturing, but these protections were often overturned in court or (simply) not enforced. When Congress took up child labor legislation starting in 1906, southern textile manufacturers fiercely resisted it; but northern companies, already bound by state restrictions on child labor, supported federal action to reduce the competition's advantage. While some business groups opposed laws for workers' injury compensation, others joined the campaign in order to coopt it. In 1911, the National Association of Manufacturers wrote a "model" compensation law that restricted injured workers' claims. Within three years business lobbyists had persuaded twenty-five states to adopt the Association's formula.

Businessmen were also ambivalent about political reforms. "Good government" progressives challenged urban political machines like the New York Democratic Party's Tammany Hall, urged the appointment of experts as public administrators, and pushed to replace mayoral administration with appointed commissioners or city managers. As the president of National Cash Register observed, such reforms put government "on a strict business basis."

Businessmen and many progressives were less enthusiastic about democracy. To quote one business paper: "We have faith in popular opinion . . . when it is instructed, sober, moral, true. But we have no faith in popular opinion when it is rash, passionate, prejudiced and ignorant." Common reforms aimed at regulating voting included literacy tests, registration far in advance of elections, and ballots supplied by election commissions instead of party clubhouses. Democratic reforms like ballot initiatives and recall elections were less widely adopted. Voter participation in elections fell from the 80 percent characteristic of the late nineteenth century to about 60 percent by 1920. Democracy did not appear in the ideal government described by one prominent progressive businessman: "the work of the state is to think for the people and plan for the people—to teach them how to do, what to do, and to sustain them in the doing."

Separation of the races, especially in the South, was the most sweeping manifestation of the Progressive Era's obsession with social order. After the Supreme Court upheld the constitutionality of Louisiana's "separate but equal" railroad cars in *Plessy v. Ferguson* (1896), white legislators enacted a myriad of laws that required the segregation of nearly every aspect of southern life, from streetcars, theaters, residences, and cemeteries to brothels and the Bibles used to swear in witnesses in court. According to some southern progressives, segregation solved the problem of violence between races. Others thought it would stabilize white society. Progressive activist Rev. Edgar Gardner Murphy of Montgomery, Alabama, wrote in 1904: "The conscious unity of race is . . . better as a basis of democratic reorganization than the distinctions of wealth, of trade, of property, of family, or class."

Segregation percolated everywhere. In 1906, the San Francisco School Board assigned Asian American children to a separate public school, an order rescinded after the Japanese government protested to President Roosevelt and agreed to restrict emigration to the United States. U.S. troops abroad carried Jim Crow with them; Cubans called it the Yankee "white fever." When Afro-Antilleans were brought to Panama to dig the canal, Panamanian authorities segregated public facilities to please American sensibilities. Back in the United States, the Commissioner of Indians ruled in 1916 that people with half or more "Indian blood" were not legally competent unless they passed a government review.

Philippine pacification was finally completed in 1914, and two years later Congress agreed to eventual independence. Aside from the purchase of the Virgin Islands in 1917, annexation had played out. Cuba proved a better model. Cubans got independence as promised in 1902. Their constitution—written under U.S. military occupation—gave the United States land for naval stations, a veto on Cuban foreign policy, and the right to send in troops at any time. American investment flowed into Cuba. This arrangement exemplified "dollar diplomacy": foreign policy designed to expand and protect U.S. investments abroad.

Military intervention backed up diplomatic initiatives. U.S. forces joined other imperial powers in suppressing China's Boxer Rebellion in 1900 and stayed for almost thirty years. In 1903, U.S. warships backed a rebellion on Colombia's Isthmus of Panama in order to create a government to sign a canal treaty already prepared by New York lawyers; the Panama Canal opened in 1914. To "protect American lives and property," U.S. troops occupied Cuba from 1906 to 1909 and again in 1917; Nicaragua almost continuously from 1912 to 1933; Mexico in 1914 and 1916–17; Haiti from 1915 to 1934; and the Dominican Republic from 1916 to 1924. When

Major General Smedley Butler looked back on his Marine Corps service in the Americas and China, he concluded, "I was a racketeer, a gangster for capitalism."

The empire needed workers as well as soldiers. No one described this requirement better than Elbert Hubbard in his essay "Message to Garcia." Just before the war with Spain, U.S. Army lieutenant Andrew Rowan had gone alone into Cuba's mountains to deliver a letter from President McKinley to the rebel general Calixto Garcia. In the March 1899 issue of Hubbard's magazine *The Philistine,* his tribute to Rowan became a meditation on the American worker. Employers, he wrote, could only be appalled by the average worker's "inability or unwillingness to concentrate on a thing and do it. Slip-shod assistance, foolish inattention, dowdy indifference, and half-hearted work seem the rule." Even worse was the malcontent, "absolutely worthless to anyone else, because he carries with him constantly the insane suspicion that his employer is oppressing, or intending to oppress him. . . . He is impervious to reason, and the only thing that can impress him is the toe of a thick-soled No. 9 boot." What civilization needed, Hubbard concluded, were diligent workers who would unquestioningly follow orders—workers who could "carry a message to Garcia." The essay so inspired American businessmen that they printed some 40 million copies to distribute to their employees.

THE LABOR MOVEMENT IN THE PROGRESSIVE ERA

The labor movement reflected changing times. It coalesced around three organizational centers: the American Federation of Labor, the Socialist Party of America (SP), and a radical union known as the Industrial Workers of the World (IWW). The AFL—the first U.S. labor federation to survive a major depression—entered the twentieth century all the more committed to its "pure and simple" unionism based on craftsmen. Activists ignored or frustrated by the Federation gathered in the SP and IWW. The three competed to lead American labor, each with a different program for winning better working conditions, richer lives, and social justice.

The American Federation of Labor focused on collective bargaining: contracts negotiated by professional representatives for well-funded unions of highly skilled workers, organized according to their separate crafts. The formula had weaknesses. In contrast to the Federation's early years craft unions now routinely crossed one another's pickets and endlessly disputed jurisdictions. Salaried union officers and staff sometimes became grafters, offering employers sweetheart deals in return for bribes. Even squeaky clean craft unions ignored less skilled workers, the majority of the labor force. United Textile Workers president John Golden explained why his union set dues too high for all but the most skilled: "I find them the most intelligent and the easiest to organize . . . [and] more value to us than the unskilled."

To organize the unorganized, the AFL used "federal labor unions" (FLUs), originally conceived as a temporary stopping place for new recruits who would later join craft unions. After 1900, the Federation chartered thousands of FLUs, now as permanent organizations for workers who did not fit into the AFL's craft structure. Samuel Gompers said of federal unions: "They extend the hand of fellowship to . . . every creed and color [and] give the lie to those who talk of A.F. of L. exclusiveness." In fact, the very existence of permanent FLUs testified to the exclusiveness of the national craft unions—their neglect of women, immigrants, and workers of color as well as the unskilled.

As of 1910, about 73,000 women workers—less than 1 percent of the female labor force—belonged to any union. To recruit women into the AFL, Boston labor activists and reformers came together in 1903 to found the Women's Trade Union League, which subsequently spread to cities across the country. AFL leaders endorsed the project; but when national unions failed to charter locals organized by the League, the Federation's Executive Council refused to press the issue or to charter the locals directly.

In 1900, only about 30,000 African Americans belonged to unions, two-thirds to the United Mine Workers (UMW). In Birmingham, Alabama, black workers were active in the UMW, federal unions, and locals affiliated with national unions of barbers, plasterers, hod carriers, iron workers, and others. Birmingham was exceptional, however. In most cities the AFL had few or no black members.

"New immigrants" from southern and eastern Europe were rarely skilled workers, and many AFL leaders considered them unfit for union membership and even admission to the United States. The Federation lobbied Congress to test immigrants for literacy, which would, according to Gompers, "shut out a considerable number of South Italians, and of Slavs, and other[s] equally or more undesirable." AFL opposition to Asian immigration and hostility to Asian American workers continued unabated. In 1903, sugar beet workers in Oxnard, California, formed the Japanese-Mexican Labor Association (JMLA), won a strike against a wage cut and applied for AFL membership. Gompers agreed to issue a charter, but only if the union would henceforth exclude Asians. When the JMLA refused to comply, he broke off all relations.

The Federation did charter a number of Latino locals in the Southwest.

In California, AFL organizer Juan Ramírez helped migrant farm workers near Long Beach and San Pedro form La Unión de Jornaleros Unidos (FLU No. 13,097) in 1911. An independent union of Tejano railroad workers in Laredo became FLU No. 11,953 in 1905. In El Paso, Texas, Anglo and Mexican American workers organized integrated locals of the Typographical Union, the Painters' Union, and the Brotherhood of Carpenters; but these locals did not include Mexican immigrants.

If prejudice begat AFL exclusiveness, so did thoughtful calculation by the Federation's leaders. They believed that craftsmen could make steady headway with narrow craft unionism—"the line of least resistance," as Gompers once called it. As the age of empire dawned, the AFL experienced a growth spurt that seemed to confirm that formula's wisdom. By 1904, the Federation reported about 1,676,000 members in 120 unions, up from 265,000 members in 58 unions in 1897. Some national unions won contracts with employers' associations: the Machinists with the National Founders' Association; the Typographers with the Newspaper Publishers' Association; the Mine Workers with bituminous coal companies in the Central Competitive Field (Pennsylvania, Ohio, Indiana, and Illinois).

The AFL also gained respectability by participating in the National Civic Federation (NCF), founded in 1900 to enlist employers, labor leaders, and prominent public citizens to promote industrial peace. Gompers and United Mine Workers president John Mitchell were charter members, along with industrial magnates like John D. Rockefeller, Jr., and Charles Schwab of U.S. Steel. The "public" was represented by university presidents, Episcopal and Catholic bishops, and retired U.S. President Grover Cleveland, now a trustee for the New York Life Insurance Company.

When 144,000 anthracite coal miners in the UMW went out on strike in 1902, the NCF swung into action. Gompers and Mitchell stymied bituminous coal miners' plans for a sympathy strike, and NCF businessmen blocked the coal companies' efforts to secure intervention by federal troops. Theodore Roosevelt (who had succeeded to the presidency with McKinley's assassination in 1901) ordered arbitration, which ended in a compromise that raised pay but did not meet the strikers' demands for union recognition and the eight-hour day. While many miners protested the settlement, Gompers and Mitchell hailed it as a vindication of "responsible" unionism.

Even as they signed union contracts and hobnobbed with labor leaders in the NCF, employers never stopped searching for methods to contain and weaken unionism. One increasingly popular method was "scientific management," pioneered by Frederick Winslow Taylor at the Midvale Steel

Works in eastern Pennsylvania. The eccentric son of a wealthy Philadelphia family, Taylor had left prep school to do industrial work at factories owned by friends of his parents. In the early 1890s, he became gang boss of Midvale's machine shop and set out to make it the most productive operation in the factory, indeed the world. The key, he decided, was to control workers' every move. First, he carefully analyzed the machinists' labor, dividing each task into a series of simple motions, all of which he timed with a stopwatch. Then he decreed the "one best way" to perform each motion and demanded that workers strictly follow his decrees. Those who complied got higher pay; resisters were punished with fines, wage cuts, or dismissal. In 1895, Taylor began to publicize the Midvale experiments, and by the early 1900s, his scientific management system was winning a following among industrial employers.

What most attracted them was Taylorism's potential to marginalize craftsmen and their unions. Once craft labor was broken down into routine steps, the lion's share of industrial production could be reassigned to less skilled workers at lower pay, and craftsmen could be relegated to ancillary roles. Under old managerial systems, skilled men had dominated production. Their detailed mastery of the labor process let them determine work methods and output quotas for themselves and their less skilled helpers. They could shut down their shops at will. But when craftsmen were isolated from semiskilled fabricators and assemblers and confined to tasks such as machine repair or tool and die work, they and their unions could hardly slow down production, much less bring it to a halt.

As scientific management undercut unions' clout on the shop floor, the National Association of Manufacturers (NAM) tried to wipe them out with the Open Shop Drive, a "crusade against unionism" launched in 1903. Within a year, the NAM established a Citizens' Industrial Association that worked with 247 employers' associations to distribute antiunion literature and compile blacklists of labor activists. The NAM worked also with the American Anti-Boycott Association, which specialized in taking unions to court. State and federal judges issued hundreds of injunctions against strikes, organizing drives, and other union activities. The U.S. Supreme Court extended the reach of these injunctions in 1908, when it ruled that members of the Hatters Union of Danbury, Connecticut, were individually liable for financial damages to a hat company the union had slapped with a boycott.

Such assaults destroyed the AFL's momentum. Contracts lapsed and strike losses mounted. Unions all but disappeared from steel, meatpacking, and Great Lakes shipping. AFL membership fell by about 222,000 between 1904 and 1906, and the loss was not fully recouped for another half decade. Shrinkage exacerbated internal divisions. Jurisdictional disputes between AFL unions grew all the more acrimonious. Defending core constituencies, AFL headquarters and national unions abandoned those at the Federation's margins; multitudes of FLUs collapsed along with all of Birmingham's black locals. More and more critics of pure and simple craft unionism squared off against the AFL conservatives.

The dissidents called for political action in conjunction with the Socialist Party and for campaigns to organize industrial unions—unions that welcomed all workers in a particular industry regardless of occupation or skill. The AFL already had some industrial affiliates—the United Mine Workers, the United Brewery Workers, the International Ladies' Garment Workers, and a few others.★ The sentiment for change was strongest in these quarters but also grew in craft unions such as the Typographers, the Machinists, and the Carpenters.

While AFL headquarters fought dissent tooth and nail, it also modified its policies to allow for political action in the two-party system. In particular, the Federation sought to exempt labor from the Sherman Antitrust Act (1890), whose ban on conspiracies to restrain free trade provided the foundation for most legal assaults on unions. In 1908, AFL spokesmen brought their cause to both the Republican and Democratic conventions. The Republicans recoiled; the Democrats gave it a lukewarm endorsement; and the AFL backed a presidential candidate for the very first time—Democrat William Jennings Bryan, who lost to the Republicans' William Howard Taft. Four years later, the AFL would back a victor as Democrats and a liberal Republican faction vied for labor's support.

This upturn in the Federation's political fortunes was closely linked to the McNamara case, the most dramatic episode in the annals of the Open Shop Drive. The National Erectors' Association had joined the drive in 1906, confronting the AFL's Bridge and Structural Iron Workers. The Iron Workers had fought back by dynamiting some eighty-seven steel structures built by nonunion labor. On October 1, 1910, twenty workmen died in an explosion that leveled the printing plant of the *Los Angeles Times,* a tireless champion of the open shop. The following spring, two Iron Workers—James B. McNamara and his older brother John J., the union's national secretary-treasurer—were indicted for murder in connection with the blast.

★ "International" unions had Canadian locals.

The brothers pled not guilty; and every branch of the labor movement, from archconservatives to revolutionaries, rallied in their defense. Then, on December 1, 1911, the McNamaras suddenly changed their pleas. Some said Gompers wept when he heard the news.

Many in the upper reaches of both the Democratic and Republican parties worried about the stability of a society in which unionists like the McNamaras—members of the AFL mainstream—resorted to violence. Running for re-election in 1912, President Taft denounced unions for "lawlessness in labor disputes." Liberal Republicans broke away to form the Progressive Party and run Theodore Roosevelt on a platform that called for workplace safety standards, old-age pensions, an eight-hour day for women and teenagers, and other labor reforms. Democrat Woodrow Wilson endorsed workers' right to organize and carried the election with backing from the AFL.

Wilson's first year in office went badly for labor. Congressional bills to exempt unions from antitrust law were repeatedly blocked. The Justice Department indicted the United Mine Workers for "conspiracy" to organize the entire coal industry. Meanwhile, in southern Colorado, union miners launched a strike against Rockefeller's Colorado Fuel & Iron (CFI). In September 1913, over 11,000 strikers and the families left CFI camps and set up tent colonies. Cheering them on was the veteran labor organizer "Mother" Mary Jones, then in her seventies and fresh out of jail for assisting a coal strike in West Virginia. The CFI battle wore on for months, with company guards and the state militia escorting scabs to work and harassing strikers. On April 20, 1914, all hell broke loose. Militiamen and guards machine-gunned and torched the tent colony at Ludlow; twenty-one people were shot or burned to death, including eleven children. As the news spread, armed trade unionists poured into the region to defend the miners. Federal troops finally stopped the fighting in May, by which time sixty-six miners or their family members had been killed. The strikers held out until December, then returned to work in defeat.

In the wake of the Ludlow massacre, Congress debated and eventually passed the Clayton Act. It stated that labor organizations should not be "construed to be illegal combinations in restraint of trade under the antitrust laws," and it barred injunctions against "peaceful and lawful" strikes. President Wilson signed the Act into law in October 1914. In the next issue of the *American Federationist,* Gompers called it "the industrial Magna Carta upon which the working people will rear the structure of industrial freedom." Prudent political action had apparently proved its value.

The political alternative shunned by the AFL was the Socialist Party, founded in 1901 by veterans of the Knights of Labor and the Peoples' Party and by leaders of socialist organizations based mainly among German and Russian-Jewish immigrants. The SP aimed to use the ballot to build a new social order based on public ownership of industry and thoroughgoing democracy. Eugene Debs, former leader of the American Railway Union, was the Party's chief spokesman and perennial presidential candidate. He had become a socialist while serving prison time for his role in the Pullman strike.

The SP organized a large network of locals and two national youth groups, the Young People's Socialist League for workers and the Intercollegiate Socialist Society for students. Starting in 1910, foreign-language associations—Italian, Finnish, German, Polish, Lithuanian, Yiddish, and others—joined the Party as autonomous federations. By 1912, the SP published over 300 periodicals in many different languages.

Party members agreed on the electoral path to socialism but not much else, and SP headquarters in Chicago did not try to impose consistency. Urban members usually favored public ownership of land, while rural members generally thought land should belong to those who formed it. Opinion on race and gender ranged from egalitarianism to outright bigotry. Austrian-born Victor Berger headed a strong socialist movement in Milwaukee, which elected him to six terms in Congress. He believed in white supremacy, reluctantly supported votes for women, and looked down on "new immigrants." New Yorker Morris Hillquit, another SP leader, was a new immigrant himself—a Latvian Jew who worked in garment shops and helped organize the United Hebrew Trades before he became a lawyer and socialist theorist. Kate Richards O'Hare edited the monthly *National Rip-Saw* for 150,000 rural readers and drew crowds at "tent meetings" where farm families camped for days of talks and entertainment. She advocated birth control and women suffrage, and accepted racial segregation. Another popular Party orator was George Washington Woodbey, a minister in the African Methodist Episcopal Church; he supported women's rights, called for unity among poor people of all races, and strongly opposed Asian exclusion. In Oklahoma, only whites could join the Renters Union of tenant farmers led by Socialist J. Tad Cumbie. In southern Texas, Party organizers such as Antonio Valdez and J. A. Hernández built interracial agrarian unions.

By 1910, the Party had more than 3,000 locals. As of 1912, more than 2,000 Socialists held public office, and Eugene Debs won 6 percent of the vote in that year's presidential election. In 1914, Russian-born labor lawyer Meyer London became the Party's second U.S. Congressman, elected from New York City's Lower East Side.

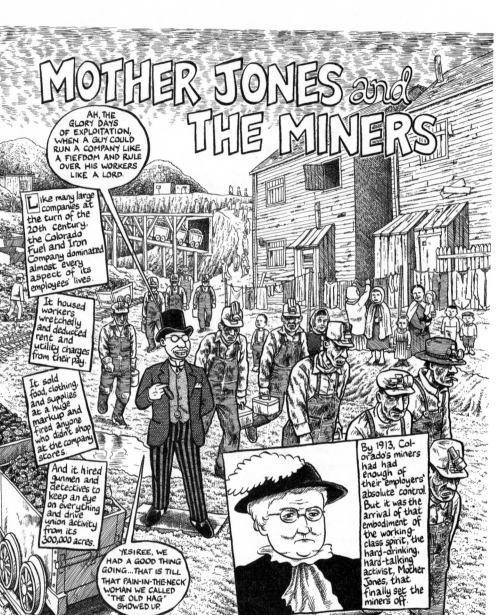

Her fiery speeches emboldened the United Mine Workers of America to call for a strike in September 1913 to force three major companies, including the Colorado Fuel and Iron Company, to negotiate on a number of demands, among which was union recognition. Many of these demands were already state law.

YOU DO WORK THAT ENABLES THE WIVES OF THE OPERATORS TO PAY $1,000 FOR DRESSES TO PUT ON THEIR ROTTEN CARCASSES...

YOU DRESS THE MINE OWNER'S WIFE AND YOU PUT YOUR WIFE IN RAGS.

LET'S GO, DEAR. I CAN SEE WE'RE NOT WELCOME HERE.

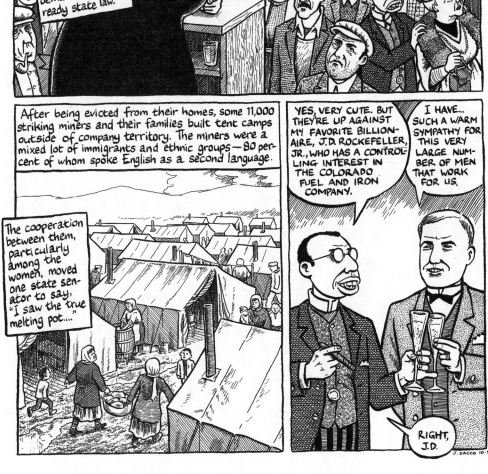

After being evicted from their homes, some 11,000 striking miners and their families built tent camps outside of company territory. The miners were a mixed lot of immigrants and ethnic groups—80 percent of whom spoke English as a second language.

The cooperation between them, particularly among the women, moved one state senator to say, "I saw the true melting pot...."

YES, VERY CUTE. BUT THEY'RE UP AGAINST MY FAVORITE BILLIONAIRE, J.D. ROCKEFELLER, JR., WHO HAS A CONTROLLING INTEREST IN THE COLORADO FUEL AND IRON COMPANY.

I HAVE... SUCH A WARM SYMPATHY FOR THIS VERY LARGE NUMBER OF MEN THAT WORK FOR US.

RIGHT, J.D.

J. SACCO 10-98

The attack on the Ludlow camp resulted in the death of one soldier, five miners, and a boy.

AND, OKAY, OUR VALIANT MILITIA RAISED A LITTLE HELL AND SET THE TENTS ABLAZE.

BOYS WILL BE BOYS, YOU KNOW.

In one makeshift cellar, two women and 11 children were found burned to death.

The killings outraged the nation and led to 10 days of open rebellion in Colorado.

Federal troops were brought in to restore order.

President Woodrow Wilson's attempts to mediate an end to the strike were thwarted by the coal operators. After 14 months, with its coffers almost empty, the union acknowledged that many of the mines were being worked at full capacity by scabs anyway and called off its strike.

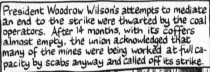

SO BACK TO WORK!

Mother Jones told all who would listen that the miners had—

—ONLY THE CONSTITUTION. THE OTHER SIDE HAD THE BAYONETS. IN THE END, BAYONETS WIN.

AND DON'T FORGET IT!

But the strike of the Colorado miners and the massacre at Ludlow had opened further the eyes of the nation to the abuses of company power.

J. SACCO 10-96

The SP rejected "dual unionism"—the formation of radical unions to rival those of the AFL. Instead, the Party "bored from within" the Federation, where Socialists promoted industrial unionism, organizing the unorganized, and political action in alliance with the SP. Socialists were active in building industrial unions. In the winter of 1909–10, SP members like Lithuanian-born Pauline Newman played a central role in New York City's "Rising of the 20,000," a strike by women shirtwaist makers that won union recognition for the Ladies' Garment Workers. Party influence also extended to craft unions; Socialists led insurgencies that ousted conservative leaders from office in the Hatters, the Sheet Metal Workers, and the Carpenters. In 1912, Socialist Max Hayes of the Typographical Union challenged Samuel Gompers for the AFL presidency and got close to a third of the vote.

The Party had a strong rural following among miners, railroad workers, and farmers, both tenants and small landowners. By 1910, the SP's largest state organization was in Oklahoma, and it was well established in Kansas, Minnesota, the Dakotas, Arkansas, and Texas. Socialist-led farmers' unions mobilized against landlords and bankers. In 1915, the North Dakota SP joined with dissident Democrats and Republicans to create the Non-Partisan League, which called for public ownership of banks and grain elevators and elected dozens of local and state officials.

SP speakers and publications identified socialism with American history and values, echoing Debs's declaration that the Party embodied "the idea of liberty and self-government, in which the nation was born." Employers' associations and business-minded civic groups replied with a barrage of literature that depicted socialism as an alien doctrine. AFL leaders loudly agreed.

Aside from this powerful opposition, the SP's mainstream strategy was itself problematic. Surveying the Party's work in the AFL, labor radical Joseph Ettor concluded, "We tried, but the more we fooled with the beast the more it *captured us.*" To serve the rank and file, or simply to remain in power, Socialist labor officials placed their unions' immediate interests above Party ideals. For example, William H. Johnston, elected president of the Machinists in 1911, endorsed industrial unionism at AFL conventions but did not promote it in his own union, where he thought it would "cause unlimited trouble." Socialist efforts to "bore from within" the political system carried similar liabilities. The Party stressed immediate reforms, defined as way stations to a socialist future; but this program lost its radical edge when antisocialist Progressives embraced many of the same reforms the SP championed.

The electoral focus could also distance the Party from potential supporters. In 1910 the Oklahoma SP campaigned to block a state constitutional amendment designed to disfranchise most black voters, then pandered to race prejudice among white voters by running the segregationist J. Tad Cumbie for governor. This alienated black political clubs that had earlier vowed support for "our Socialistic brethren." Two years later—disfranchisement now in place—Socialists added a strong civil rights plank to their election platform and hired a black organizer (W. T. Lane of Kansas) to recruit African Americans. But electoral campaigns were no longer a viable means to mobilize black communities. The recruitment drive made headway only in coal towns, where Socialist activity centered in the United Mine Workers.

When Socialists confronted popular protest beyond the boundaries of unionism and electoral politics, they generally tried to redirect it. In February 1917, thousands of immigrant housewives in New York City took action against soaring food prices with a consumer boycott, neighborhood demonstrations, and mass marches on both City Hall and the Waldorf-Astoria Hotel (where the governor was rumored to be staying). Amidst the turmoil, the SP organized the Mothers' Anti-High Price League to lobby public officials. In their work with the League, Socialists repeatedly suggested that the boycotters would do better to support unions' efforts to raise wages and the Party's campaign for women suffrage. SP strategists seldom recognized that working people could "vote" with collective action as well as ballots and "unionize" in communities as well as workplaces.

In contrast, the Industrial Workers of the World (often called Wobblies) thought the labor movement's future lay with the masses denied the vote and excluded from the AFL. At the initiative of the Western Federation of Miners (WFM)—an independent union of metal miners—some 200 labor radicals convened in Chicago in June 1905. WFM Secretary William ("Big Bill") Haywood welcomed them to "the Continental Congress of the Working Class." Among the dignitaries on the platform were Socialists Eugene Debs and Mother Jones, anarchist Lucy Parsons (widow of Haymarket martyr Albert Parsons), and the Catholic "labor priest" Father Thomas Hagerty. The convention adopted a constitution that began, "The working class and the employing class have nothing in common," and the IWW was born.

Its founders disagreed on political action. Some promoted electoral work. Others advocated syndicalism—taking "direct action" on the job to build industrial unions until they were strong enough to launch a general strike and take over business and government. As Joseph Ettor put it, "the workers of the world . . . have nothing to do but fold their arms and the world will stop." Syndicalists prevailed at the IWW's 1908 convention, the others fell away, and Wobblies went forth to organize militant industrial unions under the auspices of the "One Big Union," the IWW.

Best known for strike agitation and free speech campaigns, the IWW also staged lectures and debates and distributed pamphlets and periodicals in more than a dozen languages. Its *Little Red Songbook* included songs like "Solidarity Forever," written by the Wobbly newspaper editor Ralph Chaplin and today the anthem of American labor. IWW graphics, often contributed by avant-garde artists, still make powerful appeals for labor unity and revolution.

Wobbly agitators were dedicated, bold, and imaginative. Big Bill Haywood had organized miners for twenty years, always packing a gun. "Rebel Girl" Elizabeth Gurley Flynn, who mounted her first soapbox at age sixteen, traveled coast to coast as an IWW speaker. Black longshoreman Ben Fletcher organized across the South and led Philadelphia's Local 8 of the IWW Marine Transport Workers; his trademark slogan was "All for one and one for all." Joe Hill came from Sweden in 1902, tramped from job to job, joined the IWW around 1910, and wrote subversive lyrics to popular tunes. Half-Cherokee Frank Little called himself the reddest Wobbly and the IWW's only true American.

Wobblies scrupulously practiced solidarity: "If you are a wage worker, you are welcome . . . the IWW is not a white man's union, not a black man's union, not a red man's union, but a workingman's union." They accepted unorthodox behavior; Marie Equi, an Oregon physician who became active with the IWW during a strike by immigrant women cannery workers, wore men's clothing and lived openly as a lesbian. IWW solidarity also crossed national borders. When Mexican activists invaded Baja California in 1911 to fight the Diaz dictatorship, a hundred Anglo Wobblies joined them.

The IWW gained national notice for its role in a 1909 strike at a U.S. Steel subsidiary in McKees Rocks, Pennsylvania. When the company cut pay, Slavic steelworkers went on strike and called in the Wobblies. Strikers and their wives battled with state police for forty-five days; thirteen people were killed. After the Railroad Trainmen, an independent union, refused to transport scabs, the company caved in. The IWW's reputation grew with the 1912 "Bread and Roses Strike" in Lawrence, Massachusetts. In January, 25,000 workers—immigrants from a dozen ethnic groups—walked out of the city's textile mills to protest wage cuts. While the AFL textile union tried to quash the strike, the IWW organized "moving pickets" to foil injunctions and sent trainloads of strikers' children to safe haven in New York and other cities. After two months, the strikers won.

Militant solidarity was not always enough, however. In Merryville,

Louisiana, during the winter of 1912–13, the IWW's Brotherhood of Timber Workers struck the Santa Fe Railroad's American Lumber Company, which had fired union members for testifying in defense of workers charged with murdering a company guard. Local farmers supplied the strikers with food. African Americans, Italians, and Mexicans hired as scabs joined the strike instead. In May, posses of lawmen and company guards attacked the town, ransacking homes, beating and arresting strikers, and killing a black organizer. The Brotherhood was destroyed.

Local governments smashed other Wobbly efforts. A 1913 strike by 17,000 rubber workers in Akron, Ohio, lasted a month. Police clubbed and arrested pickets, deputized vigilantes, broke up meetings, and ran Wobblies out of town. That same year the IWW supported 25,000 workers striking the silk mills in Paterson, New Jersey. Police arrested almost 3,000 pickets and killed two; the strike collapsed after seven months.

The IWW challenged local governments in more than twenty campaigns to claim free speech and assembly under the First Amendment. In 1909, when Missoula, Montana, tried to silence Wobblies with an ordinance against public speaking, the IWW called members and sympathizers into town and flooded the jail with free speechers. In Spokane, Washington, police detained more than 600 Wobbly speakers in November 1909. Several died from torture in the "sweatbox," where guards tossed prisoners back and forth between sweltering and freezing rooms.

Wobblies won many free-speech fights, but they remained prime targets for repression. In 1914, Salt Lake City police arrested Joe Hill for murder. The prosecution presented no motive, eyewitness, or connection between Hill and the victim but still got a conviction. Shortly before his execution, Hill wired Haywood, "Don't waste any time in mourning—organize." The IWW scattered his ashes in every state except Utah; in Oregon, Dr. Equi performed the honors.

By 1915, the IWW had issued 300,000 cards, but it had only about 15,000 members. Wobbly locals were highly unstable. Strikes brought in masses of recruits, but most dropped out after they went back to work. The locals—composed of workers from various industries and shops—were ill equipped to deal with day-to-day conflicts on the job. After the strike defeats in Akron and Paterson, Wobblies set out to build sturdier unions.

The strategy came from the IWW's agricultural locals, which merged to form the Agricultural Workers Organization (AWO) in 1915 and adopted the "job delegate" system. Organizers in fixed locations directed hundreds of roving delegates, who settled job disputes while recruiting new members and collecting dues. With this system the AWO organized migrant wheat harvesters from Oklahoma into Canada, then branched out to other farm workers and lumberjacks, and grew to 70,000 members by 1917. Their dues funded AWO-style organizing drives among iron and copper miners west of the Mississippi, along with seamen and dockworkers in Atlantic, Gulf, and Great Lakes ports.

Repression continued. In 1916, police and company thugs savagely attacked striking IWW iron miners in Minnesota's Mesabi Range, and sheriff's deputies shot up a boatload of Wobblies at the town dock in Everett, Washington, killing six and wounding twenty-seven. But by 1918, the IWW had at least 100,000 dues-paying members.

At their peaks, the IWW and Socialist Party combined were less than a tenth the size of the AFL, but Samuel Gompers and his lieutenants obsessively maneuvered to counter Socialist influence and thwart Wobbly organizing. The *American Federationist* repeatedly printed attacks on the SP and IWW, most penned by Gompers himself. In 1912, he charged that Socialists were not genuine trade unionists but "fanatical . . . unscrupulous . . . vote-hunters." After the Paterson strike, he declared the IWW "destructive in theory and practice." Socialists and Wobblies responded in kind. The SP called the AFL's executives "capitalistic misleaders." For the IWW, the AFL was a nest of "union scabs." Meanwhile, the SP fought the IWW. In 1912, Victor Berger and Morris Hillquit got the Party's constitution amended to require the expulsion of members who opposed electoral activity or advocated illegal or violent methods of class struggle. A partywide referendum ousted Haywood from the SP's national executive committee in 1913, and tens of thousands followed him out of the Party.

By 1917, on the other hand, prospects looked bright for syndicalists, political socialists, and AFL conservatives alike. The IWW was growing as never before; the SP was rebuilding through its foreign language federations; AFL headquarters was celebrating Woodrow Wilson's second inauguration. But international developments had already started to shift the ground beneath their feet.

The Great War

By mid-August 1914, the great powers of Europe, along with their clients and colonies in the Balkans, Middle East, and Africa, had divided into two camps and gone to war. Four years later, the "Great War" between the Allies and the Central Powers had claimed 10 million lives in battle. Another 20 million had died of war-related starvation or disease.

The United States declared neutrality at first, but there was considerable sympathy with the Allies—Britain, France, and Russia. Financiers like J. P. Morgan helped to fund their side of the war with close to $3 billion in loans and bond purchases. Businessmen joined politicians like Theodore Roosevelt in the "Preparedness Movement" that pressed for military intervention in support of the Allies. The American Defense Society and other patriotic associations held rallies for intervention and sponsored summer camps where young men could receive military training. Newspapers carried stories of war atrocities by the Central Powers—Germany and the Austro-Hungarian Empire.

Still, many Americans opposed the calls for intervention. German Americans often sympathized with the Central Powers; most Irish Americans condemned any alliance with Britain; Russian Jews were against aid to the czar. Pacifists organized anti-intervention groups like the American Union Against Militarism and the Women's Peace Party. Much of the AFL came out against intervention too. In May 1915, eight national unions headquartered in Indianapolis jointly condemned U.S. entry into the war. Their combined membership totaled about 900,000—almost half of the AFL's rank and file. In June, the Chicago-based Labor's Peace Council organized a national labor coalition to demand strict neutrality, government ownership of munitions companies, and a ban on arms sales to the combatant nations. The many Preparedness parades that took place during the spring and summer of 1916 met fairly widespread opposition from local unions and labor councils.

Employers and authorities alike took note. Strikes by munitions workers were blamed on German agents. Several leaders of Labor's Peace Council were indicted for conspiring with a German officer to instigate strikes. When two of the defendants were convicted, the Council fell apart. Police arrested AFL radicals Tom Mooney and Warren Billings for a bombing that killed ten people at San Francisco's Preparedness parade on July 22, 1916. Despite photographic evidence of Mooney's alibi, both men were convicted; they remained in prison until 1939.

By 1917, Samuel Gompers supported intervention in the war. After President Wilson broke off diplomatic relations with Germany in February 1917, Gompers organized a summit meeting of labor officials. Invitees included members of the AFL Executive Council, national officers of seventy-nine AFL unions, and leaders of the five independent railroad brotherhoods. Gompers had left out the unions most staunchly opposed to intervention—independents like the Amalgamated Clothing Workers and AFL affiliates like the Ladies' Garment Workers, the United Mine Workers, and the Mine, Mill and Smelter Workers (formerly the Western Federation of Miners). At the summit, held on March 12 in Washington, D.C., he set forth a resolution that declared, "Should our country be drawn into the maelstrom of the European conflict, we offer our services." Ruling revisions out of order and denying union leaders' requests to consult with members, he demanded and got unanimous approval for the resolution.

Just weeks later, on April 6, Congress declared war on Germany. The U.S. Army quickly expanded from 200,000 to over 4 million, including nearly 3 million draftees. More than 2 million troops went to Europe, where close to 49,000 were killed in action and another 63,000 died of disease.

On the home front, the federal government took charge of the economy, allocating resources to war-related production, regulating its management, and taking direct control of communications and railroad systems. With the demand for labor soaring and immigration from Europe sharply curtailed by the war, industrial employers recruited new workers from the rural South, the Southwest, and Mexico. By the end of the war, about 500,000 African Americans, even more southern whites, and tens of thousands of Mexican Americans and Mexican immigrants had moved north to industrial cities.

Soaring prices and the push for breakneck war production made 1917 the most strike-torn year in U.S. history to that date, with nearly 4,500 walkouts by over 1.2 million workers. The next year saw fewer strikes (3,353), but they involved just as many people. Workers knew that labor was scarce, that the government encouraged quick concessions to strikers in war industries, and that the owners of these industries were making windfall profits. They also figured that this "war to make the world safe for democracy" should extend democracy to workplaces. In that spirit, many workers struck for the eight-hour day. As one of them later recalled, she and her shopmates in a Philadelphia hosiery mill saw no contradiction between supporting the war effort and asserting themselves through work stoppages. When local boys went off to the Army, she remembered, "We laid down our tools and paraded with our boys to the railroad station, and ate our lunch when they were gone, and took the afternoon off to show our patriotism."

Mobilizing industry, the government also mobilized public opinion in behalf of the war and backed up persuasion with repression. The Committee on Public Information flooded the country with prowar press releases, advertisements, posters, movies, and some 75,000 speakers. The Espionage Act of June 1917 and Sedition Act of May 1918 meanwhile empowered the government to censor antiwar newspapers, ban antiwar literature from the U.S. mail, and jail anyone speaking against the war. About 900 people convicted under these laws went to prison; over 8,000 more were convicted of violating draft laws. The U.S. Justice Department coordinated the American Protective League, a businessmen's group that reported disloyal activity—

about 3 million cases by the war's end. Vigilantes took action as well, with groups like the American Defense Society sending out patrols to break up antiwar gatherings.

Socialist Party leaders immediately condemned Congress's declaration of war and called for "continuous, active, and public opposition," a stand SP members ratified by a margin of eight to one. A few thousand left the Party, among them some prominent unionists like the Machinists' William Johnston and the Typographers' Max Hayes. In May 1917, Socialists joined with pacifists to launch the People's Council of America for Democracy and Peace. Opposing military conscription, defending civil liberties, and organizing against deteriorating labor conditions, it established branches in eighteen states by the end of summer 1917. Its Workmen's Council mobilized antiwar sentiment in unions. The young Socialist A. Philip Randolph and his comrade Chandler Owen founded the monthly journal *The Messenger* to promote unionism, socialism, and war opposition among African Americans. In the state and local elections of November 1917, Socialist candidates did well enough for Eugene Debs to declare, "The Socialist party is rising to power . . . growing more rapidly at this hour than ever in its history."

Antiwar agitation was drawing an increasingly harsh response, however. In early August 1917, the "Green Corn Rebellion"—an open revolt against the draft—erupted in Seminole County, Oklahoma. White, black, and Creek rebels cut telegraph wires, burned bridges, blew up oil pipelines, and declared their plan to march to Washington, D.C., feeding themselves on ripening corn along the way. Oklahoma police arrested 450 people, many of them SP members. At the end of August, a People's Council convention was banned from Minneapolis, then broken up by troops when it moved to Chicago. The War Department warned that it would suspend contracts at factories where unions endorsed the People's Council.

Subsequent measures were aimed at the Socialist Party itself. The Postmaster General banned SP publications from the mail. The Attorney General named A. Philip Randolph "the most dangerous Negro in America," and federal agents ransacked *The Messenger's* offices. The Justice Department indicted twenty-seven SP leaders under the Espionage Act; Debs was sentenced to ten years for making an antiwar speech in Canton, Ohio. Victor Berger was reelected to Congress, then convicted of speaking against the draft, and the House of Representatives refused to seat him. The SP grew in northeastern cities, but heavier losses in rural areas reduced the average monthly membership from about 80,000 in 1917 to 74,500 in 1918.

The most brutal repression fell on the IWW. Wobblies ridiculed fighting for any cause save for industrial freedom, but they did not mobilize against the war or even resist conscription in many cases. Instead, they focused on expanding the One Big Union. IWW members in northwestern lumber camps led a successful strike for the eight-hour day in summer 1917, and organizing drives continued among harvest hands, metal miners, lumber workers, stevedores, and merchant seamen. But the Wobblies' caution regarding the war provided no protection. On July 12, in Bisbee, Arizona, where the IWW was leading a peaceful strike by copper miners, deputized vigilantes packed more than 1,200 strikers into railroad cattle cars, deported them to New Mexico, and left them in the middle of the desert. That same month, Frank Little went to Butte, Montana, where martial law had been declared when copper miners went on strike. On August 1, masked vigilantes seized Little, tied him to a automobile, dragged him to a railroad bridge, and hanged him. On September 5, 1917, federal agents raided Wobbly offices and homes in sixty-four cities. The Justice Department convicted 184 IWW leaders of conspiring to obstruct the war effort. To quote Big Bill Haywood, who was sentenced to twenty years, "The Justice Department had shook the organization as a bulldog shakes an empty sack."

The AFL meanwhile flourished as Gompers campaigned to secure union support for the war, labor participation in wartime industries, and government support for union organizing. The Federation's Executive Council rejected his proposal that it repudiate strikes for the duration of the war. Otherwise his campaign generally met with success. He set up the American Alliance for Labor and Democracy, which used funds from the Committee on Public Information to saturate the AFL with patriotic literature and organize chapters of unionists who pledged to support the war. Gompers also chaired the Labor Committee of the Council of National Defense, recommended unionists for government positions, and persuaded President Wilson to give labor equal representation with employers on the War Labor Board. The Board's Code of Principles endorsed the eight-hour day, equal pay for men and women doing equal work, the right to a living wage, and the right to join a union.

During 1918, AFL membership rose by almost 40 percent, to 3.3 million. The United Mine Workers had close to 500,000 members (over 80 percent of all coal miners); the Carpenters and Machinists had more than 330,000 each. By 1919, more than 1.8 million railroad workers belonged to AFL affiliates or the independent brotherhoods. Many of the new union members came from sectors of the work force that the AFL and the railroad brotherhoods had declined to organize in the past.

Some were women. While the Amalgamated Association of Street and Electrical Railway Employees protested the hiring of streetcar "conductorettes," the Brotherhood of Railway Clerks, which had few female members before the war, recruited some 35,000 women in 1917–18. By summer 1918, even the Machinists had enrolled 12,500 women, who made up about 5 percent of the membership.

The "new immigrants" from eastern and southern Europe joined unions in unprecedented numbers. Chicago meatpacking workers—primarily Poles, Lithuanians, and Slovaks—poured into the Amalgamated Meatcutters and Butcher Workmen, which grew from 7,300 members in 1916 to nearly 63,000 by the end of the war. In March 1918, federal mediation brought pay increases and union recognition to the packinghouses. Inspired by this advance, AFL headquarters pulled together a committee of twenty-four national unions to organize the steel industry, where European immigrants also predominated.

Workers of color were not so welcome. The AFL still excluded anyone of Asian descent. Unions in meatpacking and steel signed up Latinos, but in the Southwest, where their numbers were greatest, most AFL affiliates required that Spanish-speaking members be citizens and assigned them to segregated locals. For African Americans, AFL unionism could mean segregation, wholesale exclusion, or worse. In the pulp and paper mills of Bogalusa, Louisiana, the Carpenters recruited black and white workers into separate locals; in Key West, Florida, the union refused to admit black carpenters and thus prevented their employment on an Army construction project. AFL organizers in steel signed up black workers in Cleveland and Wheeling but not in Pittsburgh, where white unionists were so hostile that the black community came to see them as the main obstacle to its advancement. The atmosphere was even more hateful in East St. Louis, Illinois. In May 1917, its central labor council vowed to tackle the "growing menace" of black migration to the city. When two policemen were killed in a gunfight in a black neighborhood on July 1, white workers mustered in union halls for a two-day rampage against African Americans. At least thirty-nine people were killed, many more burned out of their homes, and some 6,000 black residents fled the city.

THE WAR'S AFTERMATH

When the Great War ended on November 11, 1918, total union membership—in AFL affiliates, railroad brotherhoods, and other unions—topped 4 million. A steelworker in Canton, Ohio, captured the spirit of the times: "The justice of the demand for a fairer share has been established. It is not going to be given up now that the war has ended." Organizing continued full speed. By 1920, AFL membership stood at nearly 4.1 million, and total union membership exceeded 5 million. Almost 20 percent of industrial workers belonged to a union.

The years 1919–22 saw more than 10,000 strikes involving over 8 million workers—more than 4 million in 1919 alone, a fifth of the labor force outside domestic work. Strikes rolled through California citrus fields, southern cotton mills, Paterson's silk mills, New England telephone companies, Bogalusa's pulp and paper mills, El Paso laundries, Arizona cotton fields, Tampa cigar factories, even the Boston police force. In February 1919, a general strike in Seattle mobilized 100,000 workers, including AFL members, independent unions of Japanese butchers, railroad workers and others, and unorganized workers. They ran Seattle for five entirely peaceful days, calling off the strike when troops dispatched to "restore order" were nearing the city.

Workers in U.S. colonies took militant action as well. Against the advice of Samuel Gompers, Puerto Rico's Federación Libre de Trabajadores had staged wartime strikes in the sugar and tobacco industries. Veteran labor radical Luisa Capetillo had led a strike by 30,000 agricultural laborers on the eastern side of the island in 1918. In 1919, the FLT's Partido Socialista Puertorriqueño (PSP) debated independence but did not endorse it, deciding instead to return to the question once "the social democracy of labor" had been achieved. In the 1920 elections, the PSP won nearly a third of the popular vote. In the Philippines, the Congreso Obrero de Filipinas (COF) supported its Nationalist Party allies with a no-strike pledge in 1919. Even so, the COF's Domingo Simeon was implicated in a fatal bombing during a 1920 strike against the Manila Electric and Railway Company and sentenced to life in prison. The situation in Hawaii was more complicated. In January 1920, Filipino and Japanese unions on Oahu led a strike by more than 8,000 field hands—70 percent of the sugar plantation workforce. The planters used divide-and-conquer tactics to break the strike. They settled with Filipino leaders; held out against the Japanese Federation, charging that it was out to "Japanise" Hawaii; and hired Koreans, Portuguese, and native Hawaiians to replace Japanese strikers, who gave up after six months.

Stateside labor activism expanded its political dimensions. Strikers demanded the release of political prisoners, public takeovers of open shop industries, and labor participation in the European peace talks. Unions looked to political action. In January 1919, New York unions formed the American Labor Party, calling for restoration of civil rights and "democratic control of industry and commerce, by those who work." By 1920, AFL unions and the railroad brotherhoods backed twenty-three state labor parties, which merged into the Farmer-Labor Party that July.

Political realignment rippled through radical labor as well. Socialists who supported the Bolshevik Revolution in Russia broke away from the SP in September 1919 and formed two new revolutionary parties—the Communist Party (mostly immigrants) and the Communist Labor Party (mainly native-born activists). In 1923, they merged with other pro–Bolshevik factions to found the Workers' Party of America, later known as the Communist Party USA. Many Wobblies joined the new communist movement, Big Bill Haywood and Elizabeth Gurley Flynn among them.

Racial conflicts divided workers and unions. In the summer of 1919, race riots erupted in cities and towns across the country, with African Americans fighting off assaults on their communities. A five-day riot in Chicago halted cross-racial organizing in the packinghouses.

Radicalism and racial pride surged among black workers. Cyril Briggs and Richard Moore left the SP in 1919 to found the African Black Brotherhood, dedicated to socialism and black liberation; by 1923, the Brotherhood had 7,000 members, including a chapter of West Virginia coal miners. Marcus Garvey's Universal Negro Improvement Association (UNIA) won a gigantic following. Founded in 1914 in Jamaica to promote black pride and power, the UNIA had half a million U.S. members by 1921. Inside the AFL, black unionists attacked the failure to press affiliates on their color bars. At the Federation's 1920 convention, David Grange of the Marine Cooks and Stewards Union shouted from the floor, "It did not offend the dignity of any man to send the Negro into the firing lines in France."

Repression of radicals only increased after the war ended. The Justice Department established a Radical Division—headed by young J. Edgar Hoover—to compile dossiers on subversives. On the night of January 2, 1920, Attorney General A. Mitchell Palmer deployed federal agents in seventy cities across the country to arrest and detain 10,000 people identified in Department files as aliens and Communists. About 500 were deported; the rest turned out to be citizens, or immigrants without radical ties. State governments joined the hunt for subversives. New York's Lusk Committee began to investigate "un-American" activities in 1919; it was the first of many such initiatives. By 1921, thirty-two states outlawed "criminal syndicalism"—advocating illegal labor tactics, distributing literature that encouraged them, or belonging to an organization that endorsed them. In 1923, California sent 164 Wobblies and Communists to prison. Massachusetts charged Nicola Sacco and Bartolomeo Vanzetti, Italian immigrants active in

Boston anarchist circles, with a double murder during a payroll robbery; they were convicted in July 1921, despite sturdy alibis, and finally executed August 23, 1927.

Vigilante attacks on radicals also continued. On November 11, 1919, an American Legion contingent attacked the IWW office in Centralia, Washington; one legionnaire was killed and all of the Wobblies defending the office arrested. Among them was the lumberjack Wesley Everest, just back from the war and still wearing his Army uniform. That night, the town's jail turned him over to a group of "upstanding citizens" who castrated and hanged him and riddled his corpse with bullets. Six other men who defended the IWW office that day got prison sentences of twenty-five to fifty years.

Vigilantes targeted interracial unionism too, whether or not the IWW was involved. In Bogalusa, two AFL unions—the Carpenters and the International Timber Workers—united black and white workers to strike the Great Southern Lumber Company in 1919. The company organized and armed a Self-Preservation and Loyalty League to harass the strikers. On November 22, 1919, League members opened fire on Sol Dacus, the strike's most vocal black leader, killing him and four white workers who had come to his aid.

Racism even tainted the final victory of the women's suffrage movement. By 1917, both major parties endorsed votes for women, who had already been enfranchised by eleven states. With its two million members— from wage workers and housewives to professionals and socialites—the National American Woman Suffrage Association was one of the largest women's networks in the country. In January 1918, the House of Representatives narrowly passed the Nineteenth Amendment for woman suffrage; after several defeats, the Senate passed it in June 1919. Ratification came down to a single state—Tennessee—where white suffragists argued that enfranchising educated white women would help to preserve racial segregation, and the state legislature approved the Amendment by one vote. It became law in August 1920.

Attacks on radicals and interracialism heralded a massive assault on all labor activism. After the War Labor Board was dismantled in June 1919, corporate America launched a new campaign for the open shop. The first target was AFL organizing in steel. By mid-1919, the steel drive had signed up about 100,000 workers, a quarter of the industry's labor force. When the companies began to fire union activists, organizers called a strike for September 22. Within a week, 365,000 men had walked out. U.S. Steel led the counterattack. It mobilized local and state courts and police departments, which deputized company guards and private detectives. Pickets were beaten, arrested, and jailed by the thousands, and twenty strikers were killed. Immigrants came under especially heavy assault. Steel executives described the strikers as ignorant foreigners led by "red radicals," and the press agreed. The *Philadelphia Inquirer* reported that immigrant strikers were "penetrated with the Bolshevik idea." The *New York Times* considered Slavs the most dangerous—"steeped in the doctrines of the class struggle and social overthrow, ignorant and easily misled." Samuel Gompers tried in vain to persuade his friends in government to impose arbitration. In January 1920, the steel strike and organizing drive collapsed in defeat.

Hostility to immigrants took many other forms as well. It fueled the spectacularly unsuccessful experiment with the prohibition of alcohol, inaugurated in January 1920 under the Constitution's Eighteenth Amendment. Many advocates of prohibition had touted it a means of controlling unruly immigrant communities, and enforcement of the ban was now aimed disproportionately at immigrants. Immigrants were also subject to vigilante attack. Coal miners in West Frankfort, Illinois, were on strike when rumors circulated in August 1920 that Italians had committed some local bank robberies and murders. Striking miners joined nativist mobs in a three-day rampage against foreigners and drove hundreds of immigrants—including fellow strikers—out of town. Anti-immigrant sentiment passed into law at every level. An Alabama statute called for state inspection of Roman Catholic convents, said to imprison kidnapped Protestant girls. In 1913, California had barred Asian immigrants from owning land; now they were barred from leasing it. Federal immigration laws passed in 1921, 1924, and 1927 altogether excluded Asians and reduced arrivals from eastern and southern Europe to a few thousand a year. The annual number of deportations climbed from 3,600 in 1923 to 16,000 in 1929.

Employers still needed new workers, and Congress did not restrict immigration from the Americas or U.S. colonies. Filipinos on the U.S. mainland, mostly young men working in agriculture, rose in number from about 5,600 in 1920 to 45,300 in 1926. The numbers of Mexican immigrants in the border states expanded from 423,000 in 1920 to 1.2 million in 1930. But the U.S. Border Patrol, established in 1924, helped to define a new category of employee, the undocumented worker.

That most AFL members were white U.S. citizens did not shield their unions from attack. Inspired by the steel strike's defeat, employers in industry after industry formed associations to drive out unions. Corporate publicists called the open shop "the spirit of the Constitution." The *Tampa Morning Tribune* declared in August 1920, "The greatest menace today to the

perpetuation of the free institutions of the United States is to be found in the destructive propaganda, aims and practices of the American Federation of Labor." More than a hundred detective agencies meanwhile supplied companies with operatives to spy on employees, identify activists for dismissal, start fights at union meetings, beat up strikers—anything to disrupt union organizing.

Unions fought back by every means available, including gigantic strikes by textile workers, railroad workers, and coal miners in 1922. But the hopes of 1919 had evaporated. The 1920 elections brought Republicans into office. A short, sharp depression in 1921–22 threw close to a fifth of the nation's labor force out of work. Strike after strike went down to defeat, and unions were crushed or crippled. By 1923, total union membership had dropped to about 3.6 million. Unions had disintegrated in meatpacking and textiles, the United Mine Workers and Machinists had suffered major losses, and the AFL had lost a quarter of its members.

Labor's postwar changes included the passing of the three men who had long dominated the movement—Sam Gompers, Eugene Debs, and Bill Haywood. Gompers went first. Though already sick, he went to Mexico City in 1924 for the Fourth Congress of the Pan-American Federation of Labor (PAFL). Originally proposed to improve relations among labor federations in the Americas, the PAFL had actually started (with secret funding from the U.S. government) when Gompers wanted to enlist labor support for ending Mexico's neutrality in the Great War. Its first meeting, in November 1918, came too late for that, and the PAFL did little to redress Latin American grievances against the U.S. government or North American unions. In 1923, Mexico's labor federation asked for help defending the national government against a rebellion. Gompers denounced the rebels as "red" imposters and directed AFL affiliates to watch for arms shipments to the insurgents. The rebellion crushed, the Fourth Congress welcomed Gompers in triumph. But his journey had destroyed what remained of his health. Carried back to San Antonio, he died on December 13, 1924.

Debs died on October 20, 1926. He had started his ten-year sentence for sedition in April 1919; running as "Prisoner 9653," he won over 900,000 votes in the presidential election of 1920. Pardoned on Christmas Day 1921, he could not revive the Socialist Party. It lost labor influence virtually everywhere except New York garment unions, and its membership dropped from less than 27,000 in 1920 to under 8,000 in 1928. Already sick with diabetes, Bill Haywood jumped bail after his conviction for sedition and fled to the

Soviet Union, where he died on May 18, 1928. The IWW became little more than a shadow, losing members to mechanization in mining, timber and longshore work, and splitting in 1924 in a fight over central authority versus local autonomy.

All three men lived long enough to see the organizations to which they had given so much of their lives battered or broken entirely. Gompers had come to trust the government that Debs hoped to take over and Haywood planned to smash. The government turned on them all—not all at once or with equal fury, but in the end without much differentiation. Corporations dominated the political landscape. Just as the military protected their interests abroad, lawmakers, courts, and police protected them at home. As American historian W. E. B. Du Bois observed in 1924, "Modern imperialism and modern industrialism are one and the same system."

CHAPTER

AMERICA, INC.

The postwar depression gave way to a spectacular economic boom, one of the biggest in U.S. history. The boom was based on industrial production and business profits. From 1924 to 1929, auto and steel production rose by nearly 50 percent; chemicals and electrical equipment by even more. Total pretax corporate profits increased by more than half, from $7.6 billion in 1924 to $11.7 billion in 1929. Profits financed more mergers and consolidations. More than 300,000 industrial corporations operated in 1929: the largest 200—giants like U.S. Steel, Anaconda Copper, General Motors, and Westinghouse Electric—made more profits than all the rest combined. Capital itself was concentrated: more than 4,000 bank mergers and acquisitions took place between 1923 and 1929. Speculators did very well. Average stock prices nearly tripled between 1922 and 1929. By 1929, there were 486 investment corporations—stocks and bonds their only assets—and one new one started (on the average) every day.

Many workers shared in this prosperity. Average wages rose modestly but steadily during the boom years, while the cost of food and other necessities remained relatively constant. Consumer credit magnified the purchasing power of personal incomes. People of even moderate means could buy goods from clothing to radios to vacuum cleaners to automobiles, all on the installment plan. Homes too: the best-paid workers found mortgages easier to get. More and more families could afford to keep their children in school past the eighth grade.

For the labor movement, however, times were lean. Corporations elaborated their campaign to undermine unionism, with the continuing collaboration of politicians, judges, and police. During the 1920s, state and federal courts issued 921 labor injunctions, about the same number used from 1877 to 1919. Police routinely arrested strikers—7,500 during a 1926 garment workers' strike in New York City; 2,400 during a 1928 textile strike in New Bedford, Massachusetts. In major cities, special "Red Squad" police units surveilled and harassed labor radicals, identifying activists for employer blacklists and aliens for deportation. Fewer and smaller strikes failed more often—almost always, in fact. Most leaders of the AFL and railroad brotherhoods slid into a downright paralyzing conservatism, renouncing militancy and giving up on efforts to organize the unorganized. In spring 1929, William Green, Samuel Gompers's successor as AFL president, declared that the "appalling indifference of the workers themselves" ruled out the unionization of mass production.

But even as Green wrote these words, strikes for higher pay, shorter hours, and union recognition were starting to sweep through southern textile mills. And such uprisings, which occurred in other settings too, were not the only cracks in the regime of corporate America during the boom years. Throughout those years, workers engaged in many forms of subtle resistance to corporate power as well as sporadic outbreaks of open defiance. If William Green failed to take these rumblings seriously, he was scarcely alone. The labor movement's decline combined with rising prosperity to persuade many observers that worker militancy was on its deathbed. As 1929 drew to a close, however, the stock market went bust and prosperity gave way to a depression that would be the worst the U.S. had ever seen. By 1933—just a decade after the spectacular boom had begun—a third of the nation was destitute and, though unions were weaker than ever, the rumblings of discontent in working-class communities had grown too loud for anyone to ignore.

THE ROARING TWENTIES

The 1920s are usually portrayed as a light-hearted time when flappers, bootleggers, and entertainers set the trends in American life. But big businessmen were the era's biggest celebrities. Reporters interviewed them, photographers pursued them, newspapers and magazines featured their thoughts on every topic from business and national and international politics to sports and culture. Economist Stuart Chase later observed of the boom years that the business magnate had become "the dictator of our destinies," replacing "the statesman, the priest, the philosopher, as the creator of standards of ethics and behavior," and reigning as "the final authority on the conduct of American society."

In the workplace the employer ruled absolutely, his rights protected by courts and enforced by police or private operatives. But as immigration restrictions tightened over the decade, employers spent more on efficiency experts than on detectives. More and more firms adopted scientific management, not so much to break craft control of work but to get more work out of each employee. Likewise labor-saving machinery. Mechanization was better than immigrant labor: "Machinery 'stays put,' " declared one business journal in 1923. "It does not decide to go out on strike . . . go to Europe . . . or take a job in the next town." Technology and workflow design got assembly lines moving four times faster in 1928 than in 1918. Workers' average output in manufacturing rose by more than a fifth from 1923 to 1929; by more than a quarter in mining. The Aetna Life Insurance Company's scientific management of clerical work raised the output of typists and billing clerks by as much as 50 percent.

The drive for productivity prompted new attention to employee welfare programs, designed, in the words of an American Telephone and Telegraph executive, "to help our workers get their worries out of their minds so they can get on the job 'rarin' to go.' " Employers invested in workplace safety, lighting, and ventilation. They financed recreational and educational programs and medical services for employees (and sometimes their families too). They arranged mortgage loans and stock options, group insurance against illness, accident, and death, and retirement pensions (provided by more than 350 companies nationwide in 1929). There were limits. Only the largest and most prosperous companies operated extensive welfare plans, and the most generous benefits were the least common—a survey of large firms found only a fifth offering stock options or pensions. Benefits were not equally distributed within the workforce. The better the pay, the better the benefits.

Such corporate benevolence was predicated on corporate control, typically described in benevolent terms. Charles Schwab—then president of Bethlehem Steel—told a gathering of steel executives that the industry's workers counted on them to provide "welfare, progress and happiness." A U.S. Rubber spokesman put it more bluntly: "Management must lead."

Nevertheless, some show of democracy could be expedient. Perhaps the

most innovative feature of the corporate labor policies in the 1920s was the
Employee Representation Plan (ERP), first developed by the Colorado Fuel
& Iron Company (CFI) after the defeat of the 1913–14 strike. The War
Labor Board endorsed the concept—by summer 1919, there were 225
ERPs; by early 1922 about 725. By the end of the decade, ERPs covered
more than 1.5 million workers, most of them employees of the industrial
giants.

ERPs represented a new management philosophy, the "citizenship theory of labor relations." In contrast to unions, they allowed workers to help
manage their work without fighting their employers. The joint labor-
management committees established under ERPs had very limited jurisdictions. They discussed employee welfare programs, developed schemes for
improving efficiency and eliminating waste, adjudicated minor disputes,
grievances, and complaints about unfair dismissals. And not much more. An
immigrant coal miner who participated in CFI's ERP later said: "Under
union, miners have educated men who no work for the company, but give
all their time to take up grievances. Pretty hard for a man who works for the
company to take up grievances because he afraid that if he make the boss
mad, maybe he be fired, or given a bad place." Schwab himself said, "I will
not permit myself to be put in a position of having labor dictate to management."

The concern for employee welfare and the respect for employee rights
expressed in welfare capitalism supposedly demonstrated that, as one business magazine proclaimed in 1929, "the interests of the employer and employee are mutual and at bottom identical." Just in case this persuasion failed,
many employers also required workers to sign contracts pledging they did
not belong to any union, would not join a union, and would neither strike
nor encourage others to strike. By the end of the decade, over 1.25 million
people worked under these "yellow dog contracts," and dozens of court injunctions directed union organizers to avoid even talking to them.

Corporate clout in government reached such heights in the 1920s that it
was hard to tell where business left off and government began. The Republican Party held the White House and dominated Capitol Hill throughout
the decade. All three presidents were great fans of business. Warren Harding
(elected 1920, died in office 1923) presided over an administration famous
for graft, corruption, and fraudulent sales of government property. Businessmen appreciated his strong support for protective tariffs, and opposition to
government regulation of business. Calvin Coolidge inherited the office
from Harding and was elected in his own right in 1924, promising to lower
taxes and reduce the federal budget. Congress cut income taxes in half in

1926, and sharply reduced estate taxes; businessmen loved it. President Herbert Hoover had worked as a mining engineer in China, Africa, and Latin America, and served both Harding and Coolidge as Secretary of Commerce before his election in 1928. He promoted trade associations and helped U.S. companies expand their overseas markets. Andrew Mellon, whose family was worth about $450 million, was Secretary of the Treasury in all three administrations.

The Democrats were just as friendly to business, but less successful. In 1924, they nominated John Davis, chief attorney for the Morgan banking companies, for President. Their 1928 candidate—New York governor Alfred Smith—picked investor John J. Raskob to chair his campaign and head the Democratic National Committee. Raskob moved the party headquarters to the General Motors building in New York City, where it operated, in the words of one visitor, with the "efficiency which distinguishes the loftier interiors of American business enterprise."

Government took care of business in many ways. The Supreme Court voided minimum wage laws as unconstitutional, since "there can be no difference between the case of selling labor and the case of selling goods." The Justice Department gave up applying antitrust laws to corporations. The Bureau of Indian Affairs—especially under Harding's Interior Secretary Albert Fall—helped loot Native Americans. After the Midwest Refining Company found oil in the San Juan district of the Navajo reservation in 1921, the BIA appointed a Navajo Business Council to sign oil leases. Its legality was quite dubious, so the next year the Bureau held elections for a new Tribal Council, which signed the leases, while the investigation of the scandal involving Teapot Dome (a Navy oil reserve field opened to the Mammoth Oil Company) exposed Fall's regular receipt of cash gifts from oil companies. In the Oklahoma "Oilpatch," state courts adjudicated disputes over mineral rights on Indian Territory allotments. When a local banker became court-appointed guardian of Choctaw orphan Ledcie Stechi, he received the income from leasing her twenty acres of oil fields, while she died of malnutrition.

U.S. foreign policy likewise promoted U.S. business. The State Department helped broker foreign loans to increase demand for U.S. exports. After U.S. banks loaned $110 million to the German government, Ford, General Motors, General Electric, Standard Oil, Dow Chemical, the Du Pont gunpowder company, and other U.S. corporations set up German operations. State Department support for Wall Street loans to foreign governments persuaded many American bondholders that the U.S. backed the foreign bonds, which helped to sell the bonds. That turned out not to be true, but U.S.

troops did stand ready to protect American investments overseas. From 1922, Marines landed in China again and again. The occupation of the Dominican Republic ended in 1924, but Haiti remained under U.S. control until 1934. In 1924 and 1925, U.S. soldiers went to Honduras to protect American property. In 1925, U.S. troops put down a general strike in Panama. In 1926, U.S. troops returned to Nicaragua, beginning a new series of interventions that continued until 1933.

In short, every level of government operated on the principle that whatever benefitted corporations would benefit Americans one and all. As President Coolidge put it, "The business of America is business."

Business values permeated society, spread by mass media and education. Colleges and universities expanded courses in business administration, accounting, marketing, and related subjects. High schools beefed up vocational curricula to match corporate labor requirements. Corporate handouts were used in elementary school courses on science, personal hygiene, and social studies.

The media themselves were consolidated like other businesses. Newspaper chains like the Hearst syndicate bought or drove out independent publishers; by 1927, the chains controlled more than a third of newspaper circulation. Syndicated fare—advice columns, sports features, political cartoons, and editorials—dominated the "news." In the new radio industry, the government promoted consolidation. Broadcast radio began in late 1920. By the end of the decade stations broadcast from cities all across the country, and one-third of U.S. households owned a radio set. Many early stations were run by churches, ethnic associations, and labor councils, each broadcasting as many hours with as much power as it could afford. Once Congress created the Federal Communications Commission to regulate frequency, power, and schedule in 1927, the best slots went to commercial stations.

The profit in media came from advertising, which expanded tremendously as companies competed to sell the huge volume of goods they produced. Besides manipulating fantasies and anxieties to create demand for products, advertising also promoted good work habits. For ad agency executive Bruce Barton, advertising's chief value lay in its capacity to "make people dissatisfied with the old and out-of-date and . . . send them out to work harder to get the latest model—whether that model be an icebox or a rug, or a new home." Corporate public relations infiltrated advertising into the news itself, using techniques pioneered by the wartime Committee on Public Information. For many corporations, a reputation for service to the community was at least as useful as brand-name recognition. Corporate donations to parks, recreation centers, libraries, churches, Boy and Girl Scout troops, made effective advertising when reported as news. One investigator found that over half the stories in the December 29, 1929, issue of the *New York Times* originated with press agents.

If business sometimes seemed to be a religion, sometimes religion looked like business. One of the bestselling titles of 1925 and 1926 was Bruce Barton's *The Man Nobody Knows.* He portrayed Jesus as history's greatest business executive, who "picked up twelve humble men and created an organization that won the world." Many churches borrowed advertising and public relations techniques to recruit members and raise money.

Business values influenced some feminists. The National Women's Party (NWP) opposed protective labor legislation for women, echoing business arguments that labor laws restricted individual freedom and that corporate executives understood that treating women employees well was good business. When a press agent for the tobacco industry approached journalist Ruth Hale of the NWP, she recruited ten feminists to march in New York City's 1929 Easter Parade smoking cigarettes—described in the press release as "torches of freedom." In the real world, women working in offices were mostly confined to low-paying, dead-end jobs, and many employers hired only single women, and dismissed them when they got married.

Business methods could certainly make bigotry profitable. One-time preacher William Simmons made his living promoting fraternal organizations; in 1915, he started a new Ku Klux Klan, which grew to about 5,000 members in Georgia and Alabama by the end of the war. In 1920, Simmons made a deal with Atlanta-based public relations agents Edward Clarke and Elizabeth Tyler: for 80 percent of each initiation fee, they would market the Klan. Clarke and Taylor hired paid organizers ("kleagles") and trained them in market research, studying communities to identify whichever group was most hated by local white, native-born Protestants—not just people of color, but also radicals, immigrants, bootleggers, Catholics, Mormons. Kleagles encouraged women to "stand alongside our men," and admitted them to full Klan membership. They marketed a full range of regalia and literature. By mid-decade, Klan membership reached about 4 million, with chapters all across the country and influence in both Democratic and Republican parties. Enriched by shares in the proceeds, the Klan's national and regional leaders then turned on one another in an orgy of lawsuits and allegations of arson, blackmail, kidnapping, and murder. By the end of the decade membership had fallen to about 40,000.

To the extent that operations like the Klan threatened social peace, many businessmen opposed them; financial considerations could restrain even virulent bigotry. Henry Ford hated Jews. From 1920 to 1926, his *Dearborn Inde-*

pendent newspaper (distributed nationally through Ford dealers) ran articles alleging Jewish involvement in monopolies, Bolshevism, wars, foreclosures, political corruption, bootlegging, high rents, and short skirts. In 1925, American Farm Bureau attorney Aaron Sapiro sued the *Independent* for libel. To avoid paying damages, Ford publicly repudiated his accusations, though his personal opinions did not change, nor did his admiration for Nazi programs diminish.

To some people, poverty seemed to be on the verge of disappearance, thanks to the acumen and benevolence of business. President Coolidge saw a divine plan at work: "The man who builds a factory builds a temple, the man who works there worships there. We have seen the people of America build a new heaven and a new earth." Campaigning for the presidency in 1928, Herbert Hoover boasted that Washington's cooperation with Wall Street had brought Americans "nearer to the abolition of poverty, to the abolition of fear and want, than humanity has ever reached before."

True for some but not all. Five percent of households had accounts with stockbrokers, and 95 percent did not. About a third of the nation's total personal income went to the richest 5 percent of the people. The top 10 percent spent half the nation's expenditures on health care, education, and recreation. Modern research suggests that half of all U.S. families in the 1920s had to skimp on necessities. In New York City, some 2 million people lived in substandard housing. Half of U.S. households lacked indoor flush toilets; a third lacked electric lights. Workplaces were dangerous: deaths on the job averaged around 25,000 a year, work-related injuries 100,000 a year, throughout the decade.

Average real wages (adjusted for inflation) rose about one percent annually from 1923 to 1929. Some workers did better. Skilled construction workers in unions did very well: depending on their trade, their wages rose between 22 and 36 percent overall. Printers, paper makers, hosiery and knitting mill workers, autoworkers all did better than average.

Others did worse. Wages for domestic work rose about two percent over the period. For women in manufacturing, wages hardly changed. Though skilled railroad workers made much better wages, unskilled railroad laborers actually made less. Wages also declined in textile, leather, glass, tobacco, and mining. Cotton textile workers did poorly: in the South wages fell more than 10 percent, close to 5 percent in the North. Coal miners did very poorly: anthracite miners' wages dropped 14 percent from 1923 to 1929, bituminous 30 percent. Agricultural workers' wages fell in the early 1920s and did not recover—they ended the decade at about the level of 1914.

Better hourly wages did not always translate to better annual income for workers not steadily employed. The federal government did not yet keep unemployment statistics, but the national average among nonagricultural workers was probably about 7 percent. Local surveys showed some higher rates: 10–25 percent in Cincinnati's six poorest wards. Rising industrial productivity contributed to this unemployment. While manufacturing output nearly doubled from 1921 to 1929, the industrial workforce in 1929 remained about the size it had been in 1919, close to 8.6 million.

Mechanization also affected farm work—tractor use increased by a factor of ten during the decade. New crop-management methods and greater use of fertilizers also increased farm productivity. But agriculture never recovered from the postwar depression, and overproduction just made the market worse. By 1929, average farm income per capita was little more than a third the nonfarm average. Over the decade about 13 million acres of farmland were abandoned, and by 1930 almost half the country's farmers were tenants, and about half of family-owned farms mortgaged.

Farm workers suffered the most. A California grower described migrant farm workers in 1920: "They camped along the roadside, and lived in tents under which a family, invariably a large one, slept. They cooked in the open exposed to all manner of dust and filth and drew water from a creek, many times a creek that ceased to flow but [left] enough in the holes for them to drink." Child labor was common in the fields. In upper Midwest beet fields—where harvesting was especially back-breaking—investigators found about half the harvesters under fifteen, and quite a few as young as six. Government Indian schools sent students to work in the Colorado and Kansas beet fields for wages as low as 9 cents a day. Children were especially useful to beet growers—the plants were thinned with a short hoe (declared illegal many years later). Beets were harvested with a hook-topped machete, which could pick and top the beet in a single swing. Experienced *betabelaros* usually had a permanent stoop in their backs, and often fewer than ten fingers.

Even prosperity might be deceptive. Some workers could afford to flee the city for a home in one of the proliferating suburban developments, but this material comfort had an underside. Many suburban communities barred home sales to people of color, Jews, and other racial and ethnic minorities, and Klan organizers found many suburban customers. Suburban households were often deep in debt for houses, cars, furniture, appliances—consumer credit was easy to get and hard to pay off. For housewives, suburban life could be more isolated than city life, shopping less convenient and more expensive. Even with modern labor-saving appliances, housework and childcare in the 1920s still required about the same amount of time as two decades earlier—

about fifty-five hours a week—and some wives had to work outside their homes to help pay the bills.

THE LABOR MOVEMENT OF THE TWENTIES

For the labor movement, the 1920s were an era of defeat, retreat, and division. Total union membership fell from about 3.6 million in 1923 to 3.4 million in 1929; AFL unions had 2,769,000 members in 1929, 1.3 million fewer than in 1920. The losses were not evenly spread. The railroad brotherhoods and craft unions generally maintained their strength. Building trades unions actually grew. But industrial unions in mining, mass production, and agriculture suffered enormous losses. The United Mine Workers—half a million strong in 1920—had only 84,000 members in 1929. The Mine, Mill and Smelter Workers barely survived, as did industrial unions in clothing and textiles. Unions of agricultural workers virtually disappeared. Organized labor moved in increasingly conservative directions.

Before Gompers's death, the AFL experimented with independent political action, endorsing the 1924 Progressive Party presidential candidate Senator Robert La Follette of Wisconsin. When Gompers was succeeded by William Green, a Mine Workers official who had served more than a decade on the Federation's Executive Council, the *Richmond Times-Dispatch* predicted, "Capital has nothing to fear during his regime." Under his leadership, the AFL abandoned independent political action and militant demands. Cooperation with employers became the guiding principle of AFL and railroad brotherhood leaders. They endorsed scientific management and other speed-up schemes. Twenty rail unions dropped demands for permanent government control of the railroads in return for union recognition, and joined with railroad executives to draft the Railway Labor Act. Passed by Congress in 1926, the Act set up a system of compulsory arbitration and presidential intervention that made legal strikes almost impossible.★

Labor leaders echoed businessmen in their love of capitalism. Some even became capitalists themselves, starting union-owned banks and other business ventures. The Brotherhood of Locomotive Engineers pioneered this experiment, sponsoring more than a dozen banks by the late 1920s, investing more than $60 million in real estate, and buying coal mines that employed nonunion labor. Other labor banks were started by the Amalgamated Clothing Workers, the Ladies Garment Workers, the Brotherhood of Railway Clerks, and the New York State Federation of Labor.

★ In 1936, Congress extended the Act's coverage to airlines.

Some union business was less respectable. Labor racketeering had been well established in the building trades in San Francisco, Chicago, and New York before the Great War, where it functioned like any other trust combination. Employers' associations rigged bids and divided up the work, and union strikes disciplined would-be competitors, or drove them out of the industry. Unions had also sometimes hired their own thugs. "Dopey Benny" Fein enforced union rules on employers in New York's needles trades and sold favors—raiding a manufacturer cost $150 to $600 depending on size; removing an individual usually cost $200. Fein's mob could also help inside a union, persuading any trouble maker to retire, in at least one case executing a strikebreaker after a "trial." Fein even accepted out-of-town contracts, dispatching men to jobs in Philadelphia and Cleveland for $7.50 a day plus expenses. Profits from Prohibition promoted even more syndication in the crime industry, and gangsters like Al Capone in Chicago and Dutch Schultz in New York City took over some local unions entirely, raided their treasuries, and sold "strike insurance" to employers.

AFL and national union officials—like public officials—proved unable or unwilling to clean out these gangsters, and sometimes shared in the profits, while organizing activity faltered. Craft union leaders ignored most workers in their own industries, and everywhere else.

Labor radicals had not entirely disappeared. After the failure of the 1919 steel strike, William Z. Foster, one-time Wobbly and member of the steel drive's organizing committee, had tried to start a new organization, the Trade Union Educational League (TUEL), to work for industrial unionism in the AFL and amalgamation of the railroad brotherhoods, and to promote independent political action and racial harmony in the labor movement. When Foster joined the Workers (Communist) Party (after it renounced dual unionism), Communists began to build the League. TUEL activists and sympathizers were elected to office in a number of unions, including some districts of the United Mine Workers, and won top posts in the Ladies' Garment Workers and the Fur and Leather Workers. Tens of thousands of workers went on strike under TUEL leadership in New York's garment industry (1926), the silk factories of Passaic, New Jersey (1926), and the cotton mills of New Bedford, Massachusetts (1928). After AFL leaders expelled these radicals from their unions, the banished insurgents started their own "red" unions among coal miners, garment workers, and textile workers. In August 1929, the TUEL reorganized as the Trade Union Unity League (TUUL) and set out to build a left-wing labor federation to rival the AFL.

Radicals also kept a foothold in labor education. Their best-known project was the Brookwood Labor College, a residential two-year school in Katonah, New York, where about 50 students a year were financed by unions like the Mine Workers, Machinists, Ladies Garment Workers and several railroad brotherhoods. The AFL ordered its affiliates to dissociate from the school in 1928, but Brookwood had already graduated hundreds of rank-and-file activists, and the school stayed open until 1937.

Workers themselves often resisted corporate power, sometimes covertly. Writer Louis Adamic recalled his days as a factory hand in eastern Pennsylvania: "After the suppression of the radical element in 1922 or thereabouts, workers' radicalism . . . found individual, personal expression in doing as little as possible for the wages they received and wasting as much material as possible." At the Swift meatpacking plant in Chicago, women packing bacon slices enforced an agreement to turn out no more than 144 packages an hour by passing twisted, tattered slices to anyone who tried to break the quota. Many employees called their Employee Representation Plan the "Kiss Me Club," and declined to vote in elections for ERP committees.

Organizing drives and strikes continued to break out among workers abandoned by organized labor. Black railroad workers employed by the Pullman Company turned away from their ERP and started the Brotherhood of Sleeping Car Porters and Maids in 1925 under the leadership of A. Philip Randolph (by then no longer associated with the Socialist Party). The AFL refused Randolph a national charter and left the members in federal locals. But neither red-baiting nor Federation indifference deterred the union, though it took twelve years to win a national contract. In August 1927, immigrant workers from northeastern factories to southeastern mines struck to protest the execution by electrocution of Sacco and Vanzetti in Massachusetts.

Agricultural workers began organizing again in the late 1920s. Mutual benefit societies among Mexican farm workers helped form the Confederación de Uniones de Obreros Mexicanos and La Unión de Trabajadores del Valle Imperial. La Unión led 3,000 cantaloupe harvesters on strike in 1928. Tejano organizer Clemente Idar organized beet field workers in Colorado, Nebraska, and Wyoming into a multiethnic Beet Workers Association, affiliated with the AFL. Led by the "red" National Textile Workers, and organized into integrated locals, southern textile workers unleashed a wave of strikes and drives in 1929.

The labor movements in Puerto Rico and the Philippines moved into politics and slipped into accomodation and corruption. In Puerto Rico, the Partido Socialista Puertorriqueño (PSP) entered into coalition with conservative politicians, winning elections and gaining considerable political patronage—Santiago Iglesias even became the colony's resident commissioner in Washington. But the sugar industry dominated the island, and the Federación Libre de Trabajadores (FLT) failed again and again to win permanent contracts with the growers. The Depression began sooner (and lasted longer) on the island than on the mainland, but when the PSP took over Puerto Rico's Department of Labor in the early 1930s its appointees showed little interest in wages and working conditions. When the FLT finally won a sugar-industry contract in 1933 for the next year's harvest, the terms were so bad the field workers themselves briefly went on strike against it. In the Philippines the alliance of the Congreso Obrero de Filipinas with the government began to take a toll too. When Filipino field workers in Hawaii went on strike in 1924, the COF supported them. But COF founder Hermenegildo Cruz, now director of the Philippine Labor Bureau, conducted his own investigation, and reported conditions in Hawaii to be satisfactory. His consistent support of the colonial government became so controversial that the COF began to come apart, finally splitting in 1929, and existing in name only after 1932.

Ethnic divisions retarded workers' solidarity. In Hawaii, the planters discouraged labor organizing by recruiting many nationalities and giving each its own holiday—Chinese New Year, Obon (the Japanese Festival of Souls), and Rizal Day for Filipinos (marking the Spanish execution of Jose Rizal in 1896). In the U.S. some big industrial firms like Ford Motor Company hired workers of different races or nationalities to work side by side, where their common subordination to the production process might teach them to help each other resist and survive, but such shop-floor cooperation ended at the factory gate, and there were no plantwide unions to foster solidarity. Wherever workers assembled off the job, whether union hall, club, lodge, or church, racial and ethnic separatism was the order of the day. Color lines held firm; immigrants gathered by nationality and subdivided by religion; U.S. natives descended from northwestern Europe stood aloof from everyone else. The very few exceptions were mainly confined to the labor movement's radical fringe.

EARLY YEARS OF THE GREAT DEPRESSION

Organized labor's weakness in numbers and militancy helped set the stage for the Great Depression. While the Roaring Twenties saw gigantic increases in industrial output and home construction, unionism's decline placed strict limits on both wage hikes and on workers' ability to resist the speedups that helped limit industrial employment. The bottom line was that working people could not buy enough to sustain the system: earnings were simply too low and joblessness too common. By summer 1929, consumer spending had tapered off despite easy credit, home building had slumped, and manufacturers' unsold inventories had swelled to the point where many firms were cutting production and laying off workers. The U.S. economy was already teetering when the stock market crash of October 1929 pushed it over the edge.

Total national income fell from about $83 billion in 1929 to $40 billion in 1932. Working people got the worst of it. By January 1930, unemployed workers numbered 4 million. By the end of 1932, 15–17 million people were jobless, about a third of the labor force. Millions more made do with part-time jobs. Unions lost about half a million members.

Wages were cut. From 1929 to 1933, average annual earnings fell 19 percent in transportation, 30 percent in manufacturing, 35 percent in mining, 42 percent in agriculture, 48 percent in construction. There was little cushion: fewer than half of white working-class families had savings in 1929, just $336 on the average. Workers of color had less.

Local governments and charities tried to provide relief, but their efforts were overwhelmed. Homeless encampments sprang up on public or vacant land on the outskirts of cities across the country. Many households dissolved, their children going to friends, relatives, or homes run by charities. Hunger was widespread, and malnutrition encouraged the spread of diseases like tuberculosis and pellagra. New York City recorded ninety-five deaths by starvation in 1931. Despair flourished too: New York City reported 25,000 suicides in 1930–31.

The depression hit minority and immigrant communities especially hard. In 1931, African Americans were 17 percent of the population and 33 percent of the unemployed—the disproportion was even more striking in cities like Charleston, South Carolina (49 percent of the population and 78 percent of the unemployed) and Pittsburgh, Pennsylvania (8 percent of the population, 38 percent of the unemployed). Tejanos called the depression "La Chilla" ("the squeal") because it caused so much pain; in Texas an entire family could work all day picking cotton, and make just enough to buy themselves a single meal. After the blizzard of February 1932, New York City hired 12,000 men to shovel the streets; Bernardo de Vega recalled, "Many Puerto Ricans jumped at the chance to make some money . . . wrapped up in rags, their necks covered with old newspapers, swinging their shovels and shivering to the bone." David Moore remembered African Americans in Detroit in 1929, the year he turned seventeen, "going around to these markets where there was a possibility of food, picking up rotten potatoes, cutting the rotten off to salvage some part of that potato that may be good." Louise Mitchell remembered "slave markets" where black women waited on city street corners for a day's housework: "They come as early as seven in the morning, wait as late as four in the afternoon with the hope that they will make enough to buy supper when they go home . . . if they are lucky, they get about 30 cents an hour." A 1932 study of the unemployed in Chicago's meatpacking district told the story of Rose Majewski, a Polish immigrant whose husband had abandoned her and their five children. Laid off from a janitorial job that had paid up to $21.50 a week, she got work cleaning chicken carcasses for $10–12 a week, but lost that job in June 1930 and could not find another. By 1932, she and her family lived in a converted barn on $5 a week from a private charity and a monthly box of food from the county welfare bureau.

Immigrants were encouraged to leave. By winter 1932–33, about half a million Mexican nationals and their children had returned to Mexico. About 40 percent went voluntarily, often with the aid of workers' organizations like Detroit's Liga de Obreros y Campesinos. The rest were formally deported, chased out by vigilantes, or returned by charitable organizations that provided relief to Mexicans only when they agreed to leave the country. On the West Coast a wave of anti-Asian agitation and violence targeted Filipinos. In March 1934, Congress passed the Tydings-McDuffie Act, which capped immigration from the Philippines and paid the return fare for Filipino nationals in the U.S. who promised never to come back.

For the first two years of the crisis, the President and Congress insisted that relief was a local responsibility. Believing that recovery was just a matter of restoring business confidence, the Hoover administration organized conferences to persuade corporate executives to resume production and stop cutting wages, to hasten the recovery just around the corner. By 1932, something more was clearly required. The President proposed and Congress authorized the Reconstruction Finance Corporation (RFC), which made loans to private companies for expansion (and new jobs) and to local governments for relief, and financed some federal construction projects. Congress also passed the Norris-LaGuardia Act, which barred injunctions against peaceful union activities, including strikes and pickets, and outlawed yellow dog contracts. Neither helped much: unemployment continued to rise, local governments continued to run out of relief funds, and the labor movement continued to shrink.

In the early months of the depression, many corporations maintained their commitment to welfare capitalism, refraining from cutting wage rates, experimenting with job sharing to minimize lay-offs, providing loans and advances on pensions. But they could hold out only so long: in 1931, wage cuts began in earnest, followed by mass layoffs and further cuts in wages and benefits. In 1930, William Green had received a gold medal from the Theodore Roosevelt Memorial Foundation in recognition of his efforts to curb labor unrest. Now he got a letter from an out-of-work machinist about to be evicted from his home: "The bankers and industrialists who have been running our country have proved their utter inability or indifference to put the country in a better condition." Millions of people agreed.

LABOR RISING

One proposal for relief was government-sponsored unemployment insurance. AFL headquarters denounced the scheme as "socialist," but a growing number of national unions and state and local federations backed it, and it was endorsed nearly unanimously at the November 1932 annual convention. But for the most part, labor protests in the early 1930s took place outside the AFL unions, often outside the workplace as well.

Workplace revolts centered in mass production, mining, and agriculture—sectors where unionism had taken the worst beatings in the 1920s. In May 1931, 2,000 nonunion workers went on strike at a U.S. Rubber factory in Mishawaka, Indiana, to protest wage cuts and speedups. In July 1932, nonunion workers protesting wage cuts shut down more than a hundred hosiery and furniture factories in North Carolina. In Tampa, Florida, Cuban American cigar makers went on strike in 1931 when factory owners ousted the *lectores* who read aloud to the workers, probably to speed up the work since the workers hired the reader themselves.

The National Miners Union, affiliated with the Trade Union Unity League, led coal strikes in Ohio, West Virginia, Pennsylvania, and eastern Kentucky in 1931–32. The AFL's United Mine Workers staged a four-month strike against wage cuts in Illinois in 1932. When UMW officials endorsed a settlement, many strikers revolted—18,000 UMW members broke away to form the Progressive Miners of America.

In January and February of 1930, two strikes hit California's Imperial Valley, one among Mexican and Filipino field hands, the other among white packing shed workers. TUUL organizers set up an Agricultural Industrial Workers League. After its most active organizers were convicted of criminal syndicalism, TUUL organizers started the Cannery and Agricultural Workers' Industrial Union, which survived into 1935 and led twenty-four strikes, losing only three. January 1931 saw an uprising of 500 black sharecroppers in England, Arkansas. The following summer their counterparts in Tallapoosa County, Alabama, launched the Share Croppers' Union, which had about 2,000 members across the state by spring 1933, and 6,000 a year later.

The largest protest movement of the early 1930s involved the unemployed. Radical activists organized high-profile demonstrations like the Communist-led "hunger marches" of more than a million jobless workers in major cities across the country in 1930. But the movement mainly focused on grassroots organizing around local struggles. In San Francisco, for example, Communists in the Kungyu (Workers After Hours) Club supported calls for "work or bread" and unemployment insurance, and helped organize the Chinese Unemployed Alliance. CUA led demonstrations against the powerful Consolidated Chinese Benevolent Associations, demanding jobs and housing. The Communist Party built a national network of neighborhood-based Unemployed Councils that pressed relief agencies for aid, and rallied to block evictions of families for not paying rent. Socialists built similar groups in Baltimore and Chicago. A. J. Muste from Brookwood Labor College led a group of its graduates organizing Unemployed Citizens Leagues whose members used barter and labor exchanges.

Unemployed organizing sometimes shaded into workplace organizing. On March 7, 1932, for example, Detroit's Unemployed Councils joined with TUUL autoworkers in a mass protest in front of the Ford Company's River Rouge Plant. Three thousand demonstrators demanded that Ford slow down its assembly lines and rehire laid-off workers. Police and company guards fired on the crowd, wounding more than sixty and killing four.

The unemployed movement routinely organized across color lines, and its Communist-led sectors were especially active in defense of African Americans' rights. The Councils rallied to support the nine young black men sentenced to death on false charges of rape in Scottsboro, Alabama, in 1931, and Angelo Herndon, a nineteen-year-old black Communist sentenced to death under Georgia's anti-insurrection law for organizing an interracial hunger march in Atlanta in 1932. Both struggles were successful, though justice was long in coming. Herndon was freed by the Supreme Court after a five-year legal battle, and the last Scottsboro defendants were released in 1950.

Of all the protests that erupted in the early 1930s, none jolted the nation more than the Bonus March of 1932. Following the Great War, Congress had promised veterans bonuses of $50–100, payable in 1945. In summer 1932, 20,000 jobless veterans, organized in part by the left-wing

Workers Ex-Serviceman's League, converged on Washington, D.C. Many were accompanied by their families. They set up tent cities and vowed to stay put until Congress authorized immediate payment of the bonus. On July 28, troops commanded by General Douglas MacArthur, with Colonel Dwight D. Eisenhower under his command, dispersed the veterans with tear gas, burned their encampment to the ground, and ran them out of town.

As the Bonus Marchers straggled home amidst a deepening depression, radical songwriter Yip Harburg captured working people's mood in his ballad, "Brother, Can You Spare a Dime":

> They used to tell me I was building a dream,
> And so I followed the mob.
> When there was earth to plough or guns to bear,
> I was always right there on the job.
> They used to tell me I was building a dream
> With peace and glory ahead,
> Why should I be standing in line, just waiting for bread?

Anger at the Hoover administration and its business allies had been rising since the depression began; now it reached a boil. The AFL remained neutral in the presidential election of 1932, which pitted Hoover against the Democrat Franklin D. Roosevelt, an advocate of government relief programs and unemployment insurance. But while mainstream labor leaders proceeded with caution, the majority of Americans who went to the polls that year wanted a radical change. They elected Roosevelt by a hefty margin, then waited to see if the new president would make a difference.

CHAPTER

LABOR ON THE MARCH

When Franklin Roosevelt took office on March 4, 1933, the depression was deeper than ever. Jobless workers and their dependents numbered about 50 million; more than 5,500 banks had failed, wiping out many a depositor's life savings; cities and towns were starting to shut down public services for lack of funds; countless farm and home mortgages were in foreclosure; many businesses could no longer cover their payrolls. To meet the crisis, Roosevelt immediately summoned Congress to a special session that ushered in a recovery program known as the New Deal.

The New Deal was a mixed bag of reforms and emergency measures. It tightened government regulation of banks and the stock market. It created hundreds of thousands of jobs through public works projects. It revived state and local relief programs with massive federal grants that extended aid to some 27 million people—about a fifth of the national population—by 1934. Other New Deal initiatives included loans and subsidies to farmers; federal insurance of bank deposits up to $5,000; federal refinancing of home mortgages; the repeal of Prohibition by a Constitutional amendment passed by Congress and quickly ratified by the states; and an Indian Reorganization Act that provided for Native American home rule, ended compulsory individual allotments, and allowed Indian nations to form corporations modelled on the 1922 Navajo Tribal Council.

The New Deal's centerpiece was the National Industrial Recovery Act of June 1933. The NIRA aimed to resuscitate industrial production and profits by eliminating cut-throat competition among rival firms. The federal government suspended antitrust laws and called on business leaders in major industries like steel, auto, textiles, and mining to draw up "codes of fair competition," which the President then signed into law. Smaller industries soon followed suit, extending NIRA codes to 90 percent of the nonagricultural economy. The codes regulated prices, production quotas, product standards, and labor conditions.

A new federal agency, the National Recovery Administration, administered the program and touted it far and wide with parades, rallies, placards, and songs. The NRA's "Blue Eagle" insignia adorned goods marketed by companies in compliance with the program, a seal of approval for patriotic shoppers. Noncompliant companies could be prosecuted, but the government seldom pressed charges, and relied instead on negotiation and persuasion, seeking what Roosevelt called a "partnership in planning" with business.

Workers, on the other hand, would have to fight to be heard. At the government's insistence, businessmen adopted industrial codes that banned child labor and established both minimum wages and maximum hours— typically a forty-hour work week for at least $12 to $15. This certainly improved conditions in many workplaces, but in the absence of unions, employers continued to hire and fire at will, to assign and speed up work, and to keep wage scales close to the new minimums.

The New Deal's main concession to workplace democracy was NIRA Section 7(a), which declared workers' right to "organize and bargain collectively . . . free from the interference, restraint or coercion of employers." But it soon become apparent that corporate executives did not intend to obey this part of the law; and that Washington would not force the issue. The New Deal showed time and again that a federal declaration of labor rights was merely a piece of paper. To fulfill its promise, working people had to take matters into their own hands. They did just that, with a dynamism that startled the nation.

From mid-1933 through 1934, about 2.5 million men and women went out on strike, and unions sprang up by the thousands, in workplaces where employers had once driven them out or where they had never formed before. These insurgencies gave birth to a new labor movement that would transform federal politics and policies, spark a rebellion in the American Federation of Labor, and bring the country's most notorious union busters to the bargaining table. At the beginning, however, none of this looked likely: Washington was committed to a business-oriented New Deal, labor conservatives firmly controlled the AFL, and open-shop employers were gearing up for a new and final conflict.

GRASSROOTS UNIONISM

In May 1933, a month before Congress enacted the NIRA, St. Louis witnessed a strike that foreshadowed battles to come. Some 1,400 women walked off their jobs in the city's nutshelling plants to fight for a rollback of wage cuts, equal pay for black and white workers, and union recognition. None of these women had much experience in the labor movement. About three-quarters of them were African Americans, risking their jobs at a moment when black unemployment rates stood well above 50 percent. They belonged to a newborn local of the Food Workers Industrial Union (FWIU), affiliated with the Trade Union Unity League instead of the larger and stronger AFL. For all of these reasons, employers expected to win hands down, but the strike's grassroots character gave it surprising momentum.

Mass picketing buoyed the strikers' spirits and turned back scabs. Each plant had its own shop committee and picket captains chosen by the rank and file. The shop committees' chairwomen formed a central strike committee that organized mass meetings on a daily basis, and flying squadrons kept the picket lines in close touch with one another. Friends and family joined strikers on the lines and helped them build a support network that extended from unions to churches to civil rights groups. After just ten days, the strikers won a settlement that met their wage demands, including pay equity for black workers. And though employers still refused to recognize the FWIU, the wage victory galvanized its St. Louis branch. The nutshellers helped to organize other low-wage workers, strengthen the city's Unemployed Councils, and launch a militant campaign to desegregate public parks.

These patterns of struggle permeated the new labor movement that took shape during the New Deal's early years. Craft unions had become accustomed to defending only the interests of their highly skilled members and avoiding the risks of concerted action or solidarity with the masses of unskilled workers, often of suspect ethnic and racial origins. Now, grassroots industrial unionism—a marginal force since the early 1920s—took center stage. Its hallmarks were mass action, democratic decision making, and do-it-yourself organizing that reached beyond workplaces and union halls to set entire communities in motion.

In the second half of 1933, union membership grew by 775,000—an astonishing figure given the depth of the depression. The surge continued through 1934, pushing total AFL membership over the three million mark, slightly better than 1929. AFL industrial affiliates recouped their crippling losses of the 1920s. By 1935, industrial unions represented more than a third of all union members, compared to a sixth in 1929.

New members swarmed into unions old and new. As soon as the NIRA was enacted, the United Mine Workers and others sprang into action, using sound trucks, posters, and handbills to spread the message of Section 7(a): "The president wants you to join the union." Miners grabbed membership cards as fast as the union handed them out, and many started locals without waiting for organizers to arrive. The UMW added 300,000 members and penetrated new territory in Kentucky and Alabama. The International Ladies' Garment Workers grew by 100,000, reviving New York City strongholds and building new, predominantly Mexican American, locals in Los Angeles and San Antonio. The Amalgamated Clothing Workers—now an AFL affiliate—signed up 50,000 new members. Black workers in Alabama's iron mines led a Mine, Mill and Smelter Workers organizing drive. More gains followed in 1934. By summer the UMW was more than a half-million strong; the United Textile Workers had over 300,000 members, up from 50,000 a year before; and the Amalgamated Association of Iron and Steel Workers had grown from about 5,000 to more than 100,000. Mass-production workers from other industries also pounded on the AFL's door. They came in through federal labor unions (FLUs); by the end of 1934, the Federation had chartered more than 1,400 new federal locals. Their ranks included 100,000 autoworkers, 90,000 woodworkers, and 60,000 rubber workers.

Organizing accelerated on other fronts too. "Red" unions affiliated with the Trade Union Unity League (TUUL) enlisted at least 125,000 new members—coal miners in Gallup, New Mexico, steel workers in Ohio, office workers in New York City, farm workers in California. California farm workers also built new ethnic unions such as the Filipino Labor Union and La Confederación de Uniones de Campesinos y Obreros. In Laredo, Texas, Mexican workers from different trades formed La Asociación de Jornaleros. Black and white sharecroppers and tenant farmers in the Mississippi Delta founded the Southern Tenant Farmers' Union. Pork butchers in Austin, Minnesota, spearheaded the formation of the Independent Union of All Workers, which organized upper Midwest workplaces from meat plants and department stores to beauty shops and gas stations. Professionals and highly skilled tradesmen formed unions like the American Newspaper Guild; the Screen Actors Guild (led by Boris Karloff and Groucho Marx); the Mechanics Educational Society of America, founded by tool and die makers;

and the Federation of Architects, Engineers, Chemists and Technicians, formed originally as a "United Committee" of unemployed civil engineers to protest NIRA Construction Industry Code wage standards.

As unions expanded, so did community organizing under radical auspices. In New York City, the Communist-led United Council of Working-Class Women built tenant unions and rent strikes. The Birmingham branch of the Communists' International Labor Defense mobilized 3,000 members against lynch law. The unemployed movement—organized by Socialists as well as Communists—picked up momentum in cities across the country. In San Antonio, Texas, at least ten chapters of the unemployed federation Worker's Alliance of America were active, coordinated by Tejana activist Emma Tenayuca.

The organizing drives of 1933–34 spawned some 3,500 strikes, and unrest continued into 1935, which saw another 2,000. Strikes erupted in workplaces from factories to cotton fields, trucking depots to laundries, construction sites to office buildings; even among homeworkers, especially garment workers from New York to San Antonio to Mayaguez, Puerto Rico, where "inside" needleworkers brought "outsiders" into their 1933 strike over piece rates. "The country is full of spontaneous strikes," wrote one labor journalist; "wherever one goes one sees picket lines."

Conflict was especially bitter in agriculture, where New Deal policies made labor conditions worse. To shore up farm produce prices, the government paid landowners to cultivate fewer acres. Sharecroppers and tenants were evicted, field hands scrambled for fewer jobs, and farm wages—exempted from NIRA protection—fell. In 1933 alone, thirty-seven California farm strikes, most led by the TUUL's Cannery and Agricultural Workers, involved 50,000 workers—in the largest strike movement ever seen by the state's agribusinesses. Strikers and their families set up tent colonies, pooled resources, maintained mass pickets despite brutal repression, and won better pay scales in twenty-nine of the strikes. In 1933–35, strikes also hit cranberry bogs in Massachusetts, cotton fields in Arizona and the Deep South, sugar plantations in Puerto Rico, orchards in the Pacific Northwest, vegetable farms in Ohio, Michigan, and New Jersey.

Strikes by nonagricultural workers meanwhile swept through cities and towns in every part of the country. The peak came in mid-1934, when four exceptionally big uprisings grabbed national headlines.

In April, when workers in an AFL federal union at the Auto-Lite plant in Toledo, Ohio, went on strike for union recognition for the second time in three months, the company got an injunction, then resumed production with scab employees. The Lucas County Unemployed League put half a dozen people on a picket line. More joined every day, thousands by late May, enough to keep the scabs from leaving the plant. When the pickets defied National Guard orders to disperse, the soldiers attacked, killing two and wounding hundreds. Fighting filled Toledo streets for days. After the city's unions voted for a general strike, Auto-Lite accepted most of its workers' demands.

San Francisco stevedores joined the AFL's International Longshoremen's Association (ILA) seeking higher pay and shorter hours for themselves and all West Coast longshore workers. Negotiations produced no results. On May 9, 1934, at 8:00 P.M., longshoremen walked out in every West Coast port, and added a new demand: union-controlled hiring halls. Other maritime unions made their own demands; sympathy strikes spread as far as Gulf ports like Mobile, Alabama. Two months into the strike, authorities moved to open the docks. On July 5—"Bloody Thursday"—police attacked the pickets, killing two, wounding more than a hundred. Local unions called a general strike. On July 16, 127,000 workers shut down San Francisco—everything from factories to restaurants to streetcars. Vigilante bands beat strikers and ransacked union halls, and the general strike collapsed in three days. But the marine strike continued until rank and filers voted to accept federal arbitration. On July 30, strikers lined up on the waterfront and returned to work—all together, all at once. Arbitration gave the ILA most of its demands, and other unions also won improvements.

An employers' association called the Citizens' Alliance had long kept Minneapolis an open shop stronghold when drivers from a communist faction★ in a small Teamsters local set out in 1933 to organize truckers. By next spring, Local 574 had 6,000 members. On May 15, it launched a strike against trucking employers. A women's auxiliary canvassed for donations, ran a commissary for strikers' families, and gave first aid to picket-line injuries. After a Citizen's Alliance leader and another deputy were killed during a May 22 police attack on a mass picket line at the city's central marketplace, employers agreed to settle. When they stalled, Local 574 struck again on July 16. Farmers from Minnesota and nearby states restocked the strike commissary. On July 20, police shot sixty-seven strikers on a picket line; two died, and 100,000 people attended one funeral. The governor sent 4,000 National Guardsmen to enforce martial law, but few trucks moved.

★ The communists were Trotskyists, who opposed Stalinist policies in the Soviet Union and were hounded by Soviet agents all around the world.

When the Alliance accepted the strikers' main demands on August 21, thousands took to the streets for a twelve-hour celebration.

NIRA Section 7(a) was a joke in most textile mills. Workers flooded into the AFL United Textile Workers complaining of low wages, long hours, and "stretch-out"—assigning additional machines to operators until they worked nonstop the entire shift. Over the summer of 1934, walkouts spread from Alabama cotton mills throughout the South; on August 18, an emergency UTW convention voted for a general textile strike to force NIRA compliance. Beginning September 1, more than 400,000 workers idled every kind of textile mill from Alabama to Maine—the biggest strike in U.S. history. Mass pickets and parades took over mill town streets. In communities like Durham, North Carolina, the strikers had such widespread support that there was no violence. But violent confrontations were common. In Rhode Island an angry mob smashed windows and looted stores in Woonsocket's business district, and in South Carolina deputies killed six strikers in Honea Path. State after state called out the National Guard, 11,000 troops in all; another ten strikers were killed. On September 21, Roosevelt announced new officials would be appointed to enforce the NIRA in the industry and asked that the strike end. UTW leaders complied the next day. Nothing had been won. Employers continued to flout the NIRA, and southern mills often refused to rehire returning strikers.

The textile strike's defeat was the largest of many setbacks for the new labor movement, which saw many more defeats than victories. Grassroots unionism was immensely powerful but faced tremendous obstacles.

Federal officials gutted NIRA Section 7(a) with bogus interpretations of the law and lax enforcement. Corporations like U.S. Steel and General Motors rushed to establish new Employee Representation Plans. Within months of the NIRA's passage, the number of workers covered by ERPs shot up from 1.25 million to double that figure. Employers persuaded the National Recovery Administration that these "company unions" were bona fide labor organizations meeting Section 7(a) requirements.

Even when New Deal agencies favored workers, they could not enforce their decisions. As the strike wave rolled across the country, the government set up labor boards to adjudicate workplace disputes and established a National Labor Relations Board in July 1934. This board—unlike its predecessors—interpreted the NIRA in favor of unions, but lacked any authority to enforce decisions. The final word remained with the National Recovery Administration, which almost always sided with employers.

AFL conservatives undercut the new labor movement as well. The textile strikers scared UTW leadership, militant mass-production workers alarmed

AFL headquarters. In March 1934, 200,000 autoworkers were poised to strike against the open shop. AFL President William Green negotiated a truce that got them a new labor board, which denied them union recognition. Steel workers met a similar fate that summer, as did rubber workers the next year.

Green and company also frustrated plans to parlay mass production FLUs into national industrial unions. The AFL Executive Council invited craft unions to raid federal locals for their skilled members, leaving the less skilled—along with others rejected by the crafts on account of color, sex, or nationality—to fend for themselves. "The rubbish at labor's door," Teamster president Daniel Tobin called them, saying straight out the thoughts of nearly every craft union boss.

Such attitudes did not go unchallenged. As industrial affiliates like the United Mine Workers and the Amalgamated Clothing Workers revived, their leaders called for militant organizing in mass production. The TUUL amplified the chorus in the winter of 1934–35, when its radical unions dissolved and sent their members into AFL affiliates.

But labor leaders who lacked the will to organize retained the balance of power. By summer 1935, the AFL had so disappointed its new recruits in mass production that more than half a million of them had dropped out. The exodus decimated the United Textile Workers, the Amalgamated Association of Iron and Steel Workers, and federal unions in auto, rubber, and other industries.

For its part, corporate America tried to deprive the new labor movement of popular support, force it to abandon mass action, demoralize its rank and file, and pick off its most militant leaders. Antilabor propaganda made every militant unionist a violent agitator following orders from Moscow, every strike a Bolshevik plot. Employers founded or funded a host of associations to spread the gospel: the American Legion (insurance and banking money), the Sentinels of the Republic (Pew family oil interests), the American Liberty League (General Motors executives), and organizations like the U.S. Chamber of Commerce, and the Daughters of the American Revolution.

Employers mobilized state and local government support. Alabama cities Birmingham and Bessemer passed ordinances against possessing and distributing radical literature, which for local judges meant all union publications. Homestead, Pennsylvania, banned mass meetings; when federal Labor Secretary Frances Perkins came to talk with steel workers in 1933, she had to meet them at the Post Office, on federal property. California authorities helped break the farm strike wave by arresting eighteen TUUL leaders for criminal syndicalism in July 1934. Eighteen strikers were killed on picket lines during the second half of 1933; eighty-eight more over the next two years. More than 18,000 pickets went to jail in 1935.

Corporate and vigilante violence supplemented legal repression. In 1933, California agribusinesses, banks, and utility companies started the Associated Farmers, which mobilized battalions of up to 2,000 goons to attack pickets and raid tent colonies. Hate groups were ready to help. The Ku Klux Klan revived in 1934 in Dallas, Texas, to save America from labor radicals. A General Motors manager suggested to a colleague facing a union drive: "Maybe you could use a little Black Legion." A midwestern offshoot of the Klan, the Black Legion killed at least ten auto union activists in 1934–35 in the Midwest's industrial cities. Corporations also relied on professionals. After 1933, big business spent an estimated $80 million a year on agents specializing in antiunion espionage and violence. More than 200 agencies furnished tens of thousands of operatives to companies like Chrysler, Standard Oil, Firestone, Westinghouse, Campbell Soup, Quaker Oats, Montgomery Ward, Borden Milk, and Statler Hotels. A few like the Ford Motor Company and U.S. Steel preferred their own security forces.

Such assaults increased the risks of organizing and undermined many a strike, but grassroots unionism persisted. Anti-Communist propaganda failed to ignite a new "Red Scare," partly because it charged that Bolsheviks were behind the New Deal as well as the new labor movement, and the Roosevelt administration declined to support the campaign. Moreover, the new labor movement's community networks were resistant to red-baiting. Even brutality could backfire. In Birmingham, Alabama, a metal worker took his eight-year-old son to see a union organizer who had been tortured by thugs employed by U.S. Steel subsidiary Tennessee Coal and Iron. As the boy examined the wounds, his father instructed him: "Look at that, sonny. That's the company. That's what you got to learn to hate—and fight agin."

Corporations' belligerence—their war on unions, countless infractions of NIRA rules, wild charges against the New Deal—played poorly with the general public too. Letters flooded the White House demanding that the president control big business. Then, in May 1935, the Supreme Court voided the NIRA as a violation of Constitutional limits on federal power. The Roosevelt administration changed course: a second New Deal took shape, based this time on a government partnership with workers, not businessmen.

A new federal agency, the Works Progress Administration (WPA), greatly expanded public works programs to create jobs. By early 1936, the WPA had more than 3.4 million workers on its rolls. Most worked on construction projects—roads, bridges, parks, recreation centers, and other public facilities.

The WPA also organized the Federal Writers Project and the Federal Theatre Project, which employed writers, artists, actors, and musicians. It worked with the new National Youth Administration to provide part-time jobs to poor students so they could continue their educations.

Another second New Deal initiative addressed the free market's failures to provide economic security, both short- and long-term. The Social Security Act established national unemployment insurance, administered by the states and financed by a tax on employers; and pensions for workers,★ funded by taxes on both employers and workers. It also authorized federal grants to states to assist disabled individuals and destitute children (along with their mothers). The coverage was not especially generous—it excluded agricultural, hospital, and domestic workers—but the act was a breakthrough: for the first time the federal government took responsibility for working people's long-term economic security.

In another concession to popular anger at business magnates, Congress substantially raised federal taxes on corporations and wealthy individuals. It also passed the Public Utility Holding Company Act, breaking up gas and electric monopolies that charged exorbitant rates.

The centerpiece of the Second New Deal, and its most important concession to labor, was the National Labor Relations Act, usually called the Wagner Act after its author, Senator Robert Wagner of New York, and signed into law July 5, 1935. Where NIRA Section 7(a) had recognized unions, the Wagner Act gave them protection (though, like Social Security, it exempted agricultural, hospital, and domestic workers). It established secret-ballot elections for workers deciding whether to be represented by a union. It prohibited employers from interfering with organizing and banned specific common practices: using threats, coercion, or restraint against an organizing drive; sponsoring labor organizations ("company unions"); discriminating against union members in hiring, firing, or job assignments; retaliating against workers who reported Wagner Act violations; and refusing to bargain with a union voted in by the workers. Finally, Wagner established a new National Labor Relations Board (NLRB) to oversee the elections, hear and rule on complaints about violations of the Act, and petition federal courts to enforce its rulings. A coda added, "Nothing in this Act shall be construed so as to interfere with or impede or diminish in any way the right to strike."

Big business despised the second New Deal, and the Wagner Act most of all. The National Association of Manufacturers fought its passage with the

★ Survivors' pensions were added in a 1939 amendment.

biggest campaign in the history of corporate lobbying. When Wagner became law, the American Liberty League challenged it in court, and many
employers vowed to ignore it while they waited for it to be declared unconstitutional.

Workers struggling to unionize mass production were cautiously opti-
mistic. They had made gains without much help from the NIRA; more
seemed possible now. But the AFL remained an obstacle, most of its leaders
split between those who preferred to ignore mass-production workers entirely, and those who were willing to take in new dues-paying members as
long as their own prerogatives and power remained intact. Both groups
doubted mass-production workers could really be organized.

Actually, mass-production federal unions were on the move. They
founded a national auto union in August 1935 and a rubber union the following month. They fought to keep their skilled members when craft
poachers came around. More was at stake than jurisdiction or industrial versus craft structure: movement confronted paralysis. As Federated Press labor
reporter Len De Caux put it, "the will to organize" was the issue. "The Old
Guard," he observed, "was acting dog-in-the-manger over members nobody had." Labor activists intended to build unions large and militant
enough to beat the open shop: if craft conservatives blocked the way, industrial union insurgents would have to shove them aside.

Easier said than done—AFL leaders had beaten back many rank-and-file
insurgencies. But this time around, union leaders were not of one mind.
John L. Lewis—president of the United Mine Workers, the nation's largest
union—sided with the insurgents and was ready to lead an assault on the old
guard at the AFL convention. When delegates gathered in Atlantic City in
October 1935, the stage was set for a fight that would split the Federation.

THE RISE OF THE CIO

The 1935 debates between industrial and craft unionists were more acrimonious than ever. Lewis and a few like-minded union chiefs sponsored
a resolution calling for unrestricted industrial union charters for mass-
production industries. After hours of speeches pro and con, the convention
voted the resolution down, 18,024 to 10,933, and the issue seemed settled.
But delegates from the federal unions and the new auto and rubber unions
kept rising to make their case, while President Green tried to silence them
from the podium. When Carpenters' president William Hutcheson inter-
rupted a rubber worker, Lewis loudly objected. Hutcheson called Lewis
a "big bastard," and Lewis decked him with a right-cross to the jaw. That

blow—later called "the punch heard round the world"—announced that the dissidents would not be held in check.

On November 9, 1935, Lewis and seven other AFL leaders met to found the Committee for Industrial Organization (CIO) "for the purpose of encouraging and promoting the organization of unorganized workers . . . on an industrial basis." These men represented long-established unions—the United Mine Workers, Amalgamated Clothing Workers, Ladies' Garment Workers, Mine, Mill and Smelter Workers, United Textile Workers, International Typographical Union,★ Cap and Millinery Workers, and Oil and Gas Workers. But the catalyst for the CIO was the new labor movement. The grassroots uprisings that persuaded Congress to pass the Wagner Act also convinced these men that industrial organizing would pay off. Dues from more than a half-million new members so enriched the UMW and garment unions that the CIO could fund organizing campaigns without help from AFL headquarters.

The CIO started as eight unions with a million members total. Two years later, thirty-two CIO unions had 3.7 million members, the vast majority covered by collective bargaining agreements. Most newcomers were mass-production workers in industrial unions, though other kinds of workers and organizations climbed aboard too. The Steel Workers Organizing Committee (later the United Steel Workers of America) had 550,000 members and contracts with all U.S. Steel subsidiaries. The United Mine Workers had 600,000 members. The United Auto Workers and United Rubber Workers—previously AFL federal unions—had respectively 375,000 members and contracts with General Motors, Chrysler, and several smaller auto companies; and 75,000 members and contracts with Goodyear, Goodrich, and General Tire and Rubber. Other CIO forces included 400,000 textile workers; close to 500,000 members of various garment unions; 140,000 workers in electrical manufacturing; 130,000 in transportation and maritime unions; 120,000 in white-collar unions of retail workers, office workers, public employees, newspaper reporters, architects, engineers, and other professionals; 100,000 woodworkers, from loggers to furniture factory workers.

Rubber workers in Akron, Ohio, first put the CIO on the map. In the middle of February 1936, several hundred members of the United Rubber Workers (URW) threw up a picket line at the giant Goodyear tire plant after layoffs were announced. Within days, more than 14,000 Goodyear workers

★ The ITU never formally joined the CIO, but the AFL expelled it in 1938 for refusing to pay a Federation "war tax" assessment to fight the CIO.

were out on strike. Their tactics were typical of new labor. Thousands of pickets—rubber workers from Goodyear and other companies, along with their families and neighbors—encircled the plant's eleven-mile perimeter day and night, even in blizzards. When Goodyear got an injunction, the URW and Akron's central labor council promised a general strike if the National Guard enforced the injunction. The Guardsmen did not intervene. When police tried to tear down tents set up along the picket line, General Tire Company workers left their shop to help beat back the police. When the rubber barons organized a vigilante "Law and Order League," the union organized a counterforce of workers who had served in the Great War.

The strike was not just a local effort. CIO headquarters donated to the strike fund and sent staff to help the strikers. CIO researchers provided facts about Goodyear's profits and stock manipulations for publicity. CIO leaders let Goodyear and its customers know they risked national boycotts if violence broke the picket line. After a month, the company offered to shelve the layoff plan and bargain with the union. The strikers debated the offer at mass meetings and agreed to go back to work.

Both of the forces at work in the Akron victory contributed to CIO growth. Rank-and-file activists carried grassroots mobilization to new levels. CIO headquarters dedicated a large staff to organizing the unorganized. Bottom-up and top-down efforts were powerful in combination, but not a real partnership: local activists and headquarters men often built different kinds of unions.

The difference showed in CIO political action. President Roosevelt ran for reelection in 1936. John L. Lewis knew his defeat would be disastrous for labor and vigorously campaigned for him; in return, Roosevelt promised to support a CIO drive in steel. The AFL also endorsed the president, and Sidney Hillman of the CIO's Amalgamated Clothing Workers helped start Labor's Non-Partisan League to funnel union support to the president's campaign. But Lewis and Hillman faced a grassroots movement for an independent labor party, supported by five state federations, scores of central councils, and hundreds of locals in industrial unions in rubber, auto, textiles, and garments, even Lewis's Mine Workers and Hillman's Clothing Workers. Lewis gave the United Auto Workers $100,000 for organizing, contingent on a Roosevelt endorsement. Hillman converted the New York City chapter of the Non-Partisan League into the American Labor Party, suggesting the League should become the nucleus for a national labor party once Roosevelt was reelected. (After the election, the idea was dropped.)

Roosevelt won millions of working-class votes because of the second New Deal and its contrast with the relentlessly probusiness platform of his

Republican opponent. The President got over 60 percent of the popular vote, carrying every state but Maine and Vermont. Urban working-class voters—migrants from rural America as well as immigrants—came to identify themselves as Democrats. African American support for the Republican Party—steadfast since the Civil War—evaporated as federal programs brought relief to communities, and black votes went to Roosevelt even though he failed to endorse a federal antilynching law opposed by southern Democrats.

The movement for independent political action survived in third-party initiatives in Wisconsin, Minnesota, California, and Washington. New York's American Labor Party became the majority party among East Harlem's Italian, Puerto Rican, and African American voters. But national spokesmen for the CIO and its member unions remained firmly wedded to the two-party system.

As Lewis and Hillman stumped for the Non-Partisan League on Roosevelt's behalf, the CIO launched an organizing drive aimed at U.S. Steel. Lewis appointed the United Mine Workers' Philip Murray chairman of the Steel Workers' Organizing Committee (SWOC), and armed it with a war chest of $750,000. SWOC announced it would keep "centralized and responsible control of the organizing campaign" and "insist that local policies conform to the national plan of action." A staff of lawyers, researchers, publicity agents, and salaried organizers—few of them steelworkers—conducted a campaign mainly outside the mills. These tactics were designed, in Murray's words, "to banish fear from the steel workers' minds." They could join SWOC without paying initiation fees (or even dues after October 1936) and were not expected to talk up the union. Instead, SWOC staged national meetings where the CIO was endorsed by New Deal politicians and leading spokesmen for the various racial and ethnic groups represented in the mills. By the end of 1936, SWOC claimed more than 100,000 members, though the union was close to invisible on the job.

On March 2, 1937, U.S. Steel reached an agreement with SWOC, after secret meetings with Lewis (so secret not even Murray knew about them). Workers flocked into SWOC, but it remained highly centralized. Murray appointed all regional and district directors and field organizers. The national office set local dues policies, prohibited strikes without permission, and reserved the right to expel anyone breaking that rule. Murray's directors—not local officers elected by members—negotiated and signed contracts.

SWOC probably owed its victory to the autoworkers at General Motors—the world's largest corporation and bitterly antiunion. The United

Auto Workers had planned to begin a campaign in Cleveland and Detroit in the new year; after Roosevelt's reelection a series of spontaneous strikes quickened the pace. UAW leaders had discouraged strikes in Atlanta and Kansas City G.M. plants during November and early December as premature. Then a department at the Cleveland plants sat down on December 28, and the rest of the 7,000 workers joined them, vowing to stay until G.M. signed a national contract. On December 30, workers occupied Detroit's G.M. Fisher Plant No. 2. The next day, workers from Fisher No. 1 in Flint, Michigan, met on lunch break; several hundred returned to the plant, escorted guards and managers out, and settled in to stay. On January 3, 1937, with sit-downs rapidly spreading, UAW delegates met in Flint, composed formal demands, and declared a company-wide strike.

The Flint occupation was well disciplined. The shop committee patrolled to make sure no one damaged cars or equipment; drinking and gambling were forbidden. The UAW Women's Auxiliary—wives, sisters, mothers, daughters of the strikers—formed with fifty members on the second day of the strike and quickly grew to many hundreds. They raised money, provided food and childcare for strikers' families, and stood on picket lines. Genora Johnson, wife of local union leader Kermit Johnson and a member of the Socialist Party, organized a Women's Emergency Brigade, which wore red berets and carried hammers, crowbars, and two-by-fours to demonstrations and pickets. Veterans joined union groups pledging to defend the community from strike-breaking thugs and "not become a stool pigeon of the Capitalists and give them any information of our order." The strikers got outside support—First Lady Eleanor Roosevelt contributed to the strike fund. As one striker recalled, "It started out kinda ugly because the guys were afraid they put their foot in it and all they was gonna do is lose their jobs. But as time went on, they began to realize they could win this darn thing, 'cause we had a lot of outside people comin' in showin' sympathy." The pickets in front of the plant grew to ten thousand strong. By mid-January seventeen plants and well over half the G.M. workforce were on strike.

The company refused to negotiate unless the plants were vacated. Stalemated, the union made plans to take Chevrolet Plant No. 9. Spies reported the plan; G.M. security shifted in anticipation. As union members and the Women's Emergency Brigade stormed Chevy No. 9, other union militants walked into Chevrolet No. 4, which made all the engines for the Chevrolet line. Half the 4,000 workers joined them, and the rest left. After the governor refused to order troops to evict the strikers, on February 3, G.M. agreed to negotiate. A week later the company recognized the UAW at the striking plants, dropped charges and lawsuits against the strikers, and agreed to submit other demands to a labor-management conference.

The victory was enormous: Chrysler Corporation signed with the union in April, and by the end of the year the UAW had recruited 400,000 members, established a general union (Local 156) in Flint, and taken over the city's government. The sit-down tactic was widely copied. In the first two weeks after the Flint victory there were eighty-seven sit-down strikes in Detroit alone—auto parts plants, cigar factories, bakeries, and other workplaces. Over the course of 1937, about 300,000 workers staged a total of 477 sit-down strikes. The Flint victory also proved the strength of what Len De Caux, now editor of the CIO News, called "tumultuous democracy": UAW locals were virtually autonomous; all officers were elected by the membership; and the radical Unity Caucus fought with the moderate Progressive Caucus for a decade.

Whatever their internal dynamics, all CIO unions fostered workplace democracy. General Motors chairman Alfred Sloan, Jr., later recalled the fury of businessmen forced to bargain with the CIO: "Our rights to determine production schedules, to set work standards, and to discipline workers were all suddenly called into question." Unions restricted employer prerogatives.

Unions could also impose restrictions on workers. Following the Goodyear victory, officers of the United Rubber Workers squared off against the many rank-and-filers who staged departmental sitdowns to protest unsatisfactory conditions. However effective on the shop floor, these "wildcat" strikes—called without union authorization—undercut URW negotiations with Goodyear. To gain concessions from management, union officials had to deliver labor peace. Union after union clamped down on wildcats once employers agreed to negotiate.

The Wagner Act also cut both ways. NLRB elections played a big part in the CIO's growth. Unions counted on Board rulings to enforce Wagner protections. But employers broke the law more efficiently than the government enforced it. Even after the Supreme Court upheld the Wagner Act in April 1937, the NLRB was so swamped by complaints about employer violations that unions could not get rulings for months, years if the dispute went to the courts. Moreover, government help came at a price. No union could call on the NLRB—even for an election—without accepting its rules for union conduct, which prohibited strikes and boycotts in support of other unions.

Reliance on the NLRB also turned the CIO away from workers not protected by Wagner. Local and regional unions of sharecroppers, farmhands,

In December 1936, workers at one of General Motors' Flint, Michigan, factories began a sit-down strike to express their grievances to a company that refused to recognize any union. The action proved to be a watershed event in the story of American labor.

THE FLINT SIT-DOWN STRIKE

The strikers felt they worked under intolerable conditions. Management demanded workers put in 60- to 70-hour weeks for wages as low as 20 cents an hour and mandated that workers fill quotas under the notorious speedup system.

FROM NOW ON YOU THREE BOYS WILL HAVE TO DO THE WORK OF FOUR!

LOOK ALIVE!

HUP! HUP!

Management also spied on its employees and fired them for union activity.

J. SACCO 6-99

They occupied the premises and wouldn't budge. Some slept in the bodies of the vehicles they'd made. Many said they wouldn't shave till they were victorious.

A judge issued an injunction ordering the strikers out of the plant and prohibiting them from picketing... But the judge was revealed to be corrupt.

Management secured another injunction against the strikers, and hundreds of citizens were deputized and armed to take them on.

THANK YOU, AND TAKE A SHOTGUN ON YOUR WAY OUT.

NEXT!

The city manager said, "We will go into the plant shooting." The chief of police warned of a "massacre."

The governor called out the militia to prevent violence. The president leaned on both sides to reach an agreement.

And G.M. agreed to talk.

The workers had won!

They paraded through Flint

JOIN THE UNION!

WE ARE FREE!

The 44-day strike was one of the pivotal events in U.S. labor history.

G.M. agreed to accept the United Auto Workers as the automobile workers' sole bargaining agent.

UAW membership climbed from 30,000 to 500,000 within a year.

Wages in the auto industry increased by $300 million in the same period.

BOSS, HOW DO YA THINK I'D LOOK WITH A BEARD?

OH, SHUT UP.

J. SACCO 6-99

fishermen, and food processors started the United Cannery, Agricultural, Packing and Allied Workers of America (UCAPAWA) in July 1937, bringing together 110,000 members, unprotected field workers and protected plant workers alike. But UCAPAWA's central office supported farm organizing less and less, suspending it entirely in 1939. Domestic workers fared worse—the CIO did not even try to organize them.

Still, the CIO advanced working-class solidarity in important ways. CIO unions welcomed men and women of every color, creed, and nationality. This solidarity had limits. Women workers did not hold leadership positions in proportion to their numbers in CIO unions; the same was true for men of color. CIO contracts left hiring decisions to employers, and seniority clauses perpetuated the effects of discrimination. Though mass-production unions claimed jurisdiction over everyone working in their industries, they rarely reached out to the legions of women who staffed company offices.

Nevertheless, women's ranks in U.S. unions expanded from about 200,000 in 1935 to 800,000 in 1940. The CIO and its National Coordinating Committee of CIO Auxiliaries created a large and vital network of local and national women's auxiliaries, in the UAW and other unions, including the Rubber Workers, SWOC, Mine Mill, and the National Maritime Union. The auxiliaries were active in many strikes. Violet Baggett, married to a Cadillac worker, joined a UAW auxiliary when her husband went on strike. In a letter to the UAW newspaper, she wrote: "I'm living for the first time with a definite goal. I want a decent living for not only my family but for everyone. Just being a woman isn't enough any more. I want to be a human being." In Detroit and some other cities, women's auxiliaries also took on tenant and consumer issues.

CIO unions adopted constitutions outlawing exclusion, discrimination, and segregation. Their members took a CIO pledge, promising (among other things) "never to discriminate against a fellow worker on account of creed, color or nationality." They fielded organizers from diverse backgrounds and published union literature in many languages. They reached out to working-class churches and community organizations. They worked with civil rights and civic groups like A. Philip Randolph's National Negro Congress, the Southern Negro Youth Congress (based in colleges and universities), the American Committee for the Protection of the Foreign Born, the Committee for the Protection of Filipino Rights, and the Japanese American Democratic Clubs in several California cities. They supported community groups like El Congreso de los Pueblos de Habla Español, founded under the leadership of Guatemalan-born UCAPAWA organizer Luisa Moreno. El Congreso brought together more than a hundred Mexican American and Mexican groups to fight "against discrimination and deportation, for economic liberty, for equal representation in government, for the building of a better world for our youth" (to quote its eighteen-year-old executive secretary Josefina Fierro de Bright). CIO unions also cultivated connections with the radical ethnic associations affiliated with the International Workers Order, like the Slovak Workers' Society, the Garibaldi-American Fraternity Society, and the Cervantes Fraternal Society.

CIO rank and file united across racial and ethnic lines. When 200 black women from the Tobacco Stemmers' and Laborers' Industrial Union struck the Brown and Williamson Tobacco Company in Richmond, Virginia, the same number of white women from the Amalgamated Clothing Workers joined the picket line. The Maritime Workers Industrial Union (predecessor to the National Maritime Union) signed up three thousand Chinese sailors after agreeing to support their demands for equal pay and the right to go ashore in U.S. ports. When Chinese American members of the Ladies' Garment Workers struck a San Francisco factory owned by National Dollar Stores, white salesclerks honored picket lines in front of the stores. Mexican and Russian-Jewish women at the California Sanitary Canning Company in Los Angeles joined to win a UCAPAWA strike. Filipino and Japanese workers together built strong UCAPAWA locals on Hawaiian sugar plantations. In Chicago, black, white, and Mexican workers joined SWOC and the Packinghouse Workers' Organizing Committee. Journalist Ruth McKenney described white rubber workers: "Men from the southern mountains, once fair bait for the savage program of the Ku Klux Klan, applauded the speeches of Jewish garment workers, cheered the advance of Irish Catholic transport workers, sat side by side in union meetings with Negro workers."

This culture of solidarity owed a great deal to left-wing radicals, especially Communists. Though John L. Lewis had ruthlessly attacked "Reds" in the past, he hired many as CIO organizers, recognizing their militancy, discipline, and success at building interracial cooperation in the TUUL. When colleagues objected, Lewis responded, "Who gets the bird? The hunter or the dog?" Communists and their allies were elected to lead many locals and some national unions, and solidarity made the greatest advances in these settings.

Corporations had their own brand of solidarity. The "Little Steel" companies—Republic, Youngstown Sheet and Tube, Inland, and Bethlehem—planned in concert to block the union, and handed the CIO its first major defeat. Once U.S. Steel had recognized the union, SWOC turned to the industry's second tier, and called a strike against Little Steel in May 1937.

Republic Steel's chief executive officer Tom Girdler organized the joint resistance along the lines of 1919. Strikers were gassed, clubbed, and shot; thousands of workers were jailed following confrontations with police or National Guardsmen. In South Chicago on Memorial Day (May 30), police attacked a gathering of Republic strikers and their families, beating and shooting more than fifty men, women, and children—ten men died, one clubbed to death. Eight more workers were killed before the strike ended in defeat.

Little Steel strike violence was neither spontaneous nor accidental. The companies spent nearly $500,000 on weapons for strike use. Youngstown Sheet and Tube bought 8 machine guns, 369 rifles, 190 shotguns, 450 revolvers, 109 gas launchers—plus 10,000 rounds of ammunition and 3,000 tear gas canisters. Republic Steel bought more military supplies than any state or local police department in the country. So found the Senate Committee on Civil Liberties, chaired by Wisconsin's Robert La Follette Jr. (son of the 1924 Progressive presidential candidate), which began hearings in 1936. The La Follette Committee investigated corporate efforts to sabotage union organizing, and documented the "Mohawk Valley Formula," a strike strategy promoted by the National Association of Manufacturers that combined violence with elaborate propaganda campaigns.

A faltering economy compounded the CIO's trials. In 1937, following a year of recovery, Roosevelt cut government spending to balance the federal budget, with disastrous results. Recovery halted in mid-1937; by 1938 the depression was back in full force. Mexican American pecan shellers in San Antonio won a bitter strike (over a thousand strikers jailed) in early 1938, only to find themselves replaced by machines a few months later—several thousand shellers lost their jobs. Heavy industry was hit especially hard. The UAW lost three-quarters of its members. SWOC and the Rubber Workers were badly weakened. Though many CIO unions held steady, and some even grew, at the end of 1939 the CIO claimed 200,000 fewer members than two years earlier.

AFL competition also helped shrink the CIO. The Federation suspended CIO unions in 1936, and expelled them in 1937. In May 1938, the Committee for Industrial Organization became the Congress of Industrial Organizations, an independent and momentarily larger rival federation.★ The AFL started organizing. Conservative union leaders hired radicals to get things rolling. Teamster president Tobin hired communists from Minneapo-

---

★ Two CIO founding unions—the Ladies' Garment Workers and the Cap and Millinery Workers—returned to the AFL.

lis, who organized 200,000 long-haul truckers in eleven states. Craft unions developed industrial divisions. The International Brotherhood of Electrical Workers (an electricians' union) started organizing production workers in electrical equipment factories. Cautious unions grew bold. The Hotel Employees and Restaurant Employees (HERE) used a sit-down strike to win recognition and a contract with increased wages and paid vacations for lunch-counter waitresses and salesclerks at Woolworth "five and dime" stores in Detroit—the workers even got half-pay for the time they had been on strike. Some unions organizing among multiracial workforces dropped color bars. The AFL gave a charter to Field Workers Union Local 30326 in California, which had Filipino and Mexican American members. The AFL Alaska Packers Union's first, second and third vice-presidents were Japanese, Chinese, and Mexican American in 1937.

CIO and AFL unions could cooperate at the local level. Detroit HERE formed an alliance with the UAW. In Kenosha, Wisconsin, CIO locals belonged to the AFL Trades and Labor Council. But mostly the two federations fought over members and contracts in a host of industries and trades—woodworking, lumber and paper mills, packinghouses, machine tools, hauling and warehousing, public employment. The AFL promoted itself as the conservative alternative to the CIO. Machinists' president A. O. Wharton described the CIO in a letter to locals as a "gang of sluggers, communists, radicals and soapbox artists, professional bums, expelled members of labor unions, outright scabs and the Jewish organizations with all their red affiliates." As CIO ranks dwindled, the AFL's grew, from 3.4 million in late 1937 to over 4 million in late 1939, surpassing the CIO by more than half a million by the end of 1940.

Beset on all sides, the CIO abandoned militant tactics like the sit-down strike after 1937. More and more it relied on NLRB procedures and rulings to win contracts. In response, the AFL joined employers pressing Congress to restrain the Board's powers.

WHOSE AMERICA?

The government proved an unreliable ally. Businessmen and other conservatives called the economic downturn the "Roosevelt depression," arguing that the second New Deal undermined business confidence by legislating restraints on profitability. Roosevelt himself blamed the downturn on a "strike of capital," and John L. Lewis agreed. Both charged that businessmen had cut back investment to induce a depression they hoped would undo the Wagner Act and the rest of the New Deal.

The renewed depression put Roosevelt and his political allies on the defensive. Only one major reform made it through Congress after the economy slumped, the Fair Labor Standards Act (FLSA) of June 1938. The Act put a floor on wages and a ceiling on hours—25 cents an hour and 44 hours per week, with time and a half for overtime—and provided for improvement to 40 cents an hour and 40 hours a week two years later.* It also outlawed the employment of children under sixteen in most occupations, under eighteen in hazardous occupations. As enacted, the FLSA was weaker than the President had proposed. Congressional amendments limited its coverage to workers engaged in interstate distribution or production, and exempted many groups, including farm workers and agricultural processors, fishermen, domestic workers, and professionals.

In the 1938 Democratic primaries, Roosevelt campaigned for New Dealers against conservative opponents (mostly southern incumbents), with little success. In the general election, Democrats retained the majority in both the House and Senate, but New Dealers did not. Southern "Dixiecrats" joined Republicans to bring the New Deal to an end.

Ultraright sentiment surged among businessmen in 1938–40, especially sympathy for the fascist experiments in Germany and Italy. Henry Ford and International Business Machines president Thomas J. Watson accepted Nazi medals. A former president of the National Association of Manufacturers declared, "American business might be forced to turn to some form of disguised Fascist dictatorship." In 1940, midwestern businessmen from Sears Roebuck, Quaker Oats, Hormel, and other companies helped form the American First Committee to oppose intervention against Hitler.

The CIO drew fire from every part of the conservative spectrum. A Ku Klux Klan newspaper warned "CIO WANTS WHITES AND BLACKS ON SAME LEVEL." The National Association of Manufacturers distributed two million copies of the pamphlet "Join the CIO and Help Build A Soviet America." Father Charles Coughlin (the "Radio Priest") blended praise for the AFL with attacks on the CIO, communists, and the "international Jewish conspiracy" in weekly broadcasts carried nationwide. The *Labor Advocate,* newspaper of the AFL's central labor council in Birmingham, Alabama, attacked "America's Public Enemy No. 1 . . . The CIO under its Communist leaders."

---

* The AFL opposed the Act, as it had always opposed minimum-wage legislation, on the grounds that the minimum would become the maximum.

In May 1938, the U.S. House of Representatives established the Committee to Investigate Un-American Activities, chaired by Texas Democrat Martin Dies, who called a steady parade of conservative expert witnesses.★ In August 1938, the AFL's John Frey named 284 CIO organizers as Communists waiting for "the signal for revolution." The next Sunday's *New York Times* read, "COMMUNISTS RULE THE C.I.O." Then *National Republic* editor Walter Steele detailed Communist outreach from the CIO to 640 organizations, from church councils and civil rights groups to the Boy Scouts and Camp Fire Girls. In May 1939, the Committee heard from Dudley Pierrepont Gilbert, socialite spokesman for American Nationalists Incorporated, about the 150,000 foreigners mustering in Mexico to sneak across the border and seize Army arsenals, while the CIO launched a strike wave and Jewish financiers crashed the stock market. "PLOT TO SEIZE NATION BARED BY DIES," reported the *Baltimore Sun.* The Committee found that WPA writers and theater projects harbored anti-American agitators—prounion, antifascist, and critical of racial discrimination; the Federal Theatre Project closed in 1939. The Committee also investigated charges that communists controlled the La Follette Committee, which the Senate shut down in 1940.

Immigrants were especially suspect. In 1939, the House of Representatives passed the Alien Registration Act, commonly called the Smith Act. It required that all aliens (noncitizen immigrants) be fingerprinted, register with the U.S. Justice Department, and keep the government informed of their whereabouts. The Act also made it a federal crime to advocate, advise, or teach the necessity or desirability of overthrowing local, state, or national governments by force, or to belong to an organization holding such a doctrine. In effect, it was a federal antisyndicalist law. The Senate approved the Smith Act in 1940, and Roosevelt signed it into law.

If it was a crime to have revolutionary goals, many members of the CIO and its allies were guilty. They aimed to reconstruct American life from bottom to top. Len De Caux observed, "Now we're a movement, many workers asked, why can't we move on to more and more? . . . Why can't we go on to create a new society with the workers on top, to end age-old injustices, to banish poverty and war?"

Radical ambitions went hand in hand with a militant patriotism. Strikers celebrated victories by singing "The Battle Hymn of the Republic." Por-

---

★ The Committee also looked into immigrant rightists like the Italian Black Shirts and the German American Bund. The Bund endorsed the Committee's work.

traits of Abraham Lincoln adorned the pages of union newspapers and union office walls. Labor activists were routinely compared to the patriots of 1776 and abolitionists like John Brown, Frederick Douglass, and Sojourner Truth. The Communist Party called on all opponents of fascism and war to defend the "life, liberty and pursuit of happiness of the American people" and the "sacred guarantees of our Bill of Rights."

CIO-style patriotism included on active recognition of injustice and a strong sense of obligation to correct it. In his memoir *America Is in the Heart,* Filipino immigrant and activist Carlos Bulosan declared: "We must interpret history in terms of liberty. We must advocate democratic ideas and fight all forces that would abort our culture. . . . We . . . understand the many imperfections of democracy and the malignant disease corroding its very heart. We must be united in the effort to make an America in which our people can find happiness."

Unity required respect for the diversity among working people, a sentiment perhaps best articulated in "Ballad for Americans," written by radical composer Earl Robinson and poet John LaTouche for the Federal Theatre Project's 1939 musical production *Sing for Your Supper,* and turned into a hit recording by world-famous singer, actor, and political activist Paul Robeson. In the cantata, the chorus sings about American history as the soloist comments and—in response to questions from the chorus—slowly reveals his identity:

> I represent the WHOLE . . . I'm the everybody who's nobody . . . I'm an engineer, musician, street cleaner, carpenter, teacher . . . I am the et ceteras. And the so forths that do the work . . . I'm just an Irish, Negro, Jewish, Italian, French and English, Spanish, Russian, Chinese, Polish, Scotch, Hungarian, Litvak, Swedish, Finnish, Canadian, Greek and Turk, and Czech and double Czech American. And that ain't all. I was baptized Baptist, Methodist, Congregationalist, Lutheran, Atheist, Roman Catholic, Orthodox Jewish, Presbyterian, Seventh Day Adventist, Mormon, Quaker, Christian Scientist—and lots more! . . . You know who I am . . . AMERICA!

For CIO activists, this was patriotism—fighting for equal rights for every racial and ethnic group, respect for their distinct cultures and contributions, and unity on democratic grounds. Working people had a special claim because their labor built the nation, but as Bulosan put it, "America is not a land of one race or one class of men . . . We are all Americans who have toiled and suffered . . . All of us, from the first Adams to the last Filipino, native born or alien, educated or illiterate—*We are America!*"

Commitment to democracy also fostered international solidarity. The National Maritime Union honored picket lines in foreign ports, during a 1938 strike by Puerto Rican dockworkers, for example. East Harlem Congressman Vito Marcantonio of the American Labor Party defended Puerto Rican nationalists prosecuted by the colonial government. New York City's Transport Workers Union had ties to the Irish Republican Army. CIO Communists promoted American–Soviet friendship.

The gravest international issue was the spread of fascism. Under the increasing influence of militarists, the imperial Japanese government imposed direct military rule on its Korean colony in 1931; the Japanese Army occupied Manchuria the same year, and embarked on the conquest of China in 1937. Fascist Italy invaded Ethiopia in 1935, Albania in 1939. Nazis came to power in Germany in 1933, annexed Austria in 1938, Czechoslovakia the next spring, then invaded Poland in September 1939, provoking war with Britain and France. By the end of 1940, German troops occupied most of western Europe, and Italy and Japan had joined Germany in an alliance of mutual defense against any attack. The CIO opposed fascism and aggression. Its unions joined churches, women's associations, and civil rights groups in the American League Against War and Fascism, which lobbied against trade with fascist nations. The CIO worked with Chinese American groups and the National Negro Congress to boycott Japanese goods. Communists spearheaded a "Hands Off Ethiopia" campaign.

Spain got the most attention. In 1936, the fascist General Francisco Franco rebelled against the Republican government, with German and Italian aid. Labor activists were among 2,800 Americans who went to Spain to fight fascism, most as members of the Abraham Lincoln Brigade. The North American Committee to Aid Spanish Democracy supplied the republicans with hundreds of tons of food, clothes, and medical supplies. (General Motors and Texaco sent trucks and fuel to the fascists.) The CIO denounced the U.S. embargo on arms shipments to Spain, and opposed Roosevelt's recognition of the Franco regime in 1939.

The CIO also opposed domestic fascism. Its 1938 convention condemned the poll taxes used to deny African-American voting rights. CIO officers and member unions joined with the American Committee to Protect the Foreign Born to urge repeal of the Smith Act. As honorary member Paul Robeson declared at the 1941 National Maritime Union convention, ". . . we stand for mankind wherever it may suffer and wherever it may be oppressed . . . As long as we are struggling for a better life, we have one cause."

By 1940, the depression was ending, the recovery based on government spending on military procurement. Roosevelt promised to keep the U.S. out of the war, but his administration supported both an expansion of the U.S. arsenal and equipping Britain. Congress appropriated $16 billion for airplanes, warships, and other munitions. The CIO picked up momentum, growing to 4 million by the end of the year.

Roosevelt was elected to a third term in 1940, but by a narrower margin, beating Republican Wendell Wilkie by 5 million votes. John L. Lewis broke with other CIO leaders to oppose Roosevelt's nomination and endorse Wilkie in the election. If the President was reelected, he declared, he would know the CIO's rank and file backed Roosevelt, take it as a vote of no confidence in his own leadership, and resign. He kept his word; SWOC's Philip Murray took his place. The New Deal finished, Lewis gone, the nation beginning to prosper but moving toward a new world war: the labor movement headed into a new and uncertain era.

CHAPTER

HOT WAR, COLD WAR

War-related production boosted the economy out of depression on a rising tide of employment. As the nation mobilized for war, union leaders took on key roles, and unions made dramatic gains, especially in mass-production industries. By war's end the Congress of Industrial Organizations claimed six million members; its unions enjoyed new rights to representation and collective bargaining, and its leaders planned to use labor's political power to expand labor and civil rights and New Deal social programs. The postwar regime did have a place for organized labor, but it was not a leading role, and it came with political requirements that split the labor movement. The plans faltered, and even eventual reconciliation and merger between the American Federation of Labor and much of the CIO could not restore labor's momentum.

In 1940, labor—like the rest of the country—was divided over the preparations for war. John L. Lewis would not trust Roosevelt after the president failed to stop government contracts going to companies that broke labor laws. He joined with the communists to oppose any move to draw the U.S. into another war. Most union leaders opposed the peacetime draft, which Congress passed in September 1940 by a single vote. A few supported the president—Sidney Hillman of the Amalgamated Clothing Workers argued, "No man can say he is for labor, if he is not ready to defend democracy to the utmost." Hillman enjoyed Roosevelt's confidence, and served on his National Defense Advisory Council.

Meanwhile CIO unions enrolled close to a million new members. At Ford, the United Auto Workers lined up endorsements from civil rights activists and swept a May 1941 NLRB election against an AFL-chartered "United Auto Workers" led by the losing faction in the union's 1939 national election. The first Ford contract stunned observers—a union shop, dues check-off, seniority protection, grievance procedures, and the highest wages in the industry, all in return for a no-strike clause. The Steelworkers shut down Bethlehem Steel's Lackawanna, New York, plant in February and its home works in Bethlehem, Pennsylvania, in March, then went on to win one NLRB vote after another. Youngstown Sheet & Tube and Inland Steel signed union contracts without asking for elections.

Some employers resisted. When strikes affected military procurement, company executives and War Department officials urged federal intervention. Open-shop Allis-Chalmers fired union activists from a plant making Navy turbines in January 1941, and UAW Local 248 walked out. Now codirector of the Office of Production Management (OPM), Hillman tried to mediate and failed. Roosevelt ordered the plant reopened in March; the National Guard suppressed picket-line violence. The local accepted a compromise in April.

The fight at North American Aviation in Inglewood, California, was more complicated. The UAW defeated the AFL Machinists for representation in January 1941 and demanded big wage increases. The company stalled, and the local set up pickets June 5. UAW leaders wanted no part of it. Aviation Division director Richard Frankensteen denounced the strike as communist-inspired, suspended local officials, and ordered members back to work. Most refused—strikers shouted him down at a mass meeting—and Roosevelt sent the Guard to enforce the union order. Federal mediators later handed down substantial raises.

Inglewood displayed the increasingly bitter feuding between communists and anticommunists in the CIO. Roosevelt loyalists had been quick to charge their opponents with communist loyalties during the 1940 election, and that year's CIO convention passed (with no roll-call vote) the first of what CIO News editor Len De Caux called "anticommunazi" resolutions, opposing policies based on communism, fascism, and other "foreign ideologies." The Communist Party had abandoned the united front against fascism following the Nazi-Soviet nonaggression pact of August 22, 1939. When Germany invaded the Soviet Union on June 22, 1941, the Party almost overnight turned back to the antifascist war. However welcome the reds might be as allies, the switch did little to alter the widespread suspicion that the Party followed orders from Moscow.

Lewis maintained his antiwar position. In September he began a series of short strikes for union recognition in the "captive" mines owned and operated by corporations like U.S. Steel. More and more isolated in the CIO, he disaffiliated his 600,000 miners in 1942 and returned them to the AFL the next year.

Still another labor constituency criticized the war mobilization. A. Philip Randolph of the AFL's Brotherhood of Sleeping Car Porters and Maids organized a movement to "March on Washington" to protest racial discrimination and segregation in war industries, government employment, and the armed forces—over 100,000 people planned to rally in the capital on July 1, 1941. When Roosevelt agreed to ban racial discrimination by military contractors, Randolph called off the march. His compromise angered his own allies; opposition to the march from union leaders and communists, who put the fight against fascism abroad, before the struggle for justice at home made them even angrier.

Patriotic union leaders could sometimes get help from the government. Minneapolis Teamsters Local 544, led by anti-Stalinist communists from the Socialist Workers Party, threatened to join the CIO in mid-1941. At the suggestion of Teamster president Daniel Tobin, the Justice Department invoked the Smith Act, raided the Minneapolis SWP office and indicted twenty-nine Party members, most also Local 544 activists, for conspiring "to teach, advocate, and encourage the overthrow of the government by force and violence." Attorney General Francis Biddle led the prosecution and got eighteen convictions; Tobin lieutenant Jimmy Hoffa took over the local. As the American Civil Liberties Union noted, the government "injected itself into an interunion controversy in order to promote the interests of the one side which supported the Administration's foreign and domestic policies."

On December 7, 1941, the president's arbitrator announced the UMW would represent the captive mines. That very day Japanese warplanes attacked the Navy base at Pearl Harbor in Hawaii. The next day Congress declared war on Japan (and the judge in the Minneapolis trial handed down sentences). Germany and Italy declared war on the U.S. three days later. Over the next three and a half years, the war touched every part of American life and transformed the labor movement. How these changes looked depended on one's perspective: the view from union offices was rosier than the view from the shop floor.

AMERICA AT WAR

For the U.S. the Second World War began and ended in the Pacific. After Pearl Harbor, the Japanese overran British and U.S. colonial forces in the West Pacific from Malaya north to Attu and Kiska in Alaska's Aleutian Islands. With Britain and the Soviet Union facing Nazi conquest, the U.S. almost alone opposed Japanese expansion, and came late to the European theater—after the Soviets had defeated the main Nazi force at Stalingrad in February 1943. Nevertheless, the European "war against Fascism" shored up morale and sustained the ideology of a war for democracy.

The Second World War dwarfed the First. The death toll was enormous—more than 50 million overall, more than 18 million in the Soviet Union alone. Compared to the First World War, U.S. losses were considerable, though mostly military—322,000 combat dead, 675,000 wounded, 124,000 captured (more than 12,000 dying in captivity).

The nation mobilized on an unprecedented scale and at immense cost—$350 billion, about ten times more than the First World War. More than half the money was borrowed; the national debt quintupled. Corporate profits soared on cost-plus government contracts and tax credits for building or improving plants for war production. Unemployment virtually disappeared Labor shortages drew many new workers from rural areas, especially the South and Southwest. War production penetrated some rural areas too. Navajo miners working on reservation lands on the Colorado Plateau extracted a thousand tons of uranium for the government's atomic bomb project. The president set the work week at forty-eight hours, with hours over forty paid as overtime. More people made more money than ever before.

A host of agencies coordinated the effort. The War Production Board directed conversion of civilian plants to military production—autoworkers made antiaircraft guns at General Motors. The Board of Economic Warfare allocated short supplies of rubber and petroleum. The Office of Price Administration (OPA) set maximum prices for manufactured goods, controlled rents in housing-short cities, and rationed scarce goods like sugar, coffee, and gasoline. Other agencies oversaw scientific research, transportation, housing construction, aid to allies, war information, and propaganda. The War Manpower Commission (WMC) coordinated both military conscription and the war production workforce. By mid-1943, the WMC had frozen 27 million workers in critical war industries.

Almost everyone supported the war. Families planted "victory gardens" and bought "Liberty Bonds." Volunteers collected scrap metal, served on Civil Defense committees, organized blood drives, wrote "victory mail" to the troops. Some opposition came from religious pacifists like the Catholic Worker organization and the Fellowship of Reconciliation, and from a few socialists. More substantial opposition came from fascist groups like the Silver Shirts and the Christian Nationalist Crusade (though even the Ku Klux Klan endorsed the war). Selective Service classified 43,000 draftees (out of ten million) as conscientious objectors, and reported that about 350,000 tried to evade the draft.

Federal agencies working with civilian groups promoted patriotic sentiments in a giant propaganda campaign. Newspapers, magazines, posters, movies, and radio broadcasts celebrated the war as a battle for democracy and portrayed wartime America as a beacon of tolerance, fairness, and equality. But just as the antifascist war was also a fight for empire, its impact on home-front democracy was ambiguous too.

Gender, racial, and ethnic barriers to employment and advancement diminished. Publicists celebrated multiethnic cooperation: the *Detroit News* compared autoworkers with names like Kowalski, Lugari, and Bauer to an "All-American football team." Immigration standards relaxed. Congress established the "Bracero" program in 1942 to bring in Mexican farm workers, and revoked Chinese exclusion in 1943. Roosevelt promised citizenship and veterans benefits to Filipinos who volunteered to keep fighting the Japanese until U.S. forces returned. Everyone could be enlisted or drafted, though Japanese American volunteers were accepted only as an experiment, and island Puerto Ricans and African Americans served in segregated units or assignments, mostly construction and stevedoring. (African Americans also served as servants for the almost exclusively white officer corps.) Of the more than 15 million people who went into the military, 700,000 were black, 350,000 Mexican American, 48,000 Puerto Rican, 30,000 Japanese, 19,000 Native American.

About 350,000 women joined the military, and the female labor force grew by more than five million, mostly in industrial and clerical work. Popular stereotypes like "Rosie the Riveter"—working to help her fighting man—boosted morale; many women war workers came from less well-paid jobs segregated by sex and race. The auto industry employed 115 black women at the beginning of the war; a year later the UAW had 5,000 black women members.

For some the war had two fronts. African American activists promoted a "Double V" campaign ("Victory over the Axis abroad, Victory over racism at home"). In August 1942 in St. Louis, people who had organized to march on Washington marched instead on Carter Carburetor, where not one employee out of 2,650 was black. The Fair Employment Practice Committee monitored job discrimination. In 1942, the FEPC directed Allis-Chalmers and nine other companies to cease racial and religious discrimination. In 1943 hearings, the War Manpower Commission found twenty-two railroads and fourteen rail unions discriminating against African and Mexican Americans.

Some people reacted violently to the changes. When the government built the Sojourner Truth Housing Project for black workers in a white Detroit neighborhood in early 1942, it had to send the National Guard to protect the new residents from violent harassment. The next year, 25,000 white Detroit Packard workers walked out to protest black workers placed in white jobs. The strike ended four days later after UAW President R. J. Thomas got the government to issue a back-to-work order and declared strikers would be fired without union objection. Two weeks later (June 20) the city exploded—thirty hours of racial violence left thirty-four dead, twenty-five black, most killed by police. The military had trouble too. That summer racial disturbances were recorded at bases around the country and overseas—one reporter was confused when he listened to black soldiers stationed in England talk about "the enemy" until he realized they meant white Americans. Nearly every week black newspapers reported another black soldier beaten or killed off base, usually somewhere in the South. Some vigilantes wore uniforms. Early in June 1943, rumors spread in Los Angeles that "zooters" (young Mexican American men affecting a distinctive style of tailored suits) were beating up sailors. Gangs of servicemen went hunting zooters, stripping and beating any they caught, and killing several.

The federal government committed the war's most massive violation of civil liberties. In February 1942, Roosevelt ordered Japanese Americans interned—about 112,000 men, women, and children. Internment was impractical in Hawaii (more than a third of the population had Japanese ancestry), but the authorities did declare martial law, detain 3,400 community leaders, and close Japanese newspapers, schools, and temples. Some trade unionists like A. Philip Randolph (though not communists) joined social workers and church leaders denouncing the internment. Louis Goldblatt of the California CIO Council warned against turning the antifascist struggle into a race war, with little apparent effect—in the brutal Pacific campaigns government propaganda on both sides described the enemy as inferior or inhuman, and many soldiers preferred not to take prisoners alive.

Some other acts of political repression had racial tones. The government suppressed the Nation of Islam's *Final Call,* and the leader of a Black Hebrew group in New Orleans was given a fifteen year sentence for encouraging draft refusals. But no dissent was tolerated. Six thousand conscientious objectors went to prison—most of them Jehovah's Witnesses—and many served in solitary confinement on bread and water diets. Another 12,000 objectors were put in "service" camps to work jobs like fire fighting without pay.

The war did transform labor relations. Most union leaders immediately pledged not to strike for the duration. To resolve labor disputes, the president established the National War Labor Board with representatives from labor, business, and government. To protect unions from losing members, the NWLB approved "maintenance of membership"—union-shop agreements in which new hires had fifteen days to join the union or be dismissed. From 1940 to 1945, total union membership more than doubled to 15 million.

When the steelworkers—who became the United Steelworkers of America (USWA)—began bargaining with "Little Steel," they demanded more pay to cover rises in the cost of living. In July 1942, the Board allowed a 15 percent raise over the level of January 1, 1941, and applied this formula to all wartime wage demands. Unions could get around it by negotiating better nonwage ("fringe") benefits. The NWLB routinely approved settlements with improvements in paid holidays and vacations, travel and meal allowances, shift differentials, incentive pay, and bonuses. It exempted insurance and medical care from the formula entirely.

Union leaders cracked down on "hate strikes" like Detroit Packard or tried to head them off. When Bendix hired a black man into the tool room at Sylvia Woods's plant, her UAW steward said, "He's coming here to work. Anybody that doesn't like it . . . turn in your union cards and get the hell out." As she recalled, "No one quit." Some unions campaigned against racism: the UAW endorsed the "Double V" campaign; USWA urged federal prosecution of the Klan. Los Angeles CIO unions were active among Mexican Americans, protesting housing discrimination, defending youths arrested as zooters, and getting voters registered.

The number of women in unions rose from 800,000 in 1940 to 3.5 million in 1944, almost a quarter of total membership. Some unions responded with new initiatives. Women were 40 percent of the members in the United Electrical, Radio and Machine Workers (UE) in 1944, and a third of the national staff. UE filed NWLB complaints against General Electric and Westinghouse for paying women less than men for the same work, and won. Women were 28 percent of UAW membership in 1944. UAW locals hired women counsellors to help members with problems like child care and sexual harassment. In the United Cannery Workers (UCAPAWA)—renamed the Food, Tobacco, Agricultural and Allied Workers (FTA) in 1944—more than half the shop stewards were women, two out of three contracts required equal pay for equal work, and three out of four provided leaves of absence (for pregnancy, for example) with no loss of seniority.

For some CIO leaders, disciplined mobilization was not the only way labor could contribute to the war effort. Philip Murray and Walter Reuther of the UAW's General Motors division proposed industry councils, where labor would join with management to allocate resources and improve productivity. Of course, corporations would not share such management prerogatives with labor unless directed by the government, and political hostility to unions was rising. Congressional conservatives were strong enough to override Roosevelt's veto of the War Labor Disputes Act ("Smith-Connolly") in June 1943, the first antilabor legislation to become federal law since 1932. It imposed a thirty-day wait after a vote to strike, allowed the government to take over war production plants when a strike was called, banned even talking strike in federal facilities, and limited union participation in elections. The same Congress voided NLRB prohibitions on the "back-door" contracts employers signed with AFL unions to block CIO drives.

The CIO set up a Political Action Committee (CIO-PAC) to marshal union support for the President, prolabor candidates, and progressive legislation. Under Hillman's direction, CIO-PAC raised money and worked with progressive groups but its main effort—chosen after study of the 1942 elections in industrial districts—went into turning out the union vote. It lobbied legislators to let military personnel register and vote by mail. It also made special appeals to women and African Americans, who could best build on their wartime gains by joining union members in backing a revitalized New Deal. CIO-backed candidates did well in the primaries.

CIO-PAC was technically nonpartisan, and endorsed a few Republicans, but labor support for the President was a campaign theme—Republicans loved to repeat the story that Roosevelt told anyone who suggested a candidate for vice president to "clear it with Sidney" Hillman. In fact, CIO delegates to the Democratic Convention abandoned their first choice, incumbent Henry Wallace, to support Missouri Senator Harry Truman (and block South Carolina Senator James G. Byrnes). The general election was disappointing. Roosevelt was reelected and Democrats gained in Congress, but the electorate provided no mandate for a new New Deal.

As the war wore on, divisions began to strain labor peace. Some unions kept the color line. In 1943, twenty AFL affiliates and independent rail brotherhoods still excluded black members; another eight put them in Jim Crow locals. When the FEPC ordered AFL Boilermakers to cease discrimination in 1944, the union charged the Committee was run by communists. CIO unions generally endorsed women's rights to their jobs after the war, but some UAW locals colluded with employers to push women out of "men's work."

The no-strike pledge hurt. Stella Nowicki, working at the Swift plant in Chicago, saw its effect on her CIO United Packinghouse Workers local: "Grievances were hung up without being settled or turned down because the company knew we couldn't do anything." Meanwhile, production speeded up. Kaiser steelworkers could build a cargo ship in about eighty days in early 1942; by 1944 they needed only twenty-two. Industrial accidents kept pace—the Labor Department recorded more than six and a half million during the war. Through 1943, industrial accidents claimed more lives (37,600) than combat.

Most unions had to suppress local job actions to keep the pledge. Union members still staged thousands of strikes—virtually all wildcats—during the war, most over local grievances. In 1944, the Labor Department counted 4,956 strikes involving about 2.1 million workers, a record year by both counts. As Buick worker Norm Bully recalled,

> Corporations were showing no sense of patriotism or loyalty and were contributing nothing. All the sacrifices were on the part of the workers. When real and pressing grievances arose and there was no solution and management hid behind the no-strike pledge, the people felt that they were justified . . . in forcing a settlement.

Fisher Body sandblasters struck to get ten minutes paid cleanup time at the end of the shift. Ford River Rouge assembly line workers walked out when the company removed their stools, and again to protest bad ventilation. Briggs Mack crane operators refused to work more than eight hours straight. UAW locals in southern Illinois walked out when members on leave for military service returned with medical discharges and were declared unfit for work. Half of all autoworkers got involved in strikes in 1944, many in sympathy for workmates unfairly disciplined or discharged. In contrast, fewer than one in twenty electrical workers joined strikes that year. UE was a "red" union and the UAW was not—in general, communist union leaders were the quickest to crack down on anything that might disrupt the war effort.

John L. Lewis never took the pledge. To beat the Little Steel formula he led half a million miners out on strike four times in 1943. Few union leaders could have imitated him even if they had tried. He controlled his union from top to bottom. He was a master of negotiation by showdown. And union coal was not so critical to the war—the administration could afford to wait to find out what he would accept. Though his strengths were unique, his constant criticism of union cooperation with government made sense. The NWLB's approval of closed shops ("maintenance of membership") brought in thousands of new union members with no commitment to the union, but check-off docked their pay for union dues anyway. With no strike threat, employers had no reason to negotiate, so union leaders depended on politicians to win concessions. Politicians wanted production without disruption, and inevitably union leaders sometimes blocked even the most urgent and legitimate demands of their members to keep their political friends happy. The 1943 miners' strikes made a lot of politicians unhappy.

During 1944, the war turned in favor of the Allies. Germany was caught between massive Soviet armies and Anglo-American forces. They met at the Elbe River late in April 1945; Germany surrendered unconditionally on May 7. (Franklin Roosevelt did not live to see it, dying suddenly on April 12.) In the Pacific, U.S. forces had nearly reached Japan itself. On August 6 and 9, U.S. airplanes dropped atomic bombs on Hiroshima and Nagasaki, killing 80,000 and 35,000 people instantly, and tens of thousands more within days from burns and radiation. The Japanese surrendered August 14. As the Allies occupied Poland and Germany they liberated camps where the Nazis had exterminated millions of Jews—along with Gypsies, homosexuals, Slavs, and communists.

The end of the war found the U.S. with the apparatus of a planned economy—OPA alone had 73,000 employees and 200,000 volunteers—and facing the specter of postwar depression. Military contracts were cancelled, and war workers laid off—including four million women in the first eight months after VJ Day. Meanwhile tens of thousands of soldiers staged demonstrations in Manila, Seoul, Paris, and Frankfurt, demanding to be brought home to civilian life and work. Both civilians and veterans believed that their victory had earned them opportunity, equality, and a better standard of living.

Congress had already passed the "G.I. Bill of Rights," the Servicemen's Readjustment Act, in June 1944. It provided subsidized home and business loans, student stipends and job training, unemployment benefits, life insurance, hospital care, disability pensions, burial allowances, and cash bonuses—the most generous benefits war veterans (or anyone else) had ever received. More generally, President Truman proposed to continue price controls, raise the minimum wage, legislate fair employment practices, and fund unemployment compensation and a national housing program.

CIO leaders wanted to mobilize for peace. AFL leaders wanted the government out of labor relations. Businessmen looked to dismantle not only wartime controls and regulations, but the entire New Deal. The political contest started early. In Detroit's 1945 mayoral election, the UAW's Frankensteen led the nonpartisan primary vote. Backed by city newspapers and business leaders, incumbent Edward Jeffries warned that if Frankensteen won, communists would move blacks into white residential areas, lowering property values. Frankensteen lost—the vote was not even close. The labor-management conference convened by Truman in November to discuss postwar conditions broke up without agreement.

THE POSTWAR WORLD

In the first twelve months after the war, more than 4,600 strikes swept across the country. More than five million workers participated, mainly from industrial unions. The CIO Oil Workers Industrial Union started, striking on September 17, 1945, with the slogan "52-40 or Fight," fifty-two hours pay for forty hours work, followed within days by 200,000 coal miners striking for union recognition and 24,000 AFL lumber workers in the Northwest. East Coast ports shut down for nineteen days while International Long-shoremen's Association members struck against their "president-for-life" Joseph Ryan's agreement with shippers. AFL and CIO Machinists stayed out 140 days, CIO textile workers in New England 133 days, CIO glassworkers 102 days, 70,000 Midwest Teamsters 81 days. Four strikes were huge—200,000 workers in auto, 300,000 in meatpacking, 180,000 in electrical, 750,000 in steel. Everyone wanted a raise.

Wages were central to CIO plans. Rising wages would provide the consumer purchasing power to sustain prosperity. Wartime profits were more than twice the prewar average, nearly the highest on record according to government economists, suggesting that employers could pay more without raising prices. Corporate analysts argued to the contrary that profits were so low any cost increase required waiver of price controls.

The UAW targetted General Motors first; Walter Reuther demanded a 30 percent increase in hourly wages and challenged the company to open its books to prove it could not afford the raise. G.M. refused Reuther's offer of arbitration. On November 21, 1945, the UAW shut down ninety-two plants in fifty cities, and on December 8 rejected Truman's order to return to work. In January a presidential Fact Finding Panel calculated a 33 percent rise in the cost of living since 1941 and recommended that wages increase about half that amount—about 19.5 cents an hour at G.M. Reuther accepted the deal but the company refused. The United Electrical Workers demanded the same and went on strike, followed by the AFL and CIO packinghouse unions, then by the Steel Workers. The Office of Price Administration began authorizing price increases, and by mid–March the unions had settled national pattern agreements in all four industries—G.M. was the last to capitulate. Reuther became the new UAW president.

John L. Lewis scoffed at the settlements, demanded higher raises plus employer contributions to the union's welfare fund for his miners, and called 400,000 UMW members out on strike April 1. Truman seized the mines under Smith-Connolly. When the Supreme Court upheld contempt judgements against the UMW and Lewis himself, he called off the strike (but got what he wanted when the mines returned to private control a year later). When the Railroad Trainmen and the Locomotive Engineers issued a strike call in May, Truman asked Congress for authority to draft strikers into the military. The unions settled.

Some unions revived the general strike. In January 1946, 10,000 people from thirty AFL and CIO unions rallied in Stamford, Connecticut under the banner "We Will Not Go Back to the Old Days" after striking machinists were attacked by state and city police. The next month unions shut down Lancaster, Pennsylvania, for two days to stop police attacks on striking city transit workers. Later that month 20,000 AFL and CIO union members rallied in Houston, Texas, to force the mayor to negotiate with the AFL City-County Employees Union. In December, when the Oakland, California, merchants' association refused to negotiate with Retail Clerks Local 1265, 130,000 people joined a fifty-four–hour "work holiday"—"more like a revolution than an industrial dispute," to quote Teamster president Tobin.

While employers freely took out injunctions against strike-related activities, they did not generally revive old-time terrorist tactics. The New Deal and wartime labor regulations had established the right to organize and bargain collectively, and the unions' ability to defend and advance their members' interests against the biggest corporations and at the highest levels of government confirmed the new importance of organized labor's role in American society and politics. In November 1946 in Atlantic City, the CIO debated and adopted a new program. The delegates wanted fair employment practices enforced, strike-related injunctions banned, the Wagner Act extended to agricultural workers, and much more.

Delegates called for continued price and rent controls, massive investment in public housing, higher taxes on corporations and the rich, and expanded social security. They recommended federal prosecution of lynching, condemned poll taxes and other impediments to voting, and asked the Senate to expel Mississippi Klansman Theodore Bilbo. They urged affiliates to negotiate for equal pay and opportunities, endorsed an Equal Rights

Amendment for women, and called for funding maternal and child health services, day care, nursery schools, and school lunches. They endorsed better veterans benefits, military reforms to eliminate "caste distinctions" and fix the "outmoded and unjust courtmartial system," and an end to the draft. The convention backed self-determination for colonies, a Jewish homeland in Palestine, and universal disarmament. It approved CIO participation in the World Federation of Trade Unions (WFTU), which recognized Soviet labor federations.

Amid this exuberant consensus on social justice, one division threatened unity. Murray introduced a "Declaration of Policy," asking delegates to endorse democracy, Americanism, and Roosevelt's "Four Freedoms" (freedom of speech and religion, freedom from fear and want), and to "resent and reject efforts of the Communist Party . . . to interfere in the affairs of the CIO." Communist-led unions made up a fifth of CIO membership, but only two delegates voted against the declaration.

Business leaders countered CIO initiatives with public relations propaganda. After Truman gutted price controls in mid-1946, companies explained how union wage demands raised consumer prices. Wealthy conservatives funded groups like American Action—run out of the Chicago Board of Trade—to oppose CIO-backed candidates and alert the public to the dangers of communism.

Corporate lobbyists swarmed Congress. Their goal was "Taft-Hartley," the Labor Management Relations Act. It outlawed mass picketing, sympathy strikes, and secondary boycotts; banned closed shops and unions of supervisors; held unions responsible for strike-related damages; banned strikes by federal employees; let states ban union shops; authorized the president to issue eighty-day injunctions if strikes threatened national health and safety; provided NLRB protection for decertification and deauthorization elections; and required unions seeking NLRB jurisdiction to file noncommunist affidavits every year for every officer above shop steward. As New York Congressman Donald O'Toole observed, the bill was composed "sentence by sentence, paragraph by paragraph, page by page, by the National Association of Manufacturers." Congress passed it over Truman's veto on June 23, 1947.

Unlike previous anticommunist campaigns, the postwar drive fed and fed off of an aggressive U.S. foreign policy. The war was in progress when the government started planning the postwar world. Democracy "American-style" needed prosperity, which depended on trade. As a State Department official said, "we've got to plan an enormously increased production in this country after the war. . . . There won't be any question about our needing greatly increased foreign markets." In 1944, the Anglo-American allies set up the International Monetary Fund to regulate financial transactions based on the dollar, and the International Bank of Reconstruction and Development (later called the "World Bank") to promote recovery from the war's devastation. When the U.S. freed the Philippines (July 4, 1946), it kept control of tariffs and monetary policy, along with twenty military bases (and rescinded Roosevelt's promise of citizenship and benefits to more than 200,000 Filipino veterans).

Communism was the main obstacle. The Soviet Union had halted the Nazi advance, and communists everywhere, who had zealously supported (and often led) resistance to Axis occupation, looked to the Soviets—now stronger than ever—for inspiration and guidance, or for direct instructions. The generals who ran the Manhattan Project building the atomic bomb understood the immediate target might be Germany or Japan, but the ultimate target was the Soviet Union. The War Department told Murray in 1943 to stop the CIO's Federation of Architects, Engineers, Chemists and Technicians Local 25 from organizing at the Berkeley Radiation Lab, and began purging suspected communists from the maritime trades, especially after merchant seamen protested their assignment to carry French troops back to Indochina in 1945. In 1946, the U.S. set up the Strategic Air Command—its only mission to prepare to drop the new atomic bombs on the Soviet Union. In March 1947, Truman declared the U.S. must help "peoples who are resisting attempted subjugation by armed minorities or by outside pressures," and asked Congress for $400 million in military and economic aid for Turkey, which guarded the southern Soviet border, and Greece, where communist insurrection threatened a British-sponsored monarchy. In June Secretary of State George Marshall announced his $16 billion plan to aid countries that accepted what a business magazine called "a business plan *plus* . . . plus political direction, plus diplomatic guidance."

The world-wide war against Communism went back and forth. U.S. forces suppressed the Filipino Hukbalahap movement, the French drove Indochinese Communists underground, the Greek uprising failed, but Communists took over Czechoslovakia, and the Chinese Red Army marched into Beijing. India, Burma, Palestine, and Indonesia won independence, and rebellion simmered in colonial Africa. The Anglo-American North Atlantic Treaty Organization and the Soviet Warsaw Pact split Europe in 1949. Korea—divided by the Allies in 1945—remained divided after three years of war beginning in 1950, involving both U.S. and Chinese soldiers.

A steel industry journal predicted, "maintaining and building our preparation for war will be big business . . . for at least a considerable period

ahead." The military budget went from $12 billion a year in 1950 to $40 billion in 1953, the bulk of it for nuclear weapons development and U.S. bases
around the world. In 1962, *Business Week* magazine found that 24,000 companies had defense contracts, which employed more than 4 million workers.

This Cold War fostered the largest and longest red scare in U.S. history.
Beginning in 1948, Communist Party leaders were indicted, convicted, and
imprisoned for Smith Act violations. Under the 1950 Internal Security Act
("McCarran"), officers and members of 600 "Communist Action" organizations (most concerned with peace, civil rights, and labor) had to register
with the Subversive Activities Control Board. Two Communists—Julius
Rosenberg and his wife Ethel—were executed in 1953 for espionage
(though authorities considered her innocent of direct participation). Party
membership fell from its historic high of 80,000 in 1946 to about 3,000 in
1958, and its influence to just about zero.

But the campaign went far beyond the Party. The U.S. Chamber of Commerce published "Communist Infiltration in the United States" (1946),
"Communists Within the Labor Movement," and "Communists Within the
Government" (both 1947), claiming to show how far the Soviet plot had
advanced—communists already influenced if they did not actually run the
NLRB and the Labor Department. Acting on the Chamber's advice, Truman
established a "Loyalty Program" in 1947. It eventually covered more than
15 million people employed in government or by companies with government contracts. Six Congressional committees investigated the loyalty of
government employees in 1948—the best-known was headed by Wisconsin
Republican Senator Joseph McCarthy. By 1953–54, fifty-one different committees were in the hunt—the House Un-American Activities Committee
alone held 147 hearings. By then nearly 30,000 people had been accused of
disloyalty, and 10,000 had lost their jobs. Others lost the right to vote, as well
as unemployment, disability, old age, and veteran's benefits.

The red scare touched every corner of American life. In 1952, Revlon
Cosmetics changed the name of its "Russian Sable" face powder to "Dark
Dark." A city manager in Wheeling, West Virginia, noticed some vending
machines that dispensed gum and trinkets representing the world's nations.
Finding some stamped USSR, he reported the vendors to the FBI. A passerby
called New York City police when he spotted utility workers signalling sur-
veyors with red flags. The Soviet development of a nuclear arsenal sparked
a nationwide civil defense program, which taught millions of children to
"duck and cover"—duck their heads under their desks and cover their
eyes—in case of an atomic blast. Some building contractors specialized in
home bomb shelters, from $20 "foxholes" to $5,000 "honeymoon" models.

Some developments were less comical. A sexual panic accompanied the red scare and twenty-one states passed laws against "sexual psychopaths"—claiming homosexuals to be tainted with the same moral degeneracy as communists. A 1950 Congressional subcommittee declared them security risks, and homosexuals were barred from government service in 1953. Gay and lesbian activists started the Mattachine Society (1950) and Daughters of Bilitis (1955) to push for legal and civil rights. Mattachine founder (and one-time Department Store Workers organizer) Harry Hay recalled, "The first five . . . were all union members experienced in organizing underground." Revels Cayton, a leader in the CIO Marine Cooks and Stewards, observed, "If you let them red bait, they'll race bait. If you let them race bait, they'll queen bait."

Cold War diplomatic considerations did encourage some government intervention in race relations. Though Congress cut off Fair Employment Practice Committee funding in 1946, in 1947 the President's Committee on Civil Rights condemned wartime Japanese internment and warned that racist incidents (like the forty lynchings recorded in 1946) made "excellent propaganda ammunition for Communist agents." In 1948, after A. Philip Randolph and other civil rights activists threatened to organize a boycott of the draft, Truman ordered the military to desegregate (the Pentagon reported the process complete in 1955). When the Supreme Court reversed *Plessy v. Ferguson* and declared legal segregation unconstitutional in *Brown v. Board of Education* in 1954, Voice of America overseas radio broadcast the text of the decision in thirty-four languages. In 1957, President Eisenhower sent troops to enforce a court order letting black students enroll at Central High School in Little Rock, Arkansas, and then signed the first federal civil rights act since Reconstruction, letting the government seek injunctions against voting rights violations and creating a civil rights commission.

Similar considerations shaped immigration and colonial policies. After 60,000 Puerto Ricans had been drafted or enlisted for Korea, the colony received "commonwealth status" in 1952, remaining under U.S. law though its citizens could not vote in federal elections nor its representatives vote in Congress. The 1952 McCarran-Walters Immigration Act voided the 1790 law restricting naturalization to "white persons," and set new quotas—each Asian country got 100 a year. Alaska and Hawaii became states in 1959 (though the status of their indigenous peoples remained unsettled). On State Department advice, Congress reformed quotas again in 1965, allowing up to 20,000 arrivals a year from every independent nation outside the Americas.

The war against fascism never diminished labor anticommunism. After a California grassroots campaign directed by veteran UCAPAWA-FTA organizer Luisa Moreno took an NLRB election from them in October 1945, the Teamsters boycotted canneries with FTA contracts, signed a union shop agreement with the growers, attacked locked-out FTA pickets, and roused Catholic priests to tell parishioners to shun the communist-led FTA. The Teamsters won a new election in August 1946 (and the INS deported Moreno to Mexico in 1948). In Europe, the AFL's Free Trade Union Committee—run by renegade Communist Jay Lovestone—paid criminal syndicates to attack French Communist dockworkers, and Greek unions to sit out the insurrection.

Anticommunism wrecked the CIO's first major postwar drive. Philip Murray announced "Operation Dixie" in May 1946 as a "civil rights crusade." CIO organizing director Allan Heywood elaborated: "Only with a united movement, based on equal rights, can we win our fight for economic security for all." Over the summer and fall CIO unions established ten to twenty new southern locals a week, doing best with African Americans and women. The AFL launched a rival drive and relentlessly red-baited the CIO; so did employers, politicians, and the Klan. In fact, Operation Dixie excluded communists from staff, and—hoping to woo textile workers—fielded mostly white organizers (and no women). The textile drive foundered; CIO staff blamed the communists.

No labor leader liked Taft-Hartley. The UAW shut down auto plants for five hours to support 200,000 people rallying against the "Slave Labor Act" in Detroit. Lewis proposed to the 1947 AFL convention that unions nullify the law by refusing to sign noncommunist affidavits, but only the International Typographical Union (whose members' wartime wages had been frozen) backed the suggestion. Shortly afterwards he led the UMW out of the Federation.

Murray saw Taft-Hartley as a call for more effective political action. In 1948, both Truman and Republican Thomas Dewey ran on Cold War platforms. AFL and most CIO leaders supported Truman. Communist-led unions backed Henry Wallace, running on a Progressive Party platform opposing the Cold War. Truman won by a very small margin. His labor backers were disappointed to find Taft-Hartley would not be repealed, but they staunchly supported his foreign policy. In 1949, the CIO followed Belgian union leaders (paid by Lovestone) out of the WFTU when it opposed the Marshall Plan. The CIO joined the AFL in founding the International Confederation of Free Trade Unions (ICFTU). Lovestone and associates spent Marshall Plan money to get German union leaders to drop an initiative for labor unity across occupation zones and to break a citywide strike in divided Berlin.

Murray fired left-wing CIO staffers. CIO leaders like Mike Quill of the Transit Workers and Joe Curran of the National Maritime Union denounced their former allies. Industrial councils cut off left-led locals. In January 1949, United Furniture Workers Local 282 went on strike at the Memphis (Tennessee) Furniture Company. Police escorted scabs and visited local members at home late at night to ask questions, but the strikers—mostly black women—had strong backing from the community. The Memphis Industrial Council withdrew support, and the strike failed. (Memphis Furniture stayed nonunion until 1978.)

Taft-Hartley had changed the rules. Unions that refused to file affidavits were barred from NLRB ballots. UE refused, and the UAW won NLRB elections in UE shops in Hartford, Connecticut, and Brooklyn, New York. By 1949, the CIO's Communications Workers and Steelworkers, and the AFL's Machinists and International Brotherhood of Electrical Workers were raiding UE locals. The UE convention that September voted to file the affidavits, but the raids continued. When UE withheld CIO dues in protest, the Congress expelled it and chartered the rival International Union of Electrical, Radio, and Machine Workers (IUE). Murray met with Westinghouse and General Electric executives to plan IUE takeovers of UE locals. Over 1949 and 1950, the CIO expelled ten more unions: FTA; United Office and Professional Workers of America (UOPWA); Mine, Mill and Smelter Workers; Farm Equipment Workers; Fur and Leather Workers; International Longshoremen and Warehousemen (ILWU); United Public Workers (UPW); American Communications Association; National Union of Marine Cooks and Stewards; and International Fishermen and Allied Workers.

These were among the CIO unions most committed to racial and gender equity. FTA organized Mexican Americans, Filipinos, and African Americans, especially women. Marine Cooks and Stewards were exceptionally racially diverse and packed with gay men as well. Mine Mill was mostly African American in the Southeast and Mexican American in the Southwest. ILWU organized Japanese, Chinese, Filipino, Puerto Rican, Portuguese, and native Hawaiian field workers. UOPWA and UPW members were mostly white women, but UOPWA also organized Prudential Life Insurance salesmen, and UPW-organized black workers in federal cafeterias in Washington, and Afro-Antillean laborers in the Panama Canal Zone. Left-led unions helped the Party-supported National Negro Labor Council turn out 1,500 pickets to protest racist hiring policies at American Airlines in Cleveland, Ohio, in December 1952, and the Farm Equipment Workers local at International Harvester supported a 1953 campaign to get black workers hired at the new General Electric plant in Louisville, Kentucky.

These unions actively built themselves on community support. In 1951, Empire Zinc got an injunction against an eight-month-old Mine Mill strike in Bayard, New Mexico. As miner's wife Elvira Moreno wrote the local newspaper, "The order restrains our husbands . . . but it does not restrain us. . . . Women from all over the county have joined our ranks and the picket line is solid." The line stayed solid against assaults and arrests for seven months and won the miners modest gains. The left-led unions also practiced militant solidarity. When Westinghouse fired two Socialist Workers Party members as security risks from its South Philadelphia plant, UE Local 107 stopped work until the company took them back. But as the local reported, "We haven't been hearing much about this kind of thing lately, especially in the trade union movement."

Between 1951 and 1953, AFL and CIO unions conducted more than 1,200 raids on "red" locals, not always with the desired result. CIO leaders red- and race-baited FTA's largest local, Local 22 in Winston-Salem, North Carolina, so badly its members decertified it, but never joined another union. In the end only UE and ILWU survived as national unions, the ILWU limited to the West Coast and Hawaii. Expulsions and AFL raids took a big toll on CIO membership. After claiming 6.3 million members in 1946, by 1954 the CIO could count only 4.6 million. Over the same period, the AFL grew to 10.2 million.

In the new Cold War political climate, labor, management, and government gradually hammered out a new accord. UAW negotiations with General Motors set the pace. In the 1948 contract, the company gave a "cost-of-living adjustment" (COLA) and an automatic 2 percent annual raise for productivity improvements. The 1950 "Treaty of Detroit" included a COLA and pensions along with wage increases, and ran for an unprecedented five years. When Reuther demanded a re-opener in 1953, G.M. folded part of the COLAs into basic wage rates. During the 1950s, more than half of all major union contracts included some provision for COLAs. Where industries were mostly unionized, national or regional pattern contracts were the rule, and even nonunion companies like DuPont and Internal Business Machines adopted COLAs, benefits, and formal grievance procedures.

Union workers' pay outpaced inflation, but their unions paid a price in democracy and activism. Employers insisted on elaborate grievance procedures, which had to be exhausted before the union authorized a strike. Wildcats continued—the steel industry reported close to 800 during 1956–58—but were usually short and strictly local. Unions deferred to management on issues like work rules, output quotas, investment (and reinvestment) policies. They could only watch when companies like Alexander Smith Carpet left Yonkers, New York, for "right-to-work" Georgia. In 1949, Ford began moving production from its River Rouge plant—from a 1941 peak of 83,000, employment fell to 65,000 by 1950, and went under 30,000 during the 1960s. As a G.M. official put it, "give the union the money. . . . But don't let them take the business away from us." Reuther concurred: "We make collective bargaining agreements, not revolutions." Dissent from this perspective in the UAW and other industrial unions like the Rubber Workers and Steel Workers was ruthlessly suppressed.

The CIO joined the AFL in endorsing the Korean War. CIO leaders hoped to revive the wartime partnership with government and business, but the Truman administration never adopted more than partial measures to direct and control the economy. Murray negotiated a new steel settlement only after a protracted and unpopular strike.

Organized labor's cooperation with government was closer abroad. In 1954, a wave of strikes hit United Fruit plantations in Honduras. As the army arrested strike leaders, operatives rushed in from the Inter-American Regional Organization of Workers (ORIT), started in 1951 by the ICFTU, and funded by the U.S. government. They called off the strikes and set up a company union. In Puerto Rico, labor activists established a new federation in 1947—the Confederación General de Trabajadores (CGT). When CGT unions refused to comply with Taft-Hartley, AFL and CIO affiliates sent in organizers. Labor activist Juan Saez Corales—who was arrested in 1954 on Smith Act charges—wrote in 1955: "The CIO and AF of L have been imported into Puerto Rico to colonize the labor movement. Those organizations serve the purpose of the Puerto Rican government and American employers who come to Puerto Rico to pile up more wealth." Both AFL and CIO affiliates supported Puerto Rico's exemption from the federal minimum wage, the key component (along with ten-year tax holidays) of "Operation Bootstrap," the economic development program of the Partido Popular Democrático, which governed the island from 1941 to 1968.

By 1955, the two federations differed mainly in the degree to which the AFL tolerated what Mike Quill called the "3 Rs": "racism, racketeering, and raiding."

"Big Labor"

AFL and CIO leaders might agree in principle, but Green and Murray did not trust one another, and several attempts at merger had failed. Raiding between the federations was constant: one report counted 1,245 raiding attempts affecting 350,000 union members. (Raiding was also a problem inside the AFL, especially between Carpenters and Machinists.)

Both Green and Murray died unexpectedly in November 1952. Reuther took over the CIO after a fight. The AFL promoted George Meany, a one-time plumber's apprentice turned business agent, who had climbed through the organization to become AFL Secretary-Treasurer in 1939, and who boasted he had never gone on strike or recognized a picket line. In June 1953, Meany and Reuther called for a moratorium on raiding and formed a Joint Unity Committee. The Committee announced an agreement in February 1955: affiliates would keep their jurisdictions and stop raiding one another; the new federation would adopt CIO policies on racial discrimination and labor racketeering, and the AFL position on "free" unions. Meany and AFL Secretary-Treasurer William Schnitzler from the Bakery and Confectionery Workers would keep their positions; Reuther would head a new Industrial Department including all CIO unions and thirty-five AFL unions, almost half the federations' total membership. Meeting separately in New York City in early December, each federation ratified the merger, the AFL without dissent, the CIO with three nays. They reconvened December 5 as the "American Federation of Labor and Congress of Industrial Organizations," with 145 affiliated unions representing almost 16 million members—more than a third of the U.S. labor force outside agriculture. The merger statement heralded "unity of the labor movement at a time when the unity of all American people is most urgently needed in the face of the Communist threat to world peace and civilization."

Meany called for organizing the unorganized, repealing antilabor legislation, and expanding government aid to education, housing, medical care, and social security. As for labor's role in society, he professed, "I believe in the free enterprise system completely. I believe in the return on capital investment. I believe in management's right to manage." The ILGWU's David Dubinsky said it better: "Trade unionism needs capitalism like a fish needs water." Reuther predicted union membership would double or triple.

The Executive Council set up a new political operation, the Committee on Political Education (COPE), and developed a five-point labor platform—improve national defense, increase wages to strengthen the economy, guarantee civil rights, overhaul Taft–Hartley, and regulate pension and welfare plans. The 1956 Democratic platform covered most of these demands, and the Council endorsed Democrat Adlai Stevenson almost unanimously. COPE worked on getting union members to register and vote. Eisenhower won reelection, but Democrats captured both houses of Congress, with 175 successful labor-backed candidates.

The AFL-CIO's 1956 membership of sixteen and a half million was its high point as a proportion of the labor force—nearly 24 percent. Membership stagnated for more than a decade, while the percent of workers in affiliated or independent unions slowly but steadily declined. By 1960, AFL-CIO unions represented less than 21 percent of the labor force, nineteen states had declared closed union shops illegal (violating the "right-to-work"), and Reuther admitted, "We are going backward." Resistance by employers and state and local governments certainly hurt; so did union leaders' lack of enthusiasm for organizing low-paid workers in highly competitive industries. Meanwhile, the industrial work force itself was shrinking as mechanization and automation eliminated manufacturing, transportation, and mining jobs.

The Federation's failure to end racial discrimination did not help. During the unity debates, the CIO's Mike Quill tried to make AFL abolition of Jim Crow locals a condition for merger, and voted against the agreement. A. Philip Randolph protested the agreement's failure to set a timetable for ending discrimination. Meany insisted "the shortest possible time" was good enough and put George Harrison of the segregated Brotherhood of Railway Clerks in charge of his new civil rights committee. Meanwhile, southern union locals endorsed the White Citizens Council and the Virginia Federation held segregated conventions.

Union discrimination affected other minority workers. The NAACP's Herbert Hill described for Congress how the ILGWU confined Puerto Ricans and African Americans to the lowest-paid work. AFL-CIO farm worker organizing went poorly. The National Farm Labor Union, run by onetime Southern Tenant Farmers Union leader H. L. Mitchell, got only token Federation support. The AFL-CIO started its own Agricultural Workers Organizing Committee in 1959: the United Agricultural Workers of Delano got one contract with one grower.

Women received even less attention. In 1961, Bessie Hillman (Sidney Hillman's widow and an Amalgamated Clothing Workers vice president) declared: "I have a great bone to pick with the organized labor movement. They are the greatest offenders as far as discrimination against women is concerned. Today women in every walk of life have bigger positions than they have in organized labor."

Labor racketeering was a constant threat. Some employers were glad to get "sweetheart" deals, designed—as the ILGWU's Gus Tyler observed—"to give the union leader an income, to give the employer relief from a real union, and to give the workers nothing." Union welfare and pension funds opened new avenues for corruption. Senator John McClellan's Select Com-

mittee on Improper Activities in the Labor or Management Field began tel-
evised hearings in 1957. The most spectacular revelations tied Teamster
president Dave Beck to rigged elections, extortion, and criminal associations. When the Teamster national convention replaced Beck with Jimmy
Hoffa, already implicated in sweetheart contracts and welfare-fund fraud,
the AFL-CIO expelled the union. Hoffa did not go easily. He made jurisdictional agreements with some AFL-CIO affiliates, raided others, and
mounted an organizing drive in Puerto Rico. He explored joining the independent ILWU in a new transportation federation. He resisted a string of
indictments with legal ploys. The Teamsters grew.

Teamsters got the most headlines, but the McClellan Committee also investigated Hotel and Restaurant Workers, Operating Engineers, Allied Industrial Workers, United Textile Workers, Laundry Workers, and Bakery
and Confectionery Workers. The Federation expelled the laundry and bakery unions along with the Teamsters. The cleanup did not slow passage of a
new federal labor bill in 1959, the Landrum-Griffin Labor-Management
Reporting and Disclosure Act, which imposed financial disclosure and fidu-
ciary responsibility on pension and welfare fund administrators. The Act included a "Worker's Bill of Rights," which detailed what a union owed its
members (a copy of the union contract, for example), set standards for electing union officers and disciplining locals, and banned convicted felons and
Communists from union office for five years from their release from prison
or separation from the party. Though the AFL-CIO wanted the funds regulated and already banned ex-Communists and felons from office, Meany
blasted Landrum-Griffin as government interference in union business.

Government regulation did not resolve every labor dispute. In 1959,
USWA started work on a new contract. The union argued that increased
productivity and industry profits allowed raising wages to cover the higher
cost of living. Steel executives opposed any increase and demanded work
rule changes to permit the use of new technology. The steelworkers walked
off the job in mid-July, and industries like auto, which bought steel for their
own use, began slowing or shutting down too. In October Eisenhower invoked Taft-Hartley and set up a board of inquiry. When the board failed to
find a compromise, the Justice Department took out an injunction; the
union went back to work and waited for the injunction to expire. After the
Kaiser Company agreed to union terms, on January 5, 1960, other steel
companies accepted a deal with increased benefits, a deferred pay raise, and
no change in work rules.

USWA president David McDonald declared it the best steel contract
ever. Many steelworkers disagreed, and they were not the only rank-and-

file unionists to criticize their leadership. UAW members staged wildcat strikes over speedup in 1955, more in 1961, and even more in 1964 (which Reuther finally sanctioned). In 1966, the machinists shut down 60 percent of the country's air flights for five weeks in a wildcat over "chain gang conditions." In 1967, over a thousand proposed contracts were rejected by membership votes.

The AFL-CIO's political record in the 1950s had been mixed. The Federation supported and saw passed improved Social Security benefits and coverage, a minimum wage increase, and raises for federal employees. Labor support was crucial to Democrat John Kennedy's very narrow win over Vice President Richard Nixon in 1960. The administration—headed by Lyndon Johnson after Kennedy's assassination in 1963—backed several labor initiatives, expanded unemployment benefits, and let federal employees organize. Johnson supported the repeal of Taft-Hartley's "right to work" Section 14-b. (Republicans filibustered the measure to defeat.) The Federation backed some important civil rights measures including the twenty-fourth Amendment eliminating poll taxes in federal elections, and the 1964 Civil Rights and 1965 Voting Rights acts. As Johnson developed his "War on Poverty" programs with labor support, the AFL-CIO seemed to be the main U.S. institution regularly supporting a liberal social agenda. There were limits. Randolph started the Negro American Labor Council in 1960 to press for minority hiring on government building projects. After the Council endorsed the NAACP's criticism of AFL-CIO racial practices, Meany had Randolph censured at the 1961 convention for being "divisive." When Plumbers Local 2 members walked off a job at the New York City-financed Bronx Terminal Market to protest the hiring of one black and three Puerto Rican plumbers, Meany defended his old local.

The Democrats provided other opportunities for labor-government cooperation. Meany had been critical of Eisenhower's disinclination for confrontation in the Suez and Hungarian crises in 1956, and Fidel Castro's takeover in Cuba on January 1, 1959, confirmed his fears. Kennedy's Labor Secretary Arthur Goldberg helped Meany set up the American Institute for Free Labor Development (AIFLD) and provided government funding. ORIT director Serafino Romualdi headed the Institute, and businessmen with Latin American interests like David Rockefeller and United Fruit chief J. Peter Grace sat on its board. In 1962, AIFLD operatives financed strikes in British Guiana, leading the British to depose popularly elected (and socialist) prime minister Cheddi Jagan. In 1964, its Brazilian Institute for Democratic Action provided new leaders for the unions that had supported populist João Goulart, deposed in a U.S.–backed military coup. By 1965, all

AIFLD operatives were CIA professionals. The African American Labor Institute, another "AFL-CIA" program, started in 1962.

In the mid-1960s, Walter Reuther proclaimed, "The labor movement . . . is developing a whole new middle class." Yet not everyone was doing so well. A recession in 1960–61 pushed unemployment to 6.8 percent. Kennedy increased spending and cut taxes—especially corporate—to jumpstart a boom, but it did little to reduce unemployment.

Black unemployment stood at 11 percent in 1962. The tightening job market helped maintain job discrimination, derailing attempts to place more women and minority workers in jobs still mainly reserved for white men. Technological innovations continued to sweep through industry. Containerization eliminated many jobs on the docks, technical changes to trains reduced crew sizes, new printing technologies wiped out an entire craft. Fewer autoworkers made more cars, fewer steelworkers more steel. In once bustling industrial cities like Camden, New Jersey, corporate flight to lower-wage locations had begun to produce vast wastelands of crumbling factories, derelict homes and churches, streets littered with trash and vacant lots stacked high with garbage, and an omnipresent stench of social collapse.

Year by year the costs of empire mounted. The defense budget jumped from its 1950s level of $40–50 billion per year to $70 billion by 1967. Costs included lives as well as dollars: the peacetime draft tripled after 1965 as Johnson escalated U.S. intervention in Southeast Asia. More and more working-class conscripts and volunteers began coming home in body bags. The Cold War formula for social peace was more and more dysfunctional.

CHAPTER

THE SIXTIES

According to legend, American workers opposed the radical movements that shook the nation in the 1960s. Widely reproduced news photos from the era show hard-hatted construction workers attacking long-haired anti-war demonstrators in New York City. From classrooms to barrooms, Americans invoke these stereotypes as they debate the sixties. Workers are routinely cast as conservatives, and the radicals as youth out of touch with the working class.

The real story is more complicated. The turmoil associated with the 1960s ran through more than one decade. Politically speaking, the "sixties" began in the mid-1950s and extended well into the 1970s. Much of the ferment centered on campuses, but insurgent movements and ideas also reverberated from rural communities to inner cities, from churches to the military, from factories to rock concerts, from local school boards to national political conventions. Nor were all sixties activists from the college-educated middle class; working people joined and sometimes led civil rights protests, antiwar demonstrations, feminist projects, gay and lesbian initiatives, and militant movements to empower people of color and poor people across the board. Some unions plunged into social activism, working with community groups and even radical students. And despite opposition from most labor officials, the unrest spilled into other unions as well. To a large degree, then, sixties movements were workers' movements. Their causes often polarized the nation, but the divisions did not fall neatly along class lines.

IN THE SPIRIT OF MONTGOMERY

More than twenty years after canceling his 1941 March on Washington, A. Philip Randolph led a new "March on Washington for Jobs and Freedom" on August 28, 1963. Endorsed by every major civil rights organization and the AFL–CIO's Industrial Department, sponsored by the Brotherhood of Sleeping Car Porters, the United Auto Workers, and the Negro American Labor Council, this march turned out some 250,000 people, including many thousands of union members. They heard Dr. Martin Luther King, Jr., proclaim, "I have a dream that one day this nation will rise up and live out the true meaning of its creed—we hold these truths to be self-evident that all men are created equal." The civil rights movement pursued this dream through direct action. The rally in Washington capped a spring and summer of mass demonstrations across the South, with more than 20,000 arrested for protesting Jim Crow.

Direct action protests had been mounting since the mid-1950s, when black residents of Montgomery, Alabama, desegregated the city's buses. On December 1, 1955, riding home from her job as a department store seamstress, Rosa Parks was arrested for refusing to give up her seat to a white passenger. E. D. Nixon, an officer in the Sleeping Car Porters, bailed her out. Both Parks and Nixon were longtime activists with the NAACP, and they had been seeking a way to mobilize the black community. Her arrest now furnished the spark. The next day they organized a meeting to plan a community response. Out of this came a call for a bus boycott on Monday, December 5 (as it happened, the same day the AFL–CIO first met).

The boycott was solid. That afternoon its organizers formed the Montgomery Improvement Association, chose young Baptist minister Martin Luther King, Jr., to head the group, and debated whether to extend the boycott. That night thousands of people gathered, "on fire for freedom," as one newsman reported. They demanded that the boycott continue until black passengers could ride the buses on the same terms as whites. For more than a year, black workers throughout Montgomery walked for hours or carpooled to work. Some lost their jobs for taking part in the boycott, and boycott leaders were indicted (King was tried, convicted, and fined). In November 1956, the Supreme Court ruled that the law segregating Montgomery's buses was unconstitutional, and the city received a cease-and-desist order on December 20. The next day Rosa Parks took a seat at the front of the bus.

Over the next decade, the spirit of Montgomery swept through black communities across the South. In the first year alone, protests against segregation got underway in more than forty cities and towns. The Southern Christian Leadership Conference, founded in February 1957 and headed by King, started several voter registration drives coordinated by veteran NAACP organizer Ella Baker.

Beginning on February 1, 1960, in Greensboro, North Carolina, black students sat down at segregated lunch counters in southern cities and refused to leave until served. In April a conference organized by Baker formed the Student Non-Violent Coordinating Committee. SNCC protests in Albany, Georgia, in November 1961 filled the city's jails. In spring 1963, King led a "children's crusade" in Birmingham, Alabama—mass demonstrations of elementary and high-school students dispersed by fire hoses and police dogs on national television. Northern student activists dispatched groups of "freedom riders" into the South to challenge segregation in interstate transportation facilities and organized the 1964 "Freedom Summer" voter registration campaign in Mississippi.

Though youth often led the way, the movement was a family and community affair. As Sheyann Webb later recalled, "I asked my mother and father for my birthday present to become registered voters." Webb, who turned eight in 1965, lived in Selma, Alabama, where a series of mass community demonstrations for voting rights began in January and culminated two months later in a fifty-four-mile march to the steps of the state capitol in Montgomery, where the marchers were greeted by a cheering crowd including A. Philip Randolph and Rosa Parks.

Jim Crow was worst in rural Mississippi. In Sunflower County in the Mississippi Delta, more than 60 percent of the population—but less than 2 percent of the electorate—was African American. When SNCC came in August 1962 to ask who would like to register to vote, Fannie Lou Hamer, a third-generation sharecropper and the granddaughter of slaves, raised her hand and began a career as a civil rights leader. She lost her plantation job and had to leave her home; white racists spit on her, shot at her, and once nearly beat her to death. She refused to back down, and helped launch the Mississippi Freedom Democratic Party. In 1964, she and other MFDP leaders went to the Democratic Convention in Atlantic City to challenge the credentials of the official (and all-white) state delegation. When President Johnson learned the issue might be debated on the convention floor, he sent Vice President Hubert Humphrey to quash the challenge.

The vote was never an end in itself for Hamer. She also promoted the Mississippi Freedom Labor Union, founded in April 1965. That spring and summer the union mobilized plantation workers to strike for the eight-hour day at minimum wage, sick pay, health and accident insurance, equal employment practices, and an end to child and elder labor. This inspired similar strikes by cooks, maids, and custodians. When the MFLU fell apart over the winter, Hamer started "Freedom Farm," a cooperative that bought land to raise food for its members and cotton for cash.

Though the Democratic Party rebuffed the MFDP, the civil rights movement did win concessions from the Johnson administration. In July 1964, the President signed the Civil Rights Act, which prohibited discrimination by race, color, sex, religion, or national origin in voter registration, employment, public education, and public accommodations. In August 1965, he signed the Voting Rights Act, which barred states from using literacy tests and other devices to disenfranchise people of color and empowered federal officials to register voters turned away by local authorities.

Johnson also declared a "War on Poverty." The new Office of Economic Opportunity administered programs assisting poor people, especially those excluded from relief and aid programs run by state and local white supremacist governments. The Job Corps provided training and employment to youth from poor communities. Community Action Programs funded social services provided by local civil rights projects. The federal government funded adult literacy programs and the Head Start program for preschoolers. The Elementary and Secondary Education Act of 1965 gave direct federal aid to local school systems for the first time, if they were racially integrated or desegregating in good faith. Fulfilling a New Deal promise, Congress passed the Medicare and Medicaid Act in 1965: Medicare subsidized health insurance for the elderly; Medicaid paid medical expenses for indigent households.

Civil rights activists faced brutal and sometimes murderous reprisals at every step. Racists bombed King's and Nixon's homes in 1956. White mobs assaulted SNCC sit-ins in 1960. A Freedom Ride bus was firebombed outside Anniston, Alabama, and riders beaten in Anniston, Birmingham, and Montgomery in 1961. The Klan bombed a Birmingham church in 1963, killing four girls. In Mississippi, two SNCC workers were shotgunned in Ruleville in 1962, activist Medgar Evers was assassinated outside his house in 1963, and three students were abducted, tortured, and killed during Freedom Summer in 1964. Local and state police often collaborated with white supremacist vigilantes—the Alabama attacks on Freedom Riders were carried out under police supervision, and Hamer got her beating in the police station in Winona, Mississippi. Activists and protesters were arrested and jailed by the tens of thousands.

The 1964 Civil Rights Act intensified the fury. By that October, in Mississippi alone fifteen people had been murdered and thirty-seven black churches torched or bombed. Police killed protester Jimmy Lee Jackson outside Selma in February 1965. As the Selma marchers dispersed from Montgomery, Klansmen—one an FBI informant—shot and killed Viola Liuzzo, a white mother of five, daughter of a coal miner and wife of a Teamsters business agent, who had come from Detroit to show solidarity with the movement.

Amid the rising violence, black activists began to wonder if integration into the American mainstream was possible, or ever desirable. Federal concessions seemed meaningless: voting rights were not yet enforced; the War on Poverty had hardly begun; the Justice Department had not stopped white supremacist terrorism. Events in northern cities showed that intransigent racism and persistent poverty were not peculiar to the South. Hamer recalled, "I used to think that if I could go North and tell people about the plight of the black folk in the state of Mississippi, everything would be all right. But traveling around, I found one thing for sure: it's up-South and down-South, and it's no different."

In 1962 in Cambridge, Maryland, student protests against segregation at the movie theater and the skating rink roused local activists to demand not only desegregation in schools and hospitals but also jobs and housing. In June 1963, the National Guard arrived to keep the peace and stayed almost continuously for more than a year. The same month 3,000 black Boston students stayed out of public schools for a day to protest segregation; over the next school year hundreds of thousands of students staged protests in other northern cities. Also in June 1963, black New Yorkers picketed a Harlem construction site to protest their exclusion from the building trades unions. On March 6, 1964, the Congress on Racial Equality (CORE) blocked traffic on New York City's Triborough Bridge to protest conditions in Harlem—substandard schools and public services, dilapidated housing, poverty, and police brutality.

The righteous anger fueling these protests found an eloquent spokesperson in onetime railroad porter and petty criminal Malcolm Little. While in prison for burglary, he joined the Nation of Islam, renounced his "slave name," and became one of the Nation's most charismatic ministers. From Harlem's Temple Seven, Malcolm X condemned American white supremacy in all its forms and called on African Americans to practice self-respect, self-defense, and self-determination. In 1964, he broke with the

Nation; inspired by the African anticolonial struggle and the multiracial composition of orthodox Islam, he founded the Organization of African American Unity to promote political action as part of an international, multiracial movement against oppression. On February 21, 1965, he was gunned down at an OAAU meeting in Harlem.

The anger Malcolm X tried to steer to political action burst out in a wave of urban rebellions. Protests against police brutality over the summer of 1964 in Harlem, Brooklyn's Bedford-Stuyvesant section, Philadelphia, and other cities had turned violent, and most of the rebellions began as confrontations with police. In August 1965, in the Watts section of South Central Los Angeles, when police pulled over a twenty-one-year-old, then arrested his mother when she protested, thousands of people gathered, forced the police to retreat, and began four days of rebellion. They took weapons from pawn shops and military surplus outlets, built barricades, stoned police and firemen to shouts of "This is for Selma" and "Long live Malcolm X." They targeted stores known for price gouging, easy-credit schemes, and rudeness to patrons, sparing libraries, schools and black-owned businesses. The National Guard cordoned off the zone and cleared it street by street. Property damage totaled more than $35 million—thirty-four people were killed, nearly a thousand injured, over 4,000 arrested.

The summer of 1966 saw rebellions in forty-three cities, with eleven people killed and more than 400 injured. The following summer was worse. The July revolt in Newark lasted six days, and spread to nearby New Jersey cities like Paterson, Passaic, and Elizabeth. Less than a week later Detroit broke out in the worst U.S. rebellion of the century—eight days of violence suppressed by federal troops. Seventy-five major rebellions that summer claimed eighty-three lives.

As fires blazed in urban black ghettos, the southern civil rights movement shifted direction. In the summer of 1966, SNCC declared itself for "Black Power." The new agenda originated in SNCC's work with Alabama sharecroppers in the Lowndes County Freedom Organization. LCFO practiced self-defense. Sharecroppers surprised their student allies by bringing guns to meetings; as one man explained, "You turn the other cheek, and you'll get handed half of what you're sitting on." The organization ran its own candidates for public office, outside the Democratic Party. LCFO's black panther insignia and the Black Power slogan electrified legions of civil rights activists.

The slogan drew fire from the Southern Christian Leadership Conference. King publicly chided Black Power advocates for abandoning nonviolence. But even his wing of the movement charted an increasingly radical course. In 1966, SCLC opened its first campaign outside the South, joining Chicago civil rights groups to challenge discrimination in housing. In April 1967, King denounced the U.S. war in Vietnam and identified imperialism as the enemy of racial equality at home. That December SCLC inaugurated a Poor People's Campaign dedicated to the radical redistribution of wealth. The right to organize took center stage in spring 1968, when black sanitation workers in Memphis, Tennessee, struck for union recognition and SCLC leaders rallied in support. On April 4, King was assassinated in Memphis, and black communities erupted, their youth battling police in more than 100 cities with forty-six lives lost.

By the time of King's death, the movement he had helped launch in Montgomery was starting to stall. Vigilante attacks had ebbed, but police repression had reached new heights. In 1967, the FBI deployed undercover agents to "disrupt, misdirect, discredit" every major civil rights group. In February 1968, police in Orangeburg, South Carolina, fired on a peaceful black student protest at the local bowling alley, wounding twenty-eight and killing three. When Republican Richard Nixon entered the White House the following year, the FBI grew even more aggressive and the police more trigger-happy. Cooptation undermined the movement too. As black voters registered in greater numbers, the Democratic Party absorbed grassroots activism; its southern wing integrated under the control of the old establishment. But challenges to white supremacy were mounting outside the South, in communities where new organizations campaigned to empower the dispossessed.

"POWER TO THE PEOPLE"

In the late 1960s and 70s, activism surged in poor and working-class communities. Many activists got their start in groups supported by unions—Students for a Democratic Society came out of the League for Industrial Democracy, an old socialist group supported by officials from the UAW and other unions; CORE started with support from several unions including the American Federation of State, County and Municipal Employees, the UAW and the Teamsters; SNCC had links to the Highlander Folk School, a worker education center started in 1932 in Tennessee, and got support from the United Packinghouse Workers as well as from the independent United Electrical Workers and the International Longshore and Warehouse Union. More activists came fresh from the anti-imperialist wing of the peace movement, which renounced anticommunism and explored variations on the Marxist doctrine that only the organized working class could achieve revolutionary social change. The slogan "Power to the People" captured the general mood.

The Black Panther Party for Self-Defense, founded in 1966 in Oakland, California, combined radical politics and militant tactics with community service programs. The Panthers saw black America as a colony—their goal was self-determination, their first concern survival. They demanded housing, education, jobs, exemption from military service for black men, release of black prisoners, black juries for black defendants, and an end to police brutality, reparations for slavery and discrimination, and a United Nations plebiscite to determine "the will of black people as to their national destiny." Their community services ranged from schools and day care to clinics, with programs for sickle-cell anemia and high blood pressure. They supported prisoners' families with transportation and emergency cash grants, and collected clothing and shoes for school children. By 1969, their Free Breakfast program—run by welfare mothers and grandparents—served 23,000 children in nineteen cities.

The Panthers also identified with African and Asian anticolonial and anti-imperialist struggles, recruited mostly young working-class men (especially veterans and ex-convicts), and conducted community patrols wearing black berets and armed with guns and law books to monitor police activities. By late 1968, the Party had twenty-five chapters from coast to coast, and had become the chief target of local, state, and federal police, coordinated by the FBI's Counter Intelligence Program (COINTELPRO). By 1970, police had killed twenty-seven Party members. Chicago police shot Fred Hampton and Mark Clark in their beds on December 4, 1969.

The Panthers were not alone: groups in many communities adopted the combination of community service, militant protests, and special attention to youth, whether students, workers, or on the street and unemployed. (Black youth unemployment, first measured in January 1972 at 37.1 percent, fell below 30 percent only twice in the decade.) In Newark activists associated with writer and Black Power advocate Amiri Baraka (Leroi Jones) ran political and cultural projects ranging from the Committee for a Unified Newark (CFUN) to youth groups, cultural centers, community schools, repertory companies, and cooperative stores. In Detroit, SNCC veterans and a local group called UHURU started the monthly *Inner City Voice* in 1967 and founded the Republic of New Africa the next year. They also campaigned against police brutality—Detroit police held the national record for the rate at which they killed civilians.

A series of Black Power conferences spun off national organizations. The Congress of African Peoples (established 1970) had branches in fifteen cities; in coalition with other groups CAP helped mobilize 30,000 people to march in Washington, D.C., on African Liberation Day (May 27, 1972), and 30,000 more in simultaneous demonstrations in San Francisco, Toronto, and several West Indian cities. The March 1972 National Black Political Convention in Gary, Indiana, attended by about 10,000 activists, founded the National Black Assembly.

Only in the census did the category "Hispanic" form a single group. Though most spoke Spanish, Latino communities differed in origin and history. Puerto Rican migration had soared after World War II, pushed by the island's unemployment and pulled by industrial recruitment—U.S. Steel subsidiary National Tube Company and Carnegie Illinois Steel in Gary, Indiana, each brought in 500 mill hands from the island in 1947 and 1948. By the mid-1960s, more than a million Puerto Ricans lived in Northeast and Midwest cities. Most lived in New York City, where the Young Lords Party started in 1969 (borrowing the name from a Chicago youth group). The Party advocated self-defense, socialism, and self-determination for the Puerto Rican nation, and recruited workers, students, unemployed youths, and veterans returning from Vietnam. Its first community project was sweeping Spanish Harlem and South Bronx streets with brooms confiscated from the City Sanitation Department, but YLP soon set up free breakfast and clothing programs for children, tuberculosis and lead-poisoning testing, rent strikes, drug detox programs, and cultural activities—study groups, concerts, poetry readings, art shows. Most Young Lords were Puerto Rican (though the Party welcomed all Latinos); branches appeared in East Coast cities from New Haven to Philadelphia, and later in Puerto Rico. Other Puerto Rican groups developed, including La Unión Latina, Resistencia Puertorriqueña, and Puerto Ricans for Self-Determination. The pro-independence Partido Socialista Puertorriqueño, founded on the island in 1971, set up the first of many U.S. branches in 1973.

Puerto Ricans also joined El Comité, a Manhattan West Side group started in 1970 by a neighborhood softball team of factory workers and ex-gang members led by Federico Lora, a Dominican Vietnam veteran. El Comité organized against urban renewal, moving squatters into condemned buildings then daring the city to remove them by force, a tactic adopted by many housing activists afterwards. *El Comité* also agitated for better public education, health care, and day-care centers, and supported strikes by Latino workers. Among the many political refugees who fled the Dominican dictatorship installed by U.S. Marines in 1965 were branches of opposition parties such as the Movimiento Popular Dominicano.

French-speaking Haiti shares the island of Hispaniola with the Dominican Republic. Like many Dominicans, Haitian immigrants were often refugees from a U.S. client regime, the dictatorship of François Duvalier and his son Jean Claude: "Papa Doc" and "Baby Doc." Tens of thousands came to New York City after Duvalier père came to power in 1957. Proud of Haiti's standing as the second republic in the New World (and the first black republic anywhere), and affronted by the color line in U.S. society, Haitians tended to see their residence as one of transit, and to focus on ending the repression and exploitation that had forced them to emigrate. The Organization of Patriotic Haitian Women, for example, which started in New York in the early 1970s, insisted that feminist demands be subordinated to the task of Haitian liberation.

More than two-thirds of the Latinos in the U.S. were of Mexican origin, and the largest Latino movement took shape in their communities. Migration from Mexico continued, both illegal and legal. The Bracero program, based on the 1942 agreement between Mexico and the U.S., brought in over four million farmworkers before it ended in 1964. Illegal immigration was probably higher. During the 1950s, *La Migra*—the Immigration and Naturalization Service—deported almost four million people to Mexico, more than a few of them U.S. citizens or legal residents. Immigrants did participate in the Mexican American movement, but it was based mainly among people born in the U.S. Like their African American and Puerto Rican counterparts, Mexican American activists moved from a civil rights agenda towards radical nationalism.

In 1959, the Mexican American Political Association started to register voters and protest police brutality and discrimination in housing and education in southern California. A Texas group—the Political Association of Spanish-Speaking Organizations (PASSO)—formed in 1961; in 1963, Crystal City PASSO and Teamsters activists backed a slate of working-class Mexican Americans who took over the City Council.

The same year, La Alianza Federal de Mercedes (Federal Alliance of Land Grants) formed to press claims for lands confiscated after the 1848 annexation. In 1966, La Alianza, with 20,000 members in New Mexico, Colorado, Utah, Texas, and California, turned from legal to direct action. Alianza activists occupied the Kit Carson National Forest in northern New Mexico, and in 1967 raided a local courthouse to free Alianza members from detention.

Such militant actions galvanized young campus and community activists. They began to call themselves "Chicanos," turning a disparaging term for Mexican Americans into a badge of pride, and started a host of new organizations. The Brown Berets, founded in 1967 in East Los Angeles, recruited barrio youth and modelled themselves on the Panthers. They joined the 1969 National Chicago Moratorium Committee, which staged mass protests against the war. The same year in south Texas, La Raza Unida formed to promote "the natural right of all peoples to preserve their self-identity and to formulate their own destiny," and ran candidates on platforms calling for community control of schools, police, and public services.

Black and Latino resistance to oppression reverberated in the prison population. Authorities reported sixteen inmate uprisings in 1970, organized by groups like the California Prisoners Union, which spoke for "the convicted class." Inmates at California's Folsom Prison staged a three week strike demanding better conditions and treatment, including the minimum wage and the right to organize; they asked Panthers and Brown Berets to negotiate for them. In August 1971, over half the 2,200 inmates at Attica Prison near Buffalo, New York, seized half the facility and thirty-nine guards, demanding "adequate food and shelter," religious freedom, legal assistance, reading material, and fair wages for prison labor. After four days of negotiation, state troopers stormed the prison, killing twenty-nine inmates and ten guards.

Another prison made headlines when "Indians of All Nations" briefly (and for the second time) occupied the abandoned federal prison on Alcatraz Island in San Francisco Bay in 1969. Their claim was based on an old broken treaty, but even long-established treaty rights were under new attack. Between 1946 and 1960, tribes lost over 3.3 million acres of land, and reservation activists were organizing from Alaska to Florida over issues like water rights, fishing rights, and land use.

A third of the country's half-million Native Americans lived off reservations, mostly in cities. In 1968, Native American ex-convicts in Minneapolis-St. Paul started community patrols against police abuse and founded the American Indian Movement, which popularized the slogan "Red Power" and called for a return to native traditions. AIM joined the pantribal "Trail of Broken Treaties" in 1972, which took a caravan of cars and trucks to Washington, D.C., and seized BIA offices. In 1973, Oglalas tyrannized by paramilitary goons working for Pine Ridge Reservation Chairman Dick Wilson, asked AIM for help. AIM mustered at Wounded Knee and withstood a ten-week siege by the U.S. Army, though two members were killed by crossfire. Targeted by COINTELPRO and racked with dissension, AIM faded as an organization, but Native American traditions of protecting Mother Earth helped rally environmental activists to support the Navajos who defied a 1974 act of Congress mandating the removal of more than 10,000 people from their ancestral homeland on coal-rich Big Mountain in Arizona.

Native Hawaiians also asserted ancestral land claims, as well as demanding reparations for the 1890s coup and annexation. The movement targeted land seized by the U.S. military, especially 600,000 acres taken during World War II. In 1976, protesters occupied Kaho'olawe Island, used as a target range since 1941, and forced its demilitarization and decontamination.

Asian American immigrant communities had long organized their own associations and service organizations, often dominated by community business leaders. Starting in the late 1960s, young activists—most of them born in the U.S.—formed groups that crossed ethnic lines and gave birth to an inclusive Asian American movement.

Asian street gangs organized in self-help groups to fight gang warfare and drug addiction. In Los Angeles, Filipinos formed Pagkakaisa and Samoans Omai Fa'atasai, but the Yellow Brotherhood and Asian American Hardcore recruited from all Asian nationalities. By 1969, self-help organizing in San Francisco gave rise to the Asian Community Center, which ran a food co-op and summer programs for children.

Admiration for the People's Republic of China inspired some activists to create organizations like the Red Guards in San Francisco, East Wind in Los Angeles, and I Wor Kuen ("Righteous and Harmonious Fists") in New York City. They combined political organizing with service projects such as medical clinics, breakfast programs, day care, and language classes. IWK also protested Chinatown tourist bus tours in April 1970, and built the Chinatown People's Association, a coalition that mobilized mass community rallies against police brutality and for Asian workers' employment on the federally funded Confucius Plaza housing project.

Activism—sometimes explicitly racist—also intensified in white working-class communities. Alabama ex-governor George Wallace ran for president in 1968—his American Independent Party had chapters in the North and West as well as the South. That same year, Italian Americans in Newark's North Ward elected a white vigilante leader to the city council. In the mid-1970s, white residents of South Boston organized ROAR (Restore Our Alienated Rights), which violently protested busing students to integrate schools. Like-minded groups emerged in several midwestern cities.

But interracial alliances developed too. The Congress of Italian American Organizations joined black and Puerto Rican groups to push for open admissions at New York City's public colleges. Greeks and Arabs in Dearborn, Michigan, joined Native Americans and others in a community council to fight plans to tear down low-cost housing. Struggles against real estate developers in Honolulu united virtually every ethnic group on the island. Chicago's Black Panthers and Young Lords formed a "rainbow coalition"

(Fred Hampton's phrase) with the Young Patriots from the North Side's Appalachian white community. Newark's CFUN united with local Young Lords behind a "Community Choice" slate in 1970 and elected Newark's first black mayor. In cities across the country, tenants unions, parents associations, and other neighborhood groups organized for common goals across racial and ethnic lines as never before.

The most common cause of the sixties was stopping the Vietnam war. No one contributed more to popular and working-class opposition to the war than the protesters who were also veterans. Individual veterans started denouncing the war in 1965. In June 1966, the "Fort Hood 3" became the first soldiers to refuse to go to Vietnam. In 1967, Vietnam Veterans Against the War formed in New York City, the first antiwar veterans organization in U.S. history. In April 1971, VVAW organized 1,500 veterans to camp on the Mall in Washington in defiance of a Supreme Court injunction; 800 threw their service awards and combat decorations over the barricade built to keep them away from Congress, and a thousand veterans—many on crutches or in wheelchairs—led half a million people marching against the war. By then some antiwar and black power organizations operated inside the military. Mutinies compromised combat operations, and soldiers stateside refused to deploy against demonstrators.

Ruling the country and running the war were jobs for men. In radical movements, women did crucial work, but in almost every organization, men ran the show. Women confronted this inequity by challenging male leadership, launching independent projects, and forming their own organizations.

The welfare rights movement exemplified the problem. Protests by women welfare recipients proliferated in the mid-1960s, especially in black communities. By 1966, action groups had sprung up in seventy cities across twenty-six states. They gathered under the umbrella of the National Welfare Rights Organization, the brainchild of middle-class civil rights leaders. Professional men staffed the national office, and they repeatedly made policy decisions that properly belonged to the women on NWRO's elected governing board. In 1972, the women pushed the men out. New executive director Johnnie Tillmon, a welfare activist from Watts, declared in a press release that "NWRO views the major welfare problems as women's issues and itself as a strictly women's organization."

In many other quarters women found ways to work with men and enjoy autonomy too. In Los Angeles, the Asian Sisterhood ran its own counterparts to the Yellow Brotherhood's youth projects, and the Chicano movement included the Comisión Femenil Mexicana, a women's rights group. In New York, women in the Young Lords insisted that the Party platform include the demand, "We want equality for women, down with *machismo* and male chauvinism." They launched a Women's Union to press for day care, family health services, and laws to stop doctors from sterilizing women under duress. Sterilization was also a central issue for Women of All Red Nations, affiliated with the American Indian Movement, the Latin Women's Collective that worked with El Comité, and the Women's Committee of the Black United Front in Brooklyn. Down south, black and white women married to UMW activists founded Alabama Women for Human Rights to support strikes and campaign for day care, health care, and prison reform.

If feminism developed rapidly, the gay and lesbian liberation movement appeared almost overnight. Early one Saturday morning (June 28, 1969), police began a routine roundup of homosexual patrons at the Stonewall Inn, a gay bar in New York City's Greenwich Village. A lesbian patron resisted arrest, and within minutes a crowd barricaded the police inside the bar and torched it. Days later activists formed the Gay Liberation Front, "radical and revolutionary men and women committed to fight the oppression of the homosexual as a minority group and to demand the right to the self-determination of our own bodies." Gay and lesbian organizations numbered nearly 800 by 1973, thousands by the end of the decade, enrolling working people as well as students, artists, intellectuals, and street hustlers. Some groups recognized multiple kinds of oppression (or cultivated multiple sources of pride)—Gay Youth, Third World Gay Liberation, Radicalesbians, Hispanos Unidos Gay Liberados. Others, like the gay and lesbian caucus in the Young Lords, worked to bring their issues into broader struggles.

THE SIXTIES IN THE WORKPLACE

The causes that galvanized communities also resonated at work. Unions, union caucuses, and other worker organizations aligned with movements in the larger society. By the late 1960s, a strike wave was rising, and labor leaders were facing increasingly militant dissent from below. Like its predecessors, this surge of labor activism centered on workplace rights, but more broadly defined than ever before.

For some workers, organizing unions was a civil rights struggle. New York City hospital workers—mostly black and Puerto Rican women—were excluded from federal labor law protection, barred from striking by state law, and paid less than a living wage. Hospital and Health Care Workers Local 1199 started to organize private nonprofit hospitals in 1958, won better pay and benefits with a forty-six–day strike in 1959, and struck for union recognition in 1962. When 1199 President Leon Davis went to jail for contempt of court, A. Philip Randolph organized community leaders in a Committee for Justice for Hospital Workers. When Davis got a second sentence, Randolph called for a "Prayer Pilgrimage" to join the pickets, and Governor Nelson Rockefeller promised bargaining rights for hospital workers. At a victory rally, Malcolm X pronounced the lesson: "You don't get the job done unless you show the man that you're not afraid to go to jail."

In late 1968, Charleston, South Carolina, public hospital workers—mostly women, all black—formed Local 1199B and started a strike described by Coretta Scott King (Dr. King's widow) as "part of the larger fight in our nation against discrimination and exploitation—against all forms of degradation that results from poverty and human misery." SCLC provided substantial support, and after 113 days and more than a thousand arrests, the *Drug & Hospital Workers News* reported, "1199 Union Power Plus SCLC Soul Power Equals Victory in Charleston." Local 1199 became the National Union of Hospital and Health Care Employees, organizing in Maryland, North Carolina, Pennsylvania, Ohio, New Jersey, and Connecticut.

Farmworkers were also excluded from Wagner Act coverage. Community organizers César Chávez and Dolores Huerta started the National Farm Workers Association in 1962 in Delano, California. NFWA organized in the *mutualista* tradition—self-help through mutual aid—and by 1965 had about 1,700 members.

That year Filipino grape workers in the AFL-CIO Agricultural Workers Organizing Committee called a strike in Delano, and local AWOC leader Larry Itliong asked Chávez for help. NFWA joined the grape strike and spread it to thirty-seven growers. Union members slipped into the fields to talk to workers, while loudspeakers blared appeals to join the strike. Women and children set up picket lines—Huerta credited the union's nonviolence to their presence.

The growers were not moved. Chávez called for a national grape boycott. Farmworkers went to union halls, churches, and colleges all over the country to drum up support, and activists everywhere responded, picketing markets and volunteering as organizers. The union signed its first contract in 1970, with increased pay, employer-funded health care, housing and job training programs, a ban on the use of toxic pesticides like DDT, and union hiring halls. United Farm Workers (the merger of AWOC and NFWA) began a campaign against lettuce growers, recruiting mainly Mexican Americans, but also Arabs—the first UFW member killed on a picket line was Nagi Daifallah, a young Yemeni shot by police in August 1973. UFW activists joined community struggles for bilingual education, food stamps, housing and public-health projects. Jessie Lopez de la Cruz, the UFW's first woman field organizer, looked on labor and community work the same way: "The way I see it, there's more poor people than rich people. We're trying to get together, organize, stay together." Farmworker organizing groups started in Arizona and Texas; the Farm Labor Organizing Committee began organizing migrant tomato harvesters in Ohio and Michigan.

The Black Power movement had a strong workplace component too. In Boston, Pittsburgh, Chicago, and other cities, black construction workers formed independent unions to rival the AFL-CIO's building trades affiliates. Harlem Fightback started in 1965, and developed the tactic of bringing bus loads of unemployed black construction workers to a building site and shutting it down until their demands were met. (Fightback coalitions then developed in New York's Puerto Rican and Chinese communities too.)

Black workers also mobilized inside existing unions. After a wildcat strike against speedup in May 1968, black UAW members at the Chrysler Dodge main plant in Detroit found themselves targeted for retaliation by management and abandoned by the union. They formed the Dodge Revolutionary Union Movement, which forced the company to rehire most of the fired strikers. The success inspired more RUMs in many Detroit-area auto plants—they fought against discrimination by union and employer alike, and for more control over working conditions. In 1969, RUM leaders and *Inner City Voice* activists founded the League of Revolutionary Black Workers, which maintained contact with other black workers' groups like the United Black Brotherhood in Ford plants at Mahwah, New Jersey, and Lexington, Kentucky, and the Black Panther Caucus in the G.M. plant in Fremont, California.

Hit hard by layoffs during the 1969–70 slump in the auto industry, the League turned to community organizing. But black rank-and-file caucuses pushed black officials in bolder directions. An Ad-Hoc Committee of Concerned Negro Auto Workers got the UAW to stop opposing black candidates for local offices, and they began winning elections in black- and even white-majority locals. In September 1972, some 1,200 black members and officers of thirty-seven different unions met in Chicago to discuss how to "enhance black influence and power in the American labor movement"; they launched the Coalition of Black Trade Unionists to further that agenda.

Latinos formed a parallel organization, the Labor Council for Latin American Advancement (LCLAA), founded in 1973 at a conference in Washington, D.C., attended by union officers and staff. The United Steel Workers had a Chicano Caucus, organized in 1971, with chapters in nine

Some of the world's most fertile farmland is in California's San Joaquin Valley.

YES, INDEED. JUST GAZE UPON ITS BOUNTY. GOD HAS BLESSED ME WITH A MULTI-MILLION DOLLAR AGRIBUSINESS AND AN ENDLESS SUPPLY OF CHEAP MIGRANT LABOR.

Traditionally, the workers came from places like China, Japan, the Philippines, and Mexico.

YOU KNOW, THE KIND OF PLACES WHERE PEOPLE ARE AT THEIR HAPPIEST DOING BACK-BREAKING WORK FOR MISERABLE WAGES.

AND, BELIEVE ME, WE'VE DONE OUR BEST TO KEEP THEM JUST AS HAPPY HERE IN CALIFORNIA.

A SHAME, THEN, WHEN ONE OF THESE FOLKS GETS THE UPPITY NOTION THAT THINGS NEED TO CHANGE.

Such a person was Jessie Lopez de la Cruz, a Mexican-American field worker who rose from the humblest of origins to become one of the most tireless and effective organizers of migrant workers.

MIGRANT LABOR'S HEROINE

Not until she was in her mid 40's, after meeting farm labor activist César Chávez in 1962, did Jessie join what was to become the United Farm Workers. The UFW not only advocated better wages and working conditions, but also addressed the issues of immigration policy and racial dignity.

I'D BE CHOPPING COTTON AND I'D TALK ABOUT THE UNION TO PEOPLE IN ROWS RIGHT NEXT TO ME.

HEY!

WHAT'RE YOU CHATTERING ABOUT?

She was the first woman to organize workers in the field, and she spent much volunteer time following up with home visits.

Within a few years, Jessie became an official organizer and head of a union hiring hall, which directed growers who needed labor directly to UFW members.

THERE WAS A HAPPIER TIME WHEN MIDDLEMEN USED TO HELP AN AGRI-TYCOON LIKE ME PASS UP THESE OLDER WORKERS FOR YOUNGER AND STRONGER FOLKS AT A FRACTION OF THE WAGES.

STILL, HEH HEH, JESSIE AND THE UNION HAVE AN UPHILL STRUGGLE ORGANIZING MIGRANTS 'CAUSE MOST OF 'EM DON'T SPEAK ENGLISH AND DON'T STAY PUT.

ALSO, WE GROWERS AREN'T AFRAID TO CRACK A FEW SKULLS WHEN NECESSARY OR WORK WITH OTHER UNIONS, LIKE THE TEAMSTERS, WHEN WE CAN EXPLOIT THE RACIAL DIVIDE.

GOD BLESS AMERI ♪ ♫

WOMEN CAN NO LONGER BE TAKEN FOR GRANTED— THAT WE'RE JUST GOING TO STAY HOME AND DO THE COOKING AND CLEANING.

Jessie had problems within her own community too. "It was very hard being a woman organizer," she said. "Men gave us the most trouble... They were for the union, but they weren't taking orders from women, they said."

"Some women I spoke to started attending the union meetings," she said, "and later they were out on the picket lines."

J. SACCO 8.99

Years later, while living in a makeshift shack in a field near cows and horses, her 5-month-old child died.

"There were thousands of flies," Jessie recalled....

"I didn't have a refrigerator, no place to refrigerate the milk.

"She got sick...

"It was hunger, malnutrition, no money to pay the doctors."

In those days, a migrant worker's baby was twice as likely to die as the babies of others. The life expectancy of farmworkers was only 49 years.

"Growing up, I could see all injustices and I would think, 'If only I could do something about it!'" Jessie said. "But I felt I couldn't do anything."

But Jessie Lopez de la Cruz demonstrated how much a single person could accomplish — not just as a worker in an industry that traditionally takes its laborers for granted, but as a woman, a Mexicana.

"It doesn't take courage," she said. "All it takes is standing up for what you believe in, talking about things that you know are true, things that should be happening, instead of what is happening."

HUELGA
HUELGA
HUELGA

HMPH! Y'SEE WHAT I'M UP AGAINST! I TELL YA, I'M TIRED OF BEING PUSHED AROUND BY THE LITTLE GUY!

J. SACCO 6.99

cities from California to Pennsylvania and 3,000 members in Los Angeles alone. New York City was another hub of activity, with the multiunion Spanish Labor Committee in the lead.

In Puerto Rico, government repression of student antiwar activists drove a new generation of radicals into the labor movement. Beginning in 1968, a strike wave swept the island. In 1971, forty independent unions formed the Movimiento Obreros Unidos. MOU activists favored independence, opposed the island's exceptions from the federal minimum wage, brought labor support to socialist May Day activities, and fiercely defended their autonomy from the AFL-CIO. Since their strikes were opposed by the pro-statehood governing party, their mobilizations built popular support for independence. They also drew the attention of the authorities: in 1975, MOU's executive secretary Federico Cintrón Fiallo was charged with robbing a San Juan bank, held as a terrorist on half a million dollars bail, and later sentenced for criminal contempt for refusing to cooperate with a federal grand jury. Police disruption and sectarian squabbles ended MOU's effectiveness.

New organizations united women workers, both union members and others. In 1971, 600 women from twenty-four cities met in Washington, D.C., for the first national conference of domestic workers. They represented local groups formed since the late 1960s, mostly by black women with experience in the civil rights movement. These groups joined in the National Council of Household Employees, which lobbied to extend labor laws to cover domestics. In the early 1970s, clerical workers built more than a dozen citywide associations, such as Women Office Workers in New York, Women Organized for Employment in San Francisco, and Cleveland Women Working. In 1977, several groups formed 9 to 5, the National Association of Working Women, with a founding membership of 10,000.

Airline flight attendants, who had unionized in the 1940s and 1950s, formed Stewardesses for Women's Rights (SFWR) in 1974. It used lawsuits, pickets, and the mass distribution of buttons, bumper stickers, and leaflets to attack what the attendants called "sexploitation." They targeted company regulations on their hairdos, makeup, and weight, and airline advertising that depicted them as sex objects for male customer satisfaction. When ads for National Airlines invited businessmen to "fly" its attendants, SFWR replied, "Go fly yourself."

Labor feminism also brought union women together across occupations. In 1971, San Francisco activists founded the Union Women's Alliance to Gain Equality (Union WAGE), whose mission statement declared that "Women's liberation must be for the working women, beginning on the job." Based mainly in California, WAGE had outposts in the Pacific Northwest, the Midwest, and New York City. Members aided drives to unionize women workers, promoted the formation of women's caucuses, and campaigned to preserve and extend protective labor laws.

In March 1974, more than 3,200 women unionists from across the country met in Chicago to launch the Coalition of Labor Union Women. Led by the labor movement's highest-ranking female officials, CLUW lobbied for women's advancement on the job and in unions, for organizing drives aimed at women workers, and for legislation that addressed their needs. In 1980, CLUW president Joyce Miller became the first woman on the AFL-CIO's executive board.

The antiwar movement also had a labor contingent. The surviving "red" unions—UE and ILWU—always opposed the war; so did some AFL-CIO unions with left-wing histories, like Local 1199. In 1966, New York union leaders formed a Trade Union Division in the peace organization Committee for a Sane Nuclear Policy. In 1967, the Division brought 523 officers from fifty unions to Chicago for a National Labor Assembly for Peace to bring "this savage war to a swift and just conclusion, so that we may devote our wealth and energies to the struggle against poverty, disease, hunger, and bigotry." During the nationwide October 15 Vietnam Moratorium in 1969, forty unions backed the New York City demonstration, UAW and Hotel Employees and Restaurant Employees (HERE) officers spoke at the Detroit event, and a UAW leader presided over a giant Los Angeles rally. Many union leaders denounced the April 1970 invasion of Cambodia; Victor Gotbaum of AFSCME's District 37 in New York City headed the Coalition for Peace, which led a mass protest march, and fifty unions joined the sponsors of an emergency peace conference in Cleveland. In 1972, a thousand trade unionists from thirty-five AFL-CIO unions founded Labor for Peace.

Lesbian and gay rights also became labor issues, though on a smaller scale. The American Federation of Teachers first condemned employer reprisals against gay and lesbian teachers in 1970. The Gay Teachers Association (1974) formed a caucus in New York City's United Federation of Teachers. The Gay Teachers Coalition (1975) allied with San Francisco's Bay Area Gay Liberation (BAGL). Other workers took up the cause. The Gay Nurses Alliance started in 1973; both men and women joined chapters across the country. In 1974, the independent Transportation Employees Union in Ann Arbor, Michigan, negotiated the first contract to prohibit discrimination for sexual orientation—one lesbian member recalled, "There was a vision there about how trade unionism can be used to achieve civil rights." San Francisco saw the closest labor-gay alliance. After he supported a Teamsters boycott of Coors beer, the Laborers Union and the Building and Construction Trades Council joined the Teamsters to endorse gay activist Harvey Milk when he ran for the Board of Supervisors in 1975 and in 1977 (when he won). BAGL's Labor Committee held a press conference in 1976 with twenty-two union leaders to announce mutual support for negotiating contracts with antidiscrimination clauses and defeating antiunion ballot measures.

Workers rallied around health and safety issues on an unprecedented scale. In the late 1960s, the United Mine Workers backed the Black Lung Association's campaign for compensation for black lung disease, caused by breathing coal dust. UMW members in Ohio, Pennsylvania, and West Virginia staged mass strikes for compensation in February 1969. Late that year Congress passed the Coal Mine Health and Safety Act, which set up a compensation program and set new mine safety standards—mining deaths from accidents and explosions dropped by half over the next decade. The black lung campaign inspired others: the Carolina Brown Lung Association worked to get compensation for byssinosis (from cotton dust); the White Lung Association for compensation for asbestosis (asbestos was widely used in insulation).

In 1970, Congress established the Occupational Safety and Health Administration, authorized to set workplace safety and health standards and monitor compliance. OSHA was not up to the task—in its first sixteen years OSHA issued only eighteen health and safety regulations, and even at its most active could inspect less than 2 percent of U.S. workplaces in any given year. Unionists joined health professionals and scientists in a network of committees, councils, and coalitions on occupational safety and health. These "COSH" groups developed local and state standards on workplace safety and health and provided advice and training to shop stewards and other local union officers. Strikes over health and safety issues actually doubled in the first four years after OSHA's authorization.

Some unions made other allies in the struggle against toxic workplaces. The Oil, Chemical and Atomic Workers won a 1973 strike against Shell Oil after environmental groups like Friends of the Earth and the Environmental Defense Fund and community organizations like the National Tenants Association and NWRO boycotted Shell products. The next year OCAW local officer Karen Silkwood began documenting radiation hazards at the Kerr-McGee plutonium processing plant in Oklahoma City. After she was killed while driving to meet a union staffer and a *New York Times* reporter, OCAW organized a network of environmentalists and Native Americans into the Sunbelt Alliance, which targeted the nuclear industry in the late 1970s (and raised money for Silkwood's three orphaned children).

Unionism expanded dramatically in the public sector. By 1972, more than half of public employees belonged to unions—up from about one in ten in the early 1960s. The American Federation of Teachers, the American Federation of Government Employees, and the American Federation of State, County and Municipal Employees (AFSCME) became some of the largest unions in the land. Professional organizations like the National Education Association and American Nurses Association added collective bargaining to their services, though they did not formally affiliate with the labor movement.

Though strikes by public employees were almost always against the law, they broke out repeatedly anyway—among hospital workers, teachers, office clerks, social workers, fire fighters, police, and others. Each victory encouraged other groups to take their grievances to the streets. Memphis sanitation workers won their 1968 strike when the city finally recognized their AFSCME local after King's murder. Within months black garbage collectors in St. Petersburg and Atlanta launched AFSCME strikes and won with support from the SCLC and the strikers' communities.

The first national walkout by federal employees began on March 18, 1970, when postal workers in New York City staged a wildcat strike for higher pay. It quickly spread to Boston, Pittsburgh, Akron, Houston, and other cities. Within days the strikers numbered 150,000, despite federal injunctions. On March 23, President Nixon sent troops and National Guardsmen to move the mails in New York, and union officers across the country were hauled into court. The strike ended two days later, when the government agreed to negotiate; postal workers got substantial raises, and strikers got amnesty.

The postal walkout came at the peak of a strike wave that extended from 1968 into 1977. Strikes numbered over 5,000 per year and involved an average of 2.5 million workers, with more than 3 million out in both 1970 and 1971. The trend penetrated places where walkouts had been rare or unknown, and not only in the public sector. In 1969, singers, musicians, and dancers struck New York's Metropolitan Opera Company. Book publishers saw their first strike since the 1930s when Harper & Row office employees walked out in 1974. San Francisco Chinatown garment workers broke another long truce, striking the Jung Sai company in 1975. Higher pay was the most common strike demand, as military spending fueled inflation in living costs. But many strikes concerned issues of power, like union recognition and management prerogatives on the shop floor.

Women's fights for recognition could be especially bitter. In Detroit, clerical workers struck Fruehauf Trailer for six months in 1969–70; operatives at the Oneita Knitting Mills in rural South Carolina stayed out for six months in 1973. Some 4,000 Chicana garment workers in El Paso, Texas, struck Farah Manufacturing from May 1972 into March 1974. They won with the help of a Farah boycott backed by the AFL–CIO, a national network of community and campus activists, and unions as far away as Sweden and Hong Kong.

The most famous battle over managerial prerogatives was the March 1972 strike by UAW Local 1112 at the General Motors complex in Lordstown, Ohio. Virtually all of the strikers were in their late teens or twenties, many had college experience, and a good portion had served in Vietnam. They targeted the latest trend in industrial management: paramilitary shop discipline to enforce unprecedented production quotas. Though the strike lasted just three weeks and ended in a draw, it made national headlines as a youth revolt against dehumanizing work and struck a deeply responsive chord among the mostly young workers on the front lines of automated speedup.

Local 1112 president Gary Bryner said of the strikers, "They just want to be treated with dignity. That's not asking a hell of a lot." To the extent that dignity meant simple justice as well as general respect, the same could be said of all working people involved in insurgencies on the job and elsewhere in the sixties. The demands for dignity from so many fronts added up to a veritable revolution.

A HOUSE DIVIDED

In October 1974, a special issue of *Business Week* lamented the sense of entitlement that drove social unrest. The editorial declared, "Some people will obviously have to do with less. . . . Yet it will be a bitter pill for many Americans to swallow—the idea of doing with less so that big business can have more." To get its way, corporate America had launched a collective assault on what one task force called the "excess of democracy."

A chorus of business-friendly "experts" on public policy declared that the federal War on Poverty had at last been won. In fact, it had scarcely made a dent. The proportion of families living below the official poverty line dropped from about 11 percent in 1967 to 10 percent in 1973, but 23 million Americans still lived in poverty, including 10 percent of whites, 22 percent of Latinos, and 33 percent of blacks. President Nixon nevertheless decided in 1973 to shut down the Office of Economic Opportunity, and the many community projects it had supported lost their funding.

The federal cuts had especially harsh consequences in cities, where business leaders instigated reductions in public services. In New York City investment bankers staged a coup by refusing to underwrite municipal bonds unless they could dictate the city's budget. A 1975 law drafted by businessmen transferred budgetary power from elected officials to an Emergency Financial Control Board authorized to remove officials who defied its policies. By the time the board disbanded in 1978, the City had laid off 25,000 public workers and gutted spending on schools, hospitals, sanitation, mass transit, libraries, parks, and recreation.

Reduced services followed tax cuts in cities and states around the country. The cuts were often engineered by business interests. In the late 1970s, businessmen from California to Massachusetts funded groups agitating for lower property taxes, directing their appeals at white homeowners who were all too ready to believe that black and Latino people got too much attention and too much money from the government. When tax cuts were voted in, big investors in business real estate reaped the lion's share of savings, and the poorest neighborhoods took the largest cuts in public services.

Sixties-style community organizing receded under the new regimes. Urban infrastructures crumbled first and worst in the predominantly black and Latino neighborhoods that had been on the front lines of protest. Keeping a family safe and healthy in these neighborhoods now required so much extra work and worry that most people, especially women, could do little more. The diminished cadre of activists scrambled to create substitutes for defunded programs and services. Old coalitions faded as neighborhoods vied for shrinking resources, and more and more white families fled to the suburbs. Community sympathy for public workers and their unions sharply declined, making it almost impossible for them to resist layoffs, speedups, and eroding wages and benefits.

Workers in the private sector also lost ground. President Nixon tried to control inflation with a wage and price freeze in 1971. The freeze—especially on prices—was widely ignored but corporate pressure on the federal government stepped up. The Business Roundtable, founded in 1972 by the heads of General Motors, U.S. Steel, and other giant corporations, coordinated a national drive to control the legislative process. Corporate political action committees multiplied from 89 in 1974 to nearly 800 by 1978 and poured massive sums into campaign financing as well as lobbying, investing in Republicans and Democrats alike. Such investments paid off: during the 1974–75 recession, the federal government abandoned its usual attempts to stimulate the economy and cut spending. Unemployment soared to levels unseen since the end of the Depression—8.5 percent nationally and more than five times higher among young black and Latino workers. Strike activity diminished until the economy recovered in 1976.

Business's political offensive targeted a labor movement racked by internal divisions since the advent of the sixties. The AFL-CIO Executive Council refused to endorse the 1963 March on Washington. Support for integration cost the Mississippi AFL-CIO a third of its membership between 1960 and 1966. The United Farm Workers faced persistent attacks from the Teamsters, who continued their longtime practice of signing sweetheart contracts with growers trying to avoid more militant unions. Some 200 black and Puerto Rican labor leaders denounced New York City's United Federation of Teachers for its fall 1968 strike against community control of public schools.

Many thousands of workers brought complaints against unions to the Equal Employment Opportunity Commission (EEOC) established by the Civil Rights Act. The building trades repeatedly promised to desegregate but made negligible progress except when the government required integrated work crews on federally funded projects. Industrial unions drew almost as many EEOC complaints as the building trades. Feminists from Steelworkers NOW—a union caucus with loose ties to the National Organization for Women—joined black and Latino men in a lawsuit charging discrimination by the steel industry and the United Steel Workers. A 1974 settlement brokered by the EEOC set new rules for transfer, training, and promotion and obliged the union along with nine major companies to pay $30 million in back wages to groups disadvantaged under the old rules.

Divisions over Vietnam were especially acrimonious. Most AFL-CIO leaders supported the war. The AFL-CIO expanded international operations with the Asian American Free Labor Institute (AAFLI), founded in 1968 to aid the corrupt but anticommunist Vietnamese Confederation of Labor. Frustrated by George Meany's intransigence on the war, Walter Reuther took the UAW out of the Federation in 1968, and joined with the Teamsters in an Alliance for Labor Action. (The Alliance disappeared after Reuther's death in a 1970 airplane crash.)

The Nixon administration promoted labor attacks on the antiwar movement. The infamous "hardhat rampage" on Wall Street and other prowar union demonstrations in May 1970 were orchestrated by union leaders and White House operatives. (Peter Brennan, then president of the New York City Building Trades Council, later became Nixon's Labor Secretary.) The AFL-CIO made no presidential endorsement in 1972. Building trades and maritime affiliates led a Labor for Nixon campaign; most industrial and public employee unions joined with the Farm Workers and the Coalition of Black Trade Unionists in supporting the liberal antiwar Democrat George McGovern.

AFL-CIO foreign policy stuck to its Cold War mission. In Chile, where the CIA helped General Augusto Pinochet overthrow popularly elected leftist Salvador Allende in 1973, the AFL-CIO's American Institute for Free Labor Development ran programs for the truckers whose 1972 strike began the CIA's destabilization of the economy and for the maritime union leaders who supplied names of labor activists for Army death lists. Such operations remained cloaked in secrecy, more to shield AFL-CIO leaders from critics than to fool anyone in Chile. The AFL-CIO revived European operations by starting the Free Trade Union Institute in 1977 to oppose socialist and communist unions in post–fascist Spain and Portugal.

Union democracy became an increasingly explosive issue during the long wave of strikes. Many strikes were wildcats, contesting the authority of employers and labor officials alike. In April 1970, Teamsters rejected a new contract signed by their president and shut down trucking from Los Angeles to New Hampshire. In May a thousand information operators demanding higher pay and more sick days left New York Telephone switchboards. In June UMW members in Pennsylvania, Ohio, and West Virginia walked out over hospital and pension benefits and lax enforcement of the Mine Safety Act. In August 1973, UAW staffers with baseball bats escorted members to work during a wildcat strike over safety at Chrysler's Mack Avenue stamping plant in Detroit. After the October 1973 Arab-Israeli war, 2,000 members of an ad hoc Arab Workers Caucus in the Detroit UAW staged a one-day strike against union investments in Israeli bonds. In 1974, Mexican and Mexican American Steelworkers defied union leaders to strike for higher pay at Superior Fireplace in Fullerton, California, and against speedup at the Kennecott mines in Bayard, New Mexico. In July 1976, Chicana cannery workers in San Jose, California, struck against a contract negotiated by Teamsters Local 679.

Some wildcats were supported by dissident union groups. For more than six years before the San Jose strike, the Cannery Workers Committee had been pushing for rank-and-file participation and bilingual meetings in Local 679. The Superior Fireplace strike was supported by the Comité Obrero en Defensa de Indocumentados en Lucha and the Centro de Acción Autónomia—Hermandad General de Trabajadores, both Mexican workers' rights organizations. In other cases, dissident groups grew out of strikes. After the 1970 wildcat strike in the Post Office, an "Outlaw" committee led by Vietnam veterans organized in bulk-mail facilities in and around New York

City. While the Amalgamated Clothing Workers concentrated on the Farah boycott to support the El Paso strike, the strikers themselves formed Unidad Para Siempre to build a more militant and democratic local. Teamsters United Rank and File, started in Toledo, Ohio, after the 1970 wildcat strike, did not last, but Teamsters for a Decent Contract, started by long-haul drivers in 1975, became Teamsters for a Democratic Union the next year and began a long campaign to reform the union.

Like the Teamsters, Steelworkers organized against bad contracts. After Steelworker president I. W. Abel signed the no-strike Experimental Negotiations Agreement (ENA) with the major steel companies in 1973, District 31 President Ed Sadlowski and other union officers founded Steel Workers Fight Back to dump the ENA and gain union members the right to ratify contracts. Fight Back concentrated on electing Sadlowski USWA president, but failed to address the issue of affirmative action or reach out to locals outside basic steel (the majority of USWA members). In 1977, Sadlowski lost to Lloyd McBride, Abel's choice for successor, by about nine percentage points.

One reform caucus took over a national union. Pennsylvania miner and black lung activist Jock Yablonski had challenged the notoriously corrupt Tony Boyle for UMW president. On Boyle's orders gunmen murdered Yablonski and his wife and daughter on New Year's Eve, 1969. At the funeral, mourners started Miners for Democracy, which won the 1973 election with a slate headed by retired miner (and Black Lung Association leader) Arnold Miller, and then disbanded. But the new leadership made little difference in the mines, and wildcats resumed; the biggest took place in the summer of 1976, when 150,000 miners—almost every UMW member east of the Mississippi—walked out to protest injunctions against West Virginia wildcat strikers.

Union rank-and-file movements aimed at more than ousting unsatisfactory leaders. Making unions more democratic would make them more responsive to the interests of the members and better able to defend those interests. As management assaults expanded, workers needed all their collective strength.

The strike wave receded in 1978, broken by continuing high unemployment—still around 6 percent more than three years after the end of the recession. Democrats had strengthened their control of Congress following Nixon's disgrace and fall in the Watergate scandal in 1974, and Democrat Jimmy Carter had taken the White House from incumbent caretaker Gerald

Ford in 1976, but the AFL-CIO's political agenda ran into a business lobbying campaign that killed labor law reform and a minimum wage increase. Business lobbyists meanwhile won tax reform (rates on personal income reduced across the board, investment credits increased, capital gains rates lowered), cuts in federal grants-in-aid to cities, and airline and trucking deregulation.

UAW president Douglas Fraser charged that business leaders were waging "a one-sided class war" on "working people, the unemployed, the poor, the minorities, the very young and the very old, and even many in the middle-class." In October 1978, he hosted a conference attended by thirty affiliated and independent unions and seventy-one organizations from the NAACP, the National Farmers Union, and the Women's Political Caucus, to environmental, tax reform, and consumer protection groups. The following January, this "coalition of coalitions" founded the Progressive Alliance.

The Alliance fizzled; its leaders never agreed on a presidential candidate. Meanwhile, bad investments and worse marketing strategies had nearly ruined Chrysler Corporation by 1979. As the price of a rescue, banks demanded union concessions—mainly a two-year wage freeze. Fraser lobbied for the package and joined Chrysler's board to help restructure the company. The union workforce fell by nearly half to 57,000, and plants like Dodge Main closed.

George Meany retired in 1979. To take his place he named Lane Kirkland. After a brief wartime stint in the merchant marine, Kirkland had trained for the foreign service, then taken an AFL-CIO staff position researching pensions and social security. Meany had made him Special Assistant in 1960 and Secretary-Treasurer in 1969, and he had spent the next decade cultivating politicians and intellectuals who called for an all-out war against communism. The Executive Committee ratified the nomination unanimously, proving AFL-CIO conservatism had survived the sixties with its hegemony intact and ready to enlist in a new Cold War. But the world had changed, and prudential "business" unionism was not at all secure in the new order.

CHAPTER

 11

HARD TIMES

Screen actor Ronald Reagan, the former Republican governor of California, defeated Democratic incumbent Jimmy Carter in 1980 by nearly eight and a half million votes. Carter had been beset by crises—in 1979, U.S. client regimes collapsed in Iran and Nicaragua, the Soviets sent troops to prop up their own clients in Afghanistan, Iranian radicals seized the U.S. embassy in Tehran, taking fifty Americans hostage, and the economy went into recession. To their usual base of businessmen who still resented New Deal reforms, the Republicans added a new coalition of voters frustrated by the public skepticism about foreign military ventures (the "Vietnam Syndrome"), vexed by the new rights won by racial minorities, homosexuals, and women (especially abortion, decriminalized by the Supreme Court in 1973), and eager for economic relief through reduced taxes. The AFL-CIO endorsed and campaigned for Carter, but this made little difference. More and more people did not vote at all—the proportion of people eligible to vote who actually voted in presidential elections fell from nearly 70 percent in 1964 to less than 60 percent in 1980. Over half of blue-collar voters and 43 percent of voters from union households backed the actor, and the Republicans took the Senate majority.

The new regime was not friendly to unions. The Professional Air Traffic Controllers Organization had complained for years that staffing and equipment had not kept pace with expanding traffic—stress forced many controllers into early retirement. By mid-1980, the Federal Aviation Administration had set up a Management Strike Contingency Force. When 15,000 controllers walked out August 3, 1981, Reagan put the plan in action. Four hours into the strike he declared on national television that controllers who did not return to work within forty-eight hours "have forfeited their jobs and will be terminated." Most were.

The AFL-CIO had already announced a "Solidarity Day" march and rally in Washington, and the affiliated unions turned out almost half a million members and supporters on September 19. They cheered Polish independent trade unionists and PATCO strikers alike. But the Federation planned only to press Democrats to oppose Republican initiatives. As for PATCO, when some unions urged nationwide actions, President Lane Kirkland declared, "I personally do not think that the trade union movement should undertake anything that would represent punishing, injuring or inconveniencing the public at large for the sins or transgressions of the Reagan administration." Subsequent Solidarity Days became congressional lobbying blitzes, while Reagan's transgressions injured more and more members of the public at large.

LEAN AND MEAN

The Reagan team brought businessmen and their friends to Washington, and they brought business habits. Some simply looted the public treasury. The chair of the Postal Board of Governors (and crony of Attorney General Ed Meese) steered consulting contracts to his friends; the vice chair, a Reagan campaign official, took bribes from contractors. After financiers and bankers stole or gambled away $90–130 billion from federally insured and deregulated savings and loan associations, the government paid out upwards of $400 billion, much of it in interest, as the resolution of the debacle stretched into a second round of ransacking undervalued assets.

Most of the transfer of public funds to private pockets was legal. The bulk of Reagan's $8 billion worth of tax cuts went to taxpayers with annual incomes above $50,000. Almost half of all taxpayers saw their overall tax bills rise, mainly through increased payroll taxes, and another 30 percent saw little or no change. Corporations did well. In 1980, they paid over 35 percent of their profits in taxes on the average; by 1983, they paid less than 18 percent. Congress scrambled to pass new tax credits and allowances for needy firms and industries.

Businessmen wanted less government interference. Industries were deregulated: oil and gas; airlines; banking, savings and loans, other financial

TRUCKER

HEALTH CARE WORKER

J. SACCO 12-00

ELECTRONIC ASSEMBLY WORKERS

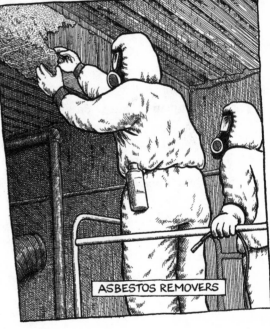

ASBESTOS REMOVERS

services; broadcasting, cable, communications; transportation. For safety, environmental, and consumer protection regulation, the White House cut agency budgets and installed administrators committed to reducing regulatory activity. When the Civil Rights Commission complained about cuts in federal civil rights enforcement staffing in 1983, the White House fired three commissioners. Some laws were just ignored. Federal contractors were required to pay "prevailing wages," usually union scale, but the military and other departments stopped enforcing the rule, and by the mid-1980s, nonunion contractors got almost all the work.

The administration left open two seats on the National Labor Relations Board until 1983, letting the case backlog grow. When corporate lawyer Donald Dotson finally became chair, the Board issued a string of decisions against unions. In 1984, the Board ruled that employers need not negotiate with unions over plant closures (Otis Elevator), could send union work to nonunion contractors (Milwaukee Spring), and could fire union members for verbal conduct (Clear Pine Mouldings). The new NLRB upheld union charges in 55 percent of the cases, down from 85 percent a decade earlier, and some unions waited five years for a final decision.

The Reagan Revolution blended ideology with greed, and a dash of ordinary incompetence, but did not alter the changes sweeping through the national economy. For most people, economic decline began with a sharp rise in oil prices after the 1973 Arab-Israeli War, followed by "stagflation"—rising inflation and unemployment. From an annual average of less than 3 percent from 1945 to 1967, inflation rose to about 5 percent in 1973, over 8 percent in 1975, and reached double digits by 1980. Unemployment remained around 5 percent through 1973, then rose to 8 percent in 1975, and reached 9 percent by 1982. Real wages began to fall in 1973, and plunged after 1975. From 1972 to 1982, average weekly earnings before taxes for nonagricultural workers fell from $196.41 to $167.87 in constant-value dollars, a 12 percent decline. For business, the crisis began earlier: around 1966, the rate of profit began to fall, partly from new competition with the rebuilt economies of Europe and Japan. The after-tax rate of return for nonfinancial corporations fell from 13.7 percent in 1966 to 7.6 percent in 1979, and funding for new capital investment came less from income and more from borrowing.

Business responded to the crisis in profits in several ways. Companies invested in other companies, buying shares in rivals, diversifying against losses in a single industry, or just shopping for profits. Corporations spent $50 billion buying into or taking over other firms in 1980, more than doubled that the next year, and doubled it again to over $250 billion in 1986. The big corporations became bigger, with more operations dispersed more widely, with heavier debts and interest payments.

Corporate ownership shifted too. By the mid–1970s, more than half of all stock purchases were made by bank trust departments. Corporate management revised the definition of "profitability." Interest paid on loans rose from 30 percent of corporate after-tax profits in 1979 to nearly 140 percent in 1986, and was still over 100 percent in 1990. A newly-acquired company had to return its regular profits plus interest on the loan that financed its purchase, a new minimum "hurdle rate." As inflation pushed up the cost of borrowing, the hurdle could rise to 25–40 percent a year.

New management restructured merged and acquired companies—closing or spinning off subsidiaries, reducing duplicate administrative, production, or distribution services or systems. Closing even a money-making facility could improve a corporate bottom line. Uniroyal shut down its profitable Indianapolis tire plant in 1978 to put the cash into making even more profitable chemical products. In 1991, G.E. announced the closure of its most profitable small appliance division, the Ontario, California, metal iron plant. A thousand black and Latino women union members lost their jobs.

Corporations also invested more abroad—G.E.'s new metal irons were made in Mexico and Brazil. Corporate profits from foreign investments tripled between 1965 and 1980, becoming almost a sixth of total profits. Corporations not only bought out or into foreign companies; they also built new facilities abroad for foreign markets or for reexport to the U.S. Already by 1970 almost half of all U.S. imports and nearly three fourths of exports were exchanges between subsidiaries of transnational corporations.

Some foreign direct investment improved access to markets or natural resources, but much of it financed the continuing quest for cheap labor. "Right to work" states (no union shops) were attractive, but labor was even cheaper in the developing world. Puerto Rico began its "Operation Bootstrap" economic development program in the 1940s, featuring tax holidays and low-wage labor. It proved to be a bonanza for U.S. investors, returning over $75 million in profits and dividends in 1960, and over $400 million in 1970. From the 1960s multinational corporations moved labor-intensive operations to new facilities in Hong Kong, Taiwan, South Korea, Singapore, Malaysia, Thailand, and the Philippines. Mexico's proximity was especially attractive. In 1966, the Mexican government opened its first industrial park for processing exports in Ciudad Juárez, across the border from El Paso, Texas. The same year, RCA opened a television assembly plant in right-to-work Memphis, Tennessee. Two years later RCA built a new facility in the Ciudad Juárez "maquiladora" zone; by 1971 RCA-Memphis had closed and RCA-Mexico had expanded. By 1974, some 500 border maquiladoras employed 80,000 workers, and Mexico expanded its "Border Industrialization Program."

World Bank and International Monetary Fund policies encouraged governments in developing countries to take the same path, improving utilities, transportation and communications infrastructure, and relaxing restrictions on foreign ownership and profit transfers. Government-backed insurance from the U.S. Overseas Private Investment Corporation provided additional support for some direct investments. U.S.-backed regimes helped enforce labor discipline. Between 1970 and 1980, U.S.-owned assets abroad multiplied five times. By 1980, more than $3.3 billion returned as profits and dividends to nonresident investors from Puerto Rico alone, nearly 70 percent of the value of the island's manufactures, going mostly to the U.S.

Business services could relocate as well as manufacturing and assembly. In 1981, Blue Shield broke a fifteen-week strike by Medicare claims processors by transferring 448 jobs out of San Francisco. Offshore data entry had started in Ireland and Barbados by 1982. By 1988, Filipino, Indian, and Scottish contractors also processed credit card slips, supermarket coupons, insurance and hospital records, and book manuscripts for U.S. companies.

Labor costs were more than just a drag on corporate profits. Thoughtful corporate economists traced the nation's economic malaise to the distribution of its prosperity. In 1979, Federal Reserve Chairman Paul Volcker declared, "The standard of living of the average American worker has to decline." Between 1978 and 1982, 6.8 million jobs were lost to plant closures. By 1981, a third of all autoworkers and half of all steelworkers were unemployed. By 1982, about two million Americans were homeless.

RACE TO THE BOTTOM

Far from board rooms and stock exchanges, economic change engulfed entire communities. In the copper towns of Greenlee County, Arizona, mine workers belonged to thirteen different unions, the largest of which was United Steel Workers Local 616, with a mostly Mexican American membership. The coordinated regional contracts ran out the last day of June 1983. The unions offered to freeze wages except for a cost-of-living adjustment, and four copper companies accepted. Phelps Dodge Copper Corporation demanded cuts and no COLA, and Phelps Dodge miners walked out a minute after midnight on July 1.

Strikes for new contracts had happened before, but the company had not tried to stay open during a strike for decades. Now Phelps Dodge got an injunction against union pickets and organized convoys under police protection to bring office employees and supervisors to work the mines. Miners' wives and supporters took over picket duty. Six weeks into the strike the company began hiring replacements; when the pickets massed to block the convoy, National Guardsmen and state police dispersed them with tear gas. The pickets returned again and again—one trooper declared, "If we could just get rid of these broads, we'd have it made."

The women organized an Auxiliary, set up a food bank and clothing exchange, fought evictions, organized relief after a flash flood, and dispatched members to strike-support rallies in New York, Boston, and California. After the Auxiliary held a Cinco de Mayo fiesta, 100 women marched off to picket the shift change at the Morenci pit mine, followed by hundreds of residents and supporters. Again the police dispersed the crowd with gas. When pickets formed up to march after a fiesta on the strike's first anniversary, a phalanx of 200 state troopers charged them.

The unions had offered in June to accept the company's terms if strikers could return by seniority. But copper prices were falling; Phelps Dodge shut down its Ajo mine, laying off 500 replacements, and reduced operations at its New Cornelia mine, laying off another 100. The Morenci pit, which incurred daily fines for polluting the San Francisco River, suspended operations in December. The Auxiliary staged a New Year's Eve "Good Bye Scabs" rally, but the strike was over. In 1987, the NLRB upheld an October 1984 decertification vote. Strikers, supporters, and unions won several civil rights cases; trial evidence detailed police collaboration with the company—getting lists of people to be arrested and filing false reports. The company's CEO concluded, "Employees at the operating level must understand how their performance toward key business goals helps the company earn a return on investment that more than covers the cost of capital. It is up to us to teach them."

Even strong unions in well-organized industries with industry-wide standards for wages, hours, and working conditions could not resist demands for concessions. Coordinated bargaining ended early in the electrical industry. In 1978, five different UAW locals in the United Technologies subsidiary Essex Wire plants staged unrelated strikes; a union rep commented, "We usually try to negotiate wages on the basis of [each] plant's ability to pay." Many wage concessions started as workers' contributions to keeping their employers open. As UAW rep Jack Horne told Chrysler Local 869 members, "Those of you who don't want to take a wage cut, go out and find another job." It was no idle threat: Ford casting plant workers in Sheffield, Alabama, refused to accept a 50 percent cut in wages and benefits, and the plant closed in 1981. But concessions developed their own competitive momentum. General Motors and Ford demanded concessions to match Chrysler, the UAW agreed, and in 1982 the membership ratified contract modifications.

The logic of concessions went beyond payroll costs. Even before the 1983 general economic recovery, when *Business Week* magazine surveyed corporate executives in 1982, 57 percent reported that they preferred concessions on work rules to wage cuts, and 19 percent agreed with the statement, "Although we don't need concessions, we are taking advantage of the bargaining climate to ask for them." In auto the buzzword was "flexibility": management redesigned production to achieve new flexibility in function, scheduling, and employment. Companies juggled just-in-time deliveries, adopted more standardized parts and processes, redeployed production to more competitive contractors, and constantly recalibrated their redesign by analyzing benchmark measures of input, output, and throughput. (The best-known benchmark was Toyota's "57-second minute"—the time assembly workers spent in motion every 60 seconds.) The individual worker did more tasks at a faster pace. The workforce saw fewer jobs with more skills, increasing contingent and part-time employment, and round-the-clock production schedules. Enthusiasts called it "lean production," and other industries adopted many "lean" practices.

Auto companies demanded that UAW locals compete for work with outside contractors—Ford locals in Detroit accepted concessions rather than see work shipped to Toyo Kogyo, a Japanese firm in which Ford had a 25 percent interest. In the 1982 settlement, Ford agreed to give thirty days notice before outsourcing union work, to give locals time to make a counter offer. The companies also insisted on "Quality of Work Life" programs, designed to promote employee commitment to company success by getting workers to team up with supervisors to find ways to cut costs and increase production. The "team concept" meant relaxing work rules. In 1985, the UAW signed an agreement covering G.M.'s new Saturn plant in Spring Hill, Tennessee, featuring team management, job classifications collapsed into a few general titles, and pay rates at 80 percent of the company base, supplemented to 100 percent or more with performance incentives. In 1987, the *Wall Street Journal* reported that twelve out of twenty-seven G.M. assembly plants had "competitive" agreements in place, most involving work rules.

The steel industry was in worse shape than auto, hit by dumping—foreign companies selling surplus production at or under cost—and faced with steep modernization costs to control pollution at older open-hearth furnaces. By 1982, the industry was running at 40 percent capacity and another 100,000 steel jobs had gone. The seven largest companies demanded $6 billion in concessions in that year's Master Steel Agreement negotiations. The union agreed to $2.5 billion in concessions, if the companies put savings into modernization. It was the last industry-wide contract. U.S. Steel bought Marathon Oil and Texas Oil & Gas, and closed a third of its remaining capacity along with several fabricating and finishing mills. Steel companies imported semifinished steel. When Armco asked a Houston local to roll foreign billets, the union refused, and Armco shut the plant. Minimills spread—small electric furnaces producing specialty items, about half nonunion, all without the overhead of pension and unemployment benefits carried by older, larger companies. In 1985, Wheeling-Pittsburgh filed for bankruptcy and moved to cancel its union contract, followed the next year by the LTV conglomerate, which owned Youngstown Sheet & Tube. In 1986, USWA settled separately with each company except USX, formerly known as U.S. Steel, which locked its workers out for six months before accepting a contract about midway in the industry range. Over the next few years LTV merged with Republic Steel and went bankrupt, foreign steelmakers acquired about a quarter of the country's integrated mills, and the profitable North Carolina–based nonunion minimill company Nucor expanded.

Each new Teamster National Master Freight Agreement covered fewer companies and permitted more regional and local concessions. The 1986 Agreement allowed individual concessions, as "loans" to employers. Even the labor aristocrats in the construction unions lost ground. More and more contractors operated as open shops, and more and more construction workers were not union members. The Carpenters lost nearly 70,000 members in just four years. In 1977, the National Contractors Association got the Laborers to pledge not to strike and to let management set crew size and dismiss employees at will. In 1978, the AFL-CIO Building and Construction Trades Department agreed to help the NCA control labor costs in heavy construction in exchange for union job guarantees.

No union member liked concessions—both the G.M. reopener and the Master Steel Agreement were nearly rejected by the unions' memberships in 1982. A wave of takeovers, diversifications, and relocations had dispersed industry ownership and operations by the early 1970s. The meatpackers' national union had become a division in a new diversified union, the United Food and Commercial Workers, product of a 1979 merger of the Retail Clerks International Union with the Amalgamated Meat Cutters, which had absorbed the United Packinghouse Workers in 1969. UFCW granted a forty-four-month wage freeze to pork processors in 1981. Within a year, the average hourly wage in meatpacking fell from $9.11 to $7.93. During 1983,

Swift Company imposed new wage cuts, while the LTV subsidiary Wilson Foods declared bankruptcy and cut hourly wages to $6.50—which qualified some meatpackers' families for food stamps.

In 1984, Hormel threatened to close its Ottumwa, Iowa, plant, got concessions from the union, then demanded other plants match them. Local P-9 at Hormel's flagship plant in Austin, Minnesota, led other Hormel locals in rejecting the demand. UFCW called Hormel local officers to a meeting and got them to take the Ottumwa rates. P-9 prepared to strike. The local's United Support Group mobilized families, retirees, and Austin youth, picketed the plant, set up defense and relief funds and a nationwide "Adopt-a-P9-Family" program. P-9 hired consultant Ray Rogers, whose New York–based Corporate Campaign publicized Hormel's ties to banks and South African companies. In August 1985, the local voted better than ten to one to strike and called a boycott against Hormel. P-9 rallied support from unions, farmers, and organizations active around peace, social justice, and environmental issues. The National Guard came to protect strikebreakers. When 6,000 activists rallied in April 1986 to shut down the plant, authorities gassed them and arrested hundreds.

UFCW president William Winn allowed the strike, but not the support activities. He got the Minnesota AFL–CIO to ban P-9 from its convention. He sequestered funds sent for P-9 support. In March 1986, he ordered the strikers back to work. They refused; three weeks later, when they defied an injunction with a mass rally at the plant gate, Winn trusteed the local. UFCW staff took over the union hall (and obliterated the famous P-9 strike mural themselves after local union painters refused the job). The new contract cut wages and benefits, and let the company fire anyone caught wearing a boycott button. Winn sent letters to every union local in the country urging trade unionists to buy Hormel products to support "union brothers and sisters."

A new round of restructuring swept the industry. Iowa Beef Packers (IBP) moved into pork, while the Cargill and Conagra feed and grain conglomerates added meatpacking to their vertically integrated food chains. When Armour meatpackers refused concessions, Armour's owner Greyhound closed the plants and sold them to Conagra, which reopened them union-free. IBP began recruiting workers directly from Mexico in 1989. Vast hog and chicken factory farms sprang up in the right-to-work South.

By 1986, average settlements in major union contracts gave a 1.2 percent raise; in major manufacturing contracts, the average was a 1.2 percent cut. Less than a third of major union contracts still had COLAs (compared to about 60 percent in 1979). Lump-sum payments replaced raises and new hires got lower pay. UFCW negotiated the most "two-tier" contracts (61 out of 261 recorded in 1983–85); Teamster two-tier contracts covered more workers.

Unions suffered big defeats. In 1983, Continental Airlines replaced strikers with new hires, and 12,000 members of the Amalgamated Transit Union at Greyhound took a pay cut after a seven-week strike failed to keep buses off the road. The same year, when the Glaziers and Glassworkers Union started a drive at Atari's video games plant, the company shut down its U.S. assembly operation. In 1985, the Brotherhood of Maintenance of Way Employees and other railroad unions lost 2,000 jobs during a strike over combining jobs on the Maine Central Railroad and at the Portland Terminal. 1986 was a very bad year. The Communications Workers at AT&T gave up their COLA in return for early notice of layoffs, after a twenty-six-day strike. TWA flight attendants went on strike over unequal pay—5,000 lost their jobs, and the Supreme Court threw out a settlement of their discrimination lawsuit. Aluminum, Brick and Glass workers struck Alcoa for five weeks before accepting the cuts in pay and benefits already accepted by Alcoa Steel Workers after a shorter strike. Greyhound workers struck again at the end of the year against more pay cuts, settled in February with a new owner, and lost deferred pay during bankruptcy proceedings. The United Paperworkers had already lost over 300 jobs during a 1986 strike at Boise Cascade in Maine; in 1988, they lost 1,200 more jobs when the union shut down a sixteen-month strike at International Paper. In 1989, Eastern Airlines pilots and flight attendants announced the "complete and unconditional termination" of their eight-month strike with Eastern's Machinists. The company announced it would not rehire strikers and filed for bankruptcy.

As Tony Mazzocchi of the Oil, Chemical and Atomic Workers observed, "Workers can see you don't need a union card to hold up a white flag." Union membership dropped 2.7 million between 1980 and 1984. By 1985, fifty AFL-CIO affiliates had fewer than 50,000 members and uncertain futures. One solution was merger: as AFL-CIO Regional Director Kevin Kistler observed, "It's a hell of a lot quicker and cheaper to add members through a merger than it is to organize new members." Many unions recruited well outside their original jurisdictions. The most aggressive organizing came from the Teamsters, Service Employees, Communications Workers, UFCW, and UAW. The International Jewelry Workers went into the Service Employees in 1980. The Barbers and Beauticians Union and the Insurance Workers International Union joined the Food and Commercial Workers in 1982 and 1983. Only 40 percent of the National Maritime Union's 25,000 members in 1987 were deep-water sailors. The Amalgamated Clothing Workers organized gravediggers working for the Catholic Archdiocese of Los Angeles in 1989.

Unions also competed over independent employee associations. For two years beginning in 1985, AFSCME, National 1199, the Communications Workers of America, and the Teamsters fought over various groups of Ohio state employees. AFSCME won many of them, but also lost locals to CWA in New Jersey and to SEIU in Massachusetts; and SEIU picked up state employee associations in Oregon (1980) and California (1982). Unions competed even in new drives. USWA, IUE, UFCW, CWA, and AFSCME all worked to organize 28,000 Blue Cross clerical workers in twenty cities, though the UAW already had a 3,000-member Blue Cross local in Michigan.

Unions made no better progress in politics. The AFL-CIO strongly backed Carter's former vice president Walter Mondale in the 1984 elections, in fact, the Federation endorsed him before the primaries. Unions activated canvassers and telephone banks, and contributed a record $35 million to candidates, but fared worse than before. Reagan beat Mondale by nearly 17 million votes overall and actually increased his support among voters from union households to 46 percent. The Teamsters reaffiliated in 1987, but the added numbers did not enhance AFL-CIO political influence—the Teamsters endorsed Republican George Bush in 1988, as they had endorsed Ronald Reagan in 1980 and 1984.

The key to working-class Republican support was racism. For AFL-CIO leaders, the racial problem was the demand for affirmative action. Unions had been the first organizations cited for contempt in cases based on Title VII of the 1964 Civil Rights Act—Plumbers Local 189 in Columbus, Ohio, and Metal Lathers Union Local 46 in New York City. Most union leaders supported affirmative action in hiring and training (sometimes under court order). USWA defended plantwide seniority and affirmative action goals for training, and went all the way to the Supreme Court to defend itself and Kaiser Corporation against a reverse discrimination lawsuit brought by white union member Brian Weber.

Promotions and layoffs were another matter, since they affected current union members. When the NAACP Legal Defense Fund campaigned to make layoffs preserve minority employment goals, the unions supported strict seniority. ("Superseniority" had been limited to union officials.) By 1984, firefighter and police unions were in court arguing against reverse discrimination in promotions as well as layoffs. Most unions stood by when the Supreme Court gutted federal antidiscrimination laws in its 1989 *Ward's Cove* decision. Filipino and native Alaskan cannery workers proved that

Ward's Cove Packing Company segregated its living and eating facilities, failed to post qualifications for hiring or transfer to higher-paid jobs, and paid white employees more on the average. The Court held that this did not prove company intent to discriminate and the workers had no legal remedy.

Unions were still dealing with racial discrimination when women took their turn. After women's organizations sued the Labor Department, President Carter set hiring goals and timetables for women on federally-funded construction projects in April 1978, and women began entering the buildings trades. They were not welcomed. In New York City a hundred members of United Tradeswomen staged a midday rally to make Jacob Javits Convention Center contractors meet federal guidelines. Once on the job, women found themselves in "trench warfare," a phrase used by an apprentice carpenter as she described the day a journeyman dropped a sledgehammer on her head and then sent her up onto a scaffold that he forgot to nail down. By 1989, women were a little more than 6 percent in only one construction trade—painters—and still less than 1 percent of plumbers and pipefitters. The AFL-CIO had its own affirmative action problem. By 1992, only three affiliates—the Retail, Warehouse, and Department Store Workers, the Association of Flight Attendants, and the American Guild of Musical Artists—had women presidents. In the eight largest AFL-CIO unions where more than half the members were women, women held between 8 percent (UFCW) and 32 percent (American Federation of Teachers) of the leadership positions.

AFL-CIO leaders supported one government initiative with enthusiasm—the renewed crusade against communism. The American Institute for Free Labor Development promoted land reform in El Salvador to defuse peasant support for leftist insurgents and paid union leaders to join the pro-government labor federation. The Institute trained union leaders in Grenada following the October 1983 U.S. invasion, set up a labor federation for Haitian dictator Jean-Claude Duvalier in 1984, and helped run conferences condemning the Sandinistas in Nicaragua. The African American Labor Institute supported Angolan anticommunist guerilla Jonas Savimbi and the Workers Union of South Africa, which competed with the anti-apartheid Congress of South African Trade Unions. The Asian American Free Labor Institute backed the Trade Union Congress of the Philippines against the Kilusang Mayo Uno federation and its campaigns against dictator Ferdinand Marcos and U.S. military bases, and funded the Fiji Trade Unions Congress campaign against the island nation's ban on nuclear weapons. In 1983, the Free Trade Union Institute began administering U.S. grants to unions worldwide. By the end of the decade FTUI funded anticommunist labor groups in eastern Europe and sponsored opposition to the independent General Confederation of Trade Unions, which had replaced the defunct Soviet federation in 1990 as the U.S.S.R. began to disintegrate.

The AFL–CIO rejoined the International Confederation of Free Trade Unions in 1984, mainly to combat communist influence, and helped affiliates participate in the international trade secretariats, networks of unions in allied industries loosely connected with the Geneva-based International Labor Organization. The secretariats proved to be more concerned with industry-wide problems and transnational employers than ideological purity. In 1990, the International Union of Food and Allied Workers' Associations admitted the left-wing Salvadoran Sindicato Industrial de Café over AFL–CIO objections.

Expanding international operations and absorbing independent associations did not build the American labor movement. Lane Kirkland recognized the need to organize new sectors of the workforce and allowed SEIU's John Sweeney and USWA's Lynn Williams to start an AFL–CIO Organizing Institute. But Kirkland's focus was fixed on the better-paid, better-educated white-collar worker, which reflected his understanding of the typical trade unionist. In his 1986 article "It Has All Been Said Before," Kirkland wrote, "As the composition of our membership shows, trade unionists are nothing more—and nothing less—than the American middle class and those who aspire to it."

This outlook did not fit the new workforce. U.S. employment patterns had been shifting rapidly, especially to the service industries. As the capitalist economy continued to mature, more and more activities became marketable commodities, urban and suburban populations needed more services, mass consumption required more elaborate distribution, and businesses required more services. As employment grew in services, it stagnated or declined in agriculture, mining, and manufacturing. These job losses came from automation and other labor-saving technological innovations and from expanding imports as well as from restructured production chains and runaway shops. Between 1979 and 1993, the number of U.S. jobs in services increased by 38 percent, while jobs producing goods, from food to fuel to manufactures, declined 12 percent.

Many of the jobs lost were union jobs; most of the jobs gained were low paid and nonunion. Between 1979 and 1987, more than 10 million new jobs were created paying $13,000 a year or less, while only 1.6 million new jobs paid more than $26,800. Union job losses helped dismantle economic arrangements that had bolstered the postwar middle class. Between 1980 and 1993, the proportion of full-time employees at large and mid-sized companies with medical insurance fully funded by the employer fell from 71 percent to 37 percent. The expectation of continuous, steadily better-paying work over a lifetime diminished. Workers abandoned by downsizings and closures rarely found jobs that paid as well. Home mortgage foreclosures measured economic distress; they tripled to over 450,000 a year between 1980 and 1995. More jobs became part-time or temporary, or both. From 1970 to 1990, as total employment increased by 54 percent, involuntary part-time employment increased 121 percent and temporary employment 21 percent. By 1993, Manpower Incorporated passed General Motors as the country's largest private employer.

Many workers in these new jobs were new to the labor force or new to the country. More and more women worked outside the home—by 1979, half of all women over sixteen; by 1990, almost 60 percent. The fastest-growing group of women workers were mothers with children under six—by 1983, half worked outside the home part- or full-time; by 1991, 60 percent. The racial and ethnic composition of the labor force changed too. After 1970, while European and Canadian immigration remained about the same, immigration from Asia and Latin America nearly doubled, and African immigration more than tripled. Immigrants were more diverse, and many were refugees from the consequences of U.S. foreign policy. By 1990, more than a quarter of U.S. Latinos were neither Mexican nor Puerto Rican in descent—5 percent were Cuban and 23 percent Central or South American. Asian immigrants included significant numbers of Vietnamese (9 percent) and South Asians (11 percent). These two trends overlapped in the electronics assembly plants of California's Silicon Valley, the Route 128 corridor in Massachusetts, and in North Carolina, where by the early 1980s about 40 percent of the workers were immigrant women, with low wages, high rates of illness, and next to no job security.

As Kirkland looked for people aspiring to the "middle class," for many people life got worse. Government policies deepened and extended the consequences of the recession. As taxes were cut, military spending expanded—some wasted in corrupt procurement (the Air Force paid $9,600 apiece for ordinary Allen wrenches), even more wasted on missile-defense schemes that never worked. The federal deficit ballooned; federal debt exploded. By 1985, more than 12 percent of annual federal spending went to interest alone.

Social spending was cut. The number of families living on $17,000 a year or less increased by a third from 1978 to 1981 to include 92 million people, more than 34 million of them below the federal poverty line. As poor families became more common, Aid to Families with Dependent Children fell, from an average $477 a month in 1980 to $374 in 1992, and more people were denied disability pensions and food stamps. Poverty spread unevenly by race and sex. When 18 percent of the total auto workforce was on layoff in 1980, almost 32 percent of black autoworkers were out of work. In majority-black "Motor City" Detroit, unemployment was 23 percent in 1982, black youth unemployment 70 percent, and the infant mortality rate about the same as for Honduras. In early 1981, while Reagan argued that high unemployment was caused by too many women looking for jobs outside the home and that government aid kept "welfare queens in designer jeans," a *New York Times* reporter interviewed Rosa, an undocumented Ecuadoran woman who lived in a Union City, New Jersey, basement with two children (one brain damaged), and worked twelve hours a day, seven days a week, sewing shirts for 20 cents apiece.

FIGHTING BACK

While top AFL-CIO leaders seemed baffled or stymied by economic and political changes, many labor activists struggled to find and use new tactics to defend themselves, organize new members, and to take control of their unions. They challenged union leaders on foreign policy, concessions, democracy, and corruption, and won some victories.

Memories of Vietnam jumpstarted labor opposition to Reagan's foreign policies. In 1981, presidents and other officials from twenty-four unions formed the National Labor Committee in Support of Democracy and Human Rights in El Salvador, run out of the New York offices of the Amalgamated Clothing Workers. In 1983, a Labor Committee delegation recommended that the U.S. suspend aid until the Salvadoran regime stopped its massive violations of labor and human rights. At that year's AFL-CIO convention, the Committee's constituent unions amended AIFLD's El Salvador report and rejected claims of progress on human rights. In 1985, Kenneth Blaylock of the American Federation of Government Employees, Ed Asner of the Screen Actors Guild, and William Winpisinger of the Machinists criticized U.S. support for the Salvadoran government from the floor of the convention. In 1987, Kirkland and AFT president Al Shanker tried to stop unions endorsing the April 25th Mobilization for Peace, Jobs and Justice in Central America and South Africa, but up to 50,000 trade unionists joined the Washington rally. At that year's AFL-CIO convention, delegates passed a resolution opposing U.S. support both the Salvadoran military and the anti-communist *contra* rebels in Nicaragua.

Some affiliates broke ranks with AFL-CIO foreign policy. Solidarity with the South African antiapartheid struggle was strong in unions with significant black membership like AFSCME and SEIU, and in unions confronting transnational employers with South African operations or investments, like the Steel Workers, Mine Workers, and OCAW. Unions sponsored speaking tours and organized support for activists like South African miners' union leader Amon Msane, detained after a U.S. tour in 1986. Similar activities supported Central American labor activists like the Stegac union workers who occupied their Guatemala Coca Cola plant for thirteen months in 1984–85 to win a strike, despite the death-squad assassinations of three union presidents. UMW observers helped the union at the Cerrejon coal mines in Colombia negotiate with Exxon in 1992, the first contract ever settled without military intervention.

AFL-CIO caution complicated relations with unions in next-door Mexico and Canada. Most Mexican unions were organs of the ruling Partido Revolucionario Institucional. In 1982, the PRI government expanded its "Border Industrialization Program" into a nationwide program to attract foreign investment. Both the "official" Confederación de Trabajadores Mexicanos and the "reform" Confederación Revolucionario de Obreros y Campesinos worked to maintain low wages and labor discipline and helped repress independent unions. The AFL-CIO recognized CTM and CROC, which generally opposed cross-border union cooperation as a threat to their control. Nevertheless, the AFL-CIO–affiliated Farm Labor Organizing Committee supported a Mexican union representing tomato pickers working for Campbell's Soup contractors while FLOC negotiated with Campbell's U.S. contractors in 1989. FLOC set up a U.S.-Mexico Exchange Program to coordinate negotiations with cucumber and pickle companies. The independent United Electrical Workers developed a "Strategic Organizing Alliance" with the Frente Auténtico de Trabajo, an independent Mexican federation. UE supported FAT drives in G.E. and Honeywell plants in northern Mexico in 1994; FAT helped UE organize the Aluminum Casting and Engineering Company in Milwaukee, where Mexican immigrants were the largest group among 450 black, white, Latino, and Southeast Asian workers.

Across the border to the north, many Canadian labor activists disagreed with the AFL-CIO's rejection of labor-based political parties, resented U.S. union's indifference to Canadian issues, and found American-style negotiation frustrating. OCAW's Canadian district disaffiliated in 1979. In 1982, Canadian UAW Chrysler locals struck to get back the 1979 COLA, and won. Their thirteen-day strike against G.M. in 1984 won a "special Canadian adjustment." They formed the Canadian UAW (later the Canadian Auto Workers) in September 1985. On a smaller scale, the Newfoundland

Fishermen's Union withdrew from UFCW in 1987, after headquarters threatened a takeover. According to NFU's Earle McCurdy, "The UFCW sees trade unionism as a business. We see trade unionism as a democratic people's organization." In USWA's 1984 special election after Lloyd Mc-Bride's death, nearly unanimous support from Canadian locals helped Canadian Lynn Williams defeat the candidate, backed by many reformers, who ran as the "All American Steel Worker."

Some unions looked to member mobilization for strength and to the wider community for support. A California cannery strike showed both the possibilities and the limits. In 1985, two Salinas Valley canners—Watsonville Canning and Richard Shaw—demanded a wage cut from $6.66 an hour to $4.25 and reductions in medical coverage. Teamsters Local 912—mostly Chicanas—went on strike September 9. Their community saw the demands as an Anglo assault and strongly supported the strike; unorganized cannery workers contributed to the strike fund, and 3,000 supporters marched in a November rally. When Watsonville Canning hired replacements, not one striker crossed over.

Shaw strikers settled for $5.85 an hour in February 1986, but the Watsonville Canning workers stayed out. Their rally in March drew 4,000 supporters. The strike committee rounded up 914 of the original thousand strikers from as far as Texas and Mexico to outvote 848 scabs in an August decertification election. After the owner went broke, Wells Fargo Bank sold the cannery to a grower. Teamsters Council 7 offered him an agreement. When the strikers learned the contract did not return them by seniority or provide medical benefits to all members, they massed around the plant to keep it closed, and six women started a hunger strike. On March 11, 1987, they accepted a new contract with seniority and medical benefits intact, but with a concession on wages.

Some union leaders preferred not to mobilize members during concessionary bargaining, but not all. Reformers recaptured the United Mine Workers presidency in 1982 when miner-turned-lawyer Rich Trumka defeated incumbent Sam Church, who was backed by the old Boyle faction and endorsed by AFL-CIO leaders. When the UMW started work on a new agreement with the Bituminous Coal Operators' Association in 1984, operator A. T. Massey—owned by Fluor Corporation and Royal Dutch Shell—refused to bargain. The union went on strike in October. Miners blocked Massey operations, and Trumka brought in an organizer from the South African National Union of Miners to run a Shell boycott, which got wide support among antiapartheid activists. When the NLRB ordered Massey to bargain in December 1985, the union ended the strike, but not the boycott.

In 1988, Pittston Coal Company demanded cuts in benefits, work rule changes, an end to overtime pay, and the right to open nonunion mines. The miners worked without a contract, filed a host of unfair labor practices charges, and set up "Camp Solidarity," where the "Daughters of Mother Jones" brought peace groups to train over 30,000 miners and supporters in civil disobedience. The strike began April 5, 1989—1,700 miners and their families blocked roads to the mines. Over a thousand were arrested the first month. Across eleven states, 40,000 miners staged wildcat strikes and shut down nonunion mines and coal-fired factories in "Memorial Day" solidarity actions. When ninety-eight miners and a local clergyman—each owning a share of company stock—occupied Pittston's main coal treatment plant, Moss No. 3, and a judge ordered them out, thousands of miners and supporters surrounded the plant until the court deadline passed. Pittston resumed bargaining in October and settled the last day of the year without most of the concessions. And over time coal operators invested more in nonunion strip-mining in the West, and UMW contracts covered less than half of national coal production.

Against leadership opposition, mobilizing the rank and file took patience and perseverance. For ten years, a Rank and File Slate in the International Brotherhood of Electrical Workers' Connecticut Local 35 worked to change how the local's business agent handed out jobs. The agent accused them of favoring blacks and homosexuals and siding with community activists to delay public construction projects. The dissidents finally won some local offices in 1992, reaffiliated the local with the Greater Hartford Central Labor Council, and continued to build membership support.

When the new Local 35 officers went to the next IBEW convention, they were surprised to meet dissidents from Chicago and Detroit locals. Most local union reformers faced almost total control of communications by their union's hierarchy. Labor support groups provided some alternatives. The Association for Union Democracy had started *Union Democracy Review* in the 1960s, but held its first national conference in 1979. The American Labor Institute, associated with OCAW insurgent Tony Mazzocchi, published books, pamphlets, and newsletters, and promoted international solidarity activities. Chicago-Gary area Steelworkers joined academics and labor activists to start the Midwest Center for Labor Research, which published *Labor Research Review* from 1982, and developed "early warning" programs to identify likely plant closures. *Labor Notes,* started in 1979, advocated militant confrontation with employers, vigorous organizing among women and minority workers, and cooperation with foreign labor activists. These and other efforts were projects of labor and sixties activists who had continued to advocate socialism and CIO-style social unionism—Walter Reuther's brother Victor was an AUD associate.

A dozen national union presidents were voted out of office in the 1980s, but the government created the biggest upset. In 1989, federal monitors for the Teamsters mandated local elections for convention delegates and nominations for national office by secret ballot, to be followed by a nationwide membership vote by mail. In 1991, Teamsters held their first direct election in decades, and reform candidate Ron Carey won the presidency.

Union reform could take strange turns. When 1199's Leon Davis retired at the end of 1981, he was succeeded in New York City's District 1199 by his longtime protégé Doris Turner. Davis had planned to pull 1199 out of its parent Retail, Warehouse and Department Store Workers Union and merge with SEIU's Hospital Workers Division. National 1199 left RWDSU in 1983 (it affiliated directly with the AFL-CIO). But Turner saw a communist plot against black leadership and won reelection over a promerger faction in April 1984. In July she pulled 50,000 members out of forty-one hospitals for nearly two months, then settled for 5 percent, close to the hospitals' original offer. When an 1199 staffer admitted helping fix the April vote, the Labor Department ordered a new election. Turner never finalized her "settlement," and uproar over the "missing 5 percent" helped elect Georgianna Johnson in June 1986. She fared little better, losing a 1987 referendum on constitutional changes curbing the president's power in a bitterly divisive racial campaign. Dennis Rivera replaced her in 1989, and 1199 rebuilt its distinctive "movement" unionism. During the same period, National 1199 successfully merged its mainly white West Virginia district with its mainly black Ohio district, through carefully planned training and social events where members learned to confide problems, share hopes, and amplify their voices in unison.

Developing wider community support took many forms. Public employees faced budget cuts, layoffs, and mounting workloads. Their unions—long accustomed to participating in local and state politics—responded with lobbying, outreach to community activists, solidarity demonstrations, strikes, and electoral challenges to faithless Democrats.

Cuts in services were the main issue, whether direct or through outsourcing, where contractors profited by skimping on wages, supervision, and standards. Philadelphia's AFSCME District Council 33 had lost a twenty-one–day citywide strike in 1986. When the mayor promised to privatize sanitation during his 1987 campaign for reelection, AFSCME Local 427 joined with Philadelphians United, a coalition of community groups fighting reductions in city services, to defeat the proposal. Local 427 activist James Sutton became D.C. 33 president in 1988, and negotiated an agreement to use early retirement incentives instead of outsourcing and layoffs to reduce the city's workforce.

Simple justice was important too, since many public employees were women or minority workers. Stephen F. Austin University in East Nacogdoches, Texas, contracted food services out to ARA Corporation in 1985, partly to avoid a court-ordered settlement of a 1972 NAACP discrimination lawsuit. After winning an NLRB election at the ARA unit, the Texas State Employees Union, a 5,000-member CWA affiliate, brought 3,000 people to town December 12, 1987—TSEU members, CWA telephone workers, other unionists, and NAACP and National Organization of Women contingents. City officials insisted the University and ARA settle: the workers got a contract, and back pay from the lawsuit too.

The most sustained union involvement in grassroots politics came out of struggles against plant closings. Youngstown, Ohio, had endured the shutdown of three steel mills and the loss of 10,000 union jobs by the end of 1979, and local clergy joined with USWA officials and the National Center for Economic Alternatives in the "Save Our Valley" coalition to try to buy and run the mills. After President Carter declined to back the plan, activists formed the "Tri State Conference on Steel," which focussed on the Monagahela valley around Pittsburgh. Tri State lobbied for extended unemployment benefits and a moratorium on foreclosures, and proposed a Steel Valley Authority (SVA) that could seize plants and sell them to employee or labor-community corporations. U.S. Steel announced in December 1983 that its Dorothy Six blast furnace in Duquesne would be torn down to clear a new industrial park. Tri State got local officials to pay for a study, while unemployed steelworkers winterized the furnace at their own expense and stood watch around the clock to make sure the company removed no machinery. The study found a growing market for semifinished steel, and SVA was incorporated by Pennsylvania in 1986. But the Authority's finance consultants insisted on retooling, then found no backers. USX demolished and buried Dorothy Six that spring.

SVA had some success. When Continental Ralston-Purina closed Braun Bakery in 1989, community and church leaders and city officials joined Bakery, Confectionary and Tobacco Workers Local 12 and SVA to fund a study that discovered that Pittsburgh had become the largest metropolitan market with no general bakery. With support from local grocers worried about fresh bread supplies in wintertime, City Pride Corporation started in

1990 and began production in 1992 in a new facility with 120 former Braun employees, now City Pride worker-owners. But the region lost more than 100,000 manufacturing jobs over the 1980s.

Local government helped UE Local 277 keep Morse Cutting Tool open in New Bedford, Massachusetts. Morse's owner, Gulf & Western Corporation, offered wage cuts or closure in 1982. The local called a strike and set up the Citizens Committee to Support the Morse Tool Workers. The Committee got the city council to authorize the mayor to save Morse by any means necessary, including seizure. After thirteen weeks, G&W signed a new contract without union concessions. When G&W announced in 1984 that it would sell or liquidate Morse, the mayor again threatened seizure, and G&W came up with an acceptable buyer.

Several cities and states passed plant closing legislation, but local and state laws could require little more than notice and severance pay. When SCOA Industries got out of the shoemaking business in 1981, its 800 employees at two Norwock Shoe Company factories in Maine got an average of $2,250 each. Corporations whipsawed local and state governments all too easily. When General Motors threatened to move operations to Montgomery, Alabama, Detroit contributed twelve years of 50-percent tax abatements and 430 acres of land (occupied by 3,200 residences) for a new Poletown plant, which opened late and operated sporadically. G.M. got property-tax reassessments everywhere in Michigan.

Beyond local politics, the Democrat-Republican duopoly was hard to crack. In Vermont, union rank and filers supported longtime activist Bernie Sanders for mayor of Burlington in 1981. When he ran for an open seat in Congress in 1988, the state AFL-CIO endorsed the Democrat and ran his campaign; the Republican barely beat Sanders, and the Democrat came in a poor third. In the 1990 rematch, local union leaders unanimously lined up behind Sanders, helping make him the first independent socialist member of Congress in more than sixty years. In national politics, the most surprising moment came when civil rights activist Jesse Jackson ran for President in the 1988 Democratic primaries. Every white candidate ran on a business platform, and the AFL-CIO made no primary endorsement. Affiliates with large numbers of black and Latino members, like District 1199 and the American Federation of Government Employees, and many black union leaders and locals joined Jackson's Rainbow Coalition. He pulled 35 percent of the votes from union households in the primaries, and led the delegate count after the UAW-dominated Michigan caucuses. The Party establishment closed around Governor Michael Dukakis of Massachusetts, and the Rainbow Coalition dissipated as an organized political force.

Efforts to gain labor influence on management accomplished less. Weirton Steel Works employees, represented by an independent company union, bought the plant from National Steel in 1985, but layoffs and restructuring continued. Union representatives on the Eastern Airlines board of directors could not vote their shares when the company was bought by antiunion Texas Air in 1986. By 1990, over 10,000 Employee Stock Ownership Plans were in operation, serving mainly to thwart hostile takeovers. Operating Engineers Local 675 in south Florida tried a different tack, using pension-fund money to finance construction using union labor. The Labor Department sued the fund trustees for technical violations. That suit was dismissed in 1985, but savings-and-loan failures halted some projects, a local Right to Work Committee protested discrimination against open shop contractors, and the Department put the pension fund into receivership in 1990.

Many union members were readier to mobilize than their leaders. New York Chinatown garment workers belonged to ILGWU Local 23–25. The union negotiated wage rates with "manufacturers" who specified material and pattern, then took the agreement to contractors who hired workers to make the clothing (the union provided medical insurance). In 1982, Chinatown contractors rejected the rates. The union announced a rally, and 20,000 turned out, mobilized by the women workers themselves. After a second demonstration on the same scale, the contractors gave in to community sentiment and accepted the agreement.

Ethnic solidarity could mobilize workers against great odds. Latino workers showed what was possible. After the Watsonville cannery strike, most of the area's food processers closed or relocated. When Green Giant (Local 912's largest employer) moved broccoli processing to Irapuato State in Mexico, workers formed Trabajadores Desplazados to campaign for severance pay and retraining. They also contacted FAT and mounted a joint corporate campaign against Green Giant, winning better displacement benefits in Watsonville and some toxic-waste cleanup at the Mexican plant. Women laid off in 1993 by Levi Strauss Company in San Antonio, Texas, formed Fuerza Unida to fight for better severance pay and more retraining.

Most union leaders thought undocumented workers could not be organized. In 1984, Nicaraguan refugee and organizer Gaspar Amaro convinced the Amalgamated Clothing and Textile Workers Union to organize Camagua, a Los Angeles mattress and waterbed company. Its owner preferred hiring undocumented immigrants because, as he observed, "the illegal worked a lot harder." The union won the January 1985 election 113–48, and the company appealed. The workers stencilled union slogans on their shirts, called in sick in groups, observed department-wide "moments of silence," and left work an hour early one day to attend Mass at the plant gate. The company began firing them for disruptive behavior. The union launched a boycott campaign in April. Fired workers located and picketed stores selling the waterbeds; by the end of June more than 200 had dropped the Camagua line. In November, the company settled. The contract did not require Camagua to take back fired workers, but they urged ratification anyway, just to beat the boss.

Building services had been SEIU's original base, and the union started a "Justice for Janitors" campaign in 1985 to reorganize the industry. Los Angeles SEIU Local 399 membership had fallen below 2,000 after an open shop drive by real estate and development companies. The workforce was mainly immigrant Mexicans. J for J came to Los Angeles in 1988, going after industry clients (who paid the bills) as well as contractors and using direct action—demonstrations, sit-ins, traffic blockages—instead of filing for elections. Some immigrants were especially militant. One organizer attributed Salvadoran's militancy to repression in their home country: "There, if you were in a union, they killed you. Here you lost a job at $4.25 an hour." After the police beat immigrant janitors at a 1990 demonstration at the Century City office complex, the union got recognition.

That same year 800 workers at the American Racing Equipment Company, mostly first-generation Latino immigrants, struck for three days to get union recognition. Six months later they affiliated with the Machinists. By that time, residential drywallers had started to organize themselves, led by immigrants from El Maguey, a village in Guanajuato, Mexico. The "Movement of Drywall Hangers" called a strike on June 1, 1992, for an increase in piece rates. Flying squads shut down construction from the Mexican border to Ventura, just north of Los Angeles. When the Highway Patrol intercepted them, they sat down on the highways. The Border Patrol raided picket lines. After learning the strikers might charge them with violating overtime provisions of the Fair Labor Standards Act, the contractors settled in November. Two thousand four hundred drywallers joined Carpenters Local 2361 and got a union contract in 1993. In 1995, 2,000 framers did the same.

Mobilized members improved their negotiating position. Some unions organized almost one on one. Hotel Employees and Restaurant Employees (HERE) Local 26 in Boston had 4,000 members, 60 percent women and 60 percent minority, speaking eighty-seven different languages and dialects. For the 1982 negotiations the Local appointed a 350-person Contract Committee reflecting membership diversity in sex, race, ethnicity, age, and kind of work. Fifty served on the negotiating committee. For the 1985 contract, hotels demanded reductions in health care coverage, lower entry-level pay, and a five-year term. The Local expanded the Contract Committee to 500, held regular meetings after shifts, always with child care, never more than an hour long, and arranged training in civil disobedience. Union members packed the lobby of City Hall while negotiators met upstairs. The new three-year contract increased wages and employer contributions to health plans and provided affirmative action in hiring and promotion, a new legal services plan, and a four-month entry rate 25 percent below the standard.

A similar style produced organizing victories at two of the country's elite institutions. Yale University blue-collar workers had been organized since the 1930s, but five drives by different unions had failed with clerical and technical workers. In 1982, the blue-collar union, now HERE Local 35, started a new drive to organize Local 34. Organizers spent more than a year talking about working conditions, recruiting an organizing committee (eventually about 450), developing the idea that clerical workers deserved respect as well as better pay. HERE filed for election in 1983 and won the May 18 vote 1,272 to 1,233, with thirty-three ballots challenged, only six short of the margin of victory. Local 34 members endured more than a year of negotiations before striking in the fall of 1984. They staged two mass arrests for civil disobedience, rallied community residents, students, and faculty to picket lines and marches, and shut down the university for three days in November. They declared a "Christmas truce" and went back to work in December after sixty-nine days; Yale signed contracts with both unions at the end of January. The AFSCME-affiliated Harvard Union of Clerical and Technical Workers used similar tactics to win a three-year campaign in 1989, then applied feminist principles to such union issues as grievances, which were handled by conflict resolution procedures.

Unions with many women members had to pay attention to gender issues. In the early 1980s, public employee unions began trying to negotiate commitments to study differentials between men and women doing similar work or using comparable education, training, and experience on the job. The campaign had only limited success. Employers rarely gave extra raises to some workers unless they could reduce them for others, and the studies themselves were complicated and unreliable. The Coalition of Labor Union Women endorsed a "Family Bill of Rights," which went beyond usual union demands for a family wage and the eight-hour day to focus on a living wage, shorter work week, and better pay for part-time work. CLUW's American Family Celebration on May 14, 1988, drew 40,000 unionists and family members. By 1993, most unions endorsed child care for their members.* But the AFL–CIO Executive Council refused to endorse reproductive choice—two of the three women on the Council voted with the majority.

The first union to get family benefits for "domestic partners" was the UAW's District 65 local at the *Village Voice* newspaper in New York City in 1982. Pressed by unions and employee associations, several public employers and some private companies added domestic partners to their benefits coverage over the next decade. SEIU hosted a reception for gay and lesbian trade unionists at AFL–CIO Washington headquarters the day before the "Great March" for Gay and Lesbian Rights in October 1987, and César Chávez addressed the half-million-strong rally. The Gay and Lesbian Labor Activist Network in Boston, San Francisco, and New York City held community forums on issues like using union labor in gay community centers and the impact of the AIDS crisis on health care workers. Activists at a spring 1991 *Labor Notes* conference organized Lavender Labor, an international network to support gay and lesbian labor activists coming out of the closet at work and in unions. An SEIU women's conference that year produced a Lavender Caucus, which had chapters around the country by 1994.

Other organizing initiatives came from outside the labor movement. In 1984, the Anti-Klan Network invited UFCW to organize Zartic Foods in Cedartown, Georgia, where the Ku Klux Klan had set up an American Workers Union with a "Fire the Wetback" campaign in 1981, and two Mexican immigrants had been murdered, their killers acquitted by local juries. The Catholic Sanctuary movement, which helped Central American refugees apply for asylum, began organizing Mayan migrant farm workers from Guatemala in south Florida in 1984, and Catholic activists in North Carolina supported strikes by Guatemalan workers at Case Farms in Morgantown and the Perdue plant in Lewiston. Black Workers for Justice started in Rocky Mount, North Carolina, to build community support for workers in the garment, automotive, pharmaceutical, and other manufacturing shops that ringed the city.

The same tradition of organizing for mutual support in poor and working-class communities that inspired the United Farm Workers produced ACORN (Association of Communities for Reform Now). Started in Chicago in 1970, ACORN developed a reputation for militant commu-

---

* Though not for their own staff. CWA staffer John Scally once remarked, "Unions, you know, are the worst employers around." In 1987, CWA staff union leaders joined delegates from six other staff unions in the International Congress of Staff Unions, to discuss common problems and generally raise morale. More than forty staff unions had affiliated by 1990.

nity-based direct action and in fifteen years grew to 60,000 dues-paying members in thirty-five cities in twenty-six states. In 1978, ACORN started United Labor Unions to help low-wage workers organize around immediate demands. ULU organizers began by surveying a local industry, then recruited workers from the industry and encouraged them to develop actions like "Recognition Days," shows of strength to get negotiations started. In 1983, ULU targeted the twelve largest vendors of home health care services in Chicago, who hired mostly welfare recipients at the minimum wage. They won their first election at National Home Care Systems in January 1984, finally signed a contract (under strike threat) in June 1985, and signed up more vendors. In Detroit a ULU group of fast-food workers got the first U.S. union contract in the industry. In New Orleans ULU organized low-wage workers in hospitals, nursing homes, and tourist hospitality centers. ACORN pioneered suing for court certification to represent members with state and local agencies, first with poor and elderly home health care clients. ACORN affiliated with SEIU in 1985.

In San Francisco, the Asian Immigrant Women Advocates started in 1982 to support organizing among Asian women immigrants working as seamstresses, waitresses, and maids. In Los Angeles, the Korean Immigrant Workers Association provided advice to immigrants cheated on their labor contracts, and campaigned to get the Koreatown business community to release relief funds to Korean workers displaced by the violence that followed the 1992 acquittal of four police officers videotaped beating motorist Rodney King. Both groups worked with HERE and SEIU locals.

Los Angeles was also home base for the Alliance of Asian Pacific Labor, which started in 1987 to build labor support for issues important in the Asian community, like language rights, political participation, and the *Ward's Cove* case. AAPL supported the Radio Korea strike, which finally failed after four weeks, the longest strike in Koreatown history. AAPL also recruited Asian American organizers, finding Vietnamese Americans to help locals in the UAW and the Aluminum, Brick and Glass Workers defeat decertification drives. Union activists founded the AFL-CIO constituency group Asian Pacific American Labor Alliance in Washington, D.C., in 1992.

Union relations with community labor groups could be strained. In 1987, affiliates from the AFL-CIO's Industrial Union Department founded Jobs with Justice (JwJ), which got union rank and filers and community activists to pledge to join at least five solidarity actions every year. The group made its debut June 23, 1987, when 3,000 Eastern Airlines machinists put on red shirts and picketed company headquarters at the Miami airport, joined by 500 community and labor activists sponsored by eighty unions and twenty-three community groups. A second Eastern rally in July brought out 12,000 people. Within a year JwJ chapters had staged more than sixty rallies, mostly in right-to-work Sun Belt states, and started Workers' Rights Boards, panels of citizens who held hearings on denials of workers' rights. Colorado JwJ started in 1988—helping CWA members working as *Denver Post* mailers fight off a 25 percent wage cut, getting the Denver U.S. Mint to hire union janitors by leafletting tourists waiting on line. But when JwJ proposed a mass rally at the Denver airport's Continental Airlines terminal to protest the company's role in breaking the Eastern strike, the Colorado AFL-CIO backed off and called a rival rally a mile away. Both events flopped, and Colorado JwJ broke up.

The Los Angeles Bus Riders Union/Sindicato de Passajeros formed in 1990 to press for more funding for public buses. BRU/SdP practiced direct action—sit-ins at intersections, office seizures—and cultivated alliances with unions representing low-wage workers and with the United Transportation Union at the Metropolitan Transit Authority. A court settlement designated BRU/SdP as representative for the bus-riding public. But BRU/SdP also opposed union initiatives like SEIU Local 660's proposal to transfer transportation funds to health care and OCAW's support for refinery owners who refused to release toxic emissions data.

Some unions resurrected more militant shop floor tactics from CIO days. UAW activists tried "running the plant backwards." When Local 282 at Moog Automotive in St. Louis faced demands for concessions in 1981, members worked without a contract, followed management directives to the letter, refused overtime, and spontaneously mustered around disputed situations. Moog management retaliated with firings and suspensions, but after six months agreed to a contract that raised pay more than a third over forty months and reinstated fired and suspended workers with back pay. UAW locals at Bell Helicopter and LTV-Vought in the Dallas-Ft. Worth area used the same tactics in 1984. The fight lasted longer—about fifteen months, including a month-long lockout at Bell—but the new contracts had no concessions, and fired workers returned with back pay.

Other unions returned to original organizing principles. IBEW had long used an apprentice program to control the supply of electrical construction workers, but it had started by organizing working electricians. In 1987, IBEW began a "bottom-up" organizing program, developed first in Boston and Atlanta. Organizers signed up workers on nonunion sites until they had enough members to call a short strike over an unfair labor practice. New members took "no-fail" exams, which qualified them on a range from beginning apprentice to full journeyman, and placed them in appropriate training. IBEW gained members in construction, while other unions were losing them. The Bricklayers and Allied Craftsmen began organizing nonunion masonry workers in New Jersey and Virginia (where racial prejudice among local Bricklayer officials required intervention by national staff).

The UAW returned to the nonunion sector of the auto industry using rank-and-file members as organizers. In 1988, UAW Local 3000 at the Detroit Flat Rock Mazda assembly plant started a drive to organize the forty Michigan-based Mazda suppliers using local members under the direction of a full-time UAW organizer. The first successes were MANA, a Mazda-owned shipping and packaging plant, and Pentsone, a Japanese-owned window assembly supplier. But UAW progress was uneven: The union was trounced in a 1989 NLRB election at the Nissan plant in Smyrna, Tennessee.

UFCW organizers learned to avoid NLRB elections and targeted employers with "pressure campaigns." After losing a 1988 election in the Kalamazoo Family Foods chain, UFCW Local 951 started a consumer boycott, which finally helped put the company out of business. Local 951 secretary-treasurer Joe Crump observed, "There is no 'free lunch' in our jurisdiction." UFCW had other ways to get recognition; union staff looked into employer compliance with a myriad of laws and codes on discrimination, wages and hours, unemployment and workers compensation, pension management, safety and health, environmental zoning and fire codes, and taxes. At the Delta Pride Catfish Farm in Mississippi, UFCW got a contract after documenting unpaid time and agreeing to represent workers in a lawsuit for back pay.

"Reaganomics" was finally discredited on "Meltdown Monday" (October 19, 1987) when the Dow Jones average fell more than 500 points, but the bills remained to be paid. "Neoliberals" proposed balancing the federal budget with new taxes, deeper spending cuts, and debt repayment. They also called for more deregulation of the international marketplace, especially restrictions on trade and investment.

The policies were bipartisan. Democrats saw how corporate contributions went Republican in 1980 and scrambled to restore balance. Democratic House leadership fast-tracked Reagan's tax cuts and solicited suggestions for additional corporate tax benefits. After Mondale's defeat, Party leaders started the Democratic Leadership Council in 1985 to make the Party more responsive to business concerns. Both Dukakis in 1988 and Bill Clinton in 1992 ran on neoliberal policies, and the AFL-CIO endorsed them both.

Vice President George Bush beat Dukakis by 7 million votes, partly by promising he would never raise taxes, then lost to Clinton by more than 5 million votes after he did. Neither election changed national economic and trade policies; both saw the major parties becoming more dependent on corporate contributions to pay for more costly campaigns.

The new policies had some success. Before-tax corporate profits had fallen from about 12 percent in 1979 to about 5 percent in 1986; by 1992, they had risen back to 8 percent. By 1989, the Dow Jones average was back to 2,500, and rose to 3,700 by 1994. But the federal deficit and the national debt remained high—federal debt as a proportion of gross domestic output went from 60 percent in 1990 to 70 percent by 1995. Military spending—which gave employment to 6 percent of the workforce in 1992—never went down, and Clinton's promise to fund military-civilian conversion projects fell through after several defense contractors declared they would rather close than convert. Interest payments took about 14 percent of the federal budget in 1995.

The new economic policy trickled down no better than the old. In 1992, 12 percent of all families, and 22 percent of all children, lived on less than the amount defined as poverty level (37 percent of median family income), including nearly half the households headed by women with minor children. Real wages continued their decline—by 1996, they were 12 percent less than in 1979. Other components of working-class economic security deteriorated. Pension coverage at large and mid-sized companies fell from 91 percent in 1985 to 80 percent in 1995, and postretirement medical coverage fell from 80 percent to 52 percent.

The new Democratic administration was no friend to labor. A bill to ban replacement workers died in Congress while the White House focused on completing the North American Free Trade Agreement, which removed restrictions on investment and trade between the U.S. and its two neighbors. The AFL-CIO opposed NAFTA, expecting it to cost U.S. jobs and overturn labor laws as restraints on trade. NAFTA passed Congress in 1993 with votes from many "friends of labor." In the 1994 Congressional elections, Lane Kirkland quelled labor opposition to NAFTA Democrats. AFL-CIO political strategy proved helpless when Republicans swept both houses for the first time in forty years.

Corporate attacks on labor rolled on. The first line of defense was keeping the union out. A study of union drives in 1993–95 found that one-third of employers fired workers for union activities, a sixth used electronic surveillance to monitor employees, and more than half threatened to close or move if the union won an election. One employer rented a trailer, painted

"Moving to Mexico" on the side, and parked it at the main entrance. (About 15 percent of employers did close in part or entirely after losing a union vote.) When the Laborers tried to organize the Perdue poultry plant in Dothan, Alabama, in June 1995, the plant's 1,000 employees—mostly African American—came to work the day before the vote to find a burning cross draped with "Union Yes" tee shirts. The union lost 646-242.

Decatur, Illinois, became one of the fiercest battlefields of the corporate campaign. Trouble had been brewing for some time at A. E. Staley Manufacturing, which was owned by British transnational Tate & Lyle and made corn syrup. In 1991, management demanded twelve-hour shifts, subcontracting rights, and the elimination of many seniority and grievance provisions. United Paperworkers Local 7837 decided to remain at work, developing an in-plant campaign of working to rule and a corporate campaign targeting major Staley customers. The same year Caterpillar rejected a UAW contract patterned after a settlement with John B. Deere Company. The UAW called a partial strike, but returned to work in April 1992 and started its own in-plant campaign. In June 1993, after Staley workers joined a rally in support of the Caterpillar local, Staley locked them out. Almost a year later the UAW finally called a strike at Caterpillar over unfair labor practices. The next month the Rubber Workers struck five Bridgestone Tire plants—including the Decatur facility—over company demands for employee copayments for health benefits, wage reductions, and a twelve-hour straight-time workday. Decatur became a war zone, with massive marches, police attacks on demonstrators, bitter divisions between the strikers and scabs or replacement workers, and among the strikers themselves.

When Staley "Road Warriors" brought their travelling solidarity show to the AFL-CIO Executive Committee's February 1995 meeting in Bal Harbor, Florida, they found union leaders pondering the sorry state of unionism and Kirkland's resignation. The plan called for him to retire gracefully at the next convention, set for New York City in October, in favor of Secretary-Treasurer Tom Donahue. Kirkland changed his mind and resigned in May, and a coalition of union leaders from the UAW, UMW, USWA, AFSCME, SEIU, and the Teamsters decided to make their own nomination, selecting SEIU's John Sweeney to head a "New Voice" slate. Kirkland appointed Donahue interim president to give him the advantage of incumbency.

Just before the convention, the Labor Resource Center at Queens College of the City University of New York held a conference on the future of the labor movement. Activists discussed union democracy, membership diversity, political action, international cooperation, and organizing the unorganized. That was the New Voice platform.

CHAPTER

12

BRAVE NEW WORLD

Only once before—in 1894, when Sam Gompers lost the AFL presidency for a year to Mine Worker John McBride—had the Federation's leadership ever really been in doubt. Interim President Tom Donahue waged a vigorous campaign, matching the New Voice slate promise for promise. But at the October 1995 convention, delegates representing 56 percent of the membership stuck with the insurgents, and John Sweeney became the fifth man in a century to head the Federation. Richard Trumka from the United Mine Workers became Secretary-Treasurer. Linda Chávez-Thompson of the American Federation of State, County and Municipal Employees took a new Executive Vice President position.

The state of the labor movement was grim. In Decatur the Bridgestone workers had already ended their strike in May. The UAW declared the Caterpillar strike "in recess," cut off strike pay, and sent local members back to work the first Monday of December. Three days before Christmas the Staley local ratified the contract they had rejected three years earlier, and sent their pickets home. Labor had lost the war in Decatur all the way down the line; in fact 1995's total of thirty-one strikes by a thousand or more workers was an all-time low. Union membership declined again in 1995, to 16.4 million workers covered by union contracts. In the private sector, the rate of union density had fallen to the level of 1930.

New Voice leaders called for organizing the unorganized. The AFL–CIO budgeted $20 million for organizing in 1996, $30 million the next year. But more than money and staff were required. Paid organizers signing up workers for NLRB elections one workplace at a time, against employers who had no reason to respect federal or local labor laws, could only slow the loss in membership. The unions had to create an "organizing culture" in which labor was part of a social movement, in coalition with religious, civil rights, and other organizations, building a network of community-based organizing centers where unions led the defense of workers' rights and interests. Easier said than done. Reversing the federation's decline required changing nearly every aspect of trade union work, from rooting out corruption and bolstering democracy in affiliates, to reaching out to allies old and new, to working out common programs among workers and unions with very different histories, expectations, and interests.

Unions faced an ever more difficult terrain. After the economy recovered from the 1991–92 recession, the stock market kept rising, and profits soared. A new corporate merger wave in the mid-1990s created even larger companies. Transnational investment increased. Foreign direct investment in developing countries increased by half in 1994–97, to more than $120 billion, and commercial loans more than doubled, to more than $100 billion. The total debt burden for all developing countries became a staggering $2 trillion. Around the world, rebellion mounted against the repressive regimes formed to contain communism and against cuts in social spending—opposition parties took power in South Korea (1997) and Venezuela (1998); dictators fell in Zaire and Indonesia in the same years.

The North American Free Trade Agreement worked pretty much as opponents predicted. In NAFTA's first five years, 200,000 U.S. jobs were lost to trade. (The government stopped trying to count jobs created after it found only 1,500.) As more manufacture and assembly relocated to take advantage of wages about one-twelfth U.S. or Canadian rates, U.S. trade with Mexico went from a billion dollar surplus to deficits over $10 billion.

Deregulation led to new crises. The Mexican peso collapsed in late 1994: businesses failed, real wages fell about a third. As international currency exchange transactions reached $1,500 billion a day, similar crises hit Thailand, Malaysia, Indonesia, and South Korea in late 1997, Russia and Brazil the next year. The International Monetary Fund and World Bank sought more "structural adjustment" as the price of rescue from national default: remove controls on markets and investments, sell state-owned enterprises, accept multilateral free-trade agreements. Meanwhile debt crushed some developing economies: debt service cost Nicaragua more than it spent on all social programs, Mozambique twice as much as it spent on health and education, and Uganda more than five times what it spent on health care.

Free-market policies widened the gap between rich and poor nations. Broad areas of sub-Saharan Africa devolved to an economy of meager subsistence and resource extraction, often at gunpoint—the Nigerian government hanged author Ken Saro-Wiwa and eight other activists who protested the environmental degradation of the Ogoniland oil region by companies like Shell, Mobil, Chevron, and Texaco. On the other side of the world, the Indonesian army disciplined workers at gold and copper mines on Irian Jaya run by Louisiana-based Freeport-McMoRan Corporation. New capitalists rich from speculative expropriation of state assets dominated the republics of the Russian Federation, while ordinary people lived more and more by barter, public services deteriorated, and both life expectancy and the birth rate declined.

The international gap was mirrored in U.S. incomes. In 1990, the average pay of the chief executive officers of the 500 biggest U.S.-based corporations was only about $2 million a year, eighty-four times the average blue-collar worker's pay. By 1999, the CEO average had gone to more than $12 million, 475 times the blue-collar average. For transnational executives the gap was bigger. In 1999, General Electric's CEO Jack Welch made about 15,000 times more than his average Mexican employee. Overall, fewer people made more, and more made the same or less. Between 1989 and 1997, the top 20 percent of families took an ever larger share of total family income. The trend was accentuated at the extremes: average family incomes in the bottom 20 percent fell slightly in real dollars, while for the top 5 percent average income rose by more than a fifth. By the end of the 1990s, though U.S. unemployment had declined, income inequality had returned to the level of the 1930s—about 100,000 millionaires alongside 36 million people living in poverty (as defined by the government). More than two million of the poor worked full-time year round, another seven million part of the year. By 1998, 2.7 percent of total private employment fell into the government category "help supply services," more than four times the 1982 figure. Many households faced their own debt crises. As banks aggressively pushed unsecured credit with high interest rates, people displaced from employment, facing divorce or medical emergencies, or carrying expensive student loans, began going broke. Bankruptcy filings increased more than a third after 1994. By 1997, one of every six families living on $25,000 or less a year paid 40 percent of their income in debt service.

MAKING CHANGE

The new AFL–CIO leadership made some changes in the Federation's foreign and domestic policies long advocated by grassroots activists and already practiced by some affiliated unions. The Federation dismantled its international operations, replacing them all with a Center for International Labor. The AFL–CIO let lapse its sponsorship of the Canadian Federation of Labor, set up in 1982 to rival the social democratic Canadian Labor Congress (the CFL folded in 1997). But the international labor establishment was ill equipped to deal with recurrent crises. Dominated by government-supported unions, the Asia Pacific Regional Organization of the International Confederation of Free Trade Unions promoted government-labor-management cooperation in maintaining each nation's competitive edge. When financial crisis swept the Asian industrial economies, APRO met in Singapore in February 1998, but could only petition international agencies to ameliorate demands for structural adjustment and set up a telephone hotline for the hundreds of thousands of displaced workers.

In Mexico, more than 3,000 plants operated in the maquiladora export zones by 1998. As privatization proceeded in long-nationalized industries, the official Confederación de Trabajadores Mexicanos lost more than 40 percent of its members, but the CTM demanded the extermination of indigenous rebels in southern Mexico, not the release of CTM union leaders jailed for opposing privatization. The Teamsters joined the United Electrical Workers in setting up a Labor Center in Ciudad Juárez with the independent Frente Auténtico de Trabajadores to promote a "culture of organizing" against a "culture of fear." The Coalition for Justice in the Maquiladoras helped Sony rank-and-file workers in Nuevo Laredo contest their official union leadership. John Sweeney visited Mexico in January 1998—the first such trip since Sam Gompers's demise—meeting both CTM and independent union leaders. Though CTM president Leonardo Rodríguez Alcaine warned that "Mexicans should . . . resolve their own problems," the Arizona AFL–CIO supported a 1999 strike against layoffs by copper miners in Cananea, Sonora (which ended when the Mexican army took over the town).

At home, AFL–CIO leaders turned their attention to the masses of unorganized low-wage workers. Despite a 1991 raise, the minimum wage had fallen to the 1950 level in constant dollar value. Sweeney published *America Needs a Raise* in 1996 during a successful AFL–CIO campaign to raise it again. The Federation also endorsed organizing welfare recipients assigned to workfare, but the efforts faltered when most courts decided the workers were not employees covered by the National Labor Relations Act.

Some union habits were hard to change. Despite years of federal and state prosecutions that had removed almost 400 Teamsters and more than a hundred Laborers officials by 1996, some unions still harbored mobsters or tolerated personal corruption. Officials from the Carpenters, Painters and Longshoremen in New York City were convicted of embezzlement and racketeering during the mid-1990s. The president of the Hotel Employees and Restaurant Employees retired in 1998 to avoid prosecution.

New Voice allies fell too, though not for labor racketeering. Sweeney and Richard Trumka strongly supported Teamster president Ron Carey over challenger James Hoffa, Jr., in 1996. In June 1997, a federal monitor voided Carey's reelection after finding that his aides had washed $700,000 in union funds through Democratic Party accounts to pay campaign expenses. Carey was barred from the union, and Hoffa won the new election held in December 1998. AFSCME trusteed New York City's District Council 37 in 1998 after officials were accused of embezzlement. It transpired that District staff and local officers had also faked ratification tallies to get the 1996 contract approved, helping Republican Mayor Rudy Giuliani win reelection. Since AFSCME set the pattern for other city unions, almost a quarter million public employees had been duped. During a lawsuit brought by dissident local members, in 1999 SEIU forced the retirement of Gus Bevona, president of New York City building services Local 32B–32J (Sweeney's home local) and at $422,000 a year the highest-paid union official in the country. At the end of 1999, New Voice supporter Arthur Coia—who had backed anticorruption investigations ordered in a consent decree—resigned from the Laborers' presidency and pled guilty the next year to avoiding taxes on a Ferrari provided by the Rhode Island company that leased cars to the union.

Dissident union reform groups could be found not only in the Teamsters, Laborers, SEIU, and HERE, but also in the Bricklayers, Carpenters, International Brotherhood of Electrical Workers, American Federation of Government Employees, Letter Carriers, Treasury Employees, Machinists, and Auto Workers. Other reformers included local and state organizations like the New Directions Caucus in Transport Workers Local 100 and the Members for Members Caucus in AFSCME's California State Employees Association. AFSCME lost the University of California clerical workers to the independent Coalition of University Employees over disagreements about union practices—CUE practiced grassroots organizing based on consciousness raising and membership mobilization, and needed only a single full-time staff person.

Unions continued to merge. In 1995, the United Rubber Workers joined the United Steel Workers, and the International Ladies' Garment

Workers and the Amalgamated Clothing and Textile Workers announced their merger into UNITE—Union of Needletrades, Industrial and Textile Employees. The Laborers absorbed the 5,000-member National Federation of Independent Unions in 1996. In 1997, New York Local 1199 affiliated with SEIU and later took over SEIU health care locals in New York, New Jersey, and Florida. In 1998, the UFCW took over the Brooklyn-based, 10,000-member Production, Service and Sales District Council, and the independent Connecticut Union of Telephone Workers (CUTW) voted to join the Communication Workers. In 1999, the United Paperworkers and the Oil, Chemical and Atomic Workers formed PACE—Paper, Allied-Industrial, Chemical and Energy International Union. The International Union of Electrical Workers (IUE) became a division of CWA in 2000. Mergers were not always easy. ILGWU and ACTWU locals took some time to merge while members sorted out differences in organizing style—UNITE changed ILGWU plans for organizing Guess contractors in Los Angeles, and Guess sent the contracts to Mexico. CUTW's leaders had actually recommended IBEW to their members. By 2000, the AFL-CIO had sixty-six affiliates, compared to 150 in 1955.

Despite overlapping jurisdictions, some merger talks failed. In 1998, the independent National Education Association, the largest union in the country, debated merger with the American Federation of Teachers. NEA conservatives who preferred a more professional approach joined liberals who objected to AFT support for U.S. foreign policy and its opposition to community involvement in public education to vote down the proposal. The Screen Actors Guild rejected a long-planned merger with the American Federation of Television and Radio Artists, and the 18,000-member American Flint Glass Workers Union (a onetime Knights of Labor affiliate) rejected merger with UFCW the same year. Merger talks failed between the two largest railroad unions, the United Transportation Union and the Brotherhood of Locomotive Engineers, and UTU later left the AFL-CIO to protest raiding sanctions. In 1999, the AFL-CIO made a small first step to resolve its recurring jurisdictional disputes by requiring that unions planning local or industry strategic campaigns register with an Oversight Committee, which could evaluate claims from competing unions.

As the New Voice campaign had recognized from the start, organizing the unorganized required a strong union commitment to civil rights, and the new leadership backed grassroots and union initiatives to send this message.

AFSCME, SEIU, and the AFT, along with the AFL-CIO's Industrial Union Department, had endorsed bans on discrimination on the basis of sexual orientation since the 1980s. AFSCME's District Council 37 had hosted a Stonewall 25 gay labor conference in June 1994, which drew more than 300 labor activists from twenty-five unions and founded Pride at Work, a national gay labor network. PAW lobbied to become an AFL-CIO constituency group and was recognized (but not funded) by the Executive Council in August 1997. PAW activists found some unions hostile to proposals for domestic partner benefits, and coming out of the closet continued to be controversial in many building trades locals. When gay activists campaigned against Hawaii's state constitutional amendment banning same-sex marriage in 1998, only the University of Hawaii Professional Association and the International Longshore and Warehouse Union joined the campaign. But when CWA member Danny Lee Overstreet was shot to death in a Roanoke, Virginia, bar by a man in a homophobic rage in September 2000, his local staged vigils and rallies and started a campaign for hate-crimes legislation.

Women's issues got more substantial support. As Karen Nussbaum, one-time president of the 9 to 5 National Association of Working Women and now director of the AFL-CIO's Working Women's Department, pointed out, the Federation had become the country's largest organization of workingwomen. In 1997, the AFL-CIO's "Ask a Working Woman" initiative collected 50,000 survey responses and held meetings and hearings in twenty cities to identify workingwomen's concerns—equal pay, layoffs and downsizing, and sick leave were most often listed—and discovered that four out of five women surveyed were interested in collective bargaining. The most visible sign of the change in attitude came in the AFL-CIO's own affirmative actions. In 1995, women headed three of its nineteen departments; by 1998, women headed ten of twenty-one. Of the four AFL-CIO regions, two were headed by minority men, one by a woman.

With AFL-CIO support, the Asian Pacific American Labor Alliance became a leading national advocate for Asian American civil rights, especially active around legislative attacks on immigrants and affirmative action. After the Japanese-owned New Otani Hotel in Los Angeles fired union activists during an organizing drive, HERE Local 11 called a boycott. APALA helped HERE persuade Japanese professional and trade associations to honor the boycott. During the February 1997 AFL-CIO Executive Council meeting, Sweeney, Trumka, and Chávez-Thompson led 2,000 people to a rally at the hotel.

The immigrants with the fewest rights were the undocumented. By Immigration and Naturalization Service estimates, about 6 million undocumented immigrants lived in the U.S. in 1999, about half in California.

Organizing low-wage workers meant challenging the INS. Though both the NLRB and the Equal Employment Opportunity Commission extended federal labor law to undocumented workers, employers hardly feared the INS—between 1995 and 1999, about 4,000 were fined for immigration violations, and nearly every fine was reduced or forgiven entirely. Deportations more than doubled from 1990 to 1997.

When UFCW organizers visited Nebraska and Iowa meatpacking plants in 1998, they found Operation Vanguard. Inspecting 24,000 employee records from forty plants, the INS operation discovered almost 5,000 without documents on file. When the Service notified the workers by mail, over 3,000 fled the area, including twenty out of twenty-two activists organizing at Greater Omaha Packing. That summer the INS disrupted a UFW drive at rose grower Bear Creek Productions in California's San Joaquin Valley by deporting hundreds of workers—many had lived and worked in the area for more than fifteen years. In 1999, the INS deported 500 members of SEIU San Francisco Local 1877 as the union began mobilizing for a contract; and in Minnesota, the Holiday Inn Express manager turned over nine employees to the INS during a HERE organizing drive. In February 2000, the AFL-CIO Executive Council declared that employer sanctions had failed, and for the first time in its history the Federation called for amnesty for illegal immigrants (and also for tougher enforcement at the already militarized Mexican border).

AFL-CIO support for organizing low-wage workers expressed the New Voice ambition to rebuild the labor movement as a social movement, but many union leaders worried that coalitions might escape their control. The AFL-CIO had declined to support groups such as Black Workers for Justice, Korean Immigrant Workers Association, Chinese Progressive Association (Boston, Massachusetts), the Chinese Staff and Workers Association, Asian Immigrant Women Association (Oakland, California), and the Pilipino Workers Center (Los Angeles), because of their radical connections. The Federation gave Jobs with Justice $100,000 in 1996, but Secretary-Treasurer Trumka wondered whether even that low level of support was worthwhile. A grassroots outcry changed his position. In 1997, the AFL-CIO Executive endorsed JwJ's demand for real jobs instead of welfare work and its Workers Rights Boards projects, and the Federation went on to encourage its affiliates to support "Street Heat" tactics.

In fact alliances became more important to many union efforts. One of the first New Voice initiatives was the Organizing Institute's Union Summer program, which recruited hundreds of college students for short summer internships with unions. The program itself got mixed reviews, but when the students returned to campus many continued to work for labor causes. In 1999, a student–faculty–community Coalition for Justice persuaded Long Island's Southampton University to dump a custodial services contract and rehire its former janitors, mostly Native and African Americans. Student activists also demanded their schools require contractors to pay a living wage—the first to adopt the policy was Johns Hopkins University in Baltimore.

What really took off was the antisweat campaign. Developed originally from the National Labor Committee's Central American solidarity work, the sweatshop campaign picked up speed in 1995, when seventy-two Thai women contract workers were discovered in a barbed-wire California compound sewing name-brand garments for seventeen hours a day at about a dollar an hour. It got another boost when NLC activists reduced television celebrity Kathie Lee Gifford to tears on her own program by showing how her Wal-Mart clothing line was made by teenage Honduran girls working fifteen-hour days. Union Summer graduates started the United Students Against Sweatshops in July 1998 to make universities and colleges impose fair labor standards on contractors licensing school logos for athletic clothing. After protests at schools like Duke, Michigan, Georgetown, and Wisconsin, students staged simultaneous actions at Stanford, Harvard, Yale, and Kent State in April 1999.

Academic support for labor, usually confined to a few college and university labor studies programs, got a boost when an October 1996 sixties-style teach-in at Columbia University drew over 2,000 participants. The organizers went on to start Scholars, Writers and Artists for Social Justice. SAWSJ distributed essays for publication in school and local newspapers, encouraged labor caucuses at national meetings of scholarly associations, and organized labor teach-ins at colleges around the country.

Religious leaders had always been key supporters in labor struggles, but the AFL-CIO's new emphasis on social justice encouraged a more organized and inclusive approach. The National Interfaith Committee for Worker Justice started in Chicago in 1996, and by 1998 had twenty-nine affiliated groups including Catholic, Protestant, Muslim, and Jewish clergy. In Los Angeles, the Clergy and Laity for Economic Justice supported HERE Local 11's campaign for better contracts for Westside hotel housekeepers with "Java for Justice," breakfast sermons delivered in hotel restaurants. In Minneapolis, silent vigils by ministers persuaded hotels to rehire workers fired for union activities. On the Sunday before Labor Day 1999, activists took the pulpits in 700 churches and synagogues to preach about the right to organize and earn a living wage. The next year the Interfaith Committee organized a public fast in support of migrant farm workers in New York State, helping persuade the state legislature to bring them under state labor law, with the minimum wage and the right to organize.

Union interests did not always fit easily into the wider world of social justice movements. Issues like capital punishment and incarceration, drug-law reform, reproductive rights, and welfare found union members themselves divided, or their interests in conflict with the community. In 1996, AFSCME prison guards helped break a prisoners' strike for minimum wage against the Minnesota subsidiary of Unicor, the country's largest prison labor company, despite strike support from the community-labor "A Job is a Right" coalition. The next year the Tennessee AFL-CIO supported prison privatization in exchange for Corrections Corporation's neutrality in union drives.

Unions sometimes disagreed with environmentalists, again over jobs. In the Pacific Northwest, unions backed timber company opposition to regulations protecting the endangered Spotted Owl and old-growth forests. Unions in polluting industries often sided with companies resisting pollution controls. USWA, UMW, UAW, UTU, and the Carpenters all joined the National Association of Manufacturers in opposing the Kyoto Protocols designed to slow global warming. But OCAW worked with the Texas United Education Fund to document increased pollution after Crown Petroleum locked out the union in February 1996. Steel Workers Local 890 joined the Albuquerque-based Southwest Research and Information Center to sue Phelps Dodge for disclosure of toxic emissions from its mines in Chino, New Mexico. United Paperworkers Local 30296 charged that toxic dumping by Arizona Portland Cement was an unfair labor practice. New Jersey unions joined a coalition called "Justice for Our Jobs, Health, and Environment" to press for statewide public hearings on hazardous wastes and catastrophic chemical accidents. The Laborers organized Local 455 in a Brooklyn, New York, recycling plant. In fact, several unions, from AFSCME to the Steelworkers, Operating Engineers, Machinists, and Teamsters, developed programs on hazardous waste removal and processing.

Labor alliances could be found almost anywhere. In 1992, activists from a revived American Indian Movement joined HERE Local 17 in a sit-in at the Normandy Hotel in Minneapolis-St. Paul the day before the Superbowl. Union members then joined AIM's protest against racist mascots in professional sports at the next day's game. In Greensboro, North Carolina, UNITE members trying to get a first contract with the local Kmart distribution center worked with the Pulpit Forum, a local ministers' group that supported a local K-Mart boycott and joined in nonviolent civil disobedience at a Kmart Superstore on Martin Luther King Day. UNITE supported Pulpit Forum campaigns for more public school funding and against racial disparities in prison sentences. Streetcorner leafletting by a local community-labor coalition provided crucial neighborhood support for UNITE Local 169's successful eight-month campaign to get contracts for Mexican immigrant greengrocery workers at several stores on Manhattan's Lower East Side in December 1999. In New York City suburbs, the Women Workers Project launched a "Justice Clinic" to provide counselling and assistance to Asian domestic workers, most undocumented, many living in virtual bondage to the whim of their employers.

Some of the most ambitious and best organized coalitions came from local labor councils in cities like Los Angeles and Oakland, New Haven, Connecticut, and Buffalo, New York, which had been building them for years. Los Angeles community and labor activists got together for a long-term effort to raise the local standard of living (the city had the widest gap between rich and poor in the country). They focused on the low-wage and growing tourist industry. In 1995, they set up the Tourism Industry Development Council, later the Los Angeles Alliance for a New Economy, an umbrella coalition of religious, labor, and community groups, to develop proposals, educate and mobilize workers and residents, demand reinvestment and land-use planning, and support union organizing. LAANE stressed that the community should benefit from public investment, got area city councils to require that workers paid with public money get health benefits and earn more than minimum wage, and worked with other community-labor coalitions on projects in low-wage industries like entertainment, light manufacturing, and health care.

Local coalitions could get the attention of local politicians. In New Haven, when the new Omni Hotel reneged on a neutrality agreement with HERE, Elm City Churches Organized got the city's Municipal Services Committee to hear testimony about corporate obligations to communities, employer resistance to union organizing, and Omni's hiring discrimination. After months of weekly pickets and reservation cancellations from groups contacted by activists, the mayor intervened and Omni agreed to HERE card-check recognition.

Workers Rights Boards' hearings could generate enough publicity to get an employer to the table, even without local government support. Aramark ran the cafeteria at Salomon Smith Barney's New York headquarters on Wall Street. When employees petitioned for recognition with HERE Local 100, Aramark management began to transfer and fire union workers. The

Jobs with Justice New York Workers Rights Board convened a hearing that drew 200 people to a downtown church to hear testimony about Aramark employee relations and NLRB procedures. Dismayed by the publicity, Salomon Smith Barney agreed that Aramark would give HERE card-check recognition.

STEPS FORWARD, STEPS BACK

Immigrant organizing, especially SEIU's Justice for Janitors campaigns, made great headlines for the new labor movement, but unions scored some remarkable victories elsewhere too.

The Laborers organized New York-area asbestos workers—mostly Ecuadoran immigrants—in 1996, and by 2000 had organized about two-thirds of the small UXO (unexploded ordnance) industry.

The Machinists settled strikes at Boeing (December 1995) and McDonnell Douglas (September 1996), both after members rejected the settlements first negotiated. The new contracts improved wages and medical benefits, and provided sixty days notice of subcontracting plans involving union layoffs. (The members had wanted job security provisions.)

UAW Local 696 at two General Motors Delphi Division brake plants at Dayton, Ohio, went on strike early in March 1996. Within days most of the North American G.M. plants had suspended operations—"lean" production and "just-in-time" inventory could be vulnerable at strategic points (in fact, the leaner, the more vulnerable). Though the strike was technically "local" and over health and safety concerns, G.M. ended it by promising yet again to hire more production and skilled workers.

In 1997, the Teamsters won a fifteen-day strike against United Parcel Service. The union paid special attention to public relations—UPS drivers visited their regular pickups to explain why they were on strike. The union demand that the company convert part-time jobs to full-time got widespread public support, and the new contract promised 10,000 new full-time jobs.

The UAW struck Johnson Control's auto seat factories in Plymouth Township, Michigan, and Oberlin, Ohio, for first contracts in January 1997. After three weeks and a Ford commitment not to buy nonunion seats, Johnson Control settled. In February, the union got a first contract at American Axle & Manufacturing, a 1994 G.M. spin-off—the contract fit the standard G.M. pattern. An eighty-seven–day strike at G.M.'s Pontiac East truck assembly plant in Michigan won 567 jobs in July. Nine days later, a five-day

THE LAST GASP?

J. SACCO 11-00

3 SACCO 11·00

UAW strike at G.M.'s Powertrain plant in Warren, Michigan, won 420 new jobs and a promise not to outsource wheel production. When G.M. removed dies for hoods and bumpers from its Flint Metal Fab Center in June 1998, UAW Local 659 walked out, joined by Local 651 at Delphi East. The fifty-four-day strike shut down twenty-seven assembly and over a hundred parts plants in North America, and cost the company almost $3 billion in lost profits. G.M. agreed to return the dies and invest in the plants. In January 2000, UAW Local 12 painters at Chrysler Daimler's Jeep plant in Toledo, Ohio, walked out after a plume of paint ignited but failed to trigger the elaborate fire suppression system. Within two hours two other Chrysler plants had suspended production, and work resumed only when the union verified that the suppression system worked.

Over the summer of 1998, CWA and IBEW workers at Bell Atlantic won a dispute on forced overtime after a two-day strike; the unions at USWest had to stay out fifteen days to get the same relief. In 1999, Steel Workers Local 8888 improved hourly rates and pensions for 9,200 workers at Virginia's Newport News Shipbuilding with a fifteen-week strike. By that time a campaign by the Southern Nevada Building Trades Council and HERE had made Las Vegas one of the highly unionized cities in the country; the AFL-CIO promised to support other "Union City" drives and started one in New Orleans.

Unionism passed a milestone when the biggest white-collar strike in U.S. history was settled early in 2000. Nineteen thousand Boeing Corporation engineers and professional workers in the Society of Professional Engineering Employees in Aerospace, which had recently affiliated with the AFL-CIO's International Federation of Professional and Technical Engineers, struck to bring their raises into line with other Boeing unions. The forty-day strike was supported by the Machinists local at Boeing, and by CWA, AFSCME, IUE, and the AFL-CIO.

Some organizing drives prospered. In October 1996, HERE Local 2 won a year-long campaign at the San Francisco Marriott Hotel. In Minneapolis, Minnesota, HERE Local 17 won contracts and raises for more than 1,500 hotel workers—many of them new immigrants from countries as remote as Tibet and Somalia—with a thirteen-day strike in June 2000. According to HERE staffer Kate Shaughnessy, the Minneapolis strikers' "unity in diversity" was their greatest strength.

In February 1999, SEIU took in 74,000 home health care workers in Los Angeles County—the biggest union victory since 1937. The election capped an eleven-year drive that had required changes in state labor laws. The union had already absorbed the forty-year-old Committee of Interns and Residents, a doctors' union based in New York City public hospitals, in 1997; in June 1999, the American Medical Association approved unions for doctors, and Boston's 15,000-member National Doctors Alliance affiliated with SEIU.

That year also saw victories at two longtime Southern targets. UNITE and its ACTWU predecessor had been trying to organize Cannon Mills plants in North Carolina since 1974, in the face of massive labor law violations and a company policy that replaced prounion workers with new hires from new ethnic groups—whites, then African Americans, then Latinos, finally Asians. The union had lost four elections. After the NLRB ordered the 1997 election rerun, the company cut back antiunion activities, and on June 23, 1999, workers at Fieldcrest Cannon's two-mill complex in Kannapolis voted for the union 2,270 to 2,102. It was the biggest private sector union victory in the right-to-work South for decades—for UNITE's lead organizer, it felt "like we just organized G.M." In November, Litton-Avondale Industries, Louisiana's largest manufacturer, ended more than seven years of defying NLRB rulings by agreeing to let the 5,000 workers at its West Jefferson shipyard decide whether to be represented by one of the eleven craft unions in the New Orleans Metal Trades Council. The first contract was ratified December 2000.

The AFL-CIO seized a onetime opportunity when the government of Puerto Rico lifted its 1960 ban on collective bargaining by public employees. A five-union consortium (AFSCME, SEIU, UFCW, AFT, and UAW) persuaded 150,000 public employees to endorse collective bargaining in May 1999, then organized representation elections. In November 1999, the Federación de Maestros became the AFT's largest affiliate. In deference to Puerto Rican labor concerns, the 1999 AFL-CIO convention passed an AFSCME resolution demanding that the Navy give up its bombing range on the island of Vieques.

However, employer resistance did not abate: some drives failed or stalled, and some strikes were lost.

Truck drivers working the Los Angeles-Long Beach port were lease- or owner-operators, "independent contractors" excluded from Wagner Act protection, and paid by the load. Most were Latin American immigrants. They had tried organizing before—striking in 1988 against excessive unpaid waiting time and in 1993 against diesel fuel price hikes. In 1995, a few activists approached CWA Local 9400 for help, and began organizing again. Within months their meetings regularly brought out hundreds of drivers. In May 1998, the drivers called a strike, both at the few companies that employed drivers and by signing up with a CWA-endorsed labor leasing company and refusing work from nonunion companies. The shippers got injunctions against pickets, brought in new drivers, and boycotted the drivers' leasing company. Despite community and church support and strike relief from CWA, when the leasing company failed, the strike failed (though intra-harbor drivers won the right to be represented by ILWU).

In January 1997, CWA lost an election for clerical and service workers at US Air. In February the nineteen-month Detroit newspaper strike ended when Gannett and Knight-Ridder management accepted the unions' unconditional offer to return to work—company stocks had soared during the strike, and many strikers were still waiting to be called back two years later. In September the UAW was embarrassed again at Nissan's Smyrna, Tennessee, plant, when fewer than half the workers signed union cards. In November, G.M. announced the closing of its Buick City plant in Flint, after years of union and city concessions. The next year, the UAW settled the Decatur Caterpillar strike on close to the company's original terms, plus a promise to rehire illegally fired strikers.

A two-year struggle at Northwest Airlines exposed other limitations. Three unions represented Northwest workers—the Air Line Pilots Association, Teamsters Local 2000 for flight attendants, and the Machinists for mechanics and ground crews, baggage handlers and clerks. They had all accepted concessions in 1993 to save the airline from bankruptcy; in 1998, they wanted restoration. The unions agreed that, if one walked, all did. The flight attendants organized Contract Action Teams to build support for the negotiations and solidarity in case of a strike. The pilots went out for fifteen days in August, winning phaseout of their two-tier pay structure and wage and benefit improvements. But the Machinists split—in November 11,000 mechanics unhappy with being "mired in an old factory union dominated by unskilled laborers" decertified the IAM in favor of the independent Airline Mechanics Fraternal Association, leaving behind 17,000 clerks and baggage handlers. Teamster negotiations went on another year, under Hoffa's personal direction and with CAT dismantled by the union. In August 1999, Local 2000 rejected the first settlement negotiated, then ratified an improved offer in May 2000.

The United Farm Workers' three-year strawberry campaign recruited only a few hundred members. In May 1999, the union was defeated at Watsonville's Coastal Berry Company by an otherwise unknown Coastal Berry of California Farmworkers Committee. Teamster drives at Federal Express and Overnite also stalled after the NLRB kept FedEx under the National Railway Act, which required that all FedEx employees vote at the same time, and after Overnite kept running during a partial strike called in October 1999 after a four-year organizing drive.

The focus on organizing was slow to pay off. Total union membership declined again in 1996 and 1997, when about 16.1 million workers belonged to unions, about 12.9 million to AFL-CIO affiliates. In the private sector, less than 10 percent of workers were in unions. The year 1998 saw a slight net gain nationwide of about 101,000 members, though union density continued to fall; 1999 was better—265,000 new members overall, with growth in private-sector union membership (12,000) for the first time in years. But to expand the proportion of union members in the working population, the Federation needed to sign up at least half a million new members a year. Job growth was taking place mostly in nonunion industries located in nonunion areas, according to an AFL-CIO study reported at the 1999 convention. Some unions devoted substantial resources to organizing—SEIU reported spending nearly half its budget on organizing, and HERE nearly a third—but many unions spent 10 percent or less. In 2000, total union membership declined again, a net loss of 200,000, and 80 percent of new union members were recruited by only ten of the 66 AFL-CIO affiliates. In private industry, where 160,000 manufacturing jobs disappeared in 2000, union density fell to 9 percent overall, though unions continued to represent significant numbers of workers in transportation and utilities (24 percent), construction (over 18 percent), and manufacturing (just under 15 percent).

The AFL-CIO became more aggressive in politics, contributing $66 million to candidates through 1998 (while corporations contributed about fifteen times more). The Federation pushed issues as well as candidates. When Congress debated raising the minimum wage, the AFL-CIO targeted thirty Republican congressional districts with media campaigns, persuading fifteen Republicans to break with their party leaders and vote for the raise. In California, union voter turnout produced a surprise June 1998 defeat of "Paycheck Protection" (Proposition 226), which required unions to get individual members' consent before making political contributions from dues income. For the 1998 elections, the AFL-CIO executive insisted that endorsements be initiated by local or state councils (after hastily endorsing a challenger to an incumbent favored by unions in his district in 1996), and included some Republican incumbents who had supported labor issues. Though the Federation failed to meet its goal of creating a Democratic majority in the House, most of its candidates won. AFL-CIO lobbying was probably instrumental in defeating the Clinton administration's "fast track" legislation requiring Congress to accept or reject trade treaties without amendment, though many Congresspeople were already reluctant to give up their places at the trade negotiations table. Republicans responded to AFL-CIO shows of strength by cutting the NLRB budget and introducing a steady stream of antiunion legislation (most failed).

Labor's Democrat dilemma did not change. John Sweeney did not interfere when activists from affiliates like OCAW and ILWU, along with the independent UE, sponsored the founding of the Labor Party in 1996—the Party planned to concentrate on local elections. The AFL-CIO endorsed the founding of New York's Working Families Party in 1998, which advocated a "fusion" strategy, building electoral strength by endorsing major-party candidates. And as political, environmental, and human rights activists prepared to rally in protest at the November meeting of the World Trade Organization in Seattle, the AFL-CIO endorsed the movement and encouraged affiliates to participate.

TURN OF THE CENTURY

The issue in Seattle was "globalization," specifically the WTO's failure to incorporate labor and environmental standards in its trade guidelines. Several local unions had experience with one or another face of globalization. The ILWU had joined the worldwide solidarity strike in support of Liverpool, England, dockworkers that briefly shut down world trade on January 20, 1997, and a second solidarity strike that shut down the West Coast on September 8. In April 1999, Teamsters Local 174 and the Inland-boatmen's Union joined with ILWU in a rush-hour "Port Workers Power" rally, and longshore workers shut down the port when Teamsters picketed nonunion shippers, and again when truck owner-operators demonstrated for union recognition. Striking steelworkers at Kaiser Aluminum got support from area environmentalists. On the day of the WTO meeting, 20,000 unionists rallied at a stadium, then marched downtown. They walked into a maelstrom of protest staged by loosely affiliated student, anarchist, and environmental groups, which caught the authorities by surprise. Between the roving protesters and the police counterattacks, the WTO adjourned ahead of schedule. The widely reported slogan found on one protester's sign—"Teamsters and Turtles Together At Last"—expressed a major theme of the day.

The Seattle showdown helped put labor rights on the free-trade agenda and roused interest in the possibilities of mass direct action, but the everyday world of organizing, strikes, and elections looked pretty much the same. In January 2000, ILA stevedores were beaten and gassed by Charleston, South

Carolina, police when the union tried to shut down a shipping contractor that switched to nonunion workers. In April, in actions targeting the World Bank in Washington, D.C., the unions rallied separately from the direct action networks and focused on opposing the administration's proposal to establish permanent trade relations with China. Despite the Democrats' record on trade issues, the AFL-CIO endorsed Vice President Al Gore's candidacy for President. Though the Teamsters, USWA, and UAW flirted with the Green Party candidacy of consumer advocate Ralph Nader, only independents UE and California Nurses Association and a few union locals actually endorsed him.

By the year's end, the Farm Workers had called off their sixteen-year boycott of California table grapes, and the Kaiser Aluminum locals had gone back to work on terms little better than what they had rejected in October 1998. A year and a half after 284 members of Longshore Local 1814 walked out of the Domino Sugar refinery in Brooklyn, New York, ninety-eight members had gone back to work and Domino owner Tate & Lyle looked likely to hold out forever, especially since the UFCW, with contracts settled at Domino plants in Louisiana and Maryland, balked at endorsing the corporate campaign and boycott suggested by the Food Workers international trade secretariat to the Tate & Lyle North America Workers Council that had formed during the Staley strike.

Intense campaigns to turn out union voters paid off—26 percent of voters in November came from union households. Gore won the most popular votes but failed to carry enough states. When the Gore campaign challenged machine-misread ballots in the Florida Supreme Court, the U.S. Supreme Court stepped in to stop manual recounts, making runner-up Republican George W. Bush the president-elect. Christmas lights went dim in California, where the newly deregulated power companies failed to meet rising demand, and Kaiser Aluminum sent workers on paid vacation while the company cashed in its subsidized power contracts.

At the 1997 AFL-CIO convention in Pittsburgh, John Sweeney had declared, "We don't need any new programs. We just need to do what we've been doing even better." Most New Voice initiatives provided little more than endorsement from the top for organizing strategies and tactics already practiced by many unions and local labor councils. The AFL-CIO opened a "Campaign for Global Fairness" to make labor standards part of a "fair trade" alternative to free trade. Its limitations could be predicted. The International Labor Organization had been founded during the Versailles Peace

Conference in 1919—in fact Sam Gompers had chaired the commission that wrote its constitution. ILO Conventions and Recommendations on minimum standards of freedom of association, the right to organize, collective bargaining, abolition of forced and child labor, equality of opportunity and treatment, were widely admired and routinely ignored. Whether just doing the same things but better would be enough in good times was still an open question. As harbingers of recession gathered in the globalized economy and signalled an end to a period of prosperity unparalleled since the 1920s, answering the question seemed more urgent than ever before.

EPILOGUE

The history of American labor is one of constant struggle, against enslavement, impoverishment, and repression, for democratic rights, economic security, and dignity. The struggle has accomplished much. From the hours and conditions of labor to the regulation of occupational safety and health, to social welfare like minimum living standards for old and young or equal opportunity, even to the democratic franchise itself, many aspects of everyday life show the results of working people organized to advance their common interests. Despite these advances, the struggles never seem to end. Working people have returned again and again to the same issues of economic security and political democracy, though under new and changing conditions.

Though conditions develop and change, the basic structure of the society has been constant. Whether called "commerce" or "free enterprise," capitalism—the economic system based on profit and private property—has dominated American society from the colonial era to the present day. The quest for private profit is by nature exclusive, expansive, and unstable—reducing all value to profit, seeking always the highest rate of return, ever prone to speculation, overproduction, disinvestment, and crisis. For people who must work for a living, the struggle to defend and advance themselves, their families, and their communities either leads to mobilization for some level of workplace, community, economic democracy, or remains confined to individual efforts, heroic and admirable but limited and precarious.

The struggle for democracy depends on solidarity. America has always been multicultural, from indigenous peoples to wave after wave of immigrants, both forced and free. Each native and immigrant group has developed its own relationship to the common culture, and different groups have fared better or worse at one time or another. But their welfare has commonly depended on their relationship to the economy. For most people, whether they work for a boss or for themselves, this relationship has been characterized by dependency, subordination, and insecurity. Though the remedy for these weaknesses has always been cooperation and unity in action, securing solidarity has always been difficult.

When working people's solidarity has been limited in scope and vision, the privileged classes—economic, social, and political elites—set the rules. When restricted by democratic controls, they have changed the rules to restore "balance" to their advantage. Working people and their movements have suffered historic defeats, from the expansion of slavery to the impoverishment of the Gilded Age to the suppression of modern movements for social justice to the devastation of deindustrialization. The stakes are higher now. Wealth and privilege are more powerful than ever. Out of the 100 largest economies in the world, only forty-nine are sovereign nations—the rest are transnational corporations, and transnational corporations control more than a fourth of the world's economic activity.

According to the *New York Times,* "America's most admired corporation" is General Electric, its year 2000 profits—$12.7 billion—the largest in the history of the world. *Fortune* magazine calls G.E. Chief Executive Officer Jack Welch "the management revolutionary of the century." Welch once explained that, "Ideally you'd have every plant you own on a barge," ready to be towed wherever labor costs were lowest. The flaw in his conceit is that labor is not just a cost factor, but work performed by people who have hopes and ambitions beyond just making someone already rich even richer, who have the collective resources, the strength in numbers, to assert their own rights and uphold their own dignity. As an officer in one of G.E.'s unions promised in response, "wherever Welch lands his barge, we'll be there to greet him."

If no victory has ever been final, neither has any defeat. The hope for a better life and the impulse to resist injustice always revive. Labor's cardinal role in this historic and democratic drama comes from the fact that labor is the engine of the system. Labor really does create all wealth. All kinds of people can organize to maintain their rights and advance their interests; only working people can also organize to abolish the system altogether. When the final conflict comes—as come it will—working people will have to be ready; the world will hang in the balance.

SUGGESTED READING

Here are suggestions for readers interested in learning more about particular periods or issues in labor history. The titles have been chosen because they are interesting, readable, and in most cases readily available. This is not a list of sources or a comprehensive bibliography. Many excellent works are out of print.

The titles are listed by broad categories. Where the title does not describe the subject, the listing is briefly annotated. No title appears more than once.

SURVEYS AND GENERAL HISTORY

Acuña, Rodolfo F. *Occupied America: A History of Chicanos.* Fourth Edition. New York: Longmans, 2000.

Amott, Teresa, and Julie Matthaei. *Race, Gender and Work: A Multicultural Economic History of Women in the United States.* Revised edition. Boston: South End Press, 1996.

Baxandall, Rosalyn. *America's Working Women: A Documentary History, 1600 to the Present.* Revised and updated. New York: W.W. Norton, 1995.

Berlin, Ira, ed. *Free at Last: A Documentary History of Slavery, Freedom, and the Civil War.* New York: The New Press, 1992.

Boyer, Richard and Herbert Morais. *Labor's Untold Story.* New York: United Electrical and Machine Workers of America, 1955. Reprinted 1975.

Brecher, Jeremy. *Strike!* Revised and updated edition. Boston: South End Press, 1997.

Brody, David. *Workers in Industrial America.* Second edition. New York: Oxford University Press, 1993.

Brown, Dee. *Bury My Heart at Wounded Knee: An Indian History of the American West.* New York: Henry Holt, 1991.

Buhle, Mari Jo, Paul Buhle, and Dan Georgakis, eds. *The Encyclopedia of the American Left.* Second edition. New York: Oxford University Press, 1998.

Buhle, Mari Jo, Paul Buhle, and Harvey J. Kaye, eds. *The American Radical.* New York: Routledge, 1994.

Buhle, Paul, and Dan Georgakas, eds. *The Immigrant Left in the United States.* Albany: State University of New York Press, 1996.

Clark, Christopher, and Nancy A. Hewitt, eds. *Who Built America?: Working People and the Nation's Politics, Economy, Culture, and Society.* Two volumes. [Revised edition] New York: Worth Publishers, 2000.

Dubofsky, Melvyn and Foster R. Dulles. *Labor in America: A History.* Sixth edition. Wheeling, Illinois: Harlan Davidson, 1999.

Foner, Philip S. *History of the Labor Movement in the United States.* Seven volumes. New York: International Publishers, 1947–1987.

Foner, Philip S. *Organized Labor and the Black Worker, 1619–1981.* Second edition. New York: International Publishers, 1982.

Gómez Quiñones, Juan. *Mexican-American Labor, 1790–1990.* Albuquerque: University of New Mexico Press, 1994.

Green, James R. *The World of the Worker: Labor in 20th Century America.* New York: Hill and Wang, 1980.

Grigsby, Daryl Russell. *For the People: Black Socialists in the United States, Africa and the Caribbean.* San Diego: Asante Publications, 1987.

Gutman, Herbert S. *Work, Culture and Society in Industrializing America: Essays in American Working-Class and Social History.* New York: Knopf, 1976.

Harris, William Hamilton. *The Harder We Run: Black Workers Since the Civil War.* New York: Oxford University Press, 1982.

Huggins, Nathan Irvin. *Black Odyssey: The African-American Ordeal in Slavery.* New York: Vintage Books, 1990.

Jones, Jacqueline. *Labor of Love, Labor of Sorrow: Black Women, Work, and the Family from Slavery to the Present.* New York: Vintage Books, 1995.

Kessler-Harris, Alice. *Out to Work: A History of Wage-Earning Women in the United States.* New York: Oxford University Press, 1982.

Laurie, Bruce. *Artisans into Workers; Labor in 19th Century America.* Urbana: University of Illinois Press, 1997.

Le Blanc, Paul. *A Short History of the U.S. Working Class: From Colonial Times to the 21st Century.* Amherst, New York: Humanity Books, 1999.

Loewen, James W. *Lies My Teacher Told Me: Everything Your American History Textbook Got Wrong.* New York: The New Press, 1995.

Montgomery, David. *The Fall of the House of Labor: The Workplace, the State and American Labor Activism, 1865–1925.* New York: Cambridge University Press, 1987.

Nash, Gary B. *Red, White and Black: The Peoples of Early North America.* Second edition. Englewood Cliffs, New Jersey: Prentice-Hall, 1982.

Robinson, Cedric J. *Black Movements in America.* New York: Routledge, 1997.

Ruiz, Vicki L. *From Out of the Shadows: Mexican Women in the 20th Century.* New York: Oxford University Press, 1999.

Saxton, Alexander. *The Rise and Fall of the White Republic: Class Politics and Mass Culture in Nineteenth-Century America.* London: Verso, 1990.

Takaki, Ronald. *Strangers from a Different Shore: A History of Asian Americans.* Updated and revised edition. Boston: Little, Brown, 1998.

Weber, David J. *The Spanish Frontier in North America.* New Haven: Yale University Press, 1992.

Zinn, Howard. *A Peoples' History of the United States, 1492 to the Present.* New York: The New Press, 1997.

SPECIAL TOPICS

Adamic, Louis. *Dynamite! A Century of Class Violence in America.* Seattle: Left Bank Distribution, 1984.

Arnesen, Eric. *Brotherhoods of Color: Black Railroad Workers and the Struggle for Equality.* Cambridge: Harvard University Press, 2001.

Avrich, Paul. *Anarchist Portraits.* Princeton: Princeton University Press, 1988.

Avrich, Paul. *The Haymarket Tragedy.* Princeton: Princeton University Press, 1984.

Barrera, Mario. *Race and Class in the Southwest: A Theory of Racial Inequality.* Notre Dame: University of Notre Dame Press, 1979.

Barrett, James R. *Work and Community in the Jungle: Chicago's Packing-House Workers, 1894–1922.* Urbana: University of Illinois Press, 1987.

Benson, Susan Porter. *Counter Cultures: Saleswomen, Managers and Customers in American Department Stores, 1890–1940.* Urbana: University of Illinois Press, 1986.

Berlin, Ira. *Many Thousands Gone: The First Two Centuries of Slavery in North America.* Cambridge: Belknap Press of Harvard University Press, 1998.

Berlin, Ira. *Slaves without Masters: The Free Negro in the Antebellum South.* New York: The New Press, 1992.

Boydston, Jeanne. *Home and Work: Housework, Wages, and the Ideology of Labor in the Early Republic.* New York: Oxford University Press, 1990.

Braverman, Harry. *Labor and Monopoly Capital: the Degradation of Work in the Twentieth Century.* New York: Monthly Review Press, 1974.

Brody, David. *Steelworkers in America: The Non-Union Era.* New York: Russell & Russell, 1970.

Bruce, Robert V. *1877: Year of Violence.* First Elephant edition. Chicago: I.R. Dee, 1989.

Buhle, Paul. *Taking Care of Business: Samuel Gompers, George Meany, Lane Kirkland, and the Tragedy of American Labor.* New York: Monthly Review Press, 1999.

Bush, Rod. *We Are Not What We Seem: Black Nationalism and Class Struggle in the American Century.* New York: New York University Press, 1999.

Calloway, Colin G. *The American Revolution in Indian Country: Crisis and Diversity in Native American Communities.* New York: Cambridge University Press, 1995.

Cameron, Ardis. *Radicals of the Worst Sort: Laboring Women in Lawrence, Massachusetts, 1860–1912*. Urbana: University of Illinois Press, 1993.

Chateauvert, M. Melinda. *Marching Together: Women of the Brotherhood of Sleeping Car Porters*. Urbana: University of Illinois Press, 1998.

Cobble, Dorothy Sue. *Dishing It Out: Waitresses and their Unions in the 20th Century*. Urbana: University of Illinois Press, 1991.

Cohen, Lizabeth. *Making a New Deal: Industrial Workers in Chicago, 1919–1939*. New York: Cambridge University Press, 1990.

Cowie, Jefferson R. *Capital Moves: RCA's Seventy-Year Quest for Cheap Labor*. Ithaca, New York: Cornell University Press, 1999.

Crawford, Vicki L., ed. *Women in the Civil Rights Movement: Trailblazers and Torchbearers, 1941–1965*. Bloomington: Indiana University Press, 1993.

Dawley, Alan. *Class and Community: The Industrial Revolution in Lynn*. Second 25th anniversary edition. Cambridge: Harvard University Press, 2000.

Denning, Michael. *The Cultural Front: The Laboring of American Culture in the 20th Century*. New York: Verso, 1996.

Dittmer, John. *Local People: The Struggle for Civil Rights in Mississippi*. Urbana: University of Illinois Press, 1994.

DuBois, Ellen Carol. *Women Suffrage and Women's Rights*. New York: New York University Press, 1998.

Du Bois, W.E.B. *Black Reconstruction: An Essay toward a History of the Part which Black Folk Played in the Attempt to Reconstruct Democracy in America, 1860–1880*. Notre Dame: University of Notre Dame Press, 2001.

Egerton, Douglas R. *Gabriel's Rebellion: The Virginia Slave Conspiracies of 1800 and 1802*. Chapel Hill: University of North Carolina Press, 1993.

Enstad, Nan. *Ladies of Labor, Girls of Adventure: Working Women, Popular Culture and Labor Politics at the Turn of the 20th Century*. New York: Columbia University Press, 1999.

Ewen, Elizabeth. *Immigrant Women in the Land of Dollars: Life and Culture on the Lower East Side, 1890–1925*. New York: Monthly Review Press, 1985.

Filippelli, Ronald L., and Mark D. McColloch. *Cold War in the Working Class: the Rise and Decline of the United Electrical Workers*. Albany: State University of New York: 1995.

Fink, Leon. *Workingmen's Democracy: The Knights of Labor and American Politics*. Urbana: University of Illinois Press, 1983.

Fink, Leon, and Brian Greenberg. *Upheaval in the Quiet Zone: A History of Hospital Workers Union, Local 1199*. Urbana: University of Illinois Press, 1989.

Finn, Janet L. *Tracing the Veins: Of Copper, Culture and Community from Butte to Chuquicamata*. Berkeley: University of California Press, 1998.

Foley, Neil. *The White Scourge: Mexicans, Blacks and Poor Whites in Texas Cotton Culture*. Berkeley: University of California Press, 1997.

Foner, Eric. *Reconstruction: America's Unfinished Revolution, 1863–1877*. New York: HarperCollins, 1989.

Fones-Wolf, Elizabeth. *Selling Free Enterprise: The Business Assault Against Labor and Liberalism, 1945–1960*. Urbana: University of Illinois Press, 1994.

Frank, Dana. *Purchasing Power: Consumer Organizing, Gender, and the Seattle Labor Movement 1919–1929*. New York: Cambridge University Press, 1994.

Friday, Chris. *Organizing Asian American Labor: The Pacific Coast Canned-Salmon Industry, 1870–1942*. Philadelphia: Temple University Press, 1994.

Georgakas, Dan, and Marvin Surkin. *Detroit, I Do Mind Dying: A Study in Urban Revolution*. Updated edition. Boston: South End Press, 1998.

Gerstle, Gary. *Working-Class Americanism: The Politics of Labor in a Textile City, 1914–1960*. New York: Cambridge University Press, 1989.

Glaberman, Martin. *Wartime Strikes: The Struggle Against the No Strike Pledge in the UAW During World War II*. Detroit: Bewick/Ed, 1980.

Glenn, Evelyn Nakano. *Issei, Nisei, War Bride: Three Generations of Japanese American Women in Domestic Service*. Philadelphia: Temple University Press, 1986.

Glenn, Susan A. *Daughters of the Shtetl: Life and Labor in the Immigrant Generation*. Ithaca, New York: Cornell University Press, 1990.

Glickman, Lawrence B. *A Living Wage: American Workers and the Making of Consumer Society*. Ithaca, New York: Cornell University Press, 1997.

Gordon, Linda. *The Great Arizona Orphan Abduction*. Boston: Harvard University Press, 1999.

Greenwald, Maurine W. *Women, War and Work: The Impact of World War I on Women Workers in the United States*. Westport, Connecticut: Greenwood Press, 1980.

Hahamovitch, Cindy. *The Fruits of their Labor: Atlantic Coast Farmworkers and the Making of Migrant Poverty, 1870–1945*. Chapel Hill: University of North Carolina Press, 1997.

Honey, Michael K. *Southern Labor and Black Civil Rights: Organizing Memphis Workers*. Urbana: University of Illinois Press, 1993.

Hunter, Tera W. *To Joy My Freedom: Southern Black Women's Lives and Labors After the Civil War*. Cambridge: Harvard University Press, 1997.

Hurtado, Albert L. *Indian Survival on the California Frontier*. New Haven: Yale University Press, 1988.

Isserman, Maurice. *Which Side Were You On?: The American Communist Party During the Second World War*. Middletown, Connecticut: Wesleyan University Press, 1982.

Katzman, David M. *Seven Days a Week: Women and Domestic Service in Industrializing America*. New York: Oxford University Press, 1978.

Kelley, Robin D.G. *Hammer and Hoe: Alabama Communists During the Great Depression*. Chapel Hill: University of North Carolina Press, 1990.

Kenny, Kevin. *Making Sense of the Molly Maguires*. New York: Oxford University Press, 1998.

Kingsolver, Barbara. *Holding the Line: Women in the Great Arizona Mine Strike of 1983*. Ithaca, New York: ILR Press, 1989.

Kornbluh, Joyce, ed. *Rebel Voices: An IWW Anthology*. New and expanded edition. Chicago: Charles H. Kerr, 1988.

Kwong, Peter. *Chinatown, NY: Labor and Politics, 1930–1950*. New York: The New Press, 2001.

Kwong, Peter. *The New Chinatown*. Revised edition. New York: Hill and Wang, 1996.

La Botz, Dan. *Rank-and-File Rebellion: Teamsters for a Democratic Union*. New York: Verso, 1990.

Letwin, Dan. *The Challenge of Interracial Unionism: Alabama Coal Miners, 1879–1921*. Chapel Hill: University of North Carolina, 1998.

Levy, Peter B. *The New Left and Labor in the 1960s*. Urbana: University of Illinois Press, 1994.

Littlefield, Alice, and Martha C. Knack, eds. *Native Americans and Wage Labor: Ethnohistorical Perspectives*. Norman: University of Oklahoma Press, 1996.

Litwack, Leon F. *North of Slavery: The Negro in the Free States, 1790–1860*. Chicago: University of Chicago Press, 1961.

López, Alfredo. *Dona Licha's Island: Modern Colonialism in Puerto Rico*. Boston: South End Press, 1987.

Matles, James J., and James Higgins. *Them and Us*. Englewood Cliffs, New Jersey: Prentice-Hall, 1974. [United Electrical Workers, 1940s–1960s]

Matthiessen, Peter. *In the Spirit of Crazy Horse*. New York: Viking, 1991. [American Indian Movement]

McPherson, James M. *Battle Cry of Freedom: the Civil War Era*. New York: Oxford University Press, 1988.

Milkman, Ruth. *Gender at Work: The Dynamics of Job Segregation by Sex During World War II*. Urbana: University of Illinois Press, 1987.

Montgomery, David. *Beyond Equality: Labor and the Radical Republicans, 1862–1872*. Urbana: University of Illinois Press, 1981.

Montgomery, David. *Citizen Worker: The Experiences of Workers in the United States with Democracy and the Free Market During the 19th Century*. New York: Cambridge University Press, 1993.

Montgomery, David. *Workers' Control in America: Studies in the History of Work, Technology and Labor Struggles*. New York: Cambridge University Press, 1979.

Moody, Kim. *Injury to All: The Decline of American Unionism*. London: Verso, 1988.

Morgan, Edmund S. *American Slavery, American Freedom: The Ordeal of Colonial Virginia*. New York: Norton, 1995.

Okihiro, Gary Y. *Cane Fires: The Anti-Japanese Movement in Hawaii, 1865–1945*. Philadelphia: Temple University Press, 1991.

Painter, Nell Irvin. *Exodusters: Black Migration to Kansas after the Civil War*. New York: Knopf, 1976.

Quarles, Benjamin. *Black Abolitionists*. New York: Da Capo Press, 1991.

Quarles, Benjamin. *The Negro in the American Revolution*. Chapel Hill: University of North Carolina Press, 1996.

Rachleff, Peter J. *Hard-Pressed in the Heartland: The Hormel Strike and the Future of the Labor Movement.* Boston: South End Press, 1993.

Roediger, David R. *The Wages of Whiteness: Race and the Making of the American Working Class.* Revised edition. New York: Verso, 1999.

Roediger, David R., and Philip S. Foner. *Our Own Time: A History of American Labor and the Working Day.* New York: Greenwood Press, 1989.

Roediger, David R., and Franklin Rosemont. *Haymarket Scrapbook.* Chicago: Charles H. Kerr, 1986.

Romero, Mary. *Maid in the U.S.A.* New York: Routledge, 1992.

Rorabaugh, W. J. *The Craft Apprentice: From Franklin to the Machine Age in America.* New York: Oxford University Press, 1986.

Rosales, F. Arturo. *Chicano! The History of the Mexican American Civil Rights Movement.* Houston: Arte Publico Press, 1996.

Rosenbaum, Robert J. *Mexicano Resistance in the Southwest: "The Sacred Right of Self-Preservation."* Austin: University of Texas Press, 1981.

Ruiz, Vicki L. *Cannery Women, Cannery Lives: Mexican Women, Unionization and the California Food Processing Industry, 1930–1950.* Albuquerque: University of New Mexico Press, 1987.

Sales, William W. *From Civil Rights to Black Liberation: Malcolm X and the Organization of African-American Unity.* Boston: South End Press, 1994.

Saxton, Alexander. *The Indispensable Enemy: Labor and the Anti-Chinese Movement in California.* Berkeley: University of California Press, 1971.

Schneirov, Richard, Sheldon Stromquist, and Nick Salvatore, eds. *The Pullman Strike and the Crisis of the 1890s: Essays on Labor and Politics.* Urbana: University of Illinois Press, 1999.

Schrecker, Ellen. *Many Are the Crimes: McCarthyism in America.* Boston: Little Brown, 1998.

Serrin, William. *Homestead: The Glory and the Tragedy of an American Steel Town.* New York: New York Times Books, 1992.

Sexton, Patricia Cayo. *The War on Labor and the Left: Understanding America's Unique Conservatism.* Boulder, Colorado: Westview Press, 1991.

Shapiro, Karin A. *A New South Rebellion: The Battle Against Convict Labor in the Tennessee Coalfields 1871–1896.* Chapel Hill: University of North Carolina Press, 1998.

Sims, Beth. *Workers of the World Undermined: American Labor's Role in U.S. Foreign Policy.* Boston: South End Press, 1992.

Stansell, Christine. *City of Women: Sex and Class in New York: 1789–1860.* New York: Knopf, 1986.

Tax, Meredith. *The Rising of the Women: Feminist Solidarity and Class Conflict, 1880–1917.* New York: Monthly Review Press, 1980.

Thomas, Hugh. *The Slave Trade: The Story of the Atlantic Slave Trade: 1440–1870.* New York: Simon & Schuster, 1997.

Tomlins, Christopher L. *Labor Law in America: Historical and Critical Essays.* Baltimore: Johns Hopkins University Press, 1992.

Torres, Andrés, and José E. Velázquez, eds. *The Puerto Rican Movement: Voices from the Diaspora*. Philadelphia: Temple University Press, 1998.

Turbin, Carole. *The Working Women of Collar City: Gender, Class and Community in Troy, New York: 1864–86*. Urbana: University of Illinois Press, 1992.

Valdes, Dennis Nodin. *Al Norte: Agricultural Workers in the Great Lakes Region, 1917–1970*. Austin: University of Texas Press, 1991.

Vargas, Zaragosa. *Proletarians of the North: Mexican Industrial Workers in Detroit and the Midwest, 1917–1933*. Berkeley: University of California Press, 1993.

Vigil, Ernesto B. *The Crusade for Justice: Chicano Militancy and the Government's War on Dissent*. Madison: University of Wisconsin Press, 1999.

Voss, Kim. *The Making of American Exceptionalism: the Knights of Labor and Class Formation in the 19th Century*. Ithaca, New York: Cornell University Press, 1993.

Weir, Robert E. *Beyond Labor's Veil: The Culture of the Knights of Labor*. University Park: Pennsylvania State University, 1996.

White, Deborah Gray. *Ar'n't I a Woman: Female Slaves in the Plantation South*. Revised edition. New York: Norton, 1999.

Wilentz, Sean. *Chants Democratic: New York City and the Rise of the American Working Class, 1788–1850*. New York: Oxford University Press, 1984.

Wood, Peter H. *Black Majority: Negroes in Colonial South Carolina from 1670 through the Stono Rebellion*. New York: Norton, 1996.

Woodard, Komozi. *A Nation Within a Nation: Amiri Baraka (LeRoi Jones) and Black Power Politics*. Chapel Hill: University of North Carolina Press, 1999.

Yellen, Samuel. *American Labor Struggles, 1877–1934*. New York: Monad Press, 1974.

Young, Alfred F., ed. *Beyond the American Revolution: Explorations in the History of American Radicalism*. DeKalb: Northern Illinois University Press, 1993.

Zieger, Robert H. *The C.I.O., 1935–1955*. Chapel Hill: University of North Carolina Press, 1995.

AUTOBIOGRAPHIES, BIOGRAPHIES, AND ORAL HISTORIES

Bird, Stuart, Dan Georgakas, and Deborah Shaffer. *Solidarity Forever: An Oral History of the Industrial Workers of the World*. Chicago: Lakeview Press, 1985.

Bulosan, Carlos. *America Is in the Heart: A Personal History*. Seattle: University of Washington, 1973.

Camp, Helen C. *Iron in Her Soul: Elizabeth Gurley Flynn and the American Left*. Pullman, Washington: WSU Press, 1995.

Chaplin, Ralph. *Wobbly: Rough and Tumble Story of an American Radical*. New York: Da Capo Press, 1972.

De Caux, Len. *Labor Radical: From the Wobblies to CIO, a Personal History*. Boston: Beacon Press, 1970.

Dollinger, Sol, and Genora Johnson Dollinger. *Not Automatic: Women and the Left in the Forging of the Auto Workers Union*. New York: Monthly Review Press, 1999.

Douglass, Frederick. *Autobiographies: Narrative of the Life; My Bondage and My Freedom; Life and Times.* Edited by Henry Louis Gates, Jr. New York: Library of America, 1996.

Equiano, Olaudah. *The African: The Interesting Narrative of the Life of Olaudah Equiano.* Tyler, Texas: X Press, 1999.

Flynn, Elizabeth Gurley. *The Rebel Girl: An Autobiography, My First Life.* New York: International Publishers, 1984.

Foner, Eric. *Tom Paine and Revolutionary America.* New York: Oxford University Press, 1977.

Hamper, Ben. *Rivethead: Tales from the Assembly Line.* New York: Warner Books, 1991.

Hudson, Hosea, and Nell Irvin Painter. *The Narrative of Hosea Hudson: His Life as a Negro Communist in the South.* Cambridge: Harvard University Press, 1979.

Jones, Mary Harris. *Mother Jones Speaks: Collected Writings and Speeches.* Edited by Philip S. Foner. New York: Monad Press, 1983.

Lee, Chana Kai. *For Freedom's Sake: The Life of Fannie Lou Hamer.* Urbana: University of Illinois Press, 1999.

Lichtenstein, Nelson. *Walter Reuther: The Most Dangerous Man in Detroit.* Urbana: University of Illinois Press, 1997.

Lucas, Maria Elena. *Forged under the Sun/Forjada Baja El Sol: The Life of Maria Elena Lucas.* Edited by Fran Leeper Buss. Ann Arbor: University of Michigan Press, 1993.

Lynd, Staughton, ed. *"We Are All Leaders": The Alternative Unionism of the Early 1930s.* Urbana: University of Illinois Press, 1996.

Lynd, Staughton, and Alice Lynd, eds. *Rank and File: Personal Histories by Working-Class Organizers.* New York: Monthly Review Press, 1988.

Nee, Victor, and Brett De Bary Nee. *Longtime Californ': A Documentary Study of an American Chinatown.* New York: Random House, 1973.

Oates, Warren and Stephen B. Oates. *To Purge This Land with Blood: A Biography of John Brown.* Second edition. Amherst: University of Massachusetts Press, 1984.

Orleck, Annelise. *Common Sense and a Little Fire: Women and Working-Class Politics in the United States, 1900–1965.* Chapel Hill: University of North Carolina Press, 1995.

Painter, Nell Irvin. *Sojourner Truth: A Life, a Symbol.* New York: W.W. Norton, 1996.

Salvatore, Nick. *Eugene V. Debs: Citizen and Socialist.* Urbana: University of Illinois Press, 1982.

Scharlin, Craig, and Lilia V. Villanueva. *Philip Vera Cruz: A Personal History of Filipino Immigrants and the Farmworkers Movement.* New edition. Seattle: University of Washington Press, 2000.

Stepan-Norris, Judith, and Maurice Zeitlin. *Talking Union.* Urbana: University of Illinois Press, 1996.

Terkel, Studs. *The Good War: An Oral History of World War Two.* New York: Pantheon Books, 1984.

Terkel, Studs. *Hard Times: An Oral History of the Great Depression.* New York: The New Press, 2000.

Terkel, Studs. *Working: People Talk About What They Do All Day and How They Feel About What They Do.* New York: Ballantine Books, 1985.

FICTION

Arnow, Harriette. *The Dollmaker.* New York: Avon Books, 1972. [First published 1954. White Appalachian family in World War II Detroit.]

Attaway, William. *Blood on the Forge: A Novel.* New York: Anchor Books, 1993. [First published 1941. Black steelworkers in Pittsburgh during the 1919 strike.]

Bell, Thomas. *Out of This Furnace.* Pittsburgh: University of Pittsburgh Press, 1991. [First published 1941. Three generations of a Slovak family in Pennsylvania steel towns.]

Bellamy, Edward. *Looking Backward, 2000–1887.* New York: St. Martin's Press, 1995. [First published 1888. Utopian future.]

Bontemps, Arna. *Black Thunder.* Boston: Beacon Press, 1992. [First published 1936. Gabriel rebellion, 1800.]

Conroy, Jack. *The Disinherited: A Novel of the 1930s.* Columbia: University of Missouri Press, 1991. [First published 1933.]

Dos Passos, John. *U.S.A.: The 42nd Parallel, 1919, The Big Money* New York: Library of America, 1996. [First published 1932. Panoramic trilogy surveying the U.S. during and after World War I.]

Fast, Howard. *The American, a Middle Western Legend.* New York: Duell, Sloan and Pearce, 1946. [John P. Altgeld and the Haymarket defendants.]

Fast, Howard. *Freedom Road.* New York: Crown Publishers, 1969. [First published 1944. Freedpeople during Reconstruction.]

Gilden, K. B. *Between the Hills and the Sea.* Ithaca, New York: ILR Press, 1989. [First published 1971. McCarthyism in a New England factory town in the 1950s.]

Gilden, K. B. *Hurry Sundown.* New York: Doubleday, 1964. [Rural South after World War II.]

Kingston, Maxine Hong. *China Men.* New York: Knopf, 1980. [Three generations of Chinese American working men.]

Le Sueur, Meridel. *The Girl: A Novel.* Albuquerque: West End Press, 1990. [Unemployed women during the Great Depression.]

Malkiel, Theresa. *The Diary of a Shirtwaist Striker.* Ithaca, New York: ILR Press, 1990. [New York City garment strike 1909–1910.]

McKenney, Ruth. *Industrial Valley.* Reprinted edition. New York: Greenwood Press, 1968. [First published 1939. Rubber workers organizing in the 1930s.]

Olsen, Tillie. *Yonnondio: From the Thirties.* New York: Delta/Seymour Lawrence, 1989. [First published 1974. Fragmentary novel about a working class girl.]

Sinclair, Upton. *The Jungle.* New York: New American Library, 1990. [First published 1906. Exposé of immigrant life in Chicago stockyards and slaughterhouses at the turn of the century.]

Steinbeck, John. *Grapes of Wrath*. New York: Library of America, 1996. [First published 1939. Migrant farm workers in Depression California.]

Vorse, Mary Heaton. *Strike!* Urbana: University of Illinois Press, 1991. [First published 1930. Textile workers on strike in Gastonia, North Carolina, in the 1920s.]

Walker, Margaret. *Jubilee*. Boston: Houghton Mifflin, 1999. [First published 1966. Black woman's life during slavery, the Civil War, and Reconstruction.]

Yezierska, Anzia. *Bread Givers: A Novel; A Struggle Between a Father of the Old World and a Daughter of the New*. New York: Persea Books, 1975. [First published 1925. Russian Jews in New York City.]

CONTEMPORARY LABOR ISSUES

Abramovitz, Mimi. *Under Attack, Fighting Back: Women and Welfare in the United States*. New edition. New York: Monthly Review Press, 2000.

Anner, John, ed. *Beyond Identity Politics: Emerging Social Justice Movements in Communities of Color*. Boston: South End Press, 1996.

Brecher, Jeremy, Tim Costello and Brendan Smith. *Globalization from Below: The Power of Solidarity*. Boston: South End Press, 2000.

Brenner, Johanna. *Women and the Politics of Class*. New York: Monthly Review Press, 2000.

Bullard, Robert D., ed. *Confronting Environmental Racism: Voices from the Grassroots*. Boston: South End Press, 1993.

Cobble, Dorothy Sue, ed. *Women and Unions: Forging a Partnership*. Ithaca, New York: ILR Press, 1993.

Dujon, Diane, and Ann Withorn, eds. *For Crying Out Loud: Women's Poverty in the United States*. New edition. Boston: South End Press, 1996.

Eisenberg, Susan. *We'll Call You If We Need You: Experiences of Women Working Construction*. Ithaca, New York: ILR Press, 1998.

Fuentes, Annette, and Barbara Ehrenreich. *Women in the Global Factory*. Boston: South End Press, 1983.

Garson, Barbara. *All the Livelong Day: The Meaning and Demeaning of Routine Work*. Revised and updated edition. New York: Penguin Books, 1994.

Gilpin, Toni, Gary Isaac, Dan Letwin, and Jack McKivigan. *On Strike for Respect: The Clerical and Technical Workers' Strike at Yale University, 1984–85*. Chicago: Charles H. Kerr, 1987.

Hathaway, Dale A. *Allies Across the Border: Mexico's 'Authentic Labor Front' and Global Solidarity*. Boston: South End Press, 2000.

Hoerr, John. *We Can't Eat Prestige: The Women Who Organized Harvard*. Philadelphia: Temple University Press, 1997.

Hunt, Gerald, ed. *Laboring for Rights: Unions and Sexual Diversity Across Nations*. Philadelphia: Temple University Press, 1999.

Juravich, Tom, and Kate Bronfenbrenner. *Ravenswood: The Steelworkers' Victory and the Revival of American Labor*. Ithaca, New York: Cornell University Press, 1999.

Kelley, Robin D. G. *Race Rebels: Culture, Politics and the Black Working Class.* New York: Free Press, 1996.

Kwong, Peter. *Forbidden Workers: Illegal Chinese Immigrants and American Labor.* New York: The New Press, 1997.

LaDuke, Winona. *All Our Relations: Native Struggles for Land and Life.* Boston: South End Press, 1999.

Levitt, Martin Jay. *Confessions of a Union Buster.* New York: Crown Publishers, 1993.

Lynd, Staughton, and Alice Lynd, eds. *The New Rank and File.* Ithaca, New York: ILR Press, 2000.

Mantsios, Gregory, and Dan Georgakas, eds. *A New Labor Movement for the New Century.* New York: Monthly Review Press, 1998.

Milkman, Ruth, and Kent Wong. *Voices from the Front Lines: Organizing Immigrant Workers in Los Angeles.* Los Angeles: Center for Labor Research and Education, UCLA, 2000.

Mink, Gwendolyn. *Welfare's End.* Ithaca, New York: Cornell University Press, 1998.

Moody, Kim. *Workers in a Lean World: Unions in the International Economy.* London: Verso, 1997.

Mort, Jo-Ann. *Not Your Father's Union Movement: Inside the AFL-CIO.* London: Verso, 1998.

Prieto, Norma Iglesias. *Beautiful Flowers of the Maquiladora.* Translated by Michael Stone with Gabrielle Winkler. Austin: University of Texas Press, 1997. First published in Spanish in 1985.

Puette, William J. *Through Jaundiced Eyes: How the Media View Organized Labor.* Ithaca, New York: ILR Press, 1992.

Quadagno, Jill. *The Color of Welfare: How Racism Undermined the War on Poverty.* New York: Oxford University Press, 1994.

Schor, Juliet B. *The Overworked American: The Unexpected Decline of Leisure.* New York: Basic Books, 1991.

Schroedel, Jean Reith. *Alone in a Crowd: Women in the Trades Tell Their Stories.* Philadelphia: Temple University Press, 1985.

Vanderbilt, Tom. *The Sneaker Book: Anatomy of an Industry and an Icon.* New York: The New Press, 1998.

Winslow, George. *Capital Crimes.* New York: Monthly Review Press, 1999. [Prison-industrial complex.]

Wood, Ellen Meiksins, ed. *Rising from the Ashes?: Labor in Age of Global Capitalism.* New York: Monthly Review Press, 1998.

Yates, Michael D. *Why Unions Matter.* New York: Monthly Review Press, 1998.

INDEX